Gesa zur Nieden, Berthold Over (eds.)
Musicians' Mobilities and Music Migrations in Early Modern Europe

Mainz Historical Cultural Sciences | Volume 33

Editorial

The **Mainzer Historische Kulturwissenschaften** [Mainz Historical Cultural Sciences] series publishes the results of research that develops methods and theories of cultural sciences in connection with empirical research. The central approach is a historical perspective on cultural sciences, whereby both epochs and regions can differ widely and be treated in an all-embracing manner from time to time. Amongst other, the series brings together research approaches in archaeology, art history, visual studies, literary studies, philosophy, and history, and is open for contributions on the history of knowledge, political culture, the history of perceptions, experiences and life-worlds, as well as other fields of research with a historical cultural scientific orientation.
The objective of the **Mainzer Historische Kulturwissenschaften** series is to become a platform for pioneering works and current discussions in the field of historical cultural sciences.

The series is edited by the Co-ordinating Committee of the Research Unit Historical Cultural Sciences (HKW) at the Johannes Gutenberg University Mainz.

GESA ZUR NIEDEN, BERTHOLD OVER (EDS.)
Musicians' Mobilities and Music Migrations in Early Modern Europe
Biographical Patterns and Cultural Exchanges

[transcript]

The print was financed by the Research Unit Historical Cultural Sciences (HKW).

Publication of the HERA-JRP »MusMig« financed by:

Bibliographic Information published by the Deutsche Nationalbibliothek
The Deutsche Nationalbibliothek lists this publication in the Deutsche Nationalbibliografie; detailed bibliographic data are available in the Internet at http://dnb.d-nb.de

© 2016 transcript Verlag, Bielefeld

transcript Verlag | Hermannstraße 26 | D-33602 Bielefeld | live@transcript-verlag.de

All rights reserved. No part of this book may be reprinted or reproduced or utilized in any form or by any electronic, mechanical, or other means, now known or hereafter invented, including photocopying and recording, or in any information storage or retrieval system, without permission in writing from the publisher.

Cover layout: Kordula Röckenhaus, Bielefeld
Type setting: Stephan Münch
Printed in Germany
Print-ISBN 978-3-8376-3504-1
PDF-ISBN 978-3-8394-3504-5

Content

Preface.. 9
GESA ZUR NIEDEN, BERTHOLD OVER

Roads "which are commonly wonderful for the
musicians" – Early Modern Times Musicians'
Mobility and Migration... 11
GESA ZUR NIEDEN

BETWEEN COLLECTIVE BIOGRAPHY AND BIOGRAPHY: CULTURAL-HISTORICAL APPROACHES TO MUSICIANS' MIGRATIONS IN THE EARLY MODERN AGE

Migration and Biography.
The Case of Agostino Steffani.............................. 35
COLIN TIMMS

"try it elsewhere [...]" – Konrad Hagius and
Musicians' Mobility in Early Modern Times in
Light of Local and Regional Profile....................... 51
JOACHIM KREMER

Competition at the Catholic Court of Munich.
Italian Musicians and Family Networks................. 73
BRITTA KÄGLER

From Munich to 'Foreign' Lands and Back Again.
Relocation of the Munich Court and Migration
of Musicians (c. 1690-1715) 91
BERTHOLD OVER

Migratory and Traveling Musicians at the Polish
Royal Courts in the 17th Century. The Case
of Kaspar Förster the Younger 135
BARBARA PRZYBYSZEWSKA-JARMIŃSKA

Foreign Musicians at the Polish Court in the
Eighteenth Century. The Case of Pietro Mira 151
ALINA ŻÓRAWSKA-WITKOWSKA

Luka Sorgo – a Nobleman and Composer
from Dubrovnik 171
VJERA KATALINIĆ

MUSICI and MusMig. Continuities and
Discontinuities 185
BERHOLD OVER, TORSTEN ROEDER

SOURCES OF MUSICIANS' MIGRATIONS BETWEEN COURT AND CITY

Musical Travels. Sources of Musicians' Tours and
Migrations in the Seventeenth and Eighteenth
Century 207
NORBERT DUBOWY

"... und bißhero mein Glück in der Welt zu suchen..." – Notes on the Biography of Jonas Friederich Boenicke 227
RASHID-S. PEGAH

The Russian Experience. The Example of Filippo Balatri 241
JAN KUSBER, MATTHIAS SCHNETTGER

Soloists of the Opera Productions in Brno, Holešov, Kroměříž and Vyškov. Italian Opera Singers in Moravian Sources c. 1720-1740 (Part I) 255
JANA SPÁČILOVÁ

Vienna Kärntnertortheater Singers in the Letters from Georg Adam Hoffmann to Count Johann Adam von Questenberg. Italian Opera Singers in Moravian Sources c. 1720-1740 (Part II) 275
JANA PERUTKOVÁ

DISSEMINATION AND TRANSFER OF MUSIC AND MUSIC THEORY BETWEEN COPIES, ADAPTATIONS AND REFERENCES

Estienne Roger's Foreign Composers 295
RUDOLF RASCH

From "Sonate a quattro" to "Concertos in Seven Parts". The Acclimatization of Two Compositions by Francesco Scarlatti 311
MICHAEL TALBOT

Spread of Italian Libretti. Maria Clementina
Sobieska Stuart — a Patron of Roman Operas 323
ANETA MARKUSZEWSKA

Migration of Musical Repertoire. The Attems
Music Collection from Around 1744 341
METODA KOKOLE

The Case of Juraj Križanić (1619-1683?) —
His Texts on Music. From Artefacts to Cultural Study
(Croatian Writers on Music and Transfer of Ideas in
Their New Environments)... 379
STANISLAV TUKSAR

People and Places in a (Music) Source. A Case
Study of Giuseppe Michele Stratico and His
Theoretical Treatises (Croatian Writers on Music
and Transfer of Ideas in Their New Environments) ... 389
LUCIJA KONFIC

List of Contributors 403

Index of Persons 409

Index of Places 425

Preface

In Early Modern Times, musical migrations have contributed considerably to the dynamics and synergy of the European cultural scene at large. By stimulating innovation, changes of style and patterns of musical and social behavior, musical migrations have contributed toward cohesion within a common European cultural identity. These migrations and movements are the focus of the international HERA project "Music Migrations in the Early Modern Age: the Meeting of the European East, West and South (MusMig)" that unites researchers from Croatia, Germany, Poland and Slovenia and is directed by Vjera Katalinić (Zagreb). This project, running from September 2013 until August 2016, is financed by the European Union and co-funded by the respective government departments of the countries involved.

In the project, the term "musician" is understood in a wide sense, including not only singers, instrumentalists and composers but also, for instance, dancers, librettists and music theorists. Moreover, the circulation of musical scores and ideas and the activities of instrument makers lie within the project's ambit. This results in a multi-stranded approach to the topic and a multi-faceted investigation that takes into full account the diversity of motivational factors underlying mobility and migration. The project's results are published in three anthologies and also in a database where the data collected on migratory musicians can be explored by the public.

The present volume is the outcome of a workshop, "Music Migrations: from Source Research to Cultural Studies", held at the Johannes Gutenberg-Universität in Mainz from 24 to 25 April 2014. In order to broaden the perspective, scholars from other parts of Europe were invited in addition to members of the project group. The reason was to ensure the contextualization of the project within current discussions on,

Preface

and studies of, migratory musicians in Europe. In this spirit, the volume assembles present-day research on methods, sources and individual cases within the project's spatial (European East, West and South) and temporal (17th-18th centuries) frames, as well as initial results from the individual sub-projects.

Some remarks on the formal aspect of the volume: In older documents cited in the articles, the often interchangeable letters "u" and "v" are standardized according to modern usage. Libraries and archives are identified by the library sigla created by RISM (Répertoire International des Sources Musicales/International Directory of Musical Sources), a catalog of which is easily accessible on the RISM website: http://www.rism.info/en/sigla.html.

Our acknowledgements begin with persons "inside" the book: namely, the contributors, who have done their utmost towards successful publication of the volume. With regard to persons "outside" the book, we wish first of all to thank Jörg Rogge, official spokesman (*Sprecher*) of the core research area Mainzer Historische Kulturwissenschaften (Mainz Historical Cultural Sciences), who kindly accepted our volume into the homonymous series, as well as Davina Brückner and Kristina Müller-Bongard in the office of the core area. We offer many thanks to Klaus Pietschmann, head of the IKM, Institut für Kunstgeschichte und Musikwissenschaft, Abteilung Musikwissenschaft (Institute for Art History and Musicology, Department of Musicology), for his unwavering support of the project. We are very grateful that Mainz University paid for a proofreading service and would like to thank Dagmar Stockfisch for her help in this regard, and for her efforts at finding a proofreading and translation agency. For the final work of correction we are much indebted to Michael Talbot. A particular mention is due to Stephan Münch, who designed the layout of the volume with considerable care. And special thanks, finally, go to our student assistants Larina Meinel, Janusz Hofmann, Maik Köster and Carlo Mertens for their invaluable work in setting up and running the database and for the creation of the present volume.

Mainz, June 2016   *Gesa zur Nieden, Berthold Over*

Roads "which are commonly wonderful for the musicians" – Early Modern Times Musicians' Mobility and Migration

GESA ZUR NIEDEN

The Early Modern Times musicians' migration is often examined in its positive role in music and cultural history research:[1] it is mostly considered as the motor for the development of European culture and identity carried by music and musicians, defined by processes of cultural communication and cultural exchange as well as the associated cultural interactions.[2] However, the fact that the mobility pertaining to the distribution of repertoire and transregional repertoire development did not generally have a positive connotation for the players in Early Modern Times is strongly evident in research in the cultural history sector of music, which – far from the biographies of outstanding musicians and virtuosos, the history of extraordinary musical institutions or the so-called "elite migration" – systematically documents the movements in the local, regional and transregional area also of anonymous composers, instrumentalists and singers.[3] Mobility for most of these musicians was not a self-deter-

---

1 The term "musician" in this case pertains to instrumentalists, singers, composers, cantors and musical theorists. This occupational group is to be investigated in its actions and networks, in which sometimes also scene painters, librettists and dancers/dance masters played an important role.
2 Cf. e.g. EMMER, 2013, pp. 21-29, or LEOPOLD, 2013, p. 38.
3 As paradigmatic, reference is made to the research in the Northern German area, among those EDLER, 1982; KREMER, 1997; ID., 1995; SOLL, 2006; PFEIFFER, 1991, pp. 11-19; WACZKAT, 2004b, pp. 157-170. Regarding the cultural-historical term of mobility and its not always positive classifica-

mined design, but a forced condition resulting from the search for permanent employment, the pursuit of a sedentary life and the desire for social advancement. This principal pursuit also blurs the border between the concepts of mobility and migration as the sedentariness represented the drive in most movements, be it visits, travels or permanent changes of location. For most Early Modern Times musicians, whose regional or transregional movements can be documented, this principally involved mobility with the objective of migration.

Such association is ultimately also displayed by the "Lebensbeschreibungen" (biographies) from the 18th century, where locations strongly connoted with the period of work, were only changed based on specific offers of a better position and were collectively also given first priority over social and particularly familial networks, as illuminated by the example of Johann Christoph Heuser, a musically versed cantor who, following his education in Stade and Jena, worked in Glückstadt during the second half of the 18th century and died in Altona in 1799:[4]

> "(*Vita*)
> I, Bernhard Christoph Heüser am born of Christian parents at Otterndorff über der Elben in the county of Hadeln [...] in 1717 on the 22 Dec: born, where my deceased: Sir Father was a merchant. Anno 1743, through God's guidance, I was elected deputy and castle or garrison cantor in the city and fortress Glückstadt, where I have faithfully held my office in school and church through Highest counsel for a total of 14 years. Ao 1745, I betrothed myself to a young widow named Dorothea Dithmar, born in Winterburgen and resident preacher's daughter, to whom, however, I was only married for 16 weeks. For the 2nd time I wed again a *Mademoisell* in Altona by the name of Frisch, whose Sir Father had been treasurer to this city several years ago. In this, thanks to God 36 yearlong happy marriage, the wife, now deceased ao 1781 on the 16 Apr: has born 5 dear children, 3 sons and 2 daughters, and of which the 4 oldest died in Glückstadt and of which a son 3 of those [...] is still alive. Ao 1757, to my surprise, I received the position as cantor in Altona and was employed as 4th colleague at

---

tion, it is stated in Bonß and Kesselring: "Mobility is only experienced as an independent dimension with positive connotations since the 18th century." BONSS/KESSELRING, 2001, p. 178.

4   Regarding Heuser's music making see NEUBACHER, 2001, pp. 275f.

the resident pedagogue by professor and director Schütz. Through the grace and mighty support of God, I have now administered my office for more than 28 years so that I have never received even the smallest reprimand due to the administration of my office, and I shall continue to do so with all diligence according to God's mercy as long as my strength permits [...] and as long as the Dear Lord will grant me life."[5]

Such striving for migration and the associated mobility were initiated and became a transregional phenomenon due to the geographically widely spread, yet limited market of the court, church and town music operations, characterised by diverse ranges of musical patronage, political-symbolic representation efforts and, partially, also due to scientific-

---

5   "(Lebenslauf.) Ich Bernhard Christoph Heüser bin von christl. Eltern zu Otterndorff über der Elben im Lande Hadeln [...] gebohrn 1717 d. 22 Dec: gebohren, woselbst mein seel: H: Vater Kaufmann gewesen. Anno 1743, bin ich durch Gottes besondere Fügung in der Stadt und Vestung Glückstadt zum Conrector und Schloß oder Garnisons-Cantor erwehlet, wo selbst ich mein Amt in Schul und Kirche durch den höchsten Beystand ganze 14 Jahre lang treulich geführet habe. Ich verheirathete mich daselbst ao 1745 mit einer jungen Witwen Namens Dorothea Dithmar gebohren Winterburgen und dort gewesen Predigers Tochter, die ich aber nur 16 Wochen in der Ehe hatte. Zum 2ten Mahl verband ich mich wieder mit einer Mademoisell in Altona Namens Frisch, deren H. Vater Cämmerer zu dieser Stadt vor einig Jahren gewesen ist. Zu dieser GottLob in die 36 Jahr vergnüglich geführten Ehe hat die nunmehr ao 1781 d 16 Apr: seelig verstorbene Frau mir 5 liebe Kinder, 3 Söhne und 2 Töchter zur Welt gebracht, wovon die 4 ältesten in Glückstadt wieder gestorben, und dazu ein Sohn 3 davon [...] noch am Leben sind ist. Ao 1757 erhielte ich ohne mein Vermuthen die Cantorat-Stelle in Altona und wurde als 4ter Colleg bey dem hiesig Paedagogio vom H: Professor u Recktor Schütz eingeführt. Allhier habe ich nun durch Gottes Gnade und mächtigen Baistand bereits über 28 Jahr mein Amt täglich verwaltet, so daß ich niemals wegen Führung meines Amtes den geringsten Verweis bekommen, und werde forderhin dasselbe nach Gottes gnädig Willen so lange mit allem Fleiß verwalten, bis meine Kräfte es zulassen [...] und der liebe Gott mir das Leben fristen wird." Archive of the Christianeum Altona, S 41: Nachlass Bernhard Christoph Heuser. Based on the contained information, the *vita* most probably originates from 1785. In this *vita*, Heuser seems to ignore his education stages in Stade and Jena and, from the onset, seems to concentrate only on the permanent positions. Cf. NEUBACHER, 2001, p. 275.

artistic interests of the princes.⁶ Also musical institutions, such as the Italian theater with its "Stagione" principle or schools ranging from the Thomas school to the Neapolitan conservatories, were set up for the fluctuation of musicians and apprentices from the very beginning.⁷ The court orchestra, city musician as well as cantor or *Kapellmeister*/musician employment in churches and cloisters represented the final destination of musician careers, with the exception of the touring companies or traveling virtuosos; a fact which is impressively illustrated in the establishment and implementation of familial networks of court as well as city musicians who bequeathed offices or procured privileges by marriage.⁸ At the same time, the principality and the city elders not only promoted the permanent settlement at a particular location, but also utilized musicians for diplomatic or representative tasks for limited periods of time, be it during the Grand Tour of individual princes, the conveyance of messages or to ensure political connections or the arrangement of particularly important festivities. In addition, also the movements of the entire court generated mobility among the traveling court musicians, while city musicians were rather induced to leave due to the influx of military units or touring companies, especially since their income resulted mainly from participations based on privileges for playing and teaching in the urban area. On one hand, these exits were greatly influenced by family ties and networks among the musicians, but were also prepared by dedications and content of musical works which created a reference to important princes and courts. Such references, this is particularly obvious up to the first half of the 18th century, were quite often generated in form of musical riddles or detailed technical demands, which necessitated a direct contact between musicians and patrons for the rendition and reception of the music.⁹

The rational for the continuation of a journey or the general mobility could vary greatly depending on the place of work, musical status

---

6   Based on the background of the vast literature to these points, a few references to the Schwerin court may suffice here: KLETT, 1999, pp. 91-96; WACZKAT, 2004a, pp. 252-263. The scope of the musical institutions, promotions as well as mere interests varied depending on the ruling system which could also differ depending on the geographic-cultural location (e.g. Kingdom of France and principalities in the German region).
7   I would like to thank Berthold Over for this information.
8   Cf. in this context the paradigmatic publication AHRENS, 2009.
9   ZUR NIEDEN, 2015, p. 124.

and level of recognition of the musician. These differences are primarily expressed via the drive for further musical education and perfection. If these predominated, mobility was connoted positively. As a consequence, the term of mobility during the 17th and 18th century has to be located in a range of reputation of certain positions, the cultural and social characterization of individual cities or courts and the musician himself. This is also evident in the example of Early Modern Times ego-documents. For example, in 1792, Heinrich Conrad Wille who – like Heuser – was also employed in Glückstadt, describes his departure from there with a specific recourse to the name of the city:

> "For a long time, the desire in me has been vivid/: as I have never been happy in Glückstadt, and will never be happy/: to travel in order to see whether Mad[ame] Fortuna has kept a good lot for me in her pot of luck/happiness."[10]

However, the extent to which the term of luck/happiness is also connected with the description of résumés between livelihood and further development as musician is evident in a *vita* "written by Joachim Quantz himself" ("von ihm selbst entworfen[en]"), which was published in Marpurg's *Historisch-kritischen Beiträgen zur Aufnahme der Musik* (History-critical contributions for the admission of the music) in 1754. Quantz uses the term "Glück (luck/happiness)" in three different contexts: (1) In view of a satisfactory future as musician,[11] (2) in descriptions of extraordinary acquaintances and friendships[12] and (3) as an adjective for a trouble-free journey.[13] All three of Quantz's points aim at the improvement of his musical abilities with which he imagined achieving the "ultimate purpose" ("Endzweck") of comprehensive musical knowledge, a

---

10 "Lange schon war der Wunsch in mir rege/: da ich nie glücklich in Glückstadt war, und auch nie sein kann/: mich auf Reisen zu begeben, um zu sehen, ob Mad[ame] Fortuna nicht in ihrem Glückstöpfchen noch ein gutes Loos für mich aufgehoben." City archives Glückstadt, No. 1015; letter of the city musician Heinrich Conrad Wille, 8 August 1792, cited from: SOLL, 2006, p. 208.
11 QUANTZ, 1754, pp. 198, 204, 228, 234, 249.
12 IBID., pp. 210, 228, 243.
13 IBID., p. 239.

permanent position at a renowned court[14] and, last but not least, also inherent "liberties" ("Freiheiten") in the execution and fulfilment of this position.[15] This "ultimate purpose" is almost exclusively achieved by changing locations from Merseburg via Poland, Dresden, Italy, France, the Netherlands, England and Berlin, which also led to new acquaintances and the expansion of his network.[16] In contrast, he spoke clearly against the unauthorised distribution of his works by the Amsterdam publisher Roger.[17] The fact that the changes of locality were positively connoted in comparison to a non-person-related distribution of his musical productions is surely due to his success as a musician, but he himself attributes this to "divine providence" ("göttliche Vorsehung") in the style

14   IBID., pp. 206, 222.
15   "In November 1741, I was appointed to Berlin for the last time by His Majesty of Prussia, who offered me such advantageous conditions, services that I could no longer refuse to accept them. Two thousand thaler *per annum* salary for life; furthermore a special payment for my composition; one hundred ducats for each flute I would deliver; the freedom of not playing in the orchestra, but only in the royal chamber music and to report to none other than his Royal Majesty, deserved forgoing a service [in the Polish court orchestra, GzN], where I never had such prospects." ("Im November des 1741 Jahres wurde ich zum letzenmale von Seiner Majestät von Preussen nach Berlin berufen, und von Höchstdenenselben mir mit so vortheilhaften Bedingungen, Dienste angeboten, daß ich sie anzunehmen mich nicht länger weigern konnte. Zweytausend Thaler jährliche Besoldung auf Lebenszeit; ausserdem eine besondere Bezahlung meiner Composition; hundert Dukaten für jede Flöte die ich liefern würde; die Freyheit nicht im Orchester, sondern nur in der Königlichen Kammermusik zu spielen, und von Niemands als des Königs Befehl abzuhangen, verdienten wohl einen Dienst [in der polnischen Hofkapelle, GzN] aufzugeben, wo ich solche Vortheile niemahls zu hoffen hatte.") IBID., pp. 247f.
16   "Dresden and Berlin were places where I would have liked to settle in time: as I could have heard more beautiful music there and learned much more than in Merseburg." ("Dresden, oder Berlin waren die Oerter, wo ich mit der Zeit meinen Aufenthalt zu finden wünschete: weil ich da viel mehr Schönes von Musik hören, und viel mehr lernen zu können glaubte, als in Merseburg.") IBID., p. 202.
17   "I do not avouch for the edition of other sonatas which have long since been published under my name in Holland." ("Zu der Ausgabe anderer Sonaten, die, unter meinem Namen, schon lange vorher in Holland herausgekommen, bekenne ich mich nicht.") IBID., p. 247.

of Mattheson's *Ehren=Pforte*, which had made his luck/happiness possible.[18] In Quantz's *vita*, luck/happiness is illustrated as the fulfilment of a "desire" ("Verlangen"), the realization of which is not within his own power, yet is simultaneously bound to certain – earthly – locations:

> "This is my *vita*: and the divine providence has led me in this manner, and my desire which I have had for many years in times when there was not the least indication, to make my fortune in Dresden or Berlin has been fulfilled at both places. I thank providence and the grace of God that I am still well at this time."[19]

The ego-documents utilized here indicate that the musicians' migration is a comprehensive complex between – depending on the location – differently applied princely, ecclesiastic and civic promotion and/or representation and individual musical as well as socially and often still religiously defined careers. In this complex, collective mobility motivations, such as sedentariness or the social rise, encounter simultaneously artistically and socially geared individual biographies, because the own "Glück" was often pursued quite individually based on the background of the distinct offer or established on musical standards which were quite different. Accordingly rich in variation are also the cultural and social levels upon which the drive for mobility, the associated motivation and the consequences between work and elite migration is reflected in the traditional sources. It is thus important to observe both perspectives – that of the musicians and that of the employers and recipients – in individual case studies in order to record the difference of the social and artistic career conditions as well as the cultural radiation of individual cities, churches/cloisters and courts. It is furthermore important to detail migration movements, such as the migration of Italian musicians to Northern Europe, or collective mobility drives, such as the search for permanent

---

18 Regarding the reflection of religious aspects in autobiographies of the Age of Enlightenment cf. SCHENK, 1957, pp. 4f.
19 "Dieses ist mein Lebenslauf; und auf diese Art hat die göttliche Vorsehung mich geführet, und mein Verlangen, das ich seit vielen Jahren, in Zeiten, da noch nicht der geringste Schein dazu war, immer gehabt habe, entweder in Dresden oder in Berlin mein Glück zu machen, an beyden Orten erfüllet. Ich danke es derselben und der Gnade Gottes, daß ich mich hier noch in erwünschtem Wohlseyn befinde." QUANTZ, 1754, pp. 249f.

employment, which also secured the working conditions for the future generations of the family, by case studies on different social and musical levels. In doing so, the Early Modern Times mobility and migration term can be continued, which also allows the distinct classification of transfers of musical genres, works and performance practices as well as innovations of instrument manufacturing and theoretical music ideas between cultural interest and social pragmatism.

The consideration of the individual social and musical standards is particularly exciting where biographic experiences or perceptions are reflected in musical works, as was the case with Johann Jakob Froberger in mid-17th century, who set the fall down the stairs of his French friend and his stormy crossing over the Rhine to music, as well as allowing the death of his life-long patron, Ferdinand III, to fade out with the triple sounding of an f".[20] During his entire life, Froberger carried the title of a Vienna court musician, most probably commissioned the fabrication of a coat of arms at the end of his career and spent his last days in an apparently balanced hierarchical relationship with the princess in Héricourt.[21] However, the example of Johann Conrad Rosenbusch, who worked in the so-called city of exiles Glückstadt for more than 20 years, who secured his privileges there by his individualism rather than musical compositions suitable for church and who was praised by Johann Mattheson for his perfect description of the motivation of his biographically designed compendium of the *Ehren=Pforte,* shows the comprehensive music term, which also reflected mobility and sedentariness with respect to a religiosity between earthly self-stylization and vertically applied worship.[22] Mattheson emphasizes Rosenbusch for the perfect education of the blind city organist in Itzehoe, before quoting Rosenbusch's letter of 9 December 1739 in the *Ehren=Pforte*:

> "I am pleased Your Highness finally allows the *Ehrenpforte,* which was established laboriously over many years: the Lord may bless such

---

20 SCHULENBERG, 2010, pp. 271-302; CYPESS, 2012, pp. 45-54. The composition dedicated to Ferdinand III carries the name *Lamentation faite sur la très douloureuse mort de Sa Majesté Impériale Ferdinand le Troisième, et se joue lentement avec discrétion.*
21 ANNIBALDI, 1998, pp. 56f.; RUGGERI, 1998, pp. 23-37.
22 EDLER, 1982, pp. 83, 110, 190-191.

work in His honor and let those who read it discover His ways on earth (**which are commonly wonderful for the musicians**) ... ."[23]

Following this cultural and music historical research status, this volume emphasizes the biographies of Early Modern Times musicians and music theorists rather than the Early Modern Times music migration as a collective phenomenon and origin of a cultural hybridity concerning composition, genres and ideas. The mobile musicians are illuminated from various conceptual aspects based on a very broad range of sources and particularly also as acting transregional in their musical and written artefacts. In this manner, it is not only possible to document motivations, intentions and strategies of musicians who taught own family dynasties at foreign courts, worked between musical compositions and clerical offices or brokered other musicians. At the same time, the social and institutional environment of the musician becomes evident through their networks, where it made a difference whether it was a medium-sized court or a small-town *Collegium Musicum* in the southern German region, or whether it pertained to the musically well-equipped Polish or Danish court. At all these locations, connections between the musician and his prince or competitive relationships between the individual musicians were aspired and managed.

In turn, the influence of dynastic and political aspects related to individual courts, churches/cloisters, cities or music event types can be determined by the approach of the collective biography. This step is particularly important in understanding the cultural radiation of also "medium-sized" courts, which only served as way stations for some musicians and were targeted by others for permanent establishment. A collective biography can therefore not only be assigned to the interface between individual *vitae* and musical institutions (court orchestra, churches, educational institutions) whose members are collectively observed, but can also be related to cross-geographical entities, because a person collective can also be compiled based on the native language, the place of education or even the still pre-governmental kingdoms, republics and principalities.[24]

---

23 "Es ist mir eine Freude, daß Ew. Hochedl. die in vielen Jahren mühsam errichtete Ehrenpforte endlich wollen ans Licht treten lassen: der Herr seegne solches Werck zu seiner Ehre, und lasse die es lesen dadurch zur Erkenntniß seiner Wege auf Erden (**welche gemeiniglich bey den Musicis wunderbar sind**) gelangen ... ." MATTHESON, 1740, p. 296 (highlight in original).
24 KÄGLER, 2015, pp. 236-268.

Such a specifically designed research customization between individual and collective biography is indeed able to provide a cultural contextualization of the mostly patchy individual biographies and to give insight into the development of culturally comprehensive attributions, functionalities of institutions or terms of taste. Much more than with respect to this field of reference between music and geographic-cultural attribution, they provide insight into that which is located between music and socio-cultural matters of fact and what can be heuristically described with the term of authenticity. As particularly illuminated by administrative sources, musicians were confronted with issues of credibility or authenticity particularly on foreign soil, which manifested themselves especially when they intended to settle permanently. Issues regarding credibility arose not least in connection with prohibitions and liberties which were granted to the strangers at the new location or decidedly attributed to them in advance, for the circumnavigation or claim of which, however, they had to demonstrate a certain affiliation. This is initially evident based on passports, which simultaneously reflect the extent of mobility which could characterize unknown musicians. For example, the "Musicus" Michael Schmoll, who most likely originated from Lille, intended traveling from Cologne to Brussels in 1788, and to continue further from there, traveled to Glückstadt in the north of Hamburg in 1789 and ultimately returned his passport in Schwerin, where it is kept in the city archives to this date:

> "Accordingly, the presenter of this pass, Michael Schmoll, is a musician from Lile in Briseau who, arriving here with his 3 children and a true pass and authentic certificates has sufficiently legitimized himself and who wishes to travel from here where the air is clean and free from pollution, so God will, to Brussels and further, in order for his music to be heard. We thus request authorities everywhere, in accordance with the reciprocal establishment of services, to allow the above mentioned presenter Michael Schmoll to pass freely and without hindrance.
> Issued with personal signature and application of the greater seal in Wiedingen am Rhein in the Nieder Erzstift Cologne on 30 October 1788 Erlenwein electoral court counsellor of Cologne, the city and Amtsschulteis at Linn and Ürdingen
> Prod.: Glückstadt, 31 May 1789"[25]

---

25 "Demnach zeiger dieses Michael Schmoll ein Musicus aus Lile in Briseau mit 3 Kindern dahier ankommend, und sich mit seinen aufrichtigem pässe

If one considers the concept of authenticity as a concept of testimony which is characterised by the correctness of the message and the credibility of the messenger,[26] it indicates the measure of foreignness with which the newly arrived was confronted within the civic and court sociality. This becomes paradigmatic in the example of the Huguenots, who settled as complete colonies in the German area particularly in the 1730s, where they were guaranteed freedom of religion. The reformed colonies included at least one priest, mostly also an organist. Particularly in case of the cantor, it was important that he was a native French speaker so he could teach the children of the colonies in French.[27] The French par-

so als sonstig authentischen urkunden genugsam dahier legitimiert, nunmehro aber von hieraus, allwo gottdank eine reine und von aller Contagion frayen Luft ist, nach Brußel und weiter, um sich in der Music hörnn zu laßen; zureisen willens, als wird hiemit jedes ortes obrigkeit [...] gebühr Suboblatione ad reciproca dienst freundlich ersuchet, obbem[elter] Zeigern Michael Schmoll allerorten frey und ungehindert paß, und repaßiren zu laßen gegeben unter eigenhändiger unterschrifft und beigedruckt größerem insingne widingen am Rhein im Nider Erzstifft Köln den 30. 8bris 1788.
Erlenwein Curkolnischer Hofrath dem Stadt und Amtsschulteis zu Linn und Ürdingen
Prod: Glückstadt d 31 Maj 1789"
City Archives Schwerin, 12.06 Paßwesen, Akte 10678. I would like to thank Berthold Over for his help in the transcription of the passport.

26 KRÄMER, 2012, pp. 15-26.
27 This argument was expressed by Cantor Gardiol, who was recruited by Consul Leers from the French-reformed colony Bützow in Mecklenburg: "It surprises me that your cantor does not want to hold the lessons, because it is an extremely necessary matter for which the cantor is responsible, because without it, the reformed children are forced to visit the Lutheran schools, which would do great injustice to the colony which has just begun to establish itself; and I believe that Pastor Bride would be well advised to force him to hold the lessons, as is the case all over Brandenburg and here; [...] once the lessons have ended, the cantor is free to give private lessons, but school may not be neglected in the process; I well believe that the cantor is not willing to devote himself to the school lessons as he can be sure to make a living in Hamburg just as well as in Glückstadt." ("Ce qui me surprend beaucoup, c'est que votre Chantre, ne veut pas tenir école, c'est pourtant une chose fort necessaire et dont le Chantre est obligé, car sans quoi les enfans des Reformés seroient obligés d'aller aux Ecoles Lutheriennes

ishes also seemed able to operate an organ, as is evident from a petition of the director of the scheduled French-reformed colony Glückstadt in the year 1762.[28] The first mass "by the Pastor Lavigne in the reformed church at Glückstadt was simultaneously an inaugural sermon which was altogether pleasing, and the *Te Deum Laudamus* was being sung under trumpets and kettle drums".[29] However, the responsible Cantor Gardiol particularly brought a comprehensive network with him, which consisted of members of his former colony in Bützow in Mecklenburg and Güstrow, in close proximity thereof, furthermore, also acquaintances from Berlin, Geneva, Wismar and Stade. Among other, Gardiol asserted

---

ce qui feroit beaucoup de tort à cette Colonie qui ne fait que de commancer à s'établir, et je trouve que Monsieur le Pasteur Bride fait fort bien de le forcer à tenir l'Ecole, comme cela se pratique dans tous le Brandebourg aussi bien qu'ici, [...] après l'Ecole fini le Chantre peut donner des leçons mais il ne faut pas que l'Ecole soit negligée, je veut bien croire que votre chantre ne voudra pas se soumettre à l'Ecole, sur tout s'il est assuré qu'il puisse gagner à Hambourg sa vie aussi largement qu'à Gluckstadt.") Letter from Gardiol to Consul Leers dated 22 April 1761, in: D-SWGa, Abt. 65.2: Deutsche Kanzlei zu Kopenhagen, Nr. 3390: Französisch-reformierte Gemeinde in Glückstadt.

28 "The German reformed church shall peacefully grant the French their meeting whenever it seems appropriate to pursue their mass; one will give them a key to the church and allow them to use the organ, and in order to avoid any discussion, one shall allow them to inspect the organ together with one or two experts to decide over its condition when the French have used it and returned it in the event that the French build a church of their own." ("Que l'Eglise allemande Reformé laissera paisiblement jouïr Les françois de s'assembler, quand bon leur semblera, pour ÿ faire leur exercisse Divin, on leur donnera une Clef de L'Eglise, et ils auront La disposition des Orgues, et afin de prevenir tout debat on faira visiter Les orgues, par un ou deux Expert, affin que Lon puisse juger dans quel état Elles sont, quand Les français auront eu La Liberter de s'en servïr, et Les auront remises, Pour que entout cas, cÿ Les francais vissent à battir une Eglise pour eux.") Letter from the Danish Consul Leers to the Chancellor Johann Hartwig Ernst von Bernsdorff in Copenhagen dated 29 October 1762, in: IBID.

29 "durch den Geistlichen Lavigne in der reformierten Kirche zu Glückstadt gleichsam eine Antritts-Predigt, mit welcher man überhaupt sehr vergnügt gewesen, [ge]halten, und das Te Deum Laudamus unter Trompeten und Paucken-Schall singen [ge]lassen". Letter of City Councilman Friedrich von Eyben from Plön to the Budget Council dated 4 August 1762, in: IBID.

this network by being able to send letters with the acceptance of persons for a joint move to Glückstadt to the locally organized Consul Leers "en original".[30] This also applied for Pastor Lavigne, whom Leers had recruited from Stockholm, however before having received the royal allocation of an annual wage from Copenhagen. When Lavigne arrived in Glückstadt, Leers was only able to pay him a small part of the promised wage. Subsequently, Leers and Lavigne accused each other of incredibility. While Lavigne asserted that "I can prove the opposite with authentic documents in my possession and the testimony of the honorable French-reformed consistory of Stockholm, which one cannot deny me",[31] Leers rolled up the entire city of Glückstadt as witness for his good deeds for the settlement of a French colony ("I take all of Glückstadt as my witness because, as Saint Paul says: show me your faith through your works, may Glückstadt judge over my conduct").[32] The testimonies became so important as Gardiol, Leers and Lavigne lacked the documented basis for their incomes and the privileges in the new colony because the King of Denmark and Norway had long since failed to renew the privileges or reply to repeated requests for a salary for the preacher and the cantor as well as financial allowances for the reimbursement of travel expenses to Glückstadt. With respect to the fulfilment of the requests, Leers – and obviously also Gardiol – stylized their intention in a deeply religious zeal ("zèle") with the opulent church-music arrangement of the masses over a long period of time, entirely in line with a divine deed on earth.[33] Ultimately, all three left Glückstadt once again; Gardiol returned to Bützow, Lavigne travelled to Hamburg and Leers sold his house "behind the house a large garden a bricked

---

30 Letter from Gardiol to Consul Leers dated 22 April 1761, in: IBID.
31 "je puis prouver le contraire et par les pièces authentiques que j'ai et par le temoignage du vénérable Consistoire Reformé François de Stockholm, qui ne me sera pas refusé". Letter from Lavigne to Consul Leers dated 21 December 1762, in: IBID.
32 "je prend tout Gluckstadt pour Temoin, Car comme dit St. Paul, fais moÿ voire ta foÿ par tes œuvres, que Gluckstadt juge de ma Conduitte". Letter from the Danish Consul Leers to the Foreign Minister Chancellor Johann Hartwig Ernst von Bernsdorff in Copenhagen dated 6 January 1762, in: IBID.
33 Letter from the Danish Consul Leers to Chancellor Johann Hartwig Ernst von Bernstorff dated 19 August 1764, in: IBID.

Lusthaus",[34] which was apparently designed to once serve the community as a church and for the extension of which he had already planned an extensive collection.[35] As also the French-reformed community of Bützow in Mecklenburg – from which Gardiol had traveled – had conducted an extensive collection in 1761-1763, among other in The Hague (Den Haag), Utrecht and Amsterdam, the extent at which purely financial reasons could rather have been decisive for the foundation of a Huguenot colony in Glückstadt, remains unclear.[36]

All these examples refer to the importance of the "degree of authenticity" of documents for the mobility, but also for the establishment of certain persons at a location. Through documents considered authentic it was possible to verify things over a certain geographical distance; however, they conversely and quite correctly also served for integration at places where the "presenter" was unknown. Accordingly, written documents, such as passports, privileges and certificates were a direct part of persons and their networks in times when authenticity was defined through authorities established according to status and, based on this, led to the sociality of citizens which not necessary belonged to the elite. Contrary to this, actions were considered much less important at times, particularly if they lacked an authorized base issued by a local or transregional authority. The above mentioned recourses to the Bible and other written testimonies speak volumes.

Based on the fact that the mobility, which was so distinctive for the Early Modern Time music history, was also characterized by such administrative as well as music-historic documents, this triple step of authority, authenticity and sociality may be considered an important basis also for the assessment of musical or music-theoretical written testimonies, which were also part of the musicians' mobility. The type of authority between author and dedicatee playing a role and the strategic-social intentions which generate sociality can probably be discerned in clear details

---

34   "Hinterm Hause einen grossen Garten ein gemauertes Lusthaus". *Glückstädtische Fortuna* Nr. 26, Mittewochen, 30 March 1763, in: IBID.

35   Project for a collection to obtain the necessary sum for the restoration of the new French-reformed church in Glückstadt ("Projet pour faire une Collecte qui puisse nous fournir les sommes necessaires pour mettre la nouvelle Eglise Reformé Françoise de Gluckstadt dans un etat decent et convenable") of Consul Leers, in: IBID.

36   Cf. D-SWa, Domanialamt Bützow-Rhün, 2.22-10/3.

under the paradigm of an Early Modern Time situation of foreignness, as the foreign musicians simultaneously strove for an image of the prince as well as an image of the relevant social networks with their compositions and treatises.[37] Also here it is important to observe the versatility of the actors:[38] a copy of arias heard on the Grand Tour was able to generate cultural authenticity in the context of the education of the prince, just as a music tractate of Tartini, adopted in theoretical scriptures of the Adriatic region, was surely related to the travel experiences of the author and possibly also with the sociality within the European Republic of Scholars perceived by him.

Based on the authenticity definition and its intersections with authority and sociality it is furthermore possible to trace the alternating role of the divine instance in the 17th and 18th century, which was strongly characterised by the volte-face of education. Sometimes, an unbroken adherence to the religion also elucidates the social accesses on foreign soil associated by the actors with the mobility; this is once again particularly concise in the example of the French-reformed commune of Glückstadt: for example, Leers does not refer to an administrative document, but immediately to the Christian lore in the Bible to stylize his actions *in situ* as testimonies, similar to the case of Rosenbusch's "wonderful" roads of the "Musicis" – even if, in the process, he thought of the earthly ways of the Lord. The authentication processes in today's, i.e. personality-related, sense are surely only observable toward the end of the 18th century. However, the tension field between sedentariness and social ascent suggested above indicates that foreignness experiences necessitated the clarification of cultural character and affiliations much earlier and that written documents played an important part in the process.

Such an outline addresses three sections which are decisive for the examination of individual *vitae* with respect to cultural-historical implications of mobility and migration:

(1) The entanglement of prosopography, structural history and biography are urgently required to record and quantify systematic as well

---

37 Rudolf Stichweh characterises foreignness in Early Modern Times through cooperation formations (see e.g. national churches in Rome, colonies) and their "Immediate status [...] with respect to the prince or king". STICHWEH, 2010, p. 115.

38 Regarding the legitimation chances of royalty resulting from the interaction with strangers cf. IBID.

as individual effects on mobility. This sector not least affects the issue of the relevance of case studies for transcending contexts, but also profits due to the immediate entanglement of musicians' migration and musical institutions such as the court, but also ecclesiastic chapels or educational institutions, also with respect to a general cultural history of the musical life in the 17th and 18th century. To this end, Colin Timms and Joachim Kremer point out the conditions and influences on individual careers based on the fact that musicians' migration was an everyday occurrence in Early Modern Times. During the 18th century, successes and failures contributed considerably to the development of individuality. While here also the of musicians' "way of life" is discussed as a unit of mobility and music experience, Britta Kägler and Berthold Over illuminate the institutional and dynastic conditions of the positioning of musicians at a foreign court and their dependency on the movement of the court, based on two collective biographies. Also foreign musicians succeeded to develop familiar networks at courts and, in doing so, co-constructed music-history relevant long-term perspectives of these courts, which excluded a career desire. Whereas Alina Żórawska-Witkowska and Barbara Przybyszewska-Jarmińska compared individual biographies with a systematic overall view of the presences of foreign musicians at the Polish court of the 17th and 18th century. This approach not only emphasizes the importance of interregional networks for the individual careers, but also the versatility of the musicians in various contexts. Vjera Katalinić documents how much-traveled musicians enhanced the local music life in Dubrovnik (Ragusa), and which basic knowledge of foreign music styles were required for this with the "local citizens". It is important to define this bilateral versatility, reacting to different institutional and cultural circumstances as well as regionally educated musicians, also in the classification and categorization structure of the database, as suggested in a contribution by Berthold Over and Torsten Roeder for the MusMig Person Data Repository.

(2) The topic has a comparative perspective on the partially very pervious areas of court, church/cloister and city, but also local, regional and transregional circles. This concerns not only the radius available for the search for sources, but also the reconstruction of cultural understandings, as they can be expressed in the context of long journeys and the achievement of career steps between divine providence and social ascent. According to a transcending contribution by Norbert Dubowy regarding

types of sources documenting musicians' mobility between visits, trips and migration and whereby their intentionality can be captured by their contextualization with networks and institutions, Rashid-S. Pegah follows the trip of a singer without permanent employment between civic and court sources and points out the importance of selective gratifications for musicians at a variety of places. Subsequently, Jan Kusber and Matthias Schnettger look at the Moscow image of an Italian castrato who rendered the tension field between the court of the Tsar, his employer, and the foreigner's quarter in autobiographic verses. The centrality of the prince was obviously not sufficient for the integration of a foreign singer, who furthermore asserted confessional, socio-cultural and educational reasons for his experiences as a foreigner. Bohemian sources are paramount at the end of this section: Jana Spáčilová assesses opera libretti of Bohemian productions in order to emphasize the importance also of regional networks and exchange structures between individual regional opera houses and traveling opera troupes for the Italian singers. This view is joined by the contribution of Jana Perutková, which focusses on the recruiting of Italian singers between Vienna, Brno (Brünn), Prague and Graz based on a court correspondence.

(3) It is advisable to also devote a detailed study to the handling of musical and music theory documents. The personal playing of music in a certain ensemble or in front of a certain audience is not the same as a report about it in an ego document or a copy of the played composition or, in turn, an aesthetic or music-theoretic essay about it in a tract. Each communicative act is characterized by different authorities, testimonies and social contexts and – this is ultimately demonstrated by Froberger's compositions on a musical level – is reflected in different narratives. Rudolf Rasch and Michael Talbot, in their contributions for the publisher Estienne Roger in Amsterdam and for the reception of Italian *concerti* of the Scarlatti brothers in England, show how target-oriented compositions, and particularly editions, could be adapted to different musical practices and cultural reception samples and/or how quickly a composition could be distributed also without the consent of the author and with a multitude of unauthorized changes. Based on Roger's received letters, Rasch verifies how important the written correspondence was for the distribution of musical repertoire. With the English copy of the *concerti* from the 1730s, Talbot documents certain pragmatism in the interlinking of works of migrated musicians with those of foreign musicians of rank-

ing, by showing how the acculturation of music occurs in an environment determined by other music-cultural experiences. In contrast, Aneta Markuszewska pursues the distribution of opera material in connection with the dedicatee Maria Clementina Sobieska Stuart, who lived in Roman exile and whose living conditions found reflexes in libretti. The extent to which music collections provide indications of biographical aspects of individual composers, touring companies or the princes themselves can be reconstructed based on the illustration of the Attems music collection from today's Slovenska Bistrica (Windisch Freistritz) near Maribor by Metoda Kokole. A similarly lively transfer of ideas is evident in the music tractates of music theorists from the Adriatic region, examined by Lucija Konfic and Stanislav Tuksar. Also here, the biographic stations of the authors, such as the personal acquaintance with Tartini in Padua or a stay in Rome and Moscow, are important elements for the understanding and cultural contextualization of the music-theoretic and music-aesthetic documents.

A total view of the contributions clarifies that the investigation of the Early Modern Times musicians' migration has to occur through biographic, institution-historical or prosopographical case studies, but that substantial and methodical connections also result from collective research in the context of digital humanities or generally by bundling essential research results. The extent to which works regarding musicians' mobility and migration can illuminate also the biography of an Andrea Bernasconi, the reception of the Mingotti touring company or Moscow's role in the European music life could already be indicated in the volume based on cross references between individual contributions.

Manuscript sources

Archive of the Christianeum Altona, S 41: Nachlass Bernhard Christoph Heuser.
City Archives Glückstadt, Nr. 1015, cited from: SOLL, 2006, p. 208.
City Archives Schwerin, 12.06 Paßwesen, Akte 10678.
D-SWa, Domanialamt Bützow-Rhün, 2.22-10/3.
D-SWGa, Abt. 65.2: Deutsche Kanzlei zu Kopenhagen, Nr. 3390: Französisch-reformierte Gemeinde in Glückstadt.

Printed sources

HERTEL, JOHANN WILHELM, Autobiographie, ed. by Erich Schenk, Graz/ Cologne 1957.
MATTHESON, JOHANN, Grundlage einer Ehren=Pforte, Hamburg 1740.
QUANTZ, JOHANN JOACHIM, Herrn Johann Joachim Quantzens Lebenslauf, von ihm selbst entworfen, in: Historisch-kritische Beyträge zur Aufnahme der Musik, vol. 1, ed. by FRIEDRICH-WILHELM MARPURG, Berlin 1754, pp. 197-250.

Literature

AHRENS, CHRISTIAN, „Zu Gotha ist eine gute Kapelle...". Aus dem Innenleben einer thüringischen Hofkapelle des 18. Jahrhunderts (Friedenstein-Forschungen 4), Stuttgart 2009.
ANNIBALDI, CLAUDIO, Froberger à Rome: de l'artisanat frescobaldien aux secrets de composition de Kircher, in: J.J. Froberger musicien européen, ed. by DENIS MORRIER, Paris 1998, pp. 39-66.
BONSS, WOLFGANG/KESSELRING, SVEN, Mobilität am Übergang von der Ersten zur Zweiten Moderne, in: Die Modernisierung der Moderne, ed. by ULRICH BECK/WOLFGANG BONß, Frankfurt a.M. 2001, pp. 177-190.
CYPESS, REBECCA, 'Memento mori Froberger?' Locating the Self in the Passage of Time, in: Early Music XI/1 (2012), pp. 45-54.
EDLER, ARNFRIED, Der nordelbische Organist. Studien zu Sozialstatus, Funktion und kompositorischer Produktion bis zum 20. Jahrhundert (Kieler Schriften zur Musikwissenschaft 23), Kassel 1982.
EMMER, PIETER C., Migration and the Making of a Common European Culture, 1500-1800, in: Migration und Identität. Wanderbewegungen und Kulturkontakte in der Musikgeschichte (Analecta Musicologica 49), ed. by SABINE EHRMANN-HERFORT/SILKE LEOPOLD, Kassel 2013, pp. 21-29.
KÄGLER, BRITTA, Von 'Geschücklichkeiten', Pfauenfeldern und einem 'Phonascus'. Kollektivbiographische Studien zu deutschsprachigen Musikern in den italienischen Musikzentren Venedig und Rom (1650-1750), in: Europäische Musiker in Venedig, Rom und Neapel 1650-1750 (Analecta Musicologica 52), ed. by ANNE-MADELEINE GOULET/GESA ZUR NIEDEN, Kassel 2015, pp. 236-268.

KLETT, DIETER, Mecklenburgische Staatskapelle Schwerin 1563-1995, in: Studien zur lokalen und territorialen Musikgeschichte Mecklenburgs und Pommerns I, ed. by EKKEHARD OCHS, Greifswald 1999², pp. 89-102.

KRÄMER, SYBILLE, Zum Paradoxon von Zeugenschaft im Spannungsfeld von Personalität und Depersonalisierung, in: Renaissance der Authentizität? Über die neue Sehnsucht nach dem Ursprünglichen, ed. by MICHAEL RÖSSNER/HEIDEMARIE UHL, Bielefeld 2012, pp. 15-26.

KREMER, JOACHIM, Joachim Gerstenbüttel (1647-1721) im Spannungsfeld von Oper und Kirche. Ein Beitrag zur Musikgeschichte Hamburgs, Hamburg 1997.

ID., Das norddeutsche Kantorat im 18. Jahrhundert. Untersuchungen am Beispiel Hamburgs (Kieler Schriften zur Musikwissenschaft 43), Kassel 1995.

LEOPOLD, SILKE, Musikwissenschaft und Migrationsforschung. Einige grundsätzliche Überlegungen, in: Migration und Identität. Wanderbewegungen und Kulturkontakte in der Musikgeschichte (Analecta Musicologica 49), ed. by SABINE EHRMANN-HERFORT/SILKE LEOPOLD, Kassel 2013, pp. 30-39.

NEUBACHER, JÜRGEN, Zur Musikgeschichte Altonas während der Zeit von Telemanns Wirken in Hamburg, in: Beiträge zur Musikgeschichte Hamburgs vom Mittelalter bis in die Neuzeit (Hamburger Jahrbuch für Musikwissenschaft 18), ed. by HANS JOACHIM MARX, Frankfurt a.M. 2001, pp. 267-311.

ZUR NIEDEN, GESA, Mobile Musicians. Paths of Migration in Early Modern Europe, in: Jahrbuch für Europäische Geschichte. European History Yearbook 16 (2015), pp. 111-129.

PFEIFFER, RÜDIGER, Einige Bemerkungen zu Telemann und Mecklenburg, insbesondere Schwerin und Strelitz, sowie zu Telemann-Quellen der Musikabteilung der Wissenschaftlichen Allgemeinbibliothek Schwerin, in: Georg Philipp Telemann. Werküberlieferung, Editions- und Interpretationsfragen. Bericht über die Internationale Wissenschaftliche Konferenz anläßlich der 9. Telemann-Festtage der DDR Magdeburg, 12. bis 14. März 1987, ed. by WOLF HOBOHM, Cologne 1991, pp. 11-19.

RUGGERI, YVES, Froberger à Montbéliard, in: J.J. Froberger musicien européen, ed. by DENIS MORRIER, Paris 1998, pp. 23-38.

SCHULENBERG, DAVID, Crossing the Rhine with Froberger. Suites, Symbols, and Seventeenth-Century Musical Autobiography, in: Fiori musicali. Liber amicorum Alexander Silbiger, ed. by CLAIRE FONTIJN, Sterlin Heights 2010, pp. 271-302.

SOLL, MIRKO, Verrechtlichte Musik. Die Stadtmusikanten der Herzogtümer Schleswig und Holstein. Eine Untersuchung aufgrund archivalischer Quellen (Kieler Studien zur Volkskunde und Kulturgeschichte 5), Münster 2006.

STICHWEH, RUDOLF, Der Fremde. Studien zu Soziologie und Sozialgeschichte, Frankfurt a.M. 2010.

WACZKAT, ANDREAS, Les Violons du Duc. Französische Musiker an mecklenburgischen Höfen, in: Jahrbuch 2002 der ständigen Konferenz Mitteldeutsche Barockmusik, ed. by PETER WOLLNY, Schneverdingen 2004a, pp. 252-263.

ID., 'Welschlands edler Geist und Frankreichs fertge Faust'. Johann Fischer und die Schweriner Hofmusik im frühen 18. Jahrhundert, in: Händel-Jahrbuch 50 (2004b), pp. 157-170.

Between Collective Biography
and Biography:
Cultural-Historical Approaches to
Musicians' Migrations in the
Early Modern Age

Migration and Biography
The Case of Agostino Steffani

COLIN TIMMS

The subject of this essay is the relationship between the study of musical migration and the writing of musical biography. The discussion revolves around the life of Agostino Steffani (1654-1728), an Italian composer, diplomat and Catholic bishop who worked mainly in Germany but spent time also in France, Savoy and the Netherlands and occasionally returned to his native country. Music was his *métier* during the first half of his career: having studied as a singer and keyboard player, he was employed as a performer and composer in Munich and Hanover. Diplomatic responsibility came his way at Munich and preoccupied him during the second half of his Hanover period. The church dominated the last third of his life, in Düsseldorf and Hanover (again), but his interest in religion had its roots in his youth. Steffani's life prompts the general observations on migration (studies) and biography with which this essay concludes.

Introduction

The word 'migration' means little more than movement from one place to another. A migrant may be an individual, a group or a mass of people, and the places involved may be large or small – continents, countries, regions, towns or institutions. In the world of nature, 'migration' traditionally refers, in UK English, to the movement of groups rather than individuals. Birds may spend the summer in one country and 'migrate' to another for the winter. Seasonal journeys are undertaken also by some fish and mammals, including *homo sapiens*.

Human beings migrate either because they feel they have to or because they want to. The causes of their migrations are many and varied but include such factors as economic hardship and fear of persecution: the migration of Huguenots after the revocation of the Edict of Nantes (1685) and of Jews in the twentieth century are well known examples. Some migrations lead to permanent settlement, others to extended visits. The dividing line between compulsory and voluntary or permanent and temporary migration is not always clear.

When human beings migrate, they take music with them. The Moors carried their music and instruments to Spain when they invaded the country in the eighth century. When Christian crusaders campaigned in the Holy Land a few centuries later, or when Europeans sailed to America, they were accompanied by music and musicians. Sometimes the music of the travelers influenced that of the indigenous population, sometimes the reverse, but in the examples given above the arrival of foreign music in a new land was incidental – a by-product of human migration. Some may claim that music 'migrates' in manuscript or print, but the movement of notated music depends on human action and is more accurately defined as dissemination, distribution, publication or transmission.

Musicians have long been required to travel as part of their employment. Members of the chapel of a monarch or magnate had to move with his household. The musicians who accompanied King Henry VIII at the Field of the Cloth of Gold in 1520 were in this position, as were those, including Monteverdi, who accompanied Duke Vincenzo Gonzaga to Hungary in 1595. A hundred years later the composer and organist Pietro Torri was led a merry dance by Elector Maximilian II Emanuel of Bavaria after his appointment as governor of the Spanish Netherlands, being taken to Brussels in 1692, to Munich in 1701, back to Brussels in 1704 and to several other places between 1706 and 1715. Nowadays, opera singers and concert artists regard travel as an essential part of their job: if they are not flying from place to place, they are not succeeding at an international level. In this sense, their journeys bear comparison with those of their predecessors and of itinerant musicians in any period.

The first substantial migration of musicians in Europe was confined to the mainland and involved northern composers traveling to Italy during the Renaissance. Well known examples include Du Fay in Bologna and Rome, Josquin Desprez in Milan and Rome, Josquin and Obrecht in Ferrara, Willaert and Schütz in Venice, the first as *maestro di cappella* of

St Mark's, the other as a student of Giovanni Gabrieli. The traffic was not immediately two-way, but in the seventeenth and eighteenth centuries, when opera, concerto, oratorio, sonata and cantata were in the ascendant, Italian composers and performers could be found all over the continent. Opera was taken to France by two Italians, Luigi Rossi and Francesco Cavalli, and the *tragédie lyrique* was created there by their compatriot Giovanni Battista Lulli, who had settled in Paris and become naturalized. Italian musicians also moved in large numbers into the courts of Austria, Germany and eighteenth-century Russia.[1]

Musicians who wanted to travel between Europe and Britain faced the obstacle of the Channel. Not many Britons migrated to the continent in the seventeenth century. Peter Philips and John Bull fled to the Netherlands, William Brade worked in north Germany and Denmark, John Dowland held an appointment at the Danish court, and after the restoration of the monarchy in 1660 the seventeen-year-old Pelham Humfrey studied for three years in France and Italy. In addition to the Channel, continental Catholics wishing to travel to Britain were confronted by the question of religion. As Oliver Neighbour remarked, 'London – distant, damp and heretical – would scarcely have been their first choice as a place of employment'.[2] Nevertheless, they came, even in the 1500s, and the Bassanos, Lupos and Ferraboscos were followed in the seventeenth and eighteenth centuries by Giovanni Battista Draghi, Luis Grabu, Nicola Matteis and Pietro Reggio, not to mention such north Europeans as Thomas Baltzar, Gottfried Finger, John Ernest Galliard, Jakob Greber, John Frederick Lampe and Johann Christoph Pepusch. These and other migrant musicians enriched the population of one of the largest, most cosmopolitan and most prosperous cities in Europe. If the future of London as the center of the cultural, economic, political, religious and social life of Great Britain was assured by the accession in 1714 of Elector Georg Ludwig of Hanover as King George I, the formation five years later of the Royal Academy of Music offered employment to a large number of foreigners, among them opera librettists, stage designers, singers, orchestral players and composers, including, of course, Handel. Handel could be described as a serial migrant, moving from Halle to Hamburg to Italy to Hanover to London. He may also have been unusual in paying a preliminary visit to London before settling and becoming a subject of his adoptive country.

---

1 STROHM, 2001.
2 NEIGHBOUR, 1978, p. 257.

Steffani's migrations

Steffani, like Handel, was both a visitor and a settler, migrating from country to country and from city to city. His first change of scene hardly counts, because he did not move far from his home town: after early schooling in Castelfranco, he transferred to nearby Padua and became a choirboy at the Basilica del Santo. In an autobiographical letter of 1706 he states that in Padua he was presented to Elector Ferdinand Maria of Bavaria, who was so impressed by his talents that he invited him to Munich.[3] This was not a case of child abduction (Steffani was only twelve years old), nor an entirely voluntary migration. The elector traveled via Castelfranco, where he discussed his proposal with the boy's parents. Acknowledging, presumably, that their son would receive an excellent education in Munich, they agreed to the plan. Steffani moved there in the summer of 1667, and his family followed him in the late 1670s. That he was based there for twenty-one years suggests that the arrangement was a success.

Steffani's migration to Munich was the first of six in which he was a settler. These form the framework of his career (see Table 1). In the same letter of 1706 he claims that he left Munich because of a wrong done to his brother.[4] Details of the incident are lacking, but it is clear that Steffani's acceptance of the post of *Kapellmeister* at Hanover in 1688 was motivated by musical considerations. The duke, Ernst August, was building a new opera house there, with state-of-the-art scenery and machines. He already had an excellent orchestra, with French or Walloon woodwind and string players, and an Italian poet – (Bartolomeo) Ortensio Mauro – who could be persuaded to write librettos, but he lacked a first-rate musician to compose opera and direct its performance. He knew Steffani and may have heard some of his music, and the composer was

---

3 "Alla prima [corte] fui condotto giovinetto dal defonto Elettore Ferdinando Maria, al quale presentato in Padova ove studio frà molti altri ragazzi, s'invogliò d'una certa tal qual di me non sò per qual destino [...]." Steffani to Count Antonio Maria Fede, 11 July 1706 (Rome, Sacra Congregatio pro Gentium Evangelizatione seu di Propaganda Fide, Archivio Storico, Fondo Spiga, vol. 39), cited in TIMMS, 2003, p. 317.

4 "Partii da quella corte di mala grazia per un aggravio fatto ad un mio unico fratello dal Conte di Sanfrè, che doveva à me solo tutte le sue fortune." IBID., p. 318.

ready to move. The works he created for Hanover in 1689-1695 were the high point of Baroque opera at the court.[5]

Table 1: The migrations and major visits of Agostino Steffani

Date	Migrations	Major visits
1667	From Padua to Munich	
1672-4		From Munich to Rome and back
1678-9		From Munich to Paris, returning via Turin
1682-3		From Munich to Hanover and back
1688	From Munich to Hanover	
1693-1710		From Hanover to Brussels and back, many times
1701-2		From Hanover to Munich and back
1703	From Hanover to Düsseldorf	
1708-9		From Düsseldorf to Rome and back
1709	From Düsseldorf to Hanover	
1722	From Hanover to Padua	
1725	From Padua to Hanover	

His migration to Düsseldorf in 1703 was also motivated by a desire to develop his career, this time as a man of the church. To explain this change of direction we must backtrack on two fronts. Steffani had served Hanover not only as a musician but also as a diplomat.[6] Even at Munich he had undertaken a diplomatic mission: in 1682-3 he had visited Hanover in order to explore the possibility of a marriage between the new Bavarian elector, Max Emanuel, and Princess Sophie Charlotte. He had become acquainted with the Hanoverian court and impressed the duke and

---

5   See KEPPLER, 1968, and WALLBRECHT, 1974.
6   See KAUFOLD, 1997.

duchess, a granddaughter of King James I of England and therefore an heir to the throne. Thus, when Elector Ernst August recruited Steffani as *Kapellmeister*, he knew that he was also an able diplomat.

Ernst August had need of skilful negotiators. His overriding ambition was that his duchy should be raised to an electorate. To this end the (Lutheran) duke required the backing of the (Catholic) emperor and electors. He had supported the emperor with troops for campaigns against the Turks in the 1680s, and he calculated that his investment in opera would impress his peers and superiors. Knowing that Steffani was well acquainted with Max Emanuel and his consort, Archduchess Maria Antonia, and that he had a flair for diplomacy, he appointed him Hanoverian *envoyé extraordinaire* to the Bavarian court in Brussels, where the elector had resided since 1692 as governor of the Spanish Netherlands. Steffani's mission was to obtain Bavaria's support for Hanover's elevation, which had been agreed in principle, and to negotiate a defense treaty between the two powers. His diplomatic responsibilities increased to the extent that he was unable to compose an opera for 1696 or 1697, and the theater at Hanover was closed on the death of Ernst August in January 1698. During the build-up to the War of the Spanish Succession, Steffani spent all his time and energy trying to persuade Max Emanuel to side with the emperor, not Louis XIV. When, on 8 September 1702, the elector besieged Ulm, Steffani knew he had failed and suffered a nervous breakdown. He recovered his equilibrium by immersing himself in his chamber duets, revising many of them and starting to make a new manuscript collection.

He did not finish this project before migrating to Düsseldorf. Here he was installed as president of the Spiritual Council for the Palatinate and the duchies of Jülich and Berg and embarked with Elector Johann Wilhelm on a mission to convert north Germany back to the Catholic faith. This was less of a change of direction than it may seem. Steffani had been a priest since 1680, Abbot of Löpsingen since 1683 and an Apostolic Protonotary since at least 1695. At Hanover his interest in the church had been constrained by the religious orientation of the court. Music had provided comfort, even therapy, during his breakdown, but the church offered alternative and possibly more reliable prospects for his future. This presumably explains why he moved to Düsseldorf. His appointment in 1706-7 as Titular Bishop of Spiga and in April 1709 as Apostolic Vicar of North Germany ensured that he would serve the Catholic church for the remaining twenty-five years of his life.

His migrations, however, were not over, for in November 1709 he returned to Hanover. There are good reasons why, as Apostolic Vicar, he based himself there. Soon after arriving in Düsseldorf he had been promoted General President of the Palatine Government and Council and charged by Johann Wilhelm with overhauling the administration, eradicating corruption and punishing its perpetrators. In the process he had made enemies and been frustrated by the elector's frequent absence. He had never experienced such difficulties before: at Hanover he had worked closely with the elector and his family and had formed friendships with many members of the court. Lying north-east of Düsseldorf, Hanover was a more convenient center from which to administer his gargantuan parish, as earlier vicars had found. Furthermore, as a condition of the electorate Ernst August had agreed to the construction in Hanover of a Catholic church; since Steffani had helped negotiate this agreement, he wanted to see it fulfilled. All in all, his return to Hanover – the city, not the court – would benefit the cause of Catholicism.

During the next thirteen years his work as Apostolic Vicar consumed nearly all his time, energy and money. By 1722 he was so exhausted and frustrated that he resorted again to migration. His destination this time was Italy: after a short period in Venice he retired to Padua, where his career had begun. He probably did not know how long he would stay, but the fact that he acquired his own accommodation suggests that he intended to settle there. After he had left Hanover, however, conditions for the Catholic community, which had been deteriorating since Georg Ludwig's departure for London, grew rapidly worse. His friends implored him to come back and restore order, and he eventually acceded to their requests. In 1725, at over seventy years of age, he made the long return journey to Hanover – his final significant migration.

Steffani's visits

Steffani also made six substantial visits, lasting months or even years, to places where he had no intention of settling. Three of these visits took place during his Munich years. The purpose of the first was entirely musical: in October 1672, at the age of eighteen, he was sent to Rome to study composition with Ercole Bernabei, director of the Cappella Giulia. Two years later, after publishing his *Psalmodia vespertina* (Rome 1674), he returned to Munich with Bernabei, who had just been appointed *Kapellmeister*. Steffani's second visit concerned both his education as a musician and his development as a courtier. The Bavarian electress, Henrietta Adelaide, a princess of Savoy who died in 1676, was a cousin of King Louis XIV. Between July 1678 and May 1679 Steffani visited both Paris and Turin, the courts to which she had been related, and was received as a Bavarian representative. In Paris he played the harpsichord for the king and assimilated the style of French music. His harpsichord playing was also admired in Turin, especially by 'Madama Reale' (the regent, Marie Jeanne Baptiste of Savoie-Nemours), but his visit was cut short by the illness of Elector Ferdinand Maria, who died before he could get back to Munich. Steffani's third visit was his mission to Hanover on the possible marriage of Ferdinand Maria's son to Sophie Charlotte. That Max Emanuel could entrust this important matter to Steffani reflects the fact that he had known him for fifteen years, as a teenager and a young man, and that the composer was now an accomplished diplomat.

All the visits of Steffani's Hanover and Düsseldorf periods were made for reasons of diplomacy. As Hanoverian special envoy to the Bavarian court in Brussels, he was constantly on the road, not just between Brussels and Hanover but also to The Hague (Den Haag), Liège, Düsseldorf, Nancy, Cologne, Bonn, Koblenz and Antwerp. In 1701, as the War of the Spanish Succession approached, Max Emanuel returned to Munich. So did Steffani, who in the following summer visited Hanover, Koblenz, Bonn, Düsseldorf and Vienna in a last-ditch attempt to bring the elector round. His failure and its consequences have already been mentioned. His most important visit as a servant of Düsseldorf was a mission to Rome to mediate between the emperor and the pope. He arrived in November 1708 and proposed a compromise that was accepted by both parties in January 1709. The pope rewarded him by appointing him a Domestic Prelate and an Assistant at the Pontifical Throne, as well as Apostolic Vicar of North Germany.

Steffani's arrangements for his journey to Rome merit scrutiny. On 16 September 1708 he wrote to Count Antonio Maria Fede, the Tuscan and Palatine diplomatic resident in Rome:

"I shall be leaving [Düsseldorf], therefore, in a few days and using post-horses; but since it is impossible for me to make this journey without stopping at Koblenz, Mainz, Frankfurt, Würzburg, Augsburg,

Innsbruck, Verona and Florence, Your Most Illustrious Lordship can well judge that I will not have the consolation of embracing you before the end of October. I shall only be bringing one chaplain, one secretary, one valet, one cook and two grooms; I shall have to put Your Most Illustrious Lordship to the inconvenience of providing me with the other personnel that I shall need, particularly a good dean. Would you send your response to this [letter] to Marquis Michele Sagramoso in Verona."[7]

That Steffani and his staff used post-horses indicates that the latter were quick and that his mission was secret: if the party had used private coaches, it would have been conspicuous. The itinerary allowed him to hold discussions with Catholic dignitaries *en route* and make an unplanned detour to Vienna. He probably left Düsseldorf in late September, was in Augsburg on 6 October and Innsbruck six days later; having picked up his post in Verona, he arrived in Rome on 7 November. On the way back he took a different route through Italy. Leaving Rome in late April, he was in Florence on 5 May and Venice by the 13th. There he stayed on the Grand Canal in the palace of Georg Ludwig of Hanover, who had invited him to use it.[8] He then spent two days in Padua before traveling overland to Mainz, where he picked up a sloop belonging to Johann Wilhelm that delivered him to Düsseldorf in early June.

---

7   "Io partirò dunque frà pochi giorni, e mi servirò di Cavalli di Posta, mà come non è possibile che io faccia questo viaggio senza fermarmi à Confluenza, à Magonza, à Francfort, à Erbipoli, à Augusta, à Inspruck, à Verona, et à Firenze, V[ostra] S[ignoria] Ill[ustrissi]ma può ben giudicare che io non potrò haver la consolatione di abbracciarla prima del fine del prossimo Ottobre. Io non condurrò seco che un Cappellano, un Segretario, un Cameriere, un Cuoco, e due Staffieri; il resto della gente che mi bisognerà, e particolarmente un buon Decano, toccherà à V. S. Ill:ma l'Incommodo di provedermene. Habbia ella la risposta di questa in Verona nelle mani del Sig[no]r Marchese Michele Sagramosa." Steffani to Count Antonio Maria Fede, 16 September 1708 (Fondo Spiga [see note 3], vol. 39).

8   Steffani's autograph letter accepting the invitation is reproduced in TIMMS, 2003, p. 93.

Steffani's journeys

In addition to his migrations and visits Steffani made countless other journeys for a variety of reasons. A summary must suffice. At Padua he acquired such a high reputation as a choirboy that he was invited to sing in Ferrara, Vicenza and Monselice and, at the ages of eleven and twelve, appeared on the Venetian stage in operas by his colleague, Carlo Pallavicino. During his Munich years he paid two or three visits to Italy, and when he left Munich in May 1688 he returned to Venice before moving to Hanover. As a Hanoverian diplomat he traveled far and wide. During his first five years at Düsseldorf (1703-8), he made one or more return journeys to Herten (the rural seat of the count of Nesselrode-Reichenstein), The Hague, Bensberg, Bamberg, Hanover and Cologne, and circular trips to Leipzig, Dresden and Heidelberg and to Hanover and Wolfenbüttel.

His most punishing schedule, however, began after his return to Hanover as Apostolic Vicar in November 1709. Some of his journeys during this period were frequent and routine, but in January 1710 he embarked on a two-year programme of visitations to the various parts of his vicariate. That month he traveled from Hanover to Brunswick, to Wolfenbüttel, to Celle and back; in February he returned to Brunswick and Wolfenbüttel; in March he went to Düsseldorf and Cologne and back. And so it went on, for month after month: the details are known, because he made a note of the dates, destinations and distances (in leagues).[9] Many of the visits were to nearby courts, monasteries or missions, but others took him farther afield. In the autumn of 1710 he traveled from Hanover to Bamberg and back and in the following year undertook a three-stage visit to Berlin: from Hanover to Celle to Berlin; from Berlin to Lindenberg (Mecklenburg) and back; and from Berlin back to Hanover via Magdeburg and Halberstadt. He entertained high hopes about this visit to Prussia but received a frosty welcome from King Friedrich I and returned from the capital empty-handed.

During the following ten years the vicar made similar journeys, but fewer of them. He usually spent part of the winter at Neuhaus and part of the summer at Herten. In October 1727 he left Hanover with the intention of returning to Italy. By the end of the month he was in Frankfurt, where he visited his close friend Lothar Franz von Schönborn, prince-bishop of

---

9 See TIMMS, 2003, p. 105.

Bamberg and elector-archbishop of Mainz, who had consecrated him as bishop. In January 1728 he was invited to Herten but did not go, and on 12 February he died in Frankfurt.

It is impossible to establish exactly how many kilometers Steffani traveled during his life, but the total may lie between 45,000 and 50,000 – about 800 kilometers a year for sixty years. This is an astonishing number, especially considering the methods of transport available and the difficulties that travel entailed.[10]

Migration and biography

Although Steffani's career was exceptional, it exemplifies a number of general points. In the Early Modern Period, at least, the main reason why musicians migrated is so that they could study or work elsewhere, often outside their native country. A 'musical' migrant could be anyone associated with the provision of music, whether a composer, singer, instrumentalist, instrument maker, copyist, choreographer or even librettist. 'Study' could mean instruction, more or less formal, with a teacher or at an institution, or simply immersion or participation in an unfamiliar musical culture. Some musicians migrated to take up posts to which they had already been appointed or to offer their services to potential patrons. Others presumably traveled in hope – the hope of finding more and better opportunities to ply their trade and make a living.

The effects of musical migration were no less diverse than the causes and were felt by both the migrant and the host. The principal effect may be summarized, perhaps, as 'the transfer of practices or ideas from one person, group or environment to another'.[11] Such transfers could take place in any of several musical domains, have a local, regional or national impact and make a short- or a long-term impression. One effect of migration in the sphere of composition was the transmission of a musical form or style from one party to another, a process that could be transformative: one example of this, perhaps, is the response of Thomas Morley and his contemporaries to the Italian madrigal, although the changes

---

10 A discussion of transport was included here when the essay was read at the workshop.
11 Other effects were felt by those whom the migrant left behind – a point easily overlooked.

undergone by secular English vocal music during the reign of Queen Elizabeth I were due less to the migration of Italian composers than to the importation of sources of their works. In the realm of performance the effects of migration might bear fruit in the design, production and playing techniques of musical instruments, in the composition of ensembles, in the circumstances of performance or in such matters as interpretation and ornamentation.

The effects of migration and travel are illustrated by Steffani's life and works. His early visits to Rome and Paris helped shape the musical language of the music, especially the operas, that he composed at Munich and Hanover in the 1680s and '90s. The effect of his visit to Paris also had more far-reaching and long-lasting consequences. His Hanover operas were staged at Hamburg in the late 1690s, and Roger published the instrumental movements from them at Amsterdam in 1706.[12] As a result, Steffani's music reached a much wider public, including composers and performers, than it would otherwise have done and contributed to the development of a musical language, combining Italian and French elements, that was 'spoken' by the next generation of composers, including Handel, Bach and Telemann. It could therefore be argued that the style of north German music in the first half of the eighteenth century was partly an effect of Steffani's visit to Paris in 1678-9.

When migration plays a part in a musician's career, it naturally belongs in an account of his life. The student of migration and the writer of biography depend on similar sources, many of them preserved in the archives of courts, educational institutions, political organizations or ecclesiastical establishments, or among the private papers of families or individuals. Unless the collection is thoroughly indexed, which is rarely the case, the best way of working in an archive is to examine a complete set of papers from beginning to end, taking note of everything of interest or of relevance to the subject. In this way one develops an understanding of the collection, of the kinds of information it contains or insights it may yield, and of how such information or insights may be interpreted. This *modus operandi* probably suits the student of migration better than the biographer, who is more likely to be looking for information on a particular individual. Unfortunately, leafing through an archive in search of specific information can be like looking for a needle in a haystack: in

---

12 *Sonata da Camera à tre Due Violini Alto e Basso del Signore Stephani Abbate &c.*, Amsterdam. RASCH assigns this undated publication to 1706.

this respect there can be a mismatch between the demands of archival research and the needs of a biographer.

A biographer's task increases in size and difficulty if his subject traveled extensively. Over the course of his career Steffani met a large number of people in various parts of Europe and corresponded with many more. The majority of the letters that he sent or received, and most of his numerous reports and memoranda on political and ecclesiastical affairs, date from his forty years in Hanover and Düsseldorf. When he set off from Hanover in October 1727, he left behind a large collection of documents that is now in the Niedersächsisches Landesarchiv (Standort Hannover), but he took with him three chests of papers which, after his death, were sent to the Sacra Congregatio de Propaganda Fide in Rome.[13] However, because he was a frequent migrant and a prolific correspondent, documents relating to him also survive elsewhere, in the archives of the many institutions or people with whom he had dealings. It is difficult to imagine any single biographer examining all the collections that might yield information on him, so no monographic biography of Steffani is likely to be complete.

This problem could possibly be solved by a team-based approach to archival research, but the solution could highlight a further difficulty. The idea of 'completeness' is suspect: a document revealing, for example, that Steffani's breakfast included hot chocolate, rather than coffee, would be of interest but might not merit inclusion in a study of his life and works. The construction of biography involves selection, and the selecting must be done by somebody with a view of the subject, based on a thorough knowledge and understanding of all the available information, who wishes to communicate his or her view to other people. This is the task of a biographer. A biographer decides which pieces of information to include, how much weight to attach to each and how to interpret them. Like a sculptor, a biographer chips away unwanted material until the subject is clear.

A biography of a musician is normally concerned with both the person and his or her music. The relationship between person and music can be reciprocal: the music can be regarded as part of the person's character of

---

13 Musical papers eventually "passed into the hands of his heirs, who did not take such account of them as they deserved" ("Le carte di Musica passarono in mano degli Eredi, che non ne tennero quel conto, che meritavano"). RICCATI, 1779, p. 26. For discussion of Steffani's estate, see TIMMS, 2003, pp. 134-135.

which it is also, in some senses, a reflection. Like all human beings, musicians are conditioned by their education, training and employment, not to mention the circumstances of their birth and existence, but a historical musician is not merely an example of a kind. One of the most important and rewarding challenges for a biographer is to identify and account for the individuality of the subject. In this respect biography may seem old-fashioned compared with other kinds of musicology, including migration studies; yet it seems likely to survive, because it brings together pairs of individuals – subject with author, author with reader, reader with subject.

This leads, finally, to the main difference between migration studies and biography. The difference has less to do with substance than with emphasis and purpose. Put simply, migration study focuses on a single kind of event or action involving any number of people, while biography deals with many kinds of event or action revolving round a single individual. It is true that there are biographical studies of musical institutions and ensembles, but normally a musical biography is concerned with a single composer or performer. If the musician in question was a migrant, an account of his or her migration will form part of the biography, but the center of attention must be the life and works as a whole. Since so many musicians of the Early Modern Period migrated so often and traveled so far and wide, the study of migration has much to offer to the writing of biography, but so does biography to migration studies: in order to understand any migration as a phenomenon one must understand the context in which it took place, and this context includes the life of the migrant(s) concerned.

Literature

KAUFOLD, CLAUDIA, Ein Musiker als Diplomat: Abbé Agostino Steffani in hannoverschen Diensten (1688-1703) (Veröffentlichungen des Instituts für historische Landesforschung der Universität Göttingen 36), Bielefeld 1997.

KEPPLER, PHILIP, Agostino Steffani's Hannover Operas and a Rediscovered Catalogue, in: Studies in Music History. Essays for Oliver Strunk, ed. by HAROLD S. POWERS, Princeton 1968, pp. 341-354.

NEIGHBOUR, OLIVER, The Consort and Keyboard Music of William Byrd, London 1978.

RASCH, RUDOLF, The Music Publishing House of Estienne Roger and Michel-Charles Le Cène 1696-1743, Part 4: The Catalogue, Saint-Hélène–Swain, pp. 75-76: http://www.hum.uu.nl/medewerkers/r.a.rasch/Roger/Catalogue-Saint-Helene-Swaen.pdf, 27.10.2014.

RICCATI, GIORDANO, Notizie di Monsig. Agostino Steffani, in: Nuova raccolta d'opuscoli scientifici e filologici, 33 (1779), pp. 1-26.

STROHM, REINHARD (ed.), The Eighteenth-Century Diaspora of Italian Music and Musicians (Speculum musicum 8), Turnhout 2001.

TIMMS, COLIN, Polymath of the Baroque. Agostino Steffani and His Music, New York 2003.

WALLBRECHT, ROSENMARIE ELISABETH, Das Theater des Barockzeitalters an den welfischen Höfen Hannover und Celle, Hildesheim 1974.

"try it elsewhere [...]" – Konrad Hagius and Musician's Mobility in Early Modern Times in Light of Local and Regional Profile

JOACHIM KREMER

1. Research basis

Music history and musical action is situated in geographic spaces and it seems superfluous to point out that also any kind of migration of musicians depends on space. Thus, mobility and migration put the idea of strict delineation of geographical spaces into perspective and even question them, as the phenomenon of immigration and migration of musicians could be found whenever and wherever, e.g. also in case of a narrow geographic limitation of local and regional research.[1] Migration is considered as a form of spatial mobility which does not represent an individual but a collective phenomenon. In the past, particularly migration movements which were either based on political-ideological reasons or which concerned large numbers of people were of interest. The former includes exile research as well as remigration research,[2] also the

---

1 The contemplations regarding mobility and migration formulated here are associated with: KREMER, 2004.
2 See, e.g. during the 16th century the migration of Jews from Spain and Portugal to the Netherlands and Turkey, or during the 17th century of the Huguenots from France to Prussia. Regarding remigration see KÖSTER/ SCHMIDT, 2005.

overseas migration, e.g. to America or Australia. The voluntary nature of migration processes – shown by the last two examples – was often not provided or merely in a restricted sense. Based on this fact, the term migration requires a minimum amount of change of locality: Only "those persons [are considered] international migrants who transfer their residence abroad for a certain minimum duration or an undetermined period of time – possibly forever. Tourists, daily or weekly commuters with a place of work in the adjacent country and persons employed in another country for a short period of time are thus not considered international migrants".[3] Only such determinations permit the enquiry about the specific reasons and motivations for the migration in view of permanence. The search for such motivations provide insights in the elementary decision-making processes of the individual and collective actions and indicate conditions and latitudes of the respective ranges, the origin as well as the destination of the mobility. As the "migrations as social processes [...] [are] answers to the more or less complex economic and ecological, social and cultural as well as religious-paradigm, ethnic and political existence and framework conditions",[4] so is the migration with respect to music history to be considered as a part-phenomenon of greater music history issues, embedded in interdisciplinary and particularly cultural-historical contexts.

Musicology has already dealt with these models of migration research derived from these settlements: with the seminar reports *Musica Baltica. Interregional musical-cultural relationships* the issue of mobility and migration became programmatic for the Baltic region research.[5] Some fields of research, such as the so-called *Mannheim School* cannot deal without the phenomenon of mobility, for example with respect to the migration of Bohemian musicians or the Mannheim contacts to Paris. The phenomenon of mobility is also related to aspects of cultural transfer, not only with respect to the increasing network of the world in terms of traffic during Modern Times.[6] If music history research speaks of "influence", "music connections" or "cultural transfer", it always also implicitly refers to the phenomenon of mobility, because the migration of musical repertoires is not conceivable without the relationship of people

---

3   MÜNZ, 2009, 29.01.2015.
4   BADE, 2002, p. 21.
5   OCHS et al., 1996, and OCHS et al., 1997. See also RAATZ, 1999.
6   ARLT, 1993, and DETERING, 1996, pp. 96-114.

over distances, i.e. without the network of geographical spaces.[7] Here, mobility could satisfy current needs, as the recruitment of numerous Italian musicians by German courts during the Early Modern Times verifies. However, there could also be moments of retardation when old repertoire was imported, i.e. in Riga, where the cantor and organ player Georg Michael Telemann staged compositions of his grandfather, Georg Philipp, even though with traces of an update.[8] It is the essence of regional and interregional research that migration research devoted to collective phenomena is an alternative concept to individual biographies and any form of "hero history" by focussing on groups of persons and, furthermore, not only those musicians who entered the history books as "heroes". In contrast, the phenomenon of migration concentrates much more on the incorporation of musical creation (individual or certain groups of musicians) in social and musical contexts. However, any depreciation of, thus, important musicians as "Kleinmeister" would ignore the potential of a contextual reconnection in favour of a constriction to issues of quality, and would classify all forms of repertoire distribution and transfer processes as aspects of music history of minor importance.[9]

2. The individual musician in the cultural landscape "Weser Renaissance": The example of Hagius (1550-1614)

In his articles pertaining to music history of the 18th century published approx. 100 years ago, Romain Rolland pursued the objective of making forgotten musicians, their *vitae* and works, known. He wanted to do justice to the musicians forgotten by historians[10] and, in doing so, he rejected the historiography that had decisively determined the just finished century: the hero history description. Thus, Johann Sebastian Bach is hardly mentioned in Rolland's articles (only as antithesis). Rolland virtually reversed the categories of historiography with Telemann, Kuhnau and Stamitz: the hero category was even replaced by the formerly often

---

7   Vol. 9 of *Arolser Beiträge zur Musikforschung* regarding "Migration [..] during the Baroque period" explicitly refers to this issue. BRUSNIAK/KOCH, 2002.
8   KREMER, 2006, pp. 159-168.
9   KREMER, 2000, pp. 161-183. Also: RASCH, 2008.
10 ROLLAND, 1919 and regarding the following: SANDBERGER, 2004, pp. 182-190.

so-called "Kleinmeister" category. However, despite the high estimation of Rolland's historiographic role, the rehabilitation determined by a sense of justice is not the major issue of my article. Rather, it is the understanding of the basic options of the musical acts and designs during the time of the "Weser Renaissance", thus, in a geographical space illustrating a certain cultural unit between Reformation and the Thirty Year's War. Focussing on this geographic space as a cultural unit also follows Hermann Aubin and his research on the Westphalia area, namely the description of a regional profile, which allows to differentiate a certain space from other spaces, to distinguish it and to capture by characteristics, which allows the recognition of accumulations, centering or (also geographical) marginalization. However, such a profile may not be understood as a rigid scope of action. Rather, numerous musicians operate in a structural frame changing more slowly than an individual *vita*. Consequently, the connection of regional profile formation and musician's mobility represents a combination of structural-historical and individual-biographic approach to music history. The musician Konrad Hagius is to serve as a type of case study, as his *vita* exhibits mobility in a remarkable manner.[11]

In 1550, Hagius was born in Rinteln; however, not much is known about his education and studies. From 1581, a musician with this name applied several times for a position in the Stuttgart *Hofkapelle*, namely in 1581 and 1591, and received from the court in Stuttgart two Gulden for "numerous compositions" as early as in 1582, i.e. still under the reign of Duke Ludwig of Wurttemberg.[12] In between, he stayed at the court of Count Edzard II of East Frisia in Emden in 1584, applied there for the position of cantor and is verifiable at the court of Duke Johann Wilhelm the Rich at Jülich, Cleves (Kleve) and Berg in Düsseldorf in 1586. This was obviously followed by extended travels soon thereafter because, in the introduction of his *Neue künstliche musikalische Intraden* (New artificial musical intrades) in 1615, Hagius writes that he had traveled Aus-

---

11   As early as in 1812, Konrad Hagius has been included by Ernst Ludwig Gerber in his *Neues Historisch-Biographisches Lexikon der Tonkünstler* (New historical-biographical lexis of musical artists) (GERBER, 1812, vol. 2, col. 480ff). Also Gustav Schilling considered him in 1836 in his *Enzyklopädie der gesamten musikalischen Wissenschaften* (Encyclopedia of the entire musical sciences); SCHILLING, 1836, p. 418.

12   The early attempts are not mentioned in: GOLLY-BECKER, 1999. See here BOSSERT, 1910, p. 339 and BOSSERT, 1900, pp. 273, 283ff.

tria, Bohemia, Hungary, Poland, Prussia and Lithuania. After a further sojourn to Stuttgart, Hagius is again mentioned in a letter in 1586, where the secretary and teacher of Count Simon VI of Lippe recommended him, which – according to Hans Joachim Moser – had even led to employment at Count Simon. Once again, after a certain period of time, Hagius went to Stuttgart where, in 1600, he was accepted into the *Hofkapelle* as bass singer. In 1602, he received a commendation as well as extra pay for copying a fifteen-voice composition for viols.[13] However, he only appeared as a composer in Stuttgart in the register of the court lute player Paul Jenisch for whom he composed the canon *Christus ist mein Leben* (Christ is my life) in 1602, which was later bound into the register as endpaper (see figures 1 and 2).[14] This register dating to the years 1575 to 1647 originates from Paul Jenisch, a theologian and musician, who worked as a lute player in the *Hofkapelle* from 1613 following his career as a theologian, and who died in 1647.[15] The sad fortune mentioned in the inscription ("miserum fatum"), can definitely be interpreted biographically and provides insight into a forced geographical (and subsequently professional) mobility of the register owner: because Jenisch and Hagius shared an adherence to the Catholic confession,[16] and Jenisch had to leave Augsburg in 1595 due to the publication of a mystical text and subsequently settled in Lauingen. Here, he was also visited by the Gdansk *Kapellmeister* Nikolaus Zangius and it is surely not a coincidence that Hagius married there on 20 April 1602.[17] In 1603, Hagius once again received an extra payment from the court in Stuttgart; however, soon thereafter, on 20 June, he was dismissed, presumably during the preparations for the glamorous festivities in occasion of the bestowed Order of the Garter (*Hosenbandorden*) to Duke Friedrich I of Wurttemberg, one of his greatest achievement in foreign affairs.[18] Following a short employment at the court of Friedrich IV of the Palatinate in Heidelberg

13   BOSSERT, 1910, p. 356.
14   D-Sl, Cod. Hist. 4º 299, fol. 9r and 9v.
15   See KREKLER, 1999, pp. 38ff. as well as GOTTWALD, 1969, p. 93.
16   Renate Federhofer-Königs notes that Hagius converted from Lutheran to Catholic faith and was even ordained a priest in 1572; FEDERHOFER-KÖNIGS, 1957, p. 35, note 11.
17   GOTTWALD, 1969, p. 93.
18   See here RÜCKERT, 2010, particularly chapter "Ritter beider Orden" (Knight of both medals), IBID., pp. 381-395.

Figure 1 (for the caption see figure 2)

and the Kurmainz *Amtshof*, which, however, is not proven by sources, Hagius was once again accepted in the Stuttgart *Hofkapelle* on 9 November 1607. However, negative tendencies following the death of the duke in 1608 caused the final termination of his employment: although Ludwig Finscher points out that Hagius, as well as numerous other musicians, had followed a variety of denominations,[19] however, this inter-denominationally orientation of the *Hofkapelle* – not least due to the mobility and different origins of the musicians – became difficult in Wurttemberg after 1608: The new Duke Johann Friedrich ordered that "Papists were no longer to be tolerated".[20] The established Hagius was initially granted protection, yet under the proviso that the Duke would be able to terminate his employment at any time. This termination occurred soon thereafter on 20 February 1609. Meanwhile, Hagius had made contact with the ambitious Count Ernst III of Holstein-Schaum-

---
19   FINSCHER, 1989, p. 385.
20   BOSSERT, 1911, p. 157.

Figure 2: Konrad Hagius, Canon à 4, Christus ist mein Leben. *Register page, Württembergische Landesbibliothek Stuttgart, Cod. Hist. 4° 299, fols. 9r and 9v (with the kind permission of the Württembergische Landesbibliothek Stuttgart).*

burg by bestowing to him his *Tricinien* collection in 1604. On the other hand, it is most remarkable that Hagius failed to dedicate either this collection nor any other of his music sheets to the Wurttemberg Duke Friedrich I as his long-standing employer, even though other sheets can be related to the specific place of work, so the Gdansk *Glückwunschung: zu einem glückseligen Eingang des 94. Jahrs* (Felicitations: to a beatific start of the 94th year) (Thorn 1594) or the Ulenberg Psalter, which indicates a Catholic, in the eyes of some music researchers also counter-reformatory application. However, the latter mentioned dedication would have been unthinkable in Wurttemberg after the Austrian administration of the dukedom during the 16th century, following the impending re-catholicization and the subsequent reconversion of the dukedom into a fiefdom (*Reichslehen*) in the Treaty of Prague (*Prager Vertrag*) (1599) purchased by Friedrich I for 400,000 Gulden. Such religious-denomination-associated compositions would only have received marginal significance in 1600 Wurttemberg and the "cleaning" of the *Hofkapelle* in 1609 can even be interpreted as an expression of Lutheran self-localization. It is remarkable that Hagius, with the *Psalmen Davids* published already in 1589, was geared toward contexts that were quite different from the Wurttemberg circumstances with regard to religious denomination-politics as well as musical aspects. It is therefore safe to assume that the subsequent Stuttgart employments could only have been transitional stations for him. In contrast, the introduction to the *Tricinien* indicates that Hagius had met Count Ernst III many years before. In addition, contacts to the cloister Möllenbeck had been established as early as 1596, from which a recommendation had been made to Count Simon VI of Lippe, to whom he had dedicated the compositions. This obviously long-standing relationship lasting beyond the terminations in Stuttgart paid off for Hagius in this last stage of his life: negotiations had commenced in 1608 in order to employ a "Wolgeübtenn unndt Kunstreichen Capellmeister", i.e. a well versed and artistic *Kapellmeister* in Bückeburg.[21] Hagius would probably have left Stuttgart much sooner, but he was only released from employment Easter 1609; long time before he had signed the Bückeburg *revers* at this point in time, namely on 17 January 1609, thus one month prior to his actual termination, upon which the letter of passage had been penned immediately.[22] At that time, there were obviously not enough reasons to hold Hagius in Stuttgart. Although the stage of life now following with the assumption of office Easter 1609 was short, it was successful in every aspect, yet: it almost seems as if Hagius had finally found his purpose after many years of preparation and contact maintenance. As the new *Hofkapellmeister* in Bückeburg Hagius established the first *Hofkapelle*, but received his release from court services and the nomination as "Composer [...] at the court music" as early as 1611. Easter 1612, he retired to his native town of Rinteln with a significant annual wage and had to deliver a print publication annually. However, he died during the first six months or in summer of 1616.

One constructive moment of this musician's *vita* is his mobility which led him staying at one place hardly longer than a few years. Although Hagius did not visit the politically and artistically most aspiring

---

21 See the letter by the Prior of cloister Möllenbeck, Hermann Wedemhoff, in: LAAKMANN, 2000, p. 1 and the rendition IBID., pp. 305ff.
22 LAAKMANN, 2000, pp. 283, 306ff.

courts (Munich, Copenhagen or Kassel), he approached courts which were either culturally interested or promoted the establishment and/or re-establishment of their *Hofkapellen*. The ultimate structure change of the *Hofkapellen* described by Wolfgang Hirschmann toward mixed *Kapellen* (*cantorey*) or the establishment of instrumental court music[23] can also be recognized in Bückeburg under Ernst III and in Detmold under Count Simon. Although the court in Stuttgart, under the direction of the *Hofkapellmeister* Balduin Hoyoul and Leonhard Lechner, was also one of the aspiring courts which even tried to compete with Munich, a less methodical music policy was pursued under the government of Duke Friedrich I; one eagerly hired musicians (also from Italy), but this international orientation was only marginally deliberated.[24] This also becomes evident in the fact that – on the one hand – many musicians were hired for a short period in Stuttgart (among those also Hagius) and – on the other hand – that many traveling musicians visited the court; however, among those are hardly any names still known today.[25] Hagius, as bass singer, hardly played a significant or even leading role in this musical policy. In addition, he did not possess the qualities favored by the duke of Stuttgart: He was neither Italian nor one of the English actors, which were popular there at this time.[26] His activity was more traditional than those of the Englishman John Price, who was used as lute player at special festivities, such as during a performance of the musical play *Phoebus und Lucina* in 1609 in the context of the wedding feast for Duke Johann Friedrich. Price was admired in Marin Mersenne's *Harmonie universelle* because he could play through three octaves on a three-hole-flute and Philipp Hainhofer was impressed because Price was able to play *viola*

---

23 HIRSCHMANN, 2015, pp. 189-198.
24 See here KREMER, 2010a, pp. 315-334.
25 See here the analysis of the court files and the list of traveling musicians who livened up the music scene at court in Wurttemberg by dedicating compositions to the Duke or received wages for courtesies; see lists in: BOSSERT, 1910, pp. 359-362. In all, the list hardly includes musicians from the great music centers such as Vienna, Munich or Paris. At most, Valentin H[a]ussmann stands out among them who presented the duke with a composition in 1594, thus on the way to or from the *Reichstag* in Regensburg, and who repeated such a gift in the following year. A pendant illustrates the evaluation of the granting of passports: KOUDAL, 1993.
26 KREMER, 2010b, pp. 235-256. Here also HENKE, 2014.

da gamba with one hand while simultaneously playing "English pfeiflin" with the other.[27] This makes Price appear as a personified musical curiosity of a type collected by Friedrich also for his princely "art chamber" (*Kunstkammer*); in a minor capacity, he represents a certain type of music or even a certain – possibly newly created – repertoire. One diversion may be permitted: if Hagius, beside his activity as musician, would have also taken on the role of an alchemist, his chances at the court in Stuttgart would surely have increased enormously, because Duke Friedrich I employed a large number of alchemists whose physical existence, however, was constantly jeopardized: if unsuccessful, they ended up on the gallows.

3. The role of the sovereign personality

Hagius stayed at no other court as often as he did in Stuttgart, where the politico-cultural ambition constantly offered new possibilities for confirmation, but the lack of systematic planning of the princely music policy represented a mixture of security and uncertainty for him. This was not the case at Bückeburg, where Count Ernst awarded him with the central musician office to establish the *Hofkapelle*. Hagius used this artistic latitude by hiring other musicians: the singer Martin Glatz and the alto Georg Mayer followed him from Stuttgart. The letter of passage further mentions bringing one alto and one tenor each to Bückeburg.[28] The Italian Josephus Marini from Venice also reached Bückeburg via the court in Stuttgart.[29] In June 1609, Hagius obtained information on Bückeburg via Marini, who was lent to the Zollern court at the time. This permits the conclusion of a profound difference between the conditions at Stuttgart and Bückeburg. As much as the structural conditions were able to affect the work of a musician, his mobility and his *vita*, so formative was also the person of the sovereign during Early Modern Times, his individual propensities and preferences. The significance of this personal compo-

---

27   MERSENNE, 1636, Vol. 3: Traité des Instruments à chordes, pp. 231ff. Hainhofer states as follows: "spielet auf der viola di gamba und pfeiffet wie gemelt zugleich mit der rechten hand auf einem englischen pfeifflin", he "habe ihn Ao 1615 in Stuttgart auch also spilen hören"; MEYER, 1962, col. 1623.
28   LAAKMANN, 2000, pp. 71ff., note 258.
29   LAAKMANN, 2000, p. 73.

nent is particularly evident in the fact that, following the death of the sovereign, the successors set different priorities and sometimes dissolved *Hofkapellen*; this, for example, was the case in Detmold under Count Simon VII or in Heidelberg with the accession of Friedrich V of the Palatinate in 1610. Luckily, the development in Stuttgart (i.e. the personnel restructuring), after the death of Friedrich I in 1608, coincided for Hagius with the option of changing over to Bückeburg. Here, he met with a regent who strove for the intensive expansion of the *Hofkapelle* and whose role is retrospectively applauded by Johann Rist in 1666:

> "In this hour, I must praise the deceased, knowledgeable Lord and Prince Ernst, Count of Schauenburg and Holstein, Lord of Gehmen and Bargen; this energetic prince loved his musicians whom he employed at his magnificent court from various nations, but particularly from Germany and England in such a manner that he paid them like his very reasonable chancellors and advisors and clothed like his peers [...]; this is why it was also required that two *Kapellmeister* were present for his incomparable music, of which each received wages of 1200 Reichsthaler *per annum*. The other musicians were paid 1000, some 1200 Reichsthaler each/ [...] The prince had furthermore clothed the mentioned musicians in magnificent clothes/ [...] and it is not to be mentioned that the gentlemen *Kapellmeister* and also some of the other musicians wore a presentable golden chain and held such esteem with the entire court society as well as the citizens and residents of the country that the prince himself found pleasure in it because it resulted in the fact that the prince had such music at his court as could hardly be found at the imperial or other princely courts."[30]

---

30 "Jch muß noch diese Stunde loben/den Weiland hochqualificirten Herren/ Fürsten Ernsten/Graffen zu Schauenburg und Holstein/Herren zu Gehmen und Bargen/welcher tapferer Fürste seine Musicanten/die er von unterschiedlichen Nationen/sonderlich Teütschen und Engelländern/an seinem prächtigen Hofe hielte/dermahssen liebte/daß Er sie/wie seine hochvernünftige Kantzler und Räthe/besoldete/und wie seine Edelleute kleidete. [...] Also mussten auch bey seiner unvergleichlichen Music/zwene Kapelmeister sein/derer ein jedweder zwölfhundert Reichsthaler jährliche Besoldung hatte/den anderen Musicanten gab Er einem jeglichen Tausend/etlichen auch zwölffhundert Reichsthaler/[...] Uber dieses alles/ließ hochgedachter Fürst besagte Musicanten prächtig kleiden/[...] zu geschweigen/daß die

Based on the chronological distance, Rist's eulogy may not entirely illustrate reality, but it provides an impression of the role of the person, as it describes Count Ernst as the center of this musical promotion. Also Hagius attests to such an attitude of the prince in the introduction of his *Neue deutsche Tricinien* of 1604: he had "seen and known how Your Worship, apart from the other liberal arts, appreciates and loves music with particular delight".[31] Accordingly, Count Ernst showed interests which were also shared by his brother-in-law, Landgrave Moritz of Hesse, whose court he had experienced, or which were pursued by his cousin, Heinrich Julius of Braunschweig-Wolfenbüttel: in such a concept, music was understood as a part of the liberal arts, beyond all political and representative productions.[32] Helge bei der Wieden explicitly compares the music policies of the Bückeburg Count Ernst III of Holstein-Schaumburg with those of his brother-in-law, Landgrave Moritz of Hesse and, summing up, declares:

"However, maybe this is part of the secret of Ernst's success: he does not scatter himself. He prefers an excellent instead of a mediocre *Kapelle*, also when he could additionally afford a slightly glamorous theater. [...] He sets other priorities."[33]

Herren Kapelmeistere/auch etliche von den anderen Musicanten/ihre staatliche güldene Kette trugen/wobey sie in solchem Respect und Ansehen bey der sämtlichen Hofeburß/auch Bürgern und Landes-Leuten waren/daß der Fürst selber seinen Lust und Wolgefallen daran hatte/zumahlen dahiedurch ward zu wege gebracht/daß der hochlöbliche Printz eine solche Music an seinem Hoffe hatte/derer gleichen kaum am Kaiserlichen/wil geschweigen anderen Fürstlichen Höfen müchte erfunden werden." RIST, 1666, preliminary report (without pagination), quoted also in: LAAKMANN, 2000, p. 2.

31 "gesehen und erfahren/wie Ew. G. nebens den andern Freyen Künsten/derselben auch die Musicam [...] nicht für die schlechteste zu schätzen/mit sonderbahrem lust hat gelieben lassen". Quote according to LAAKMANN, 2000, p. 68.
32 See SCHMIDT, 2010, pp. 279-298.
33 "Aber vielleicht liegt hier ein Teil des Geheimnisses von Ernsts Erfolg: Er zersplitterte sich nicht. Eine hervorragende Kapelle war ihm lieber als eine mittelmäßige, auch wenn er sich dann zusätzlich noch ein wenig glanzvolles Theater hätte leisten können. [...] Er setzte andere Schwerpunkte." BEI DER WIEDEN, 1994, pp. 41ff.

Compared to these two court positions, the Stuttgart findings under Friedrich I with respect to the artistic program are rather diffuse. Friedrich consistently promoted the economy of his country in the spirit of mercantilism, particularly the cultivation of flax as well as its processing and at the same time metal processing; after all, it was important to recover the 400,000 Gulden which he had paid to Habsburg for full sovereignty over the dukedom.[34] Yet, he was personally less fond of music. However, he was eager to learn, which is evident by the descriptions of his travels to Italy, the Netherlands and England.[35] However, his musical education or activity, as explicitly noted in the report of his travels to England for Queen Elisabeth I, is not verifiable.

4. Specialization and professionality

Even though Hagius was employed as a singer in Stuttgart, his *vita* shows that he principally saw himself as a composer. As early as in 1584, he applied – although in vain – as "Componista" for choir service in Emden; in 1594, he devoted a composition to the burgraves, mayors and senators of the city of Thorn; in 1604, he devoted his *Newe deutsche Tricinien* to Ernst III; and the second edition of the Psalter is devoted to the Kurmainz Archbishop Johann Schweickhart. The organist and composer Wolfgang Getzmann also included Hagius among the few specifically mentioned "musicae coryphaeis" in his *Fantasien* print of 1613.[36] In contrast to this nationwide profile, from Stuttgart it is only known that he had presented the Wurttemberg duke an eight-part composition in 1603.[37] Although – on the occasion of the denomination-related dismissals in Stuttgart in 1609 – it was pointed out that Hagius was a "good composer", yet a composer activity at the court in Stuttgart is not verifiable, with the exception of the page from the Jenisch register (figures 1 and 2). However, particularly this genre of composition indicates that the work as a composer was not specifically required: in Stuttgart,

---

34 LORENZ, 2010, p. 7.
35 RÜCKERT, 2010.
36 This print assumes the sequence technique of the English *fancies*. WOLFGANG GETZMANN, *Phantasiae sive Cantiones mutae* […], Frankfurt 1613, information according to: SL (REIMANN), 2002, col. 851.
37 Regarding the application in Emden, see NIEMÖLLER, 1969, p. 215 and the Stuttgart dedication BOSSERT, 1910, pp. 339, 357.

Hagius was employed as a singer, rather at the center of the traditional music repertoire and not in areas where innovations were pursued.

Hagius extensively worked as composer and editor of instrumental music before or after his time in Stuttgart and his collective print *Newe künstliche, Musicalische Intraden, Pavanen, Galliarden, Passamezen, Courant und Uffzüg* (Nuremberg 1616) served those interests which were obviously not sought in Stuttgart: because, the print emphasizes the novelty of the music, its latitude with respect to genre and degree of style (from parade to fugue) and aims to vocal and instrumental design. It combines the compositions of various composers (such as the four-part movement *In laudem Musices* of the Bückeburg *Kapellmeister* Tobias Hoffkuntz) and, with its five-part dances (among those works by Alessandro Orologio, Johann Grabbe and Thomas Simpson), it participates in the instrumental music production of its time. Interestingly, it also conveys a composition by Gioseffo Biffi whom Hagius surely knew or knew of from Stuttgart: Biffi had been employed there since 1 August 1597, but it is noted that he disappeared in a "dishonest manner" as early as 6 November 1600, thus five days before the employment of Hagius.[38] Biffi is therefore one example of a foreign musician who practiced internationality, and who, with his madrigal prints published prior to his Stuttgart employment,[39] stood for a repertoire which was, however, rather marginal in Stuttgart. Contrary to the Wurttemberg court, in 1607, Count Simon VI of Lippe sent his musician Johann Grabbe to Venice for a two year education and, subsequently, Grabbe's *Primo libro de' madrigali* published in 1609 is verifiable in Bückeburg.[40] Biffi's Italian madrigal *Questi freggi celesti* on the Stuttgart music table created in 1599 and preserved until today together with the collection of the duke's *Kunstkammer*, remains an exception in the Stuttgart repertoire.

The aspiring music policy of the Bückeburg Count Ernst of Holstein-Schaumburg obviously permitted the connection of denominational openness and creative ambition.[41] The last print of Hagius is obviously tailored to this situation, because only 15 of the overall 60 compositions

---

38 BOSSERT, 1910, p. 348. Konrad Hagius included a *Galliarda amorosa a 4* by Biffi in his *Newe künstliche, Musicalische Intraden, Pavanen, Galliarden, Passamezen, Courant und Uffzüg* [...] (Nuremberg 1617).
39 BIFFI, 1596, and ID., 1600.
40 LAAKMANN, 2000, p. 218.
41 BEI DER WIEDEN, 1994, pp. 39-43, regarding Hagius IBID., p. 41.

originate from Hagius, among those a *Pavan de Schawenburg* and a *Gaillarde di Rentle* [Rinteln]. In Stuttgart, there is only a small reference to the independent instrumental music during the reign of Friedrich I, which is connected to Hagius: for the copying of a fifteen-part composition for viols he received a commendation and extra payment of one Gulden in 1602, when 14 instrumental musicians were hired.[42] A Stuttgart inventory of 1589 registered only few viols, and even if one were to assume a blurred equalization of "Geygen" and "Violen" (violins and viols) in this source, the cast of the copied compositions must have been extraordinarily large with respect to the size of the viol ensemble. This applies for the entire ensemble repertoire of the time, not just for the circumstances in Stuttgart. However, there were no independent instrumental music prints in Stuttgart at that time. This is also due to the fact that Stuttgart was not a trading center similar to the commercial and university cities, for example Frankfurt, Leipzig or Nuremberg. In contrast, Hagius' last edition carries international repertoire, namely respective a *Galliarde* by the English-Dutch lute player Gregorius Huwet (Heuwett, Howett, Huwer), whom Hagius could have met previously at the wedding at Jülich, by Gideon Lebon and by Alexander Orologio six intrades set with German text. It therefore fits the Bückeburg musical policy which favored instrumental as well as English music, and which was not verifiable in Stuttgart.

5. Mobility and work options or "try it elsewhere"

In light of the different latitudes in Wurttemberg and Schaumburg-Holstein it is once more emphasized in clear words: this contribution does not attempt the "honor rescue" of the musician Hagius, who never played a central role, neither in music history of his time nor in modern historiography. It is also not about appropriating a musician for a territory (such as Wurttemberg) in order to write a broken down hero-story. As the number of Hagius' compositions is limited, a person-related illustration can only be

---

42 BRENNECKE, 1956, col. 1312 and BÖLLING, 2001, col. 395-397. Presumably, this meant 15 parts (partes) and not a real fifteen-part composition for viols. Regarding Hagius see BOSSERT, 1910, p. 339. Regarding "Geygen" and "Violen" (violins and viols) at the Stuttgart court see GOLLY-BECKER, 1999, p. 208.

about the representation of the different opportunities and circumstances encountered by a musician in various situations. This allows the contextualization of the mobility behavior of a musician. Hagius' *vita* is ruled by employments and changes, by settlement and mobility. This heterogeneity is also reflected in his œuvre. It includes occasional works at the beginning of the year 1594 or for Jenisch's register, the psalm designated for congregation vocals and lessons, his first book of 12 *Magnificat*-scorings, which were printed in Dillingen and dedicated to the brothers Marcus and Christoph Fugger, the *Neue deutsche Tricinien*, which provide a variety of movement techniques for secular and theological text, and the collective print with numerous compositions (also instrumental works) of other composers of 1616. It is difficult to detect any uniform musical profile; one could almost say that it was only consequential that the heterogeneity of the *vita* had also caused a heterogeneous Œuvre. Even the extremely favorable opportunity of changing to the Bückeburg Court failed to produce a radical change in this context, not least due to the early death of the composer. To some extent, Hagius' activity as composer runs parallel to the local options, ignores his musical actions as bass singer and demonstrates artistic multi-professionalism. Since Hagius had never held an active position prior to his employment at Bückeburg, his mobility behavior and the latitude of his compositions are like two sides of a coin: they are an expression of the constant search for the improvement of his career as musician. However, in this context, Hagius is neither an individual nor a special case: during Early Modern Times, many musicians have made conscious decisions and were mobile. In 1723, Johann Sebastian Bach voluntarily and with conviction changed from the Köthen court to the cantor office to Leipzig (also this change resulted in more than just a spatial modification),[43] and a *vita* such as that of Johann Adolph Scheibe was virtually determined by the moment of mobility. Even though the article in *Die Musik in Geschichte und Gegenwart* describes Scheibe's profession with terms such as "musical writer and composer",[44] it must be noted that this by no means took care of living expenses during the 18th century, because both activities were normally not associated with a musician office. Several applications for an organist position in Leipzig and the position as *Kapellmeister* in Prague, Gotha, Sondershausen and Wolfenbüttel indicate Scheibe's constant search, and only few years of his life were associated

---

43 See SCHNEIDERHEINZE, 1982, pp. 247-258.
44 MACKENSEN, 2005, col. 1201.

with an office: he worked as *Kapellmeister* in Copenhagen between 1740 and 1748. The publication of his book *Der critische Musicus* (1737-1740), considered to be innovative by modern historiography, and the no less innovative establishment of a vocational music school in Sønderborg in 1757 is thus opposed by mobility and a high degree of financial and economic uncertainty. As these findings are to be considered less a special, but rather a regular case, it was publically contemplated during the 18th century: in his *Universal-Lexicon*, Johann Heinrich Zedler reflects on talent, disposition and the extent in which they could be realized with an individual "lifestyle". Here, he practically encourages mobility and speaks openly of the option to change a preordained progress of his own *vita* and offensively steer it into a direction, which justifies the Godly provenance of the musical disposition:

"If your chosen way of life in your home country is not successful, try it elsewhere. The world belongs to the Lord everywhere and the prophet usually counts least in the homeland. If your merits are not recognized in this land, you are not bound to it. Try it elsewhere. If you are oppressed at this place, you may be raised at another. If the present time is not ready for your sciences, work for the future."[45]

Meanwhile, the example of Konrad Hagius indicates that the mercantilism and *embourgeoisement* of the music culture during the 18th century has not just created, but possibly intensified this awareness in such a manner that now the individuality of the mobility was discussed.[46] Mobility and musical experience are reflected in the "Lebensart" (lifestyle) category and the verification of musical experiences evident through migrations became extremely important in the musician autobiographies of the early 18th century. One example, *ex negativo*, to verify this fact:

---

45 "Gehet es mit der ergriessenen Lebens=Art in deinem Vaterlande nicht fort, versuche es anderwärts. Die Erde ist überall des Herrn, und der Prophet gilt gemeiniglich im Vaterlande am wenigsten. Erkennet man in diesem Lande deine Verdienste nicht, bist du doch nicht an dasselbige gebunden. Versuche es anderwärts. Unterdrucket man dich an diesem Orte, wird man dich an jenem vielleicht erheben. Sollten auch vielleicht gegenwärtige Zeiten deiner Wissenschaft noch nicht fähig seyn, arbeite aufs künfftige." ZEDLER, 1737, col. 1276.
46 The musician's biographies and autobiographies of the 18th century are impressive examples in this case.

the *vita* of Georg Philipp Telemann, so poor in international experience compared to that of George Frideric Handel, relied extremely on the allocation of broad space to the encounter with Polish and Moravian music in Upper Silesia. Mobility and musician's experience are thus becoming a partial moment of Telemann's "Lebensart" for the reader by way of the extensive and spirited narration through the author.[47]

Printed sources

BIFFI, GIOSEFFO, Il primo libro delle canzonette a sei voci per cantar [...] da lui novamente composta, Nuremberg 1596.
ID., Madrigali a sei voci [...], Nuremberg 1600.
MATTHESON, JOHANN, Grundlage einer Ehren=Pforte, Hamburg 1740.
MERSENNE, MARIN, Harmonie Universelle contenant la Théorie et la Pratique de la Musique, Paris 1636, reprint, ed. by FRANÇOIS LESURE, Paris 1975, vol. 3: Traité des Instruments à chordes, Paris 1975.
RIST, JOHANN, AllerEdelste Belustigung Kunst- und Tugendliebender Gemüther, Frankfurt 1666.
ZEDLER, JOHANN HEINRICH, art. Lebens-Art, in: Grosses vollständiges Universal LEXICON Aller Wissenschafften und Künste, ed. by ID., vol. 16, Halle/Leipzig 1737, cols. 1273-1276.

Literature

ARLT, WULF, Italien als produktive Erfahrung franko-flämischer Musiker im 15. Jahrhundert (Vorträge der Aeneas-Silvius-Stiftung an der Universität Basel 26), Basel/Frankfurt a.M. 1993.
BADE, KLAUS, Historische Migrationsforschung, in: Migration in der europäischen Geschichte seit dem späten Mittelalter. Vorträge auf dem Deutschen Historikertag in Halle a.d. Saale, 11. September 2003 [i.e. 2002] (IMIS-Beiträge 20), ed. by ID., Osnabrück 2002, pp. 21-43.
BEI DER WIEDEN, HELGE, Ein norddeutscher Renaissancefürst. Ernst zu Holstein-Schaumburg 1569-1622 (Kulturlandschaft Schaumburg 1), Bielefeld 1994.

---

47 Regarding Telemann's autobiography, see MATTHESON, 1740, p. 360 and regarding "Lebensart" KREMER, 2014, pp. 259-280.

BÖLLING, JÖRG, Hagius, Konrad, in: Die Musik in Geschichte und Gegenwart, ed. by LUDWIG FINSCHER, Personenteil 8, Kassel et al. 2001, cols. 395-397.

BOSSERT, GUSTAV, Die Hofkantorei unter Herzog Ludwig, in: Württembergische Vierteljahrshefte für Landesgeschichte, Neue Folge, IX (1900), pp. 253-291.

ID., Die Hofkapelle unter Herzog Friedrich 1593-1608, in: Württembergische Vierteljahrshefte für Landesgeschichte, Neue Folge, XIX (1910), pp. 317-374.

ID., Die Hofkapelle unter Johann Friedrich 1608-1628, in: Württembergische Vierteljahrshefte für Landesgeschichte, Neue Folge, XX (1911), pp. 150-208.

BRENNECKE, WILFRIED, Hagius, Konrad, in: Die Musik in Geschichte und Gegenwart, ed. by FRIEDRICH BLUME, vol. 5, Kassel et al. 1956, cols. 1311-1315.

BRUSNIAK, FRIEDHELM/KOCH, KLAUS-PETER (eds.), Probleme der Migration von Musik und Musikern in Europa im Zeitalter des Barock. 15. Arolser Barock-Festspiele 2000. Tagungsbericht in Zusammenarbeit mit dem Institut für deutsche Musikkultur im östlichen Europa Bonn (Arolser Beiträge zur Musikforschung 9), Sinzig 2002.

DETERING, HEINRICH (ed.), Grenzgänge. Skandinavisch-deutsche Nachbarschaften (Grenzgänge. Studien zur skandinavisch-deutschen Literaturgeschichte 1), Göttingen 1996.

FEDERHOFER-KÖNIGS, RENATE, Johannes Oridryus und sein Musiktraktat (Düsseldorf 1557) (Beiträge zur rheinischen Musikgeschichte 24), Cologne 1957.

FINSCHER, LUDWIG, Die Musik des 15. und 16. Jahrhunderts (Handbuch der Musikwissenschaft 3), Laaber 1989.

GERBER, ERNST LUDWIG, Neues Historisches-Biographisches Lexikon der Tonkünstler, vol. 2: E-I, Leipzig 1812.

GOLLY-BECKER, DAGMAR, Die Stuttgarter Hofkapelle unter Herzog Ludwig III. 1554-1593 (Quellen und Studien zur Musik in Baden-Württemberg 4), Stuttgart 1999.

GOTTWALD, CLYTUS, Humanisten-Stammbücher als musikalische Quellen, in: Helmuth Osthoff zu seinem siebzigsten Geburtstag (Frankfurter Musikhistorische Studien), ed. by URSULA AARBURG/PETER CAHN, Tutzing 1969, pp. 89-103.

HENKE, ROBERT/NICHOLSON, ERIC (eds.), Transnational Mobilities in Early Modern Theater, Surrey 2014.

HIRSCHMANN, WOLFGANG, Die 'gemischte Kantorei' und ihr 'Capellmeister'. Neue Organisationsformen der Kirchenmusik im 16. Jahrhundert zwischen geistlicher und weltlicher Sphäre, in: Der Kirchenmusiker. Berufe – Institutionen – Wirkungsfelder (Enzyklopädie der Kirchenmusik 3), ed. by FRANZ KÖRNDLE/JOACHIM KREMER, Laaber 2015, pp. 189-198.

KÖSTER, MAREN/SCHMIDT, DÖRTE (ed.), "Man kehrt nie zurück, man geht immer nur fort." Remigration und Musikkultur, München 2005.

KOUDAL, JENS HENRIK, Musikermobilitet i Østersøområdet i 1600-og 1700-tallet, in: Dansk Årbog for Musikforskning XXI (1993), pp. 9-32.

KREKLER, INGEBORG, Stammbücher bis 1625 (Die Handschriften der Württembergischen Landesbibliothek, Sonderreihe 3), Wiesbaden 1999.

KREMER, JOACHIM, Zur Mobilität und Repertoireverbreitung im 19. Jahrhundert. Der Lüneburger Organist Louis Anger (1813-1870) im Urteil Mendelssohn-Bartholdys, Schumanns und Hummels, in: Niedersachsen in der Musikgeschichte. Zur Methodologie und Organisation musikalischer Regionalgeschichtsforschung. Internationales Symposium Wolfenbüttel 1997 (Publikationen der Hochschule für Musik und Theater Hannover 9), ed. by ARNFRIED EDLER/ID., Augsburg 2000, pp. 161-183.

ID., Regionalforschung heute? Last und Chance eines historiographischen Konzepts, in: Die Musikforschung 57 (2004), pp. 110-121.

ID., Georg Michael Telemanns Weg von Hamburg nach Riga: Mobilität als Problem einer Regionalgeschichtsforschung, in: Orgelbau, Orgelmusik und Organisten des Ostseeraums im 17. und 19. Jahrhundert. Internationale musikwissenschaftliche Konferenz Musica Baltica – Interregionale musikkulturelle Beziehungen im Ostseeraum, Greifswald-Lubmin, 8. bis 11. September 2002 (Greifswalder Beiträge zur Musikwissenschaft 14), ed. by MATTHIAS SCHNEIDER/WALTER WERBECK, Frankfurt a.M. et al. 2006, pp. 159-168.

ID., Madrigal und Kulturtransfer zur Zeit Friedrichs I. von Württemberg. Zu einem Konzert mit Werken von Schütz, Monteverdi, Grabbe, Lechner und Zeitgenossen, in: Hofkultur um 1600. Die Hofmusik Herzog Friedrichs I. von Württemberg und ihr kulturelles Umfeld (Tübinger Bausteine zur Landesgeschichte 15), ed. by ID. et al., Ostfildern 2010[a], pp. 315-334.

ID., Englische Musiker am württembergischen Hof in Stuttgart. Musikermobilität und der strukturelle Wandel der Hofkantorei um 1600, in:

Hofkultur um 1600. Die Hofmusik Herzog Friedrichs I. von Württemberg und ihr kulturelles Umfeld (Tübinger Bausteine zur Landesgeschichte 15), ed. by ID. et al., Ostfildern 2010[b], pp. 235-256.

ID., "Von dem Geschlecht deren Bachen". Kommentierte Quellen zur Musikerbiographik des frühen 18. Jahrhunderts, Neumünster 2014.

LAAKMANN, ASTRID, "… nur allein aus Liebe der Musica". Die Bückeburger Hofmusik zur Zeit des Grafen Ernst III. zu Holstein-Schaumburg als Beispiel höfischer Musikpflege im Gebiet der "Weserrenaissance", Münster 2000.

LORENZ, SÖNKE, Herzog Friedrich I. von Württemberg (1557-1608): ein Fürst zwischen Ambition und Wirklichkeit. Zur Einführung, in: Hofkultur um 1600. Die Hofmusik Herzog Friedrichs I. von Württemberg und ihr kulturelles Umfeld (Tübinger Bausteine zur Landesgeschichte 15), ed. by JOACHIM KREMER et al., Ostfildern 2010, pp. 1-23.

MACKENSEN, KARSTEN, Scheibe, Johann Adolph, in: Die Musik in Geschichte und Gegenwart, ed. by LUDWIG FINSCHER, Personenteil 14, Kassel et al. 2005, cols. 1201-1205.

MEYER, ERNST HERMANN, Price, John, in: Die Musik in Geschichte und Gegenwart, ed. by FRIEDRICH BLUME, vol. 10, Kassel et al. 1962, cols. 1622-1623.

MÜNZ, RAINER, Internationale Migration, [April 2009], http://www.berlin-institut.org/fileadmin/user_upload/handbuch_texte/pdf_Muenz_Internationale_Migration_09.pdf, 29.01.2015.

NIEMÖLLER, KLAUS WOLFGANG, Untersuchungen zu Musikpflege und Musikunterricht an den deutschen Lateinschulen vom ausgehenden Mittelalter bis um 1600 (Kölner Beiträge zur Musikforschung 54), Regensburg 1969.

OCHS, EKKEHARD et al. (eds.), Musica Baltica. Interregionale musikkulturelle Beziehungen im Ostseeraum. Konferenzbericht Greifswald-Gdansk 28. November bis 3. Dezember 1993 (Deutsche Musik im Osten 8), Sankt Augustin 1996.

ID. et al. (eds.), Musica Baltica. Interregionale musikkulturelle Beziehungen im Ostseeraum (Greifswalder Beiträge zur Musikwissenschaft 4), Frankfurt a.M. et al. 1997.

RAATZ, KATHLEEN, Musikermigrationen im deutschen Ostseeraum in der ersten Hälfte des 19. Jahrhunderts. Die Kleinstadt Greifswald – ein Schnittpunkt zahlreicher Reiserouten (Europäische Hochschulschriften, Reihe XXXVI, 195), Frankfurt a.M. et al. 1999.

RASCH, RUDOLF (ed.), The Circulation of Music in Europe 1600-1900. A Collection of Essays and Case Studies (Musical Life in Europe 1600-1900. Circulation, Institutions, Representation, vol. II), Berlin 2008.

ROLLAND, ROMAIN, Voyage musical aux pays du passé, Paris 1919.

RÜCKERT, PETER, Ausstellungskatalog Fürst ohne Grenzen – Duc sans frontières: Herzog Fridrich I. von Württemberg (†1608), in: Hofkultur um 1600. Die Hofmusik Herzog Friedrichs I von Württemberg und ihr kulturelles Umfeld (Tübinger Bausteine zur Landesgeschichte 15), ed. by JOACHIM KREMER et al., Ostfildern 2010, pp. 335-405.

ID., Fürst ohne Grenzen: Herzog Friedrich I. von Württemberg auf Reisen, in: Hofkultur um 1600. Die Hofmusik Herzog Friedrichs I. von Württemberg und ihr kulturelles Umfeld (Tübinger Bausteine für Landesgeschichte 15), ed. by JOACHIM KREMER et al., Ostfildern 2010, pp. 207-234.

SANDBERGER, WOLFGANG, "Held" und "negative Kontrastfigur". Zur Konzeption der Musikerbiographie im 19. Jahrhundert, in: Biographie und Kunst als historiographisches Problem. Bericht über die Internationale Wissenschaftliche Konferenz anlässlich der 16. Magdeburger Telemann-Festtage Magdeburg, 13. bis 15. März 2002 (Telemann-Konferenzberichte 15), ed. by JOACHIM KREMER et al., Hildesheim et al. 2004, pp. 182-190.

SCHILLING, GUSTAV, Encyclopädie der gesammten musikalischen Wissenschaften oder Universal-Lexicon der Tonkunst, Bd. 3, Stuttgart 1836.

SCHMIDT, DÖRTE, Zwischen Wissen, Repräsentation und Kommunikation. Moritz von Hessen-Kassel und die Bedeutung der Musik für das Herrscherbild der Zeit, in: Hofkultur um 1600. Die Hofmusik Herzog Friedrichs I. von Württemberg und ihr kulturelles Umfeld (Tübinger Bausteine zur Landesgeschichte 15), ed. by JOACHIM KREMER et al., Ostfildern 2010, pp. 279-298.

SCHNEIDERHEINZE, ARMIN, 'Ob es mir nun zwar anfänglich gar nicht anständig seyn wolte ...' – Bemerkungen zum Kapellmeister im Kantor Johann Sebastian Bach, in: Bach-Studien 7 (1982), pp. 247-258.

SL (MARGARETE REIMANN), Getzmann, Wolfgang, in: Die Musik in Geschichte und Gegenwart, ed. by LUDWIG FINSCHER, Personenteil 7, Kassel et al. 2002, cols. 850-851.

Competition at the Catholic Court of Munich
Italian Musicians and Family Networks

BRITTA KÄGLER

In the seventeenth century, Italian music with its interaction of music, scenery and costumes was *en vogue* at European courts. As a result of the breakthrough of Italian *drammi per musica*, the phenomenon of Italian musicians spreading all across Europe, from Scandinavia to Spain, from England to Russia, is fairly abundant and well known. On the other hand, systematical approaches referring to micro-historical perspectives on social and artistic integration of foreign musicians are still unexpectedly meagre and poorly researched. This article addresses foreign musicians at the court of Wittelsbach in Munich from as early as mid-seventeenth century up to late eighteenth century and comments on (mostly unsuccessful) efforts to establish lasting family networks. I am referring to the musicians themselves and the European courtscape as their major markets. This focus helps to complement the findings Tanya Kevorkian recently released about Munich town musicians.[1]

---

1 KEVORKIAN, 2012, pp. 350-371. The city itself maintained four pipers and one drummer for all public and private occasions before 1600. Court trumpeters and city pipers sometimes helped out on occasion. And it was not exceptional for city pipers to be both in the city service and court service at the same time. As the article in *The New Grove* strengthens: The city musicians did not form their own guild until after the Thirty Years War. LEUCHTMANN/ MÜNSTER.

Introduction: research and sources

A few words should be said about current research on migration history, which is focusing to a great extent on the dimensions and the variety of migration processes in Early Modern Times.[2] Several studies which dealt especially with lower class migration proved that migration was not exceptional, but quite normal. The body of sources typically favored in migration history includes literature of biographical texts, eye-witness accounts, correspondence, and itinerary sources such as route descriptions or toll registration. Crises including wars and famines, along with religious and political expulsions and work migration among laborers have been emphasized as decisive factors to spark migration.[3] Migration of elites, however, has found far less academic attention to date. Studies about the formation of networks shed more light on itinerant merchants or scholars who were educated abroad. Regarding traveling musicians, the focus was not so much on the single star composer – such as Handel and Hasse; it concentrated much more on the traveling "folk musicians" or the showmen with their touring theaters, who attracted attention. Early Modern musicians have repeatedly been at the center of historical, cultural-historical and musicological research,[4] as these musicians had a lasting influence on the musical culture of Central Europe.[5]

---

2   Transnational migrations: OBERPENNING, 2001, pp. 123-126; MOCH, 1992, pp. 6-9. Regional migrations e.g. from Napels to Venice can be found in research dealing with Early Modern composers: STROHM, 1997, pp. 61-80; GESTRICH, 2013, pp. 297f., 300f.

3   Among them were hawkers and mercenaries as well as vassals, maidservants or craftsmen who were looking for work. Drawing on work by Klaus J. Bade and Leslie Page Moch over the last decades, migration history focused on a wide range of topics, from individual immigration, to integration strategies of migrating groups, to the rise of immigration during the nineteenth century in Europe.

4   Latest publications are dealing with foreign musicians at Hungarian courts. KIRÁLY, 2014, pp. 253-270. An overview on research concerning Hungarian court music and the musical life of its high nobility can be found in KIRÁLY, 2005, pp. 439-443; KIRÁLY, 2003, pp. 79-82.

5   Thus, the Bohemian musicians had a lasting influence on the musical culture of Central Europe during the eighteenth century. Leopold emphasizes in her recent publications that the "Mannheim School" in the middle of the eighteenth century would not have been possible without the Bohemian

Challenging the traditional sparse sources on migrating musicians, the ANR/DFG-sponsored MUSICI Project has produced a systematic survey of foreign musicians in Italy with focus especially on Venice, Rome and Naples between 1650 and 1750.[6] By bringing together famous and well-known musicians such as Johann David Heinichen (1683-1729), George Frideric Handel (1685-1759) or Johann Adolf Hasse (1699-1783), whose careers certainly belong to the best-documented,[7] and those less successful, less known – and less-documented – into the center of discussion, made an important contribution to our understanding of the role played by migrating musicians throughout Europe during the seventeenth and eighteenth century. The project members developed the structure of a relational database for migrating musicians, their patrons, and customers, as well as networks of reciprocity between patrons themselves and their dependents. Nevertheless, an extensive database such as this requires further collaboration with researchers from different disciplines. Intense exchange is guaranteed in the HERA MusMig project, which has been set up by Croatian, German, Polish, and Slovenian historians and musicologists in 2014.

Searching for names and context in micro-historical perspective

My first objective is the identification of foreign musicians who worked in Munich during the seventeenth and eighteenth century. I am considering those musicians who worked at court temporarily as well as those who established themselves and stayed in Bavaria for the remainder of their careers. Secondly, I am going to examine if foreign musicians were able to succeed in placing some of their family members in salaried jobs also at foreign courts – or if there is evidence to suggest that positions which passed down for generations were reserved for local musicians only. To explore these two consecutive aspects, it is necessary to look outside the corpus of standard sources to the still largely unexplored re-

---

  immigrants. LEOPOLD, 2013, pp. 31 and 38. See also NAGEL, 1982, pp. 32-40; WÜRTZ, 1982, pp. 7-11; LARSEN, 1962, pp. 303-309.
6 See www.musici.eu, 07.07.2016.
7 And even Handel's stay in Rome is not well documented, but lies rather in the shadows of history.

cord administration. The Wittelsbach court in Munich offers an especially appropriate framework in as far as its record administration – including annual account books dating back to 1556 – which is completely preserved for a consecutive 250 years. For each calendar year, there is a record for every single person who received a salary[8] from the court, sometimes even several pay slips handed down through history. Due to the selective survival of other sources, "Hofamtsregistraturen" – files of the registry – and "Besoldungsbücher" – salary records – are the best sources for the reconstruction of names and positions, as well as reports about the lives of foreign musicians. As the court of Munich was one of the most important Catholic courts within the Holy Roman Empire, close connections to other Catholic courts in Europe can be assumed, especially close relationships with Italy.[9] Thus, not surprisingly, a significant number of foreign musicians in Munich came from the Italian peninsula. Munich's *Hofkapelle*[10] and its personnel structure mainly followed that of the Viennese imperial court; it was just a little smaller. In the seventeenth and eighteenth century, about 1,500 persons were formally employed at the Bavarian court, which depicted a hierarchy that was, in a number of smaller households,[11] completely focused on the sovereign and his family. The largest European courts comprised hundreds of official musicians. Many of those who regularly attended the court for special events and festivities were not formally employed. Though most courts can be seen as places of quick turnover and invariable exchange, every once in a while, local musicians managed to establish family dynasties of musicians, such as the Kröner and Pez families throughout the eighteenth

---

8   Sometimes, even unpaid positions are listed.
9   The Italian peninsula was far from being one Early Modern territory reigned by one sovereign, but consisted of different duchies, republics, the Kingdom of the Two Sicilies and the Papal States. Nevertheless the idea of "Italy" was linked to the Italian language and culture that is why contemporary German sources absolutely adhered to the description "Italy" as "Welschland".
10 The German word "Hofkapelle" means on the one hand a court chapel as a building, on the other hand it stands also for a chapel as a musical ensemble associated with a noble court.
11 Next to the princely household there were also the households of the electress, the children, and possible other households e.g. one of the widow of the late elector. KÄGLER, 2011, pp. 7, 47f., 60.

century in Munich. Based on the international job market for European musicians it is possible to estimate how many foreign musicians – both instrumentalists and vocalists – joined the extended household compared with the number of German musicians formally employed at court.

However, please allow me to first explain where we are and who we are dealing with in the Bavarian electorate: during the sixteenth century, the Bavarian court comprised just about 500 people and did not seem to rank highly among other contemporary courts in Europe. The same has to be said about the Bavarian *Hofkapelle* and its musicians. Though, first evidence of a *Kapelle* dates from the time of Duke Albrecht IV (1465/1467-1508),[12] the standing of the *Kapelle* waned after Ludwig Senfl,[13] director of the *Hofkapelle*, died in 1543.

Nevertheless, in time, the Bavarian court became undoubtedly one of the most important Catholic courts within the Empire, which gave the Wittelsbach opportunity to closely align themselves with the Habsburg emperors, whose concern it was to strengthen the Roman Catholics in the course of the Counter-Reformation. Furthermore, an absolutistic court life was already shaped in Munich throughout the sixteenth century. This was particularly early with regard to the characteristics later known as signs of absolutism, and at least very early compared to other German-speaking courts. After the imperial court in Vienna, it was first and foremost Bavaria that adopted the imperial model and developed a cultural impact which was competing with the Habsburg court.[14] When, from the seventeenth century onwards, Italian music triumphantly conquered Europe, Duke Albrecht V of Bavaria (*1528, reg. 1550-1579) felt obliged to attempt the creation of a musical establishment in Munich *en par* with that at the most important courts in Europe, at least those of middle power status. As a result, Albrecht began upgrading his *Hofkapelle* from the 1560s by increasing the number of singers, the number of musicians playing the trombone,

---

12 The first court chapel included already two far traveled Bavarian musicians who had worked in London. LEUCHTMANN/MÜNSTER.
13 Different spellings: Senfli, Sennfel. Current research is dealing with Senfl's work, generating a complete catalog of his works. Preliminary results can be enquired online: http://www.senflonline.com, 08.01.2015. FISHER, 2014, pp. 79f., 83.
14 KÄGLER, 2011, p. 11.

and especially the strings.[15] During his reign, Albrecht V was clearly responsible for transforming the court of Munich into a leading cultural center, which became increasingly "European in its musical outlook".[16]

The culture at the ducal court in Munich is often characterized by a coexistence of traditional as well as open-minded concepts.[17] The latter were definitely expressed in the dukes' artistic patronage, particularly focusing on musicians who could enrich the *Hofkapelle* and its perception. Musicians outnumbered medical practitioners, writers, even confessors. However, salary records, travelogues and letters prove an astonishing standard of court music and an increase in efforts to improve musical performance and style.[18] Considering the development up to the eighteenth century, salary records and court administration records confirm the assumption that foreign musicians at court did change in number and function. First, there were only a few foreign musicians – among them for instance Orlando di Lasso (1532-1594), who joined Albrecht's *Hofkapelle* in 1556[19] and was officially appointed as *Hofkapellmeister* in 1563. Under his auspices and the generous endowment of music by the duke the court ensemble, which originally had a strong Netherlandish

---

15 Duke Albrecht V was clearly responsible for transforming the small duchy of Bavaria during his reign into a leading cultural center: „Auch für andere deutsche und europäische Höfe läßt sich ungefähr ab Mitte des Jahrhunderts eine systematische Vergrößerung der Kapellen belegen. Neue organisatorische Strukturen zeigen, daß Instrumentalisten nun selbstverständlich zur Hofmusik dazugehörten. Ab 1552 wird z.B. am Münchner Hof nicht mehr zwischen Kantorei und Instrumentalisten unterschieden; sie bilden von nun an eine institutionelle Einheit. Der allgemein zu beobachtende Ausbau der Hofmusiken diente zuerst der Repräsentation im weltlichen Bereich, wurde jedoch auch für die Kirchenmusik bedeutsam." WIERMANN, 2005, p. 3.
16 LEUCHTMANN/MÜNSTER.
17 LÜTTEKEN, 2006, p. 14.
18 Research depends on various archival sources like the salary records provided in the Bavarian State Archives (inventory: D-Mhsa, Kurbayern Hofzahlamt), travelogues edited in several themed transcripts (e.g. travelogues edited by KARL VON REINHARDSTÖTTNER/KARL TRAUTMANN in *Jahrbuch für Münchener Geschichte*).
19 The earliest record of Lasso's residence in Munich dates back to 1557 suggesting he joined the court of Munich in 1556. BOETTICHER, 1963, pp. 84-94, 121-137; FISHER, 2014, pp. 90-92; PIETSCHMANN, 2006; O'REGAN, 1999, pp. 132-157.

contingent, recruited more and more Italians.[20] And Munich had indeed much to offer to the musicians it attracted from abroad, as Albrecht V made a name for himself with the collection of antiques, art, valuable books and manuscripts, still an essential part of the Bavarian state library and the Bavarian state art collections. Publishers as Johann Andreas Schobser and especially Adam Berg and his successors (Nicolaus Henricus the Younger †1654, Johann Jäcklin †1710) founded Munich's reputation as a publishing center,[21] Adam Berg specialized in music publications, including e.g. numerous editions of Lasso's works.[22]

To date, research has been concentrating particularly on these top composers like di Lasso. However, there were more and mostly fameless musicians, whose number increased during the seventeenth century, which in turn led to fierce competition between local musicians and the increasing number of musicians, conductors and choir masters from the Italian peninsula for access to the Munich court. Important factual data on migration patterns of musicians in southern Germany can be gathered by carrying out a detailed prosopographical survey and a study of foreign musicians employed at the Wittelsbach court in Munich.

Nevertheless, it is no easy task to trace those musicians who were formally employed at court. When analyzing the salary records, it is possible to reconstruct who occupied which position(s) and how much they were paid quarterly, but it is rarely possible to gather detailed information about their tasks, their language skills, concerns or if (and where) these musicians proceeded on their career path once they can no longer be traced in Munich's administration records. In addition to the names and salaries of foreign musicians, only some records – especially records from the eighteenth century – reveal information about the beginning and the end of their employments.[23]

---

20 LEUCHTMANN/MÜNSTER: "From then on Munich was a musical center of significance, with a chapel that could stand comparison with those of the emperor, the King of France and even the pope."
21 KÄGLER et al., 2012, p. 1503.
22 Different notations: Adamus Berg, Adam Montanus, Johannes Montanu (†1610). RESKE/BENZING, 2007, p. 625f.
23 The records rarely give insight into the reason why a musician left the court. For instance, the reasons for female singers at times were marriage, but also death. Additional information includes the marital status often with a mention of the husband's or wife's name, for female employees the maiden

A first list of foreign musicians suggests that it is mostly Italians who regularly found employment at the Wittelsbach court.[24] Also a small number of Dutch instrumentalists can be found. Many of these musicians are only mentioned for short term visits, implying that actors, singers and instrumentalists may have belonged to a troupe of actors giving a guest performance only. Most of the musicians traceable in the salary records stayed for more than six years. Singers and well-paid conductors and instrumentalists in high positions, such as composers, directors of the *Hofkapelle* and some of the string players, stayed longer and were members of the court ensemble in Munich until the end of their careers.

The salary records, however, are not our only record for foreign musicians. There are also contemporary catalogs of musical instruments. One of the most significant catalogs was set up in 1655.[25] All instruments belonging to the Bavarian court are listed with utmost care. But it is important to note that even this rudimental list reveals some information about foreign musicians: One of the valuable harps was mentioned as being stored in a case and kept at the home of an Italian priest (see figure 1). The former Italian priest and later court harpist mentioned in the short passage was surely Giovanni Battista Maccioni (employed: 1651-1674), born in Orvieto, subsequently living in Rome for years.[26] The result of comparing this catalog with the administration records is that Maccioni was formally employed at the Bavarian court since 17 May 1651. He was both listed as member of the princely household as well as member of the *Hofkapelle*. After ten years in Munich he returned to Rome where he continued working for the Bavarian elector. In his role as an agent of the Wittelsbach court, he recruited several Italian musicians including e.g. Ercole Bernabei (c. 1622-1687) who left his post as *maestro di cappella* in St. Peter in Rome for the lead of the Munich *Hofkapelle*.[27]

---

name, too, as well as relationships, if father or mother were also employed at court. Finally, in some cases, the taxation is reported, making it possible to calculate the relation between gross and net income. KÄGLER, 2011, p. 57f.

24 These musicians are part of preliminary research results that will expand as I progress.

25 WACKERNAGEL, 2003, pp. 13-37 (facsimile).

26 For Bavarian connections and Maccioni's activity as Bavarian agent in Italy see EITNER, 1902, p. 263; DAOLMI; REINHARDSTÖTTNER, 1887, pp. 93-172.

27 Unfortunately, I could not find any reliable information on whether being head of the Munich *Hofkapelle* was better paid or linked with special privileges for the Italians.

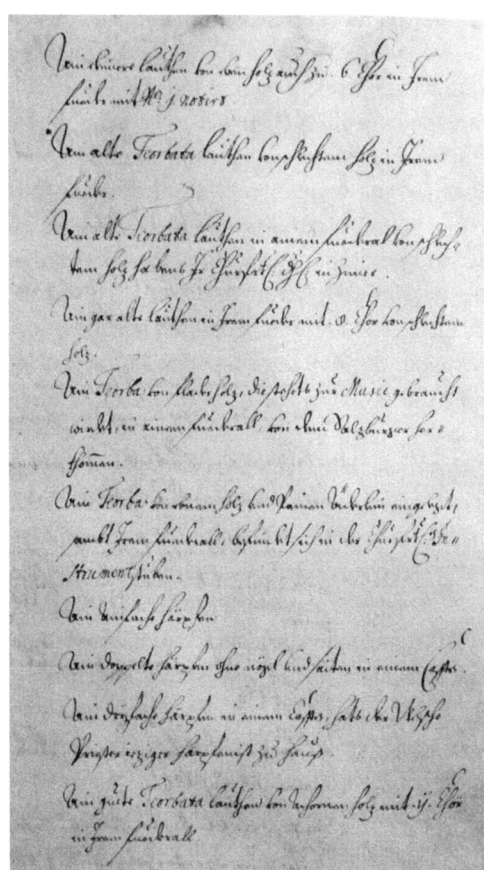

*Figure 1:
Catalog of musical instruments, 1655 – "Inventarium über die Churfürstliche Instrumentenstuben, so beschriben worden Anno 1655", fol. 10v (WACKERNAGEL, 2003)*

Together with the overall picture of foreign musicians it can be stated that more and more Italians came to Munich up to the mid-eighteenth century. One of them was Andrea Bernasconi (c. 1706-1784), a representative example of a successful and well-paid employee. Bernasconi was an Italian composer, mainly of operas. In 1753, he came to the court of Munich and was appointed to the post of *Hofkapellmeister* two years later. He successfully produced several compositions of the conservative *opera seria*. Gerber[28] reports that Johann Adolf Hasse's wife, the soprano Faustina Bordoni (1697-1781), liked Bernasconi's operas, and

---

28   GERBER, 1790-92, col. 146.

that his arias pleased her as much as those of her husband.[29] Clearly, Bernasconi was not a genius of his century. Subsequent judgments, which were taken out of context, overemphasized that Bernasconi composed some enjoyable, light and dramatic operas as well as those which failed, were dull and trivial with no dramatic effect.[30] However, it is very likely that Bernasconi not only satisfied the requirements of the Bavarian court, but that he was also very popular and seemed to reflect the spirit of his age in particular. So, how did Andrea Bernasconi come to the Munich court? – Well, little is known of Bernasconi's education. He was *maestro di cappella* at the Ospedale della Pietà in Venice for nearly ten years.[31] His wife, Maria Josepha Wagele (c. 1722-1762), was German. He met and married her in Italy before he was invited as assistant *Kapellmeister* of vocal music in Munich. He was probably recruited by one of the elector's agents, much like a century ago, when Maccioni recruited several musicians in Rome for the Bavarian court. However, with the exception of his appointment, commencing in August 1753 and coinciding with the opening of the residence theater, none of this can be verified. One year later, he became the music teacher of Princess Maria Anna Josepha (until July 1755) and Princess Josepha Maria (until January 1765). Even the monarch himself, Max III Joseph, received music lessons from him.

Formally employed musicians and those who regularly attended the court without an official function also took part in Early Modern decision-making processes, as well as other servants. Their closeness – or distance – to the prince was an important indication of the status they held within court society. Court musicians were under the command of the High Steward (*Obersthofmeister*). In principle, the musicians did not belong to the aristocracy and, thus, were outside of the framework of noble hierarchy at court. Hence, they had no position of trust or direct access to the prince based on their range of musical tasks. Several studies on court history have shown, however, that there could be situations where those characteristics underlying courtly hierarchy were disregarded. These included the age, the tenure of serving at court (anciennity), the social rank

---

29   SADGORSKI, 2010, p. 261; LIPPMANN, 1987, pp. 17-65.
30   For efficacious judgements in the nationalistic spirit of the 19th century: "... viel Angenehmes, Leichtes, Effectvolles, neben viel Verfehltem, Leerem, Gehaltlosem", VON WURZBACH, 1856, p. 325.
31   Since 1744, SADGORSKI, 2010, pp. 48, 254.

of the family of origin, the age of the family if noble etc.[32] In this respect, the function-oriented hierarchy at court was easily brought off balance by preference and favor.[33] Taking a close look at the particular situation, when the prince and a selection of his court members traveled, reveals a special feature of court musicians: Who and how many officeholders accompanied the prince during travels was connected with procedural tasks on one hand and how prestigious the entourage was considered on the other. In order to be seen as representative in Early Modern Times, not only the liveries of the servants had to be right, there were always musicians and trumpeters[34] necessary, too.[35] As a result, musicians could seek out the proximity to the prince; and being close to the elector could be an indication of their possible influence at court, for spending time with the prince and his family was a first step in the most common careers at courts. The personal proximity was of major interest: the elector was the most powerful advocate for any servant at the Munich court. Contemporaries saw the advocacy and mediation by the elector as a perfectly legitimate procedure, whether applied to court-internal matters, public matters or political decision making processes.[36]

Bernasconi revealed a strong preference for positions close to the sovereign. But was he able to build a professional network or to secure positions at the court for his relatives? It is difficult to analyze the personal networks of Bernasconi, as we do not have many reliable sources. He shaped the court life for 19 years, and during this period many Italian musicians were attracted to the Bavarian court. Nevertheless, it is only possible to provide evidence of *one* protégé: Bernasconi cared about the musical education and the *début* of his stepdaughter Antonia Bernasconi (1740/1-1803), née Wagele, married Rieler. He instructed her in singing and arranged the opportunity of a very public *début* in Munich: She was singing the Aspasia in Bernasconi's own opera

---

32 HENGERER, 2004, p. 187.
33 KÄGLER, 2011, p. 408; WINTERLING, 1997, pp. 11-25.
34 Trumpeters were not listed in the same category as musicians (singers and instrumentalists), they were separate in the account books as were drummers. Both trumpets and drums had a long tradition of military importance. See WATANABE-O'KELLY et al., 2004, pp. 89, 167, 337, 435.
35 HENGERER, 2004, p. 136.
36 Referring to advocacy, closeness/distance and mediation see HENGERER, 2004, pp. 376-381, 443-446, 494-499; SCHLÖGEL, 2008, pp. 155-224.

Temistocle in January 1762 and started her successful career as a soprano in serious operas.[37]

Here, the focus shifts to the networks of foreign musicians at the Bavarian court. Is Bernasconi's promotion of his stepdaughter a paradigm for networks of musicians? Did foreign court musicians succeed in establishing family members, placing some of them as colleagues at court? Analyzing the salary records, it can be proved that foreign musicians at court worked together as husband and wife only in rare cases, and hardly ever with other relatives. In the late eighteenth century, there was the married couple Le Brun (Le Brüne): Ludwig August was employed as oboist at the *Hofkapelle*, Franziska (née Danzi) was a soprano singer. Both are traceable for exactly the same period from 1780 up to the year 1791.[38] They came to Munich at the same time, as both of them had already been a working couple in Mannheim.[39] A hundred years earlier, Luigi Orlandi was employed for more than two years before also his wife received a post as a singer at the Munich court.[40] When Angela Orlandi died 13 years later, her husband resigned, left Bavaria and returned to Italy.[41]

However, it is striking that networks of local musicians are quite different and more far-reaching: Examples include the families Kröner and Pez, just two of many that placed relatives at court, starting as court musicians

---

37 Mozart said "he would have trusted her with a part in the German performance of *Idomeneo* that he was planning." Antonia Bernasconi, as Mozart said (letter from 29 August 1781), really sang well only in serious operas. Aside from that his letter is severely critical of her intonation and German declamation. See MÜNSTER; SADGORSKI, 2010, pp. 92, 107. Mozart's letter is online available (facsimile and transcript): http://dme.mozarteum.at/DME/briefe/letter.php?mid=1186&cat=, 08.11.2015.

38 D-Mhsa, HR I 469/614.

39 See OVER, in print.

40 D-Mhsa, Hofzahlamt Kurbayern: Luigi Orlandi was court poet with the additional title of a secretary (1684–1697). His wife Angela Orlandi joined the court of Munich in 1686 as a vocalist. She received the honorary title as *Kammersängerin* and died in the first quarter of the year 1697 in Munich. D-Mhsa, HR I 471/751.

41 As my project's close examination of the situation at the Wittelsbach court will be complemented by a broad reference framework of musicians working at the courts of Eichstätt, Ansbach, Bamberg and Stuttgart, it might be possible to find related musicians at these courts, too.

and later gaining access to even more lucrative positions close to the elector. Starting points for this networking were often individual musicians in a position of trust. For example, the violinist Anton Kröner placed brothers and/or cousins, at least one son and daughter[42] in the Munich court and helped in the award of a noble rank for himself and his family. It may have been an advantage that all family members were violinists: Anton Kröner started as court violinist before being employed as chamber violinist.[43] Since the 1750s, Anton Kröner helped to establish Franz Karl Kröner, who started at the same time as Anton as an *Instrumentalakzessist*, i.e. assistant instrumentalist, before also being employed as a violinist. He, Franz Karl was ennobled in 1750 and became vice-concertmaster at court in 1764.[44] The same office was held later by Johann Nepomuk Kröner (1775-1780) and Johann Kröner (1780-1785).[45] Maria Josepha Kröner (née Berberich) was a singer and chamber virtuoso, too, according to the salary records.[46] Finally, Joseph Kröner held the office of "Ballmeister" at the University of Ingolstadt between 1778 and 1780.[47] Taking such a close look at the Kröner family members reveals a strong preference for similar or the same positions, staying true to their strength of playing the violin. Here, they had to compete with foreign musicians, mainly from Italy.

---

42 It might be a daughter-in-law, too, as the exact relationship could not be proven so far.
43 I assume the position as *Kammerviolinist* was a kind of honorary title at court for some violinists as chamber secretaries among other secretaries at court. These positions were not related to further duties but included chamber access and therefore closer proximity to the princely family. Anton Kröner was violinist from 1745 to 1770, *Kammerviolinist* (EITNER: Violoncellist) from 1744 to 1769. He died on 30 September 1770. Sources: D-Mhsa, HSK, DS 1754/I/9, DS 1768/XII/13, HR I 467/501.
44 *Instrumentalakzessist* 1738, violinist from 1748 to 1778, vice-concertmaster during the year 1764. Sources: D-Mhsa, HSK, DS 1753/I/16, DS 1765/III/6, HR I 467/502.
45 Kröner, Johann von: "Vizekonzertmeister bei der Instrumentalmusik der Hofmusik" from 1780 to 1785. Sources: D-Mhsa, HSK. Kröner, Johann Nepomuk (might be identical with Johannes von Cröner): court and chamber violinist from 1751 to 1774, vice-concertmaster at court from 1775 to 1780. Sources: D-Mhsa, HSK, DS 1751/VIII/19, HR I 465/326, HR I 467/500.
46 D-Mhsa, HSK, DS 1755/V/30, HR I 463/136.
47 Kröner, Joseph (died on 2 November 1780): Sources: D-Mhsa, Hofzahlamt Kurbayern.

I previously mentioned another German family: members of the Pez family can be found throughout the second half of the seventeenth up to the middle of the eighteenth century. Johann Baptist Pez started as trumpeter at court and cleared the way for his children. Johann Christoph became a musician too, though the sources do not reveal which instruments he used to play. Between 1689 and 1692, Johann Christoph Pez was staying in Rome. Nothing is known about his stay in Italy but it suggests itself as a time for advanced education. Back in Germany, he returned to Munich for a while and became *maestro di cappella* at the court of Cologne shortly afterwards.[48] A close relationship between Munich and Cologne was rather normal at that time as the two electors were brothers and their personal relationship led to a steady exchange of artists, musicians, architects and other employees.[49] Franz Anton Pez is a son of Johann Christoph Pez; he also started as musician in Munich before leaving court music to become a toll collector for the court administration.[50] This position was a first step for the family to start a career outside of the pure music setting: His sister was lady-in-waiting at the princely household in Munich,[51] her daughters both worked at court as servants between 1720 and 1748.[52] Members of the Pez family showed a strong preference for positions close to the sovereign, culminating both in positions in the personal household of the princely family, and in the court and state administration. There, they detached themselves from the keen competition among musicians at court, where Italian origins, at least Italian family background and Italian experience, were still favored over the years of the turn of the century.

48   See OVER, in print.
49   Pez (Pöz), Johann Christoph. – Musician at court from 1689 to 1693, in 1694 he left Munich and was until 1705 at the Wittelsbach court in Cologne. – Sources: D-Mhsa, Hofzahlamt Kurbayern, HR I 463/156.
50   Pez, Franz Anton. – Court and chamber musician from 1718 to 1724 (he left the court to become a toll collector in the small Bavarian town Neuötting). – Sources: D-Mhsa, Hofzahlamt Kurbayern, HR I 463/152.
51   Pez, Anna Maria (mother of Christina Theresa Pez and Maria Anna Lombé, died at the beginning of 1728). She served at court as a chamber maid at from 1722 to 1728. – Sources: D-Mhsa, Hofzahlamt Kurbayern.
52   Pez, Theresia Christina (daughter of Anna Maria Pez, sister of Maria Anna Lombé). – Chamber servant of duchess Maria Anna from 1720 to 1736, left the court marrying and becoming a wife and returned widowed in the year 1746. – Sources: D-Mhsa, Hofzahlamt Kurbayern, HR I 8/40/8. Pez, Anna. – Chamber servant 1748. – Sources: D-Mhsa, HR I 8/40/8.

Conclusion

This insight into administrative sources shows their potential for analyzing Early Modern court musicians. For them, it was not just a question of obtaining a regular salary. Musicians were attracted to the court because of the privilege to serve at the center of the electorate. And as the society's elite was attracted to the court, musicians were able to join the noble networks and be part of representation processes at court. I noted earlier how it is often observed that local musicians were more successful in establishing lasting family networks than foreign musicians and their family members. The comparison between foreign and local musicians at the court in Munich hereby offers unique perspectives. Difficulties involved in trying to reconstruct migratory movements of Early Modern musicians always depend on variety and divergence of archival sources. Though the various factors that could determine the success or failure of integration processes at the Munich court cannot only be figured out by analyzing salary records and dominant positions of single families, yet this has value in itself: The difficulties of foreign musicians in establishing lasting family networks during the seventeenth and eighteenth century provides a framework against which we can judge alterations or continuity that may occur in later centuries.

Manuscript and printed sources

Salzburg, Internationale Stiftung Mozarteum, Bibliotheca Mozartiana: Wolfgang Amadé Mozart an Leopold Mozart, Wien 29. August 1781, in: Digital Mozart Edition: http://dme.mozarteum.at/DME/briefe/letter.php?mid=1186&cat=, 08.11.2015.

GERBER, ERNST LUDWIG, Historisch-biographisches Lexikon der Tonkünstler, vol. 2, Leipzig 1790-92, reprint Graz 1977.

WACKERNAGEL, BETTINA, Musikinstrumentenverzeichnis der Bayerischen Hofkapelle von 1655. Faksimilie, Transkription und Kommentar (Veröffentlichungen der Gesellschaft für Bayerische Musikgeschichte), Tutzing 2003.

Literature

BOETTICHER, WOLFGANG, Aus Orlando di Lassos Wirkungskreis. Neue archivalische Studien zur Münchener Musikgeschichte, Kassel et al. 1963.

DAOLMI, DAVIDE, Maccioni, Giovanni Battista, in: Dizionario Biografico degli Italiani 67 (2006), www.treccani.it/enciclopedia/giovanni-battista-maccioni_%28Dizionario_Biografico%29/, 08.11.2015.

EITNER, ROBERT, Biographisch-bibliographisches Quellen-Lexicon der Musiker und Musikgelehrten der christlichen Zeitrechnung bis zur Mitte des neunzehnten Jahrhunderts, Leipzig 1902.

FISHER, ALEXANDER J., Music, Piety, and Propaganda: The Soundscape of Counter-Reformation Bavaria, New York 2014.

GESTRICH, ANDREAS, Migration und Kulturkontakte in der Musikgeschichte. Ein Kommentar aus der Perspektive der Historischen Migrationsforschung, in: Migration und Identität. Wanderbewegungen und Kulturkontakte in der Musikgeschichte (Analecta musicologia 49), ed. by SABINE EHRMANN-HERFORT/SILKE LEOPOLD, Kassel et al. 2013, pp. 295-301.

HENGERER, MARK, Kaiserhof und Adel in der Mitte des 17. Jahrhunderts. Eine Kommunikationsgeschichte der Macht in der Vormoderne (Historische Kulturwissenschaften 3), Konstanz 2004.

KÄGLER, BRITTA, Frauen am Münchener Hof (1651-1756) (Münchener Historische Studien 18), Kallmünz 2011.

ID. et al., München, in: Handbuch kultureller Zentren der Frühen Neuzeit, vol. 2: Halberstadt – Münster, ed. by WOLFGANG ADAM/SIEGRID WESTPHAL, Berlin/Boston 2012, pp. 1471-1518.

KEVORKIAN, TANYA, Town Musicians in German Baroque Society and Culture, in: German History 30 (2012), pp. 350-371.

KIRÁLY, PÉTER, Foreign Musicians and Their Influence in Sixteenth- and Seventeenth-Century Hungary, in: A Divided Hungary in Europe. Exchanges, Networks and Representations (1541-1699), ed. by GÁBOR ALMÁSI et al., Newcastle upon Tyne 2014, pp. 253-270.

ID., A magyarországi főnemesség 17. századi zene- élete. Vázlatos áttekintés néhány főúri család forrásai alapján [The musical life of the Hungarian high nobility in the 17th century. A cursory overview based on sources of some aristocratic families], in: "Idővel paloták ..." Magyar udvari kultúra a 16-17. században ["Over Time Palaces ..." Hungarian court culture in the 16th and 17th century], ed. by ILDIKÓ HORN/NÓRA G. ETÉNYI, Budapest 2005, pp. 439-443.

ID., 16-17. századi udvari zenénk kutatásának problematikájáról [Problems concerning the research of our 16th-17th century court music], in: Magyar Zene [Hungarian Music] 41 (2003), pp. 79-82.

LARSEN, JENS PETER, Zur Bedeutung der "Mannheimer Schule", in: Festschrift für Karl Gustav Fellerer, ed. by HEINRICH HÜSCHEN, Regensburg 1962, pp. 303-309.

LEOPOLD, SILKE, Musikwissenschaft und Migrationsforschung. Einige grundsätzliche Überlegungen, in: Migration und Identität. Wanderbewegungen und Kulturkontakte in der Musikgeschichte (Analecta musicologia 49), ed. by SABINE EHRMANN-HERFORT/SILKE LEOPOLD, Kassel et al. 2013, pp. 30-39.

LEUCHTMANN, HORST/MÜNSTER, ROBERT, Munich, in: Grove Music Online, www.oxfordmusiconline.com/subscriber/article/grove/music/19360, 08.11.2015.

LIPPMANN, FRIEDRICH, Hasses Arienstil und seine Interpretation durch Rudolf Gerber, in: Colloquium Johann Adolph Hasse und seine Zeit (Analecta Musicologica 25), ed. by FRIEDRICH LIPPMANN, Laaber 1987, pp. 17-65.

LÜTTEKEN, LAURENZ, Abgrenzung versus Verflechtung. Die Münchner Hofkapelle des 16. Jahrhunderts zwischen lokalem Profil und europäischer Perspektive, in: Die Münchner Hofkapelle des 16. Jahrhunderts im europäischen Kontext, ed. by THEODOR GÖLLNER/BERNHOLD SCHMID, Munich 2006, pp. 7-19.

MOCH, LESLIE PAGE, Moving Europeans in Western Europe since 1650, Bloomington/IN 1992.

MÜNSTER, ROBERT, Bernasconi, Antonia, in: Grove Music Online, www.oxfordmusiconline.com/subscriber/article/grove/music/02865, 08.11.2015.

NAGEL, KARL-HEINZ, Die Familie Grua: Italienische Musiker in kurpfälzischen Diensten, in: Mannheim und Italien – Zur Vorgeschichte der Mannheimer. Bericht über das Mannheimer Kolloquium im März 1982 (Beiträge zur Mittelrheinischen Musikgeschichte 25), ed. by ROLAND WÜRTZ, Mainz et. al. 1984, pp. 32-40.

OBERPENNING, HANNELORE, "People were on the move". Wanderhandelssysteme im vor- und frühindustriellen Europa, in: Kleinräumige Wanderungen in historischer Perspektive (imis-Beiträge 18), ed. by HANNELORE OBERPENNING/ANNEMARIE STEIDL, Osnabrück 2001, pp. 123-140.

O'REGAN, NOEL, Orlando di Lasso and Rome, in: Orlando di Lasso Studies, ed. by PETER BERGQUIST, Cambridge 1999, pp. 132-157.

OVER, BERTHOLD, Employee Turnover in *Hofkapellen* of the Wittelsbach Dynasty. Types of and Reasons for (Impeded) Migration (1715-1725), in: Music Migrations in the Early Modern Age. People, Markets, Patterns, Styles, ed. by VJERA KATALINIĆ, Zagreb in pr.

PIETSCHMANN, KLAUS, Römische Spuren im Repertoire der Münchner Hofkapelle zur Zeit des Trienter Konzils, in: Die Münchner Hofkapelle des 16. Jahrhunderts im europäischen Kontext, ed. by THEODOR GÖLLNER/BERNHOLD SCHMID, Munich 2006, pp. 105-117.

REINHARDSTÖTTNER, KARL VON, Über die Beziehungen der italienischen Litteratur zum bayerischen Hofe und ihre Pflege an demselben, in: Jahrbuch für Münchener Geschichte 1 (1887), pp. 93-172.

RESKE, CHRISTOPH/BENZING, JOSEF (ed.), Die Buchdrucker des 16. und 17. Jahrhunderts im deutschen Sprachgebiet, Wiesbaden 2007, pp. 625-626.

SADGORSKI, DANIELA, Andrea Bernasconi und die Oper am Münchner Kurfürstenhof 1753-1772, Munich 2010.

SCHLÖGEL, RUDOLPH, Kommunikation und Vergesellschaftung unter Anwesenden. Formen des Sozialen und ihre Transformation in der Frühen Neuzeit, in: Geschichte und Gesellschaft 34 (2008), pp. 155-224.

STROHM, REINHARD, Dramma per Musica. Italian Opera Seria of the Eighteenth Century, New Haven/London 1997.

WATANABE-O'KELLY, HELEN et al., Europa Triumphans. Court and Civic Festivals in Early Modern Europe (Publications of the Modern Humanities Research Association 15,1), Aldershot 2004.

WIERMANN, BARBARA, Die Entwicklung vokal-instrumentalen Komponierens im protestantischen Deutschland bis zur Mitte des 17. Jahrhunderts (Abhandlungen zur Musikgeschichte 14), Göttingen 2005.

WINTERLING, ALOYS, "Hof". Versuch einer idealtypischen Bestimmung anhand der mittelalterlichen und frühneuzeitlichen Geschichte, in: Zwischen "Haus" und "Staat". Antike Höfe im Vergleich, ed. by ID. (HZ Beihefte 23), Munich 1997, pp. 11-25.

WURZBACH, CONSTANTIN VON, Bernasconi, Andrea, in: Biographisches Lexikon des Kaiserthums Oesterreich, vol. 1 (1856), p. 325.

WÜRTZ, ROLAND, Mannheim und Italien. 80 Jahre Musikforschung zur Vorgeschichte der Mannheimer, in: Mannheim und Italien – Zur Vorgeschichte der Mannheimer. Bericht über das Mannheimer Kolloquium im März 1982 (Beiträge zur Mittelrheinischen Musikgeschichte 25), ed. by ROLAND WÜRTZ, Mainz et. al. 1984, pp. 7-11.

From Munich to 'Foreign' Lands and Back Again
Relocation of the Munich Court and Migration of Musicians (c. 1690-1715)

BERTHOLD OVER

At the end of the 17th and beginning of the 18th century, Elector Max Emanuel of Bavaria moved his court several times. When he became governor of the Spanish Netherlands in 1692, he relocated his court to Brussels. In 1701, during the War of the Spanish Succession, he returned to Munich. When Max Emanuel had to flee from Munich due to the conquest of Bavaria by the emperor troops in 1704, he returned to the Spanish Netherlands and later moved to France. His wife, Therese Kunigunde was forced into exile in Venice in 1705. When the court was re-established after the peace agreement in 1715, both returned to Munich. It is obvious that the regents did not travel alone, but were accompanied by an, although reduced, entourage. Court officers, butlers, coachmen and other servants, including musicians, naturally traveled with them or met the regents at a later date. Other personnel was recruited to uphold a court befitting its status at the respective locations and, perhaps, returned to Munich with the regents. These movements are to be examined herein, focussing on the consequences with respect to the migration of musicians.

Speaking of migration in this context, this keyword is naturally not to be understood in terms of 'exodus', 'emigration' or 'immigration' in the modern sense; migration in this paper rather means – with stronger emphasis on the historical context – the relocation from one territory to another. While this relocation can initially be understood as inland migration (as, in this case, it partially occurs within the borders of the Holy Roman Empire), one could secondly consider it as a migration beyond its borders (e.g. from/to France or Italy) and thirdly as a migration from one sovereign territory to another (e.g. from the electorate of Bavaria to the electorate of Saxony).

1692: from Munich to Brussels

For the Spanish Netherlands, ruled by governors since the 16th century, a constant change of music-cultural orientation must be stated. Each governor set his own cultural 'brands' which are characterized by his preferences and experiences as well as the 'import' of personnel from his country of origin.[1] The organization of the court in Brussels made a distinction between ecclesiastic and secular musical activities. Chapel and court possessed two distinct ensembles which were each managed by a *Kapellmeister*. While the salaries of the chapel musicians were paid from the royal Spanish budget, the costs for the chamber musicians were generally at the expense of the governor.[2] The musicians were recruited from local sources; however, the governors often brought them to Brussels from their own territories (Spain, Italy, Austria, German territories). Thus, it is no surprise that the chapel and chamber music included Spanish musicians,[3] which were otherwise rather underrepresented, if not non-existent.

However, the intention of this paper is not the reconstruction of the personnel of the chapel and chamber music with reference to the governorship of Max Emanuel. Rather, the focus is on two types of musicians in Brussels who were on the payroll of the Munich court: Those who

---

1   To date, there is no comprehensive study regarding the music culture of the governors.
2   THIEFFRY, 2002, pp. 165 and 168; STRYCKERS, 2013. According to LIPOWSKY (1820, pp. 11, 17-19 [only partially with reference]), Max Emanuel received 70,000 Reichstaler per month for his income from the Spanish crown. HÜTTL (1976, pp. 213-218) refers to two million fl. and a monthly payment of 30,000 fl. from Munich. However, these contributions were not sufficient to finance the governor's court, forcing him to take up numerous credits.
3   CLERCX, 1950, p. 152.

had been ordered to Brussels from the Munich *Hofkapelle* and newly recruited members. Due to their payment from budgets located in Munich, the latter promise to have a closer connection to the Bavarian court. The payment of personnel costs from the Munich budget makes it seem feasible that the respective musicians went to Munich in the event of a relocation of the court. A scenario that would not be plausible if their wages would have been financed through the royal Spanish budget and/ or that of the Spanish Netherlands. Musicians such as Pietro Antonio Fiocco,[4] Jean François Van der Linden[5] or Johann Philipp Kerckhoven,[6] who worked at the court in Brussels, or the transient soprano Domenico Mucciolanti in 1700,[7] are therefore ignored hereafter, as they were not paid by or employed from Bavarian funds. Also those musicians are excluded who, like Jeanne-Françoise Dandrieu, Nicolas Clérambault or Élisabeth Jacquet de la Guerre had contact to Max Emanuel during exile (1704-1715).[8]

The sources for the reconstruction of the respective musician corps in Brussels are quite exhaustive. Besides some lists documenting the Brussels court and other documents in the Secret House Archives (Geheimes Hausarchiv) of the Wittelsbach family, there are many small clues in the salary ledgers of the Munich court which comprise numerous marginal notes next to the paid amounts. Further sources are available in various decrees and applications. As far as permissible, based on the estimation of the files, the relocation of the court to Brussels had obviously no direct effect on the local chapel and chamber music.[9] It seems that both ensembles were more or less taken over completely and only missing personnel

---

4   RASCH, 2002; COUVREUR, 2001; STELLFELD, 1941.
5   CLERCX, 1942, p. 173.
6   In 1698-1700, Kerckhoven took the trouble for remuneration for works as a tuner (1693-1699). D-Mhsa, Kriegsarchiv, F 69, F 87; MÜNSTER, 1976, p. 296; ZUBER, 2012, p. 133. In the applications, he refers to his kinship with Abraham van Kerkhoven who worked in the chamber music of the governor Archduke Leopold Wilhelm between 1649 and 1652. THIEFFRY, 2002, pp. 166 and 174f.; regarding the musician dynasty "Van de Kerckoven"/"Van den Kerckhoven" see also CLERCX, 1942, p. 170 and CLERCX, 1950, pp. 164f.
7   D-Mhsa, Kriegsarchiv, F 69 (payment decree dated 15 April 1700); also ZUBER, 2012, p. 133.
8   See CESSAC, 2012.
9   HÜTTL (1976, p. 210) makes a general comment that nobody was dismissed from the Brussels court during the relocation.

was replaced. These were either recruited from the local musicians or ordered from Munich to Brussels.

Pietro Torri and Giovanni Paolo Bombarda traveled to Brussels together with Max Emanuel (see table 1). There, Torri worked as a valet, organist and *Kapellmeister* until the end of March 1701.[10] Bombarda (who was probably originally engaged in the entourage of Ercole Bernabei 1680 as a musician at the Munich court [in 1680?], but subsequently directed the electoral financial affairs from 1688) covered the financial requirements of the Elector and governor, was involved in the Opéra du quai au Foin from 1694 until 1697 and had the Théâtre de la Monnaie established, opening in 1700, which he directed and managed.[11] At the very beginning of his governorship, Max Emanuel employed the trumpeter Louis Petit in 1692, who was budgeted to the Munich *Hofkapelle* from 1695 and who previously must have been paid from other sources.[12] In 1694 at the latest, Felix Emanuel Deibner[13] and

---

10 Specification/Waß von Ihre Ch: Drl: [...]; Verzaig/aller Persohnen, [...]. 12. July/1698; Chrfrl: Hoffstadt zu Brüssel (listed amongst the "Churfl: Ca[m]mer Diener"); Verzaichnuss/Der Churfrt: [...]. Regarding the Brussels time in general, cf. MÜNSTER, 1976, pp. 296f. Unproductive with reference to Torri is GROOTE, 2003.

11 D-Mhsa, Kurbayern, Hofzahlamt (hereinafter KBH) 730 (Besoldungsbuch [payroll ledger] 1692), fol. 66r; COUVREUR/VAN AELBROUCK, 1996, particularly pp. 8-19; ZUBER, 2012, pp. 132f.; HÜTTL, 1976, pp. 213f.; regarding the construction of the theater HENNAUT/CAMPIOLI, 1996.

12 D-Mhsa, Kriegsarchiv, F 69 (employment decree dated 7 October 1693); KBH 733 (Besoldungsbuch 1695), fol. 112r; Kriegsarchiv F 96, decree dated 27 January 1696 with attached "Specification" of 28 October 1695: Petit belonged to the court of the electress; Fürstensachen 677c, fol. 12r (decree dated 17 August 1701); Verzaichnuss./Was hernach folgent: [...] pro anno 1697 [...]; Verzaig/aller Persohnen, [...] .12. July/1698; Verzaichnuss/Der Churfrt: [...]; Verzaichnuss./Der angschafften [...]. See also ZUBER, 2012, p. 133, and MÜNSTER, 1976, pp. 296f. SCHARRER (2012, p. 49) sees the employment of Petit as well as Le Cocq, Normand, Fivé and Poulain (see below) in connection with the Brussels opera maintenance from 1695, which can definitely not be the case with Petit.

13 D-Mhsa, KBH 732 (Besoldungsbuch 1694), fol. 60v; Kriegsarchiv, F 87; Specification/Waß von Ihro Ch: Drl: [...]; Verzaichnuss./Was hernach folgent: [...] pro anno 1697 [...]; Verzaichnuss./Der angschafften [...]. Deibner died in 1703 (KBH 742 [Besoldungsbuch 1703], fol. 80r) and

Vinzenz Lampert[14] from Munich arrived in Brussels. Next to their regular salary of the Munich *Hofkapelle*, both also received special payments for their living expenses. The theorbo player Giuseppe Trevisani can be verified in Brussels in 1695, 1697 and 1698 and was still traveling in 1702, after the return of the court to Munich.[15] In 1695, Gerhard Sové

> was one of the "three Teybner brothers" ("drey Teybner gebrüder") Johann Anton Franz, Felix Emanuel Cajetan and Sigmund Joseph Victor Amadee, who were sent for education to Paris together with Dominique/Dominikus Mayr in 1684-1685 (see SCHARRER, 2012, pp. 46f.) and employed as violinists on 25 January 1686 (employment decree in Fürstensachen 677e, fol. 43r). At the time of relocation of the court, Hans Caspar and Felix Emanuel Deibner are found in the *Hofkapelle*; Mayr was a member of the *Hofkapelle* up to his death in 1698. See D-Mhsa, KBH 728 ff. (Besoldungsbuch 1690 ff.). All are sons of Wolfgang Teubner, who came from Saxony and worked, prior to his employment in Munich in 1658, in Brussels in the chapel of Archduke Leopold Wilhelm. At the same time, Johann Caspar Kerll was active in the Archduke's chapel as organist. In 1656, Kerll was employed as *Vizekapellmeister* at the Munich court and was promoted to *Kapellmeister* in the same year (D-Mhsa, KBH 694 [Besoldungsbuch 1656], fol. 72v). Probably as a consequence, also Teubner came to Munich in 1658 (D-Mhsa, KBH 696 [Besoldungsbuch 1658], fol. 141r: "Härpfenist" [harpist] and valet with a salary of 600 fl., the second highest amongst the instrumentalists). See THIEFFRY, 2002, pp. 166-167; HARRIS/GIEBLER; D-Mhsa, Fürstensachen 676 (the "Hatschier" Joseph Leb on origin and relationship).

14 D-Mhsa, KBH 732 (Besoldungsbuch 1694), fol. 60v; Verzaichnuss./Der angschafften [...]; Verzaichnuss/Der Churfrt: [...]; Verzaichnuss./Was hernach folgent: [...] pro anno 1697 [...]; Specification/Waß von Ihro Ch: Drl: [...]. In a decree of 1686, Lampert (Lambert) is described as a French musician. See D-Mhsa, Fürstensachen 677e, fol. 48r (8 May 1686), also SCHARRER, 2012, p. 48. In 1689, he was in Max Emanuel's service, when he was obviously dismissed together with other musicians; however, he is continuously kept in the ledgers from 1690. D-Mhsa, Kriegsarchiv, F 83 (decree draft, 19 August 1689); KBH 728 ff. (Besoldungsbuch 1690 ff.). In 1705, he was dismissed by the Austrian administration (see below); since 1711, he belonged with interruptions to the court of Elector Joseph Clemens of Cologne, Max Emanuel's brother, in Valenciennes and Bonn. See BRAUBACH, 1967, p. 42, and the Bonn court calendars 1719-1724 ("Lambert", without first name, concertmaster).

15 D-Mhsa, KBH 733 (Besoldungsbuch 1695), fol. 68v (entry under Georg Elias Gottfried Neuner, which contained special payments for his tuition by Tre-

(Sauvé?) traveled to the Spanish Netherlands. As is evident from a letter of the Munich *Obersthofmeister* (High Steward), he had originally planned a mere three to four month stay in Antwerp,[16] but seems to have subsequently traveled on to Brussels, where he served in Max Emanuel's *Hofkapelle* until 1701.[17] Also in 1695, the Walloons or Frenchmen Franz Anton Le Cocq[18] and Remy Normand (Oboist)[19] as well as in 1696 Peter Fivé[20] and Toussain Poulain[21] were employed at the expense of the

visani, which, however were omitted due to the absences of the theorbist). VAN AELBROUCK (2012, p. 123) mentions without a source that Trevisani participated in the opera performances in Brussels in 1697. Verzaig/aller Persohnen, [...] .12 July/1698; D-Mhsa, KBH 741 (Besoldungsbuch 1702), fol. 79r.

16   D-Mhsa, GHA, Obersthofmeisterstab 2164, letter of the High Stewart, 13 April 1695, see Letters in the appendix.

17   D-Mhsa, KBH 741 (Besoldungsbuch 1702), fol. 79v. In earlier documents (1685), Sové is described as a French musician. See SCHARRER, 2012, p. 48 ("Gerard Sonne").

18   D-Mhsa, Kriegsarchiv, F 69 (employment decree dated 1 December 1695); KBH 733 (Besoldungsbuch 1695), fol. 64v; see also ZUBER, 2012, p. 133. However, Le Cocq is already mentioned in a "Specification" dated 28 October 1695 as paid court musician at the court of the electress (D-Mhsa, Kriegsarchiv, F 96, decree dated 27 January 1696). Specification/Waß von Ihro Ch: Drl: [...]; Verzaichnuss/Der Churfrt: [...]; Verzaichnuss/Was hernach folgent: [...] pro anno 1697 [...]; Verzaichnuss./Der angschafften [...]. Le Cocq had left the *Hofkapelle* again as early as 1701. The Besoldungsbuch 1702 (KBH 741) does not contain payments to him; the Besoldungsbuch of 1703 (KBH 742, fol. 76r) notes: "No longer in service" ("Ist nit mehr in diensten"). A Jacques Cocq was in the Brussels chapel and chamber music between 1647 and 1652. It is not known whether he was related to Franz Anton. Regarding the older Cocq see THIEFFRY, 2002, pp. 166, 169-170 and 174-175; regarding the musician dynasty of "Lecoq" see CLERCX, 1942, p. 170. Hand-written tabulature books for guitar of the "Musicien Jubilaire de la Chapelle Royale" "Francois Le Cocq" are preserved in B-Bc (Ms. Littera S, No. 5615, dated 1729 and 1730) and B-Br (Ms. II. 5551, approx. 1730-1740) (BOETTICHER, 1978, pp. 53f., 66).

19   D-Mhsa, Fürstensachen 677e, fol. 85r (decree dated 19 November 1696), 86r (decree dated 18 January 1697); KBH 734 (Besoldungsbuch 1696), fol. 66r.

20   D-Mhsa, KBH 734 (Besoldungsbuch 1696), fol. 61v; Verzaichnuss./Der angschafften [...].

21   D-Mhsa, Fürstensachen 677e, fol. 90r; KBH 734 (Besoldungsbuch 1696), fol. 61v; Kriegsarchiv, F 87 (several documents and notes from 31 Octo-

Munich *Hofkapelle*. In the same year, Franz Simon Schuechpaur was ordered to Brussels, where he probably stayed until 1698.[22] In 1697, the singers Filippo Pantani and Philipp Jacob Seerieder (bass) were called to Brussels. In addition to their wages from Munich, they received remuneration from the budget of the chapel music,[23] so that it is possible to safely state that they had worked in the Spanish *Kapelle* which was, however, also utilised for secular occasions.[24] Peter Le Vray was initially employed in Brussels as aspirant in chamber and chapel from 1694,[25] before becoming valet. From 1697 he additionally worked as musician paid by the Munich *Hofzahlamt* (court payment office).[26] The singers Clementin Hader[27] and Giovanni Giacomo Riccardini[28] as well as a certain "Herr

---

ber 1699 to 20 April 1700); Verzaichnuss/Der Churfrt: [...]; Verzaichnuss./Der angschafften [...]. Poulain, who traveled to Munich with Max Emanuel, probably traveled to Brussels once again after the relocation of the court, as evident from a decree dated 15 December 1702 regarding a special payment (Fürstensachen 677e, fol. 114r).

22   D-Mhsa, GHA, Obersthofmeisterstab 2164, decree Max Emanuel's dated 18 June 1696 (see Letters in the appendix); Verzaig/aller Persohnen, [...] .12. July/1698: "Puenspaur Simon".

23   D-Mhsa, Fürstensachen 677e, fol. 89r (decree dated 16 December 1697); KBH 735 (Besoldungsbuch 1697), fol. 62r, 64r; Specification/Waß von Ihro Ch: Drl: [...]. Both receive allowances in October 1699 (D-Mhsa, Kriegsarchiv, F 69, decree dated 20 and 25 October). Regarding Pantani see also ZUBER, 2012, p. 133.

24   Regarding the tasks of both *Kapellen* see THIEFFRY, 2002.

25   D-Mhsa, Kriegsarchiv, F 69, employment decree dated 19 November 1694; Verzaichnuss./Der angschafften [...]; see also ZUBER, 2012, p. 133.

26   Verzaichnuss/Der Churfrt: [...]; D-Mhsa, KBH 735 ff. (Besoldungsbuch 1697 ff.). As aspirant, Lambert initially received 300, then 500 and, from 1701, 700 fl. wages; see D-Mhsa, Fürstensachen 677b/I, fol. 264r (decree dated 4 May 1701).

27   Chrfrl: Hoffstadt zu Brüssel: ".1. Clementin"; Verzaig/aller Persohnen, [...] .12 July/1698: "H: Clementin". See also OVER, 2007, p. 274; MÜNSTER, 1976, p. 305. According to KÖCHEL (1869, pp. 63, 68), Hader was employed in the Vienna *Hofkapelle* between 1672 and 1687, but he is recorded in Munich as early as the beginning of 1686. See D-Mhsa, Fürstensachen 677e, fol. 44r (decree dated 3 February 1686 regarding the reimbursement of his travel expenses).

28   Specification/Waß von Ihro Ch: Drl: [...]; Verzaig / aller Persohnen, [...] .12. July/1698: "Herr chacometto [Giacometto]".

Pezl", which probably refers to Johann Christoph Pez,[29] and a certain "Herr Rodier",[30] surely dance master François (Franz) Rodier, who is also verified in wage ledgers,[31] were in Brussels in 1698 at the latest. During this time, the documents list at least two other musicians, whose identity cannot be clarified. It could possibly be choirboys, to which the specification "Choralisten" and "Discantisten" may refer.[32] The participation of Evaristo Felice Dall'Abaco in the chapel or chamber music mentioned occasionally in secondary literature cannot be verified in archives, but is quite probable as Dall'Abaco was engaged in the theater.[33]

---

29   Verzaig/aller Persohnen, [...] .12 July/1698. In 1689-1692, Pez was "in Rome for his further training" ("zu seiner mehrer[en] perfectionirung zu Rhom") and was in the service of the Elector of Cologne in 1695. See D-Mhsa, Fürstensachen 677e, fol. 60r (decree dated 28 May 1689); KBH 728 ff. (Besoldungsbuch 1690 ff.); KBH 732 (Besoldungsbuch 1694), fol. 61v, and BRAUBACH, 1967, p. 47. It is possible, however not verified in documents, that he traveled to Brussels in 1698. In 1702, he returned to Munich and received a waiting pay up to the vacancy of an adequate position, see KBH 741 (Besoldungsbuch 1702), fol. 77v; also Fürstensachen 677e, fol. 113r (decree dated 1 September 1702).

30   Verzaig/aller Persohnen, [...] .12 July/1698.

31   According to VAN AELBROUCK (2012, pp. 121f.) Rodier came to Brussels in 1692 and returned to Munich in 1699. However, christenings are only documented in Brussels for the years 1696-1698. The ledgers of the court payment office record a "Franz" Rodier from at least 1690 to at least 1727 (D-Mhsa, KBH 728 ff.). In 1700, a dance master of the same surname died in Düsseldorf ("Monsr Rodié", see EINSTEIN, 1908, pp. 403f.), who may have been related to François.

32   Verzaig/aller Persohnen, [...] .12 July/1698.: "Musici 2"; Specification/Waß von Ihro Ch: [...]: "zwey Choralisten". However, in a decree dated 4 May 1699 it is decided that "the two treble boys who were victualed by him [Torri] should return to Munich" ("die zwey Discantisten Knaben aber bey ihme in der Cosst gewest, wider nacher München gehen sollen"; D-Mhsa, Kriegsarchiv, F 53). MÜNSTER (1976, p. 296) points out the fact that Pietro Torri took care of two choir boys, among them one of the Asam brothers in 1698/99.

33   ZUBER, 2012, p. 133; SCHARRER, 2012, p. 48. Pietro Zambonini, mentioned by MÜNSTER (1976, p. 296) could not be verified in the documents.

1701: from Brussels to Munich

Following the outbreak of the War of the Spanish Succession, Max Emanuel left the Spanish Netherlands due to political-strategic reasons and returned to Munich. The reasons were based on the political orientation of the elector who, once his son Joseph Ferdinand, who was designated as the heir to the Spanish throne by King Charles II, died in 1699, changed sides and became an ally of France. The latent threat through Austria, adjacent to Bavaria, rendered the personal presence of the elector in his territory unavoidable.[34]

Musicians from Brussels came to Munich with the relocation of the court. As well as the electoral musicians, who had been ordered to the Spanish Netherlands (Deibner, Lampert, Pantani, Riccardini, Rodier, Sové, Schuechpaur, Seerieder, Trevisani), those, who had been engaged by Max Emanuel in Brussels, came to the Bavarian residence city (Le Vray, Normand, Poulain). Others (Bombarda, Le Cocq, Petit) remained in Brussels, even though they formally belonged to the Munich court personnel, as they had been paid by the court budget. A variety of personal reasons were sure to be responsible for or against a move to Munich. While Le Vray and Normand left the service in 1705, and Poulain in 1706,[35] when Max Emanuel had to hastily retreat from his residence city during the chaos of the War of the Spanish Succession and the *Hofkapelle* was entirely dissolved in June 1706, only Normand returned to court in 1715. Normand is an interesting figure because he had a career in Brussels as well as in Munich. Initially employed as vocalist, he changed over to the instrumentalists in 1697.[36] In 1715, next to his function as musician, he took up the role as valet in Munich, which provided him with direct access to the court's power center, the elector. At the same time, he took over the office of residence caretaker, which led to the doubling of his wages.[37]

---

34 See here in detail SCHRYVER, 1996, pp. 99-140.
35 D-Mhsa, KBH 744-746 (Besoldungsbuch 1705 [fol. 75r, 79v, 85v], 1705 [6 June-31 December, fol. 55r] and 1706 [fol. 61r]).
36 D-Mhsa, KBH 734 and 735 (Besoldungsbuch 1696 and 1697).
37 As valet and musician, Normand received 450, as residence caretaker 400 fl. See D-Mhsa, KBH 755 (Besoldungsbuch 1715), fol. 124r, 133v. See also the contribution by Britta Kägler in this volume, pp. 73-90.

1704/05: in Dutch-French and Italian exile

Based on the disastrous military losses which culminated in the occupation of Bavaria by the Habsburgs, Max Emanuel was forced to flee from Munich in 1704. Initially, he went to Brussels to reassume his position as governor of the Spanish Netherlands – this time allied with France. The battles, which were lost here, forced him once again to leave and seek protection in France.[38] Musicians of the Munich *Hofkapelle* accompanied him (see table 2):[39] Pietro Torri, Peter Le Vray, Giuseppe Trevisani, Valeriano Pellegrini, Stefano Frilli, Franz Anton Le Cocq, Evaristo Felice dall'Abaco, Clementin Hader (von Hadersberg) as well as a number of trumpeters. The latter were already members of the court (Abraham Ebenpöck, Franz Ories, Dominikus Zehetner)[40] or doubtlessly belonged to the troops of the Bavarian-French alliance in the War of the Spanish Succession and moved with Max Emanuel in their specialised function as troop-specific signal trumpeter (Matthias Anton Fink, Johann Caspar Burger, Hyacinth Hochpain).[41] Also oboe players served military purpo-

---

38 Regarding the political situation, see SCHRYVER, 1996, pp. 140 ff.; HÜTTL, 1976, pp. 281 ff.
39 Payments and employments for the years 1704-1709 are documented in Bombarda's ledger in D-Mhsa, MF 19581, particularly from fol. 132, and for the years 1710-1712 in MF 19582 (without foliation). The musicians were accompanied by the servant Paul Führschildt/Fischenschildt, who received money for his return trip to Bavaria in 1705 and applied for a position as blower on 31 December 1705 (D-Mhsa, MF 19581, fol. 33v; MF 19590, n. 11, with certificate from Valeriano Pellegrini and Stefano Frilli).
40 Ebenpöck was employed at the Munich court before 1690; D-Mhsa, KBH 728 ff. (Besoldungsbuch 1690 ff.). Ories' employment occurred 1690; D-Mhsa, KBH 728 ff. (Besoldungsbuch 1690 ff.). He could possibly be identified as the "trompete felbries", who was paid in 1709; D-Mhsa, MF 19589 (letter dated 18 November 1713 regarding payments in Mons). The same source notes a salary payment to the "Trompete Dominique [Zehetner]". Zehetner was employed at the Munich court in 1704; D-Mhsa, KBH 743 (Besoldungsbuch 1704), fol. 133v (entry under Johann Pocorni).
41 Fink was possibly related with the trumpeter and violinist Johann Franz Fink, who is verified at the court in Bonn in 1697. BRAUBACH, 1967, p. 37. Regarding the trumpeter's function see ALTENBURG, vol. 1, pp. 88-93; with respect to their important functions in the court ceremonial (here at the Dresden court), which justified their generally high salary see MÜCKE, 2006.

ses. They can be verified in the exile court since 1705, were recruited under German and Wallonia-French forces and dismissed in 1711: Matthias Valentin Bartscher, Gottfried Ludwig Santer (from 1705), Johann Joseph Maillien (from 1706), Johann Anton Marchand (from 1710), Laurent Le Clerc (1711).[42] Other musicians joined the court only later and/or were recruited locally: Vinzenz Lambert[43] and Remi Normand[44] (from 1706) as well as the newly employed Pierre (?) Dechars (from 1704, dance master),[45] "Bonel" (from 1705), "Legrand" (from 1707), Cornelius Gerbl (from 1705, timpanist) and Franz Xaver Lorenz (from 1707, trumpeter). However, only Lorenz seems to have had a connection with the Elector's court as he should have been related to the timpani player Johann Anton Lorenz, who had worked in the *Hofkapelle* at least since 1690.[46] The also paid Gregoire Blovy (from 1704) seems to have been a musical buffoon "who played the fagot with his mouth as if he had an instrument."[47] It looks as if further musicians had only been hired at the end of Max Emanuel's stay (see below), others again were temporarily in his service or were in contact with him (see above). One of these musicians is the violin player Jean-Baptiste Anet, who was not formally employed, but received a pension.[48]

---

42 According to Bombarda's ledger (D-Mhsa, MF 19582), a sixth oboe player was on the payment list in 1711 when all were dismissed in August. The oboe players served in the "squadron of mounted privates" ("Grenadiers à cheval esquadron"). In the case of Bartscher and Santer it can be assumed that they were not Walloons or Frenchmen. "Barcher" was employed in 1717 retrospectively as at 1 April in Munich. D-Mhsa, Fürstensachen 677e, fol. 174r (employment decree dated 16 April 1717).

43 In the source "Monsieur Lambert", surely the violinist Vinzenz Lampert, as mentioned above.

44 Normand, also dismissed by the Austrian administration in 1705 has been in Max Emanuel's service since 1695, see above.

45 Dechars (de Chars, Deschars) was dance master at the Opéra du quai au Foin during the time of the governorship. See VAN AELBROUCK, 2012, p. 122; ZUBER, 2012, p. 138.

46 D-Mhsa, KBH 728 ff. (Besoldungsbuch 1690 ff.). Regarding the role of family relationships in the context of musicians' recruiting, see OVER, i.pr.

47 "welcher mit den Maull den fagot blaset, als ob er ein instrument hette"; D-Mhsa, MF 19581, fol. 187r.

48 He was recruited by Max Emanuel in France in 1710 and, together with other musicians, dismissed on 22 March 1715 (see ANTOINE, pp. 88f.). Next

Also Electress Therese Kunigunde left Munich. Her trip to Italy in 1705 served the purpose to deliberate her situation with her mother Maria Casimira, who resided in Rome after the death of her husband, King Jan Sobieski of Poland. The occupying force Austria allowed the electress to depart, but refused re-entry under the pretense of a lacking visa, which forced her into exile in Venice. There, she was met by dismissed court musicians from Munich which documents that also the electress practiced keen musical art as well as that the Munich musicians made musically-stylistic experiences in Venice, which enhanced their professional profile. The exile court documents the singers Pietro Lemoles (1706, 1711-12, 1714/15) and Massimiliano Gaetano Manzin (Maximilian Manzini/Mancini, 1707/08), who had surely already been born in Germany,[49] as well as the instrumentalist Franz Simon Schuechpaur (1708-09, table 3).[50]

1715: from exile to Munich

The end of the War of the Spanish Succession brought the reinstatement of their rights for Max Emanuel and his wife, which made the return to Munich possible. As the court personnel had been reduced to a minimum due to the Austrian occupation, the establishment of a new, representative court had to commence. In the process, a new constitution of the *Hofkapelle* was necessary, which had been completely liquidated in 1706 as mentioned above. Contrary to all expectations from a historically removed aspect, the dismissed musicians had taken on new positions only in exceptional cases, so that approx. 70% of the musical personnel of 1706 could be re-engaged in 1715.[51]

---

to the final payment in March 1715, a payment is documented in August 1711: "To the violinist Baptist for his pension" ("Dem Violinisten Baptist à conto dessen pension"; D-Mhsa, MF 19582).

49 Manzini was the son of Dario Manzini, a singer in the *Hofkapelle* who died in 1695. As well as a grace payment for his mother, he was initially paid a reduced wage of 200 fl. (he may have been in training), which was increased to 400 fl. in 1701. D-Mhsa, Fürstensachen 677e, fol. 80r (decree dated 15 December 1695); KBH 733-740 (Besoldungsbuch 1695-1701).

50 Over, 2007, particularly pp. 265f.; Over, 2012, p. 91; regarding the exile time in general Kägler, 2011, pp. 446-469.

51 Over, i.pr.

This was reinforced by the personnel originating from the various cultural spheres of the regents, with whom they came into contact during their exile: Max Emanuel brought musicians from the Spanish Netherlands and France, Therese Kunigunde those from Italy into the *Hofkapelle*. The personnel was often recruited specifically for the Munich court (see table 4).

The targeted engagement of musicians on the 'free market' can be demonstrated by the search for singers conducted by Electress Therese Kunigunde in Venice (see table 3). Numerous letters and other documents, which have been addressed elsewhere,[52] prove that the electress, who was extraordinarily well acquainted with the opera scene of the lagoon city and had acquired critical musical competence contacted successful singers who performed in the theaters of the city, as well as (due to cost reasons) those still in training. This is how Bartolomeo Bartoli (soprano-castrato), Francesco Maria Venturini (bass) and Vincenzo Corradi (instrumentalist and alto-castrato) arrived at the Munich court. She also consulted her sister in law, Violante Beatrix of Bavaria, who resided as the widow of Ferdinando de' Medici in Siena, and took over from her services the tenor Francesco Cignoni. A further musician, whom Therese Kunigunde recruited in Venice, was the violin player Giuseppe Brescianello who, following a short interval in Munich, became concertmaster in 1717, then *Oberkapellmeister* in 1721 in Stuttgart.[53] Ultimately, it has to be mentioned that the Electress obviously had contact to Antonio Vivaldi, whom she recommended to her husband as possible *Hofkapellmeister*. However, Max Emanuel declined with reference to the already employed 'opera expert' Pietro Torri.[54]

The origin of the new musicians was noted in the ledger 1715 not quite consistently. Thus, reference is made to the presence of musicians in a "Netherland ledger": these include the previously mentioned musicians who had partially returned to Munich as well as those who were obviously employed not long before the end of the exile time: the blower Adam Niedermayr (who was obviously not Flemish or Walloon), the scribe Franz Couvin and the Italian instrumentalist Thomas de Piani.[55]

---

52 OVER, 2007, and OVER, 2012.
53 OVER, 2007, pp. 276-281; OVER, 2012, pp. 98f.; D-Mhsa, KBH 755 (Besoldungsbuch 1715), fol. 54r, 114v, 115r, 122r. Regarding the employment of Brescianello in Stuttgart see OWENS, 2011, pp. 172f.
54 OVER, 2004; OVER, 2007, pp. 282f.; OVER, 2012, pp. 99f.
55 D-Mhsa, KBH 755 (Besoldungsbuch 1715), fol. 113r, 118r, 118v, 123r. Regarding the employment of de Piani see also OVER, 2007, p. 281. (De) Piani

However, the majority of the newly employed musicians came with the elector from France, as indicated by respective notes. Thus, it is particularly those trumpeters already employed during the exile court, who are indicated with a respective side note in ledger 1715 ("court trumpeter who came along from France").[56]

Two other trumpeters seem to come from a similar context, however it is not mentioned from which territory they came to Munich. Thus, Lorenz Böhmer and Johann Michael Leser were employed from the regiment of Count of Arco – this is probably the Bavarian Field Marshall Johann Baptist von Arco, who died on 21 March 1715 –[57] as well as Johann Georg Leitenroth from the cuirassier regiment of Count of Taufkirchen – most probably the Colonel and Brigadier Ferdinand Johann of Taufkirchen, whose "Tauffkirchen-Kürassiere" existed since 1 November 1711 and were dissolved with the decree of 15 June 1715.[58]

The engagement of a court oboist band could have been based on French as well as military experiences, as recorded in ledger 1715 ("five oboists coming from France"): the earlier mentioned Johann Joseph Maillen, Gottfried Ludwig Sander and Johann Anton Marchand, who are verifiable in the French Bavarian troops, were supplemented by Marin

---

came from Naples, where he was taught at the Conservatorio della Pietà dei Turchini until 1705. He remained in Munich until 1716 (KBH 756 [Besoldungsbuch 1716], fol. 93v) and can be found in the Vienna *Hofkapelle* from 1717 until his death in 1760. His cousin (?), Giovanni Battista Piani, has been in the service of Louis-Alexandre de Bourbon, Comte de Toulouse since 1704 and is found in the Vienna *Hofkapelle* from 1720. Regarding both Piani see PIANI, 1975, p. vii, as well as KÖCHEL, 1869, pp. 76f., 83, 86.

56   "aus Franckhreich mitko[m]mener hoff=Trompeter" and similar. D-Mhsa, KBH 755 (Besoldungsbuch 1715), fol. 196v-197v.

57   Böhmer: D-Mhsa, Fürstensachen 677b/II, fol. 57r (employment decree dated 9 May 1715); KBH 755 (Besoldungsbuch 1715), fol. 197v. Leser: Fürstensachen 677b/II, fol. 56r (decree dated 9 May 1715). Regarding Johann Baptist von Arco see ARETIN, 1953.

58   D-Mhsa, employment decree with reference to his fifteen-year activity as military trumpeter dated 11 October 1715 in Fürstensachen 677b/II, fol. 113r; KBH 755 (Besoldungsbuch 1715), fol. 198r. Regarding Taufkirchen see STAUDINGER, 1904, vol. 2, pp. 816-818. Taufkirchen had accompanied Max Emanuel in various functions in the Spanish Netherlands and into exile (see IBID., vol. 1, p. 82; vol. 2, pp. 784, 801, 810, 814, 1192).

Pourveu and Ignaz Balthasar.[59] With the employment of oboists at court, which – as far as the rather inconsistent information in the documents on the instruments available in the *Hofkapelle* allow – had not been present prior to 1706, Max Emanuel joins a general tendency observable at German courts around 1700,[60] but adopts this tendency late.

Also French-inspired was the employment of a French theater troupe (the "französischen Co[m]moedianten")[61] which, next to actors, comprised of personnel which could also be utilised for ballet and opera performances: the dancers Jean Pierre and Pierre Dubreil as well as Marie Le Fevre, the "Simphonist" Pierre Gravier, the stage designers Pierre Laurent ("decorateur"), Nicolas Roger and Pierre Henry (both "Soudecorateur"), the wardrobe ladies Catherine Duclos and Marie Laurent as well as the prompter Bonne Dauflise.[62] That this personnel was also interesting for the realization of non-French plays and other performances is proven by the fact that the two Dubreil (now dance master), Laurent (from 1721 "Theatres und Scennen Decorator") and Henry continued to be employed after the dismissal of the troop in 1720.[63] Also the "Symphonist" Pierre Rey, who replaced the retired

---

59 "auser franckhreich geko[m]menen .5. Hautboisisten". D-Mhsa, Fürstensachen 677e, fol. 137r (employment decree dated 12 September 1715); KBH 755 (Besoldungsbuch 1715), fol. 123v-124r. Here, it is pointed out that the oboists had already been in the service of Max Emanuel prior to their employment in Munich. Regarding oboist bands as independent corporations see DUBOWY, 2001, pp. 92f., and BRAUN, 1971. Regarding oboists in the Bavarian and Netherland regiments, which had occasionally existed since 1689 and which were only permitted in the personal regiment of the elector and that of the electoral prince since 1699/1700, see STAUDINGER, 1904, vol. 1, pp. 97f., 117, 121f.; vol. 2, pp. 815, 1336.

60 BRAUN, 1971, pp. 45-50.

61 During the French exile, Max Emanuel had engaged a theater troupe between 1708 and 1712. This troupe comprised a major part of the personnel from the time of the governorship (ZUBER, 2012, pp. 138-140) and is not identical with the Munich troupe.

62 D-Mhsa, KBH 755 (Besoldungsbuch 1715), fol. 149r-149 1/2r.

63 The ongoing employment was surely connected with the preparations for the wedding of the heir to the throne, Prince Elector Karl Albrecht with Archduchess Maria Amalia of Austria in 1722. This event was celebrated with scenic spectacles of all kinds (see WERR, 2010, pp. 233-248; SOMMER-MATHIS 1994, pp. 53-67). The imperial decision to marry Maria Amalia to

Gravier in 1719 was taken over and recorded in the Hofkapelle as violinist from 1722.[64]

In addition, two further instrumentalists were recruited in France: Jacques Loeillet (Le Lieu, Loeilliet, Loeillier or similar, oboe; he receives "the salary he enjoyed in France"), who originated from Ghent (Gent) and possibly met Max Emanuel as early as in the Spanish Netherlands, and Gabriel Dubuisson ("chamber musician with the salary he enjoyed in France").[65] Two musicians can be recognized as coming from French-speaking areas by their name, whereby it has to remain open when and where they were engaged and whether they came from Wallonia or France. Worth mentioning are the dance master at the University of Ingolstadt, Carl Gouvillet, and the "discantist" Johann Romedi Piubelin (who was probably a choir boy as he only remained in Munich until 1721).[66]

However, not only the exiles of the regents were decisive factors; also others determined the recruiting of musicians. Some musicians had belonged to the court of the princes in their exile in Klagenfurt and Graz and now followed them to Munich: the dance master Johann Ferdinand Le Comte from Vienna (since 1707), the double-bass player Franz Anton Hindermair (since 1711) and the lute player Wolff Jacob Lauffensteiner, who had taught the princes in music since 1712.[67] The violinist Johann

---

Bavaria and her older sister Maria Josepha to the competing Dresden court was already made on 28 February 1719 (STASZEWSKI, 1996, p. 94).

64 D-Mhsa, KBH 759 (Besoldungsbuch 1719), fol. 118r; KBH 760 (Besoldungsbuch 1720), fol. 126r, 128r, 130r; KBH 761 (Besoldungsbuch 1721), fol. 120r-121r; KBH 762 (Besoldungsbuch 1722), fol. 113v, 123r-124v.

65 "die in franckhreich genossene besoldung" resp. "Ca[m]mer Musico mit der in franckhreich genossenen besoldung". D-Mhsa, Fürstensachen 677e, fol. 138r (employment decree for "Lellie" dated 19 September 1715), fol. 144r (employment decree for Dubuisson dated 10 January 1716); KBH 755 (Besoldungsbuch 1715), fol. 118v, 124v. Regarding Loeillet see SKEMPTON/ROBINSON and SL/(PRIESTMAN), 2004, col. 380, who specify 1726 as employment year in Munich; OVER, 2007, p. 281; JANZEN, 1983, p. 503; MÜNSTER, 1976, p. 305.

66 D-Mhsa, Fürstensachen 677e, fol. 132r (employment decree for Piubelin dated 10 June 1715); KBH 755 (Besoldungsbuch 1715), fol. 115r, 142r.

67 ZEDLER, 2012, pp. 342, 349, 351, 356; ISER, 2000, p. 98; FLOTZINGER, 1966, pp. 212-239; D-Mhsa, KBH 755 (Besoldungsbuch 1715), fol. 66r, 120v, 149 1/2v. Following the time in exile, Lauffensteiner was employed as valet to Ferdinand Maria and, for his teachings to the prince (lute and other instruments) and own compositions, received a pay rise of 100 fl. to

Pluemb or Bluemb, who also worked at the court of the princes, had been in the Munich *Hofkapelle* since 1704 and was one of the musicians who were dismissed in 1706.[68] In 1715, he also returned.

Two further court and field trumpeters, whose employment is only indirectly related with the exile of the regents, were recruited from the troops of the occupying forces. Elias Anton Taunickh and Lorenz Bruno Kern came from the entourage of Prince Maximilian Karl of Löwenstein[69] who, as administrator of the dukedom Bavaria, was responsible for the hard Austrian occupation.[70]

A different case is the Bohemian Anton Alexius Haveck (Havek), *Kapellmeister* of the *Hochstift* Regensburg, whose *vita* is closely connected with Max Emanuel's brother, Joseph Clemens. Until 1702, Haveck was "employed in Munich in the [Jesuit?] school" and subsequently worked in Regensburg upon recommendation by Count Törring,[71] the bishopric seat of which was held by Joseph Clemens since 1685. 1715, when Joseph Clemens had to surrender this office due to ecclesiastical-legal reasons,[72] Haveck returned to Munich as an organist,[73] where he possibly held a waiting position, similar to Johann Christoph Pez in 1702.[74] Haveck left the Munich court as early as 1717 in order to accept a position at the Bonn court of Joseph Clemens, where he died in 1723.[75]

---

450 fl. on 20 July 1715 and by 150 fl. to 600 fl. on 23 April 1717 (D-Mhsa, Fürstensachen 677b/II, fol. 99r, 213r).

68 ZEDLER, 2012, pp. 342, 349; ISER, 2000, p. 98; D-Mhsa, KBH 743-746 (Besoldungsbuch 1704-1706 [resp. fol. 83v, 80r, 55r, 61r]); KBH 755 (Besoldungsbuch 1715), fol. 120r.

69 Taunickh: D-Mhsa, KBH 755 (Besoldungsbuch 1715), fol. 198v; Kern: fol. 199r. Employment decrees from 7 and/or 8 July 1715 in D-Mhsa, Fürstensachen 677b/II, fol. 94r, 96r.

70 Regarding Prince Löwenstein see ZUBER, 1987.

71 "in München bei der Schul angestellt". METTENLEITER, 1866 (p. 120, without reference, but "processed from archival documents and other sources").

72 ENGELBRECHT, 1999, p. 14.

73 D-Mhsa, Fürstensachen 677e, fol. 133r (employment decree dated 12 June 1715); KBH 755 (Besoldungsbuch 1715), fol. 121r.

74 Regarding Pez see OVER, i.pr., and the contribution of OVER/ROEDER in this volume.

75 D-Mhsa, KBH 758 (Besoldungsbuch 1718), fol. 94r: „ist aus dem dienst gangen". His name is recorded in the Bonn court calendars from 1717 to 1724 ("Haveck", "Haveck senior", without first name) as instrumentalist

Other musicians were newly employed at court due to family relationships, whereby the most interesting case should be that of the violinist and oboist Nikolaus Joseph Thomas. Thomas was surely related with Ferdinand Matthias Thomas, who was employed in 1703 and reemployed in 1715; both were sent to the Spanish court to Madrid by Max Emanuel (in diplomatic mission?).[76] Due to the political alliances and constellations, the stay would have fallen in the period after 1701,[77] when Bourbon Philipp V ascended his throne in Madrid,[78] while his Habsburg counterpart Archduke Karl III (the latter Emperor Karl VI) resided in Barcelona since 1705.[79] The organist Johann Christoph Kerll ("Kerl") was also employed due to his kinship with Johann Caspar Kerll (he was his son), organist at the Munich *Hofkapelle* from 1656 to 1674, where he died in 1693. According to Siegbert Rampe and Andreas Rockstroh, Johann Christoph was educated at the expense of the court and employed as early as 1702.[80] The latter cannot be verified in the ledgers; however, reference is made that he worked for the court orchestra unpaid for two years – and that his employment was the consequence of his father's long service.[81]

Ultimately, there are musicians whose origins are not specified in the sources and who possibly came from Munich and surrounding areas. These included the two hornists Johann Kaspar and Matthias Ganspöck,

---

and valet. He died in 1723, see court calendar 1724 (rubric "*Abgestorbene Hoff-Bediente vom Jahr* 1723."). See also BRAUBACH, 1967, who refers to Haveck's name in a nondescript list of 1716 (p. 40) and assumes that the family originated in Bavaria (p. 60).

76 Ferdinand Matthias: D-Mhsa, Fürstensachen 677e, fol. 117r (28 January 1703); Nikolaus Joseph: D-Mhsa, KBH 755 (Besoldungsbuch 1715), fol. 121v.

77 Both Thomas' have obviously left no traces at the Spanish *Hofkapelle* and are not mentioned in SÁNCHEZ-BELÉN, 2005, SANHUESA FONSECA, 1997, KENYON DE PASCUAL, 1995, SÁNCHEZ-BELÉN/SAAVEDRA ZAPATER, 1995, JAMBOU, 1989, and KENYON DE PASCUAL, 1987.

78 He arrived in Madrid on 22 January 1701 and moved in officially on 18 February. See SCHNETTGER, 2014, p. 121 (chronology); SCHRYVER 1996, p. 117.

79 Regarding the court of Archduke Karl III see CASADEMUNT I FIOL, 2011, and SOMMER-MATHIS, 1996.

80 RAMPE/ROCKSTROH, 2003, col. 31.

81 See D-Mhsa, Fürstensachen 677e, fol. 130r (employment decree dated 20 May 1715).

instrumentalist Paul Reininger and the trumpeter Veith Augerneder.[82] It is also unknown how the singer Lucrezia Panizza, who originated from Trent, was engaged.[83]

However, the latter may have encountered similar happy circumstances as in case of Filippo Balatri, who was engaged at the Munich court while traveling through. Balatri, who provides ample information with respect to migration research and who left behind an autobiography in verse form, was at the court of the Wittelsbach branch Pfalz-Neuburg in Düsseldorf from July until September 1715, where he was ordered by Cosimo III de' Medici to return home to Tuscany.[84] Elector Johann Wilhelm of the Palatinate was, due to his ancestors, connected to the Bavarian Wittelsbach branch as well as the Florentine Medici due to his marriage to Maria Anna Luisa, Cosimo's daughter. Cosimo's son Ferdinando, who died as early as 1713, had furthermore married Max Emanuel's sister, Violante Beatrix. The diverse familial connections possibly caused that Johann Wilhelm issued a letter of recommendation for Balatri which was to secure for him a benevolent reception at the Munich court.[85] Possibly arriving in Munich in October 1715, Balatri presented the letter to the electoral prince Karl Albrecht; he was then introduced to the Elector by Pietro Torri. The Elector auditioned the castrato and, again via Torri, asked him to stay. Following negotiations with Cosimo,

---

82 D-Mhsa, Fürstensachen 677e, fol. 128r (employment decree for Reininger dated 8 May 1715), 129r (employment decree of both "Ganßspekh" dated 8 May 1715); KBH 755 (Besoldungsbuch 1715), fol. 120r-v, 121v, 198r, 199r.

83 She is specified as "Lugrezia Panizza di Trento" in the only libretto, which mentions her name (*La Partenope*, Trent 1713). See SARTORI, Nr. 17824. Regarding her Munich employment until 1716 see D-Mhsa, Fürstensachen 677e, fol. 139r (employment decree dated 30 October 1715): retrospective employment as at 1 June; KBH 755 (Besoldungsbuch 1715), fol. 116v; KBH 756 (Besoldungsbuch 1716), fol. 92r. She can be verified from 1723 to 1740 in the Vienna Hofkapelle (KÖCHEL, 1869, p. 76) and was possibly related to Jacob Anton Panizza "of Trent", who requested the financing of his education by the Vienna court in 1675. See KNAUS, 1967-69, vol. 2, p. 34.

84 BALATRI, vol. 2, fol. 94v. The duration of the stay is evident from the fact that Balatri arrived in Düsseldorf prior to the name day of the Electress (26 July) (fol. 92v) and stayed for three months, according to his own information (fol. 94r).

85 BALATRI, vol. 2, fol. 94v-95r.

to whom Balatri felt obligated as his governor and who probably released him without fuss, he initially procured – according to his own words (this cannot be verified by the documents) – employment for his brother Ferrante, in order to ultimately join the *Hofkapelle* in Munich as a singer:[86]

> A Monaco arrivato, io presento
> al Conte Alberto il Foglio Palatino.
> Il Torri (ch'in compor' hà del Divino)
> all'Elettor' mi guida (a un' lieto evento.)
>
> Il Gran' Massimiliano, d'ascoltare
> il canto mio si degna; e buon' desìo
> al Torri ne dimostra acciocche io
> risolvami in Baviera di restare.
>
> Quello, che è suo Mastro di Cappella,
> contento mene fà proposizione.
> Rispondo, che il Granduca è mio Padro:ne,
> e gl'appartiene l'Asino e la sella.
>
> Scrivine (mi risponde) prontamente,
> e son' sicuro che il tuo Signore
> privato non vorrà di tant'Onore,
> servendo à sì Gran Prence, e suo Parente.
>
> Inpenno un' Foglio, e con rassegnazzione
> à quanto piaceranne al mio Sovrano.
> Risponde, ch'egli gode in dar' la mano
> di tanto mio vantaggio all'occasione.
>
> [...]
>
> Ne mostra del piacere l'Elettore,
> e mi fà dir', quanto ch'io voglio avere?
> Rispondo, che non vuò ch'il suo volere,
> purche inpieghi il German; per cui hò amore.

---

86 BALATRI, vol. 2, fol. 101r-102v.

Subito al caro Frate fà assegnare
trecento buon' Fiorini per ciasch'Anno;
Con questo, ch'abbia il peso (e grave danno)
di dormir', meglio bere, e più mangiare;[87]

[...]

Veggio dunque il German' accomodare,
in stato dannon far' ch'il <u>Cavaliere</u>.
A Fiorenza (al ministro) fo sapere,
<u>ch'hò piazzàto l' Fratel', senza sudare</u>.

Mille Fiorini all'Anno mi fà dare
l'Elettore, Clemente e Generoso.
Il servirlo può dirsi un' ver riposo,
essendo le fatiche poche, e rare.[88]

Conclusion

The investigations of the relocation of the court of the Bavarian elector couple leads – perfunctory – to a seemingly mundane result that musician migrations are linked to the traveling regents. However, if one considers the traveling musicians/musician groups as individual cases, the different motivations leading to migration become obvious. It seems not without reason that Max Emanuel 1694/95 had ordered the musicians Deibner, Lambert and possibly Sové to Brussels. With this action, he summoned personnel to the Spanish Netherlands which had been educated in France and was probably to be assigned for his opera plans, which were realized in form of operas by Jean-Baptiste

---

[87] However, Ferrante Balatri was only employed on 15 December 1716 and is recorded in the ledgers as vocalist ("musicus") from 1717. D-Mhsa, Fürstensachen 677e, fol. 149r; KBH 757 (Besoldungsbuch 1717), fol. 91r. In 1721, he sang in the opera *L'amor d'amico vince ogni altro amore* (SARTORI, Nr. 1333, "Fernante Ballatri").

[88] With decree dated 6 February 1716, Filippo Balatri was employed retrospectively from 1 October 1715. D-Mhsa, Fürstensachen 677e, fol. 145r; KBH 755 (Besoldungsbuch 1715), fol. 116v.

Lully in the Opéra du quai au Foin and in the Théâtre de la Monnaie since 1695.[89] The strong French orientation, which is also manifest in the employment of French-Walloon personnel (Le Cocq, Le Vray etc.), is not reduced by the presence of foreign instrumentalists such as Schuechpaur and Trevisani. These expanded their stylistic and performance-technical competences in Brussels, as can be verified for Torri on a compositional level.[90] The singers whom Max Emanuel fetched to Brussels are mostly Italians or personnel educated in Italy (Hader, Pantani, Riccardini), with the exception of bassist Seerieder. Overall, this correlates with Max Emanuel's preference for Italian singing and French instrumental performances.[91]

On one hand, the migration of musicians from Brussels to Munich is motivated by the return of the musicians called to Brussels and, on the other, by the employment rooted in Munich, whereby aspects such as appeal – one obviously held a position for life as court musician – and loyalty – court service seems to have been more or less synonymous with a fiduciary relationship – were decisive for the migration.[92]

Exile also provided musicians with the option of an expansion of competencies abroad due to accompanying and/or following the regents. For example, the German Schuechpaur was able to expand his spectrum, which had already been enriched in the Spanish Netherlands, by stylistic and performance-technical experiences in Italy.

The reorganization of the *Hofkapelle* in 1715 indicates the diversity of "sources" from which the musicians were recruited, who subsequently migrated to Munich. Next to a large contingent of court musicians who remained "loyal" during the time of exile (i.e. without entering into a new employment), the respective personal experiences of the regents in the different countries were decisive, leading to a certain selection of musicians/musician groups (oboist band, actor troupe, Italian singers). Also here, the French orientation with respect to the instrumentalists and the Italian orientation with respect to the singers become evident, particularly also by the fact that Max Emanuel expressed reservations with respect to the Italian violinist Brescianello.[93]

---

89   VAN AELBROUCK, 2012, pp. 122-124; COUVREUR, 2001, pp. 154-163.
90   JAHRMÄRKER, 2012.
91   OVER, 2007, p. 281; SCHARRER, 2012.
92   See also OVER, i.pr.
93   OVER, 2007, p. 281.

The musicians newly engaged in 1715 furthermore show that musicians in the entourage of the elector naturally reflected the stations of his exile. Some musicians accompanied him into Dutch exile or were hired there. Some seemed to join the entourage of the elector in France, as in case of the oboist band or the French actor troupe, which brought a reflection of the French lifestyle to Munich. Despite this, it is rather unlikely that a "court trumpeter who came along from France" or a timpanist with a German name was only recruited in France. It seems rather more likely that he joined the court with the troop movements of the Bavarian-French alliance during the war in Bavaria, the Spanish Netherlands and France.[94] The reasons for this can surely be found in the military function of the instruments and the related signal-call competency.[95] Also the employment of Louis Petit in Brussels, who remained there after Max Emanuel's departure but was paid until his death, is possibly motivated by his specific knowledge of Spanish-Dutch signal calls – next to the fact that he could be used for courier services due to his linguistic skills.[96] Ultimately, the admission of trumpeters would only have been possible for the occupying forces if these mastered Bavarian signal calls – surely *the* motive why Prince Löwenstein had already hired them.

Many special cases exhibited other constellations and dynamics connected to musician migrations. Musicians were able to come to Munich in the entourage of the princes (Hindermair, Le Comte, Lauffensteiner), be employed due to dynastic contexts (Haveck), return following missions at foreign courts (Thomas) or receive the offer of an engagement while traveling through (Balatri).

However, collectively it has to be stated that migration of the musicians connected with the Munich court seems to have been in most cases motivated by their dependency on the regent couple and their children rather than by personal (career) objectives (which could, at the most, be presumed in case of Sové and Haveck).[97] The relocation of the electoral family court resulted in migrations; their preferences and desires were responsible for the change of residence of musicians.

---

94   See here SCHRYVER, 1996, pp. 140 ff.; HÜTTL, 1976, pp. 377 ff.
95   During the times of Max Emanuel, military personnel were at any rate predominately recruited among native children. ALBRECHT, 1988, pp. 662f.; HÜTTL, 1976, pp. 308-313.
96   D-Mhsa, Kriegsarchiv, F 69 (employment decree dated 7 October 1693).
97   See here also OVER, i.pr.

Appendix

Table 1: Musicians in Brussels 1692-1701 (B = Brussels, BN = Bonn, M = Munich, R = Rome)

Name	1691	1692	1693	1694	1695	1696	1697	1698	1699	1700	1701	1702	Remarks
Bombarda, Giovanni Paolo	M	B	B	B	B	B	B	B	B	B	B	B	opera entrepreneur in Brussels: 1694-97 Opéra du quai au Foin, 1700-1706? Théâtre de la Monnaie
"zwey Choralisten"										B	B		
Deibner, Felix Emanuel	M	M	M	B	B	B	B	B	B	B	B	M	supplementary grant for maintenance in Brussels paid until March 1701
Fivé, Peter						B	B						died in 1697
Hader, Clementin								B					since 1698 in Brussels at the latest, no entry in the salary books
Lampert, Vinzenz	M	M	M	B	B	B	B	B	B	B	B	M	supplementary grant for maintenance in Brussels paid until March 1701
Le Cocq, Franz Anton					B	B	B	B	B	B	B		employed at the expense of the Munich *Hofkapelle*
Le Vray, Peter							B	B	B	B	B	M	

From Munich to 'Foreign' Lands and Back Again

"Musici 2"								B					
Normand, Remy	M					B	B	B	B	B	B	M	employed at the expense of the Munich *Hofkapelle*
Pantani, Filippo		M	M	M	M	B	B	B	B	B	B	M	
Petit, Louis		B	B	B?	B	B	B	B	B	B	B	B	salary paid in Brussels until 1702, since 1703 no further payments
Pez, Johann Christoph?	R			M	BN	BN	BN	B	BN	BN	BN	M	"Herr Pezl"
Poulain, Toussain						B	B	B	B	B	B	M	employed at the expense of the Munich *Hofkapelle*
Riccardini, Giovanni Giacomo	M	M	M	M	M	M	M	B	B	B	B	M	
Rodier, François	M	B?	B?	B?	B?	B	B	B	M?	M?	M?	M	"Herr Rodier"
Sové, Gerhard	M	M	M	M	B?	B?	B?	B?	B?	B?	B		traveled to Antwerp in 1695, died in 1701
Schuechpaur, Franz Simon		M	M	M	M	B	B	B	B?	B?	B?	M	
Seerieder, Philipp Jacob	M	M	M	M	M	M	B	B	B	B	B	M	
Torri, Pietro	B	B	B	B	B	B	B	B	B	B	B	M	
Trevisani, Giuseppe	M	M	M	M	B?	B	B	B	?	?	?	?	

Table 2: Musicians in Max Emanuel's exile in the Netherlands and France (1704-1715)

Name	Function	Remarks
Chamber musicians		
Torri, Pietro	director of the chapel	payments documented: 1704-1708
Levray, Peter	chamber assistant, musician	payments documented: 1704-1708
Trevisani, Giuseppe	[theorbo player]	payments documented: 1704-1708
Pellegrini, Valeriano	[singer]	payments documented: 1704-1706
Frilli, Stefano	[singer]	payments documented: 1704-1706
Le Cocq, Franz Anton	instrumentalist	payments documented: 1704-1707
Dall'Abaco, Evaristo Felice	chamber musician	payments documented: 1705-1709
Hadersberg, Clementin von	chamber musician [singer]	payments documented: 1704-1707, 1709, 1711, also with Max Emanuel in 1710*
Bonel, ?	musician	employed 1st June 1705, payments documented: 1705-1707, 1710
Lambert, Vinzenz?	violin?	employed 1st January 1706, payments documented: 1706
Normand, Remi	chamber musician	employed 1st February 1706, payments documented: 1706-1707, 1709
Legrand, ?	musician	employed 1st January 1707, payments documented: 1707-1708
Trumpeters		
Ebenpöck, Abraham	trumpet	payments documented: 1704-1707, 1711
Ories, Franciscus	trumpet	payments documented: 1704-1708, 1709?

Zehentner, Dominicus	trumpet	payments documented: 1704-1707, 1709
Fink, Matthias Anton	trumpet	payments documented: 1704-1707
Burger, Johann Caspar	trumpet	payments documented: 1704-1707, 1711
Hochpain, Hyacinth	trumpet	payments documented: 1704-1707
Gerbl, Cornelius	kettledrum	employed 6 March 1705, payments documented: 1705-1707
Lorenz, Franz Xaver	trumpet	employed 1st April 1707, payments documented: 1707-1708, 1711
Other artistic staff		
Dechars, Pierre?	dance master	employed 1st October 1704, payments documented: 1704-1709, 1711
Blovy, Gregoire	buffonesque musician	payments documented: 1704-1706
Anet, Jean-Baptiste	violin	payments documented: August 1711 (pension), March 1715 (final payment)
Military musicians		
Le Clerc, Laurent	oboe	payments documented: 1711
Santer, Gottfried Ludwig	oboe	payments documented: 1705-1706, 1710-1711, unidentified (without month and year)
Bartscher, Matthias Valentin	oboe	payments documented: 1705-1706, 1710-1711, unidentified (without month and year)
Mallien, Johann Joseph	oboe	payments documented: 1706, 1710-1711, unidentified (without month and year)
Marchand, Johann Anton	oboe	payments documented: 1710-1711, unidentified (without month and year)

* In November 1710 he receives a payment, in June 1711 the reimbursement for his travel costs to Paris. D-Mhsa, MF 19582.

Table 3: Musicians in Therese Kunigunde's exile in Venice (1705-1715)

Name	Function	Remarks
Musicians from Munich		
Lemoles, Pietro	singer	payments documented: 1706, 1711-12, 1714/15; 1709 presence in Venice documented
Manzini, Maximilian	instrumentalist	payments documented: 1707/08
Schuechpaur, Franz Simon	instrumentalist	payments documented: 1708-1709
Newly recruited musicians		
Cignoni, Francesco	tenor	employed in November 1713
Bartoli, Bartolomeo	soprano	employed 1st May 1714
Venturini, Francesco Maria	bass	employed 1st October 1714
Brescianello, Giuseppe	violin	employed 19 November 1714
Corradi, Vincenzo	instrumentalist (later alto)	employed 12 March 1715

Table 4: Newly employed musicians in 1715

Name	Function	Remarks
Provenance: Spanish Netherlands		
de Chars [Pierre Deschars?]	pages's dance master	see table 2
Couvin, Franz	copyist	

de Piani, Thomas	instrumentalist	1717 in Vienna *Hofkapelle*
Niedermayr, Adam	blower	
Provenance: France (trumpeter)		
Burger, Hans Kaspar	trumpet	see table 2
Fink, Matthias Anton	trumpet	see table 2
Hochpain, Hyacinth	trumpet	see table 2
Lorenz, Franz Xaver	trumpet	see table 2
Gerbl, Cornelius	kettledrum	see table 2
Provenance: France (oboe band)		
Balthasar, Ignaz	oboe	
Maillen, Johann Joseph	oboe	see table 2
Marchand, Johann Anton	oboe	see table 2
Pourveu, Marin	oboe	
Santer, Gottfried Ludwig	oboe	see table 2
Provenance: France		
Loeillet, Jacques	instrumentalist	from Ghent, maybe already in service in the Spanish Netherlands, but no payments documented
Dubuisson, Gabriel	instrumentalist	
Provenance: France (French actors)		
Du Breil, Jean Pierre	dancer	

Du Breil, Pierre	dancer	dismissed in 1720
Le Fevre, Marie	dancer	
Gravier, Pierre	"Simphonist" (instrumentalist)	substituted by Pierre Rey in 1719
Henry, Pierre	stage designer	
Laurent, Pierre	stage designer	
Roger, Nicolas	stage designer	dismissed in 1720
Du Clos, Catherine	costumer	dismissed in 1720
Laurent, Marie	costumer	dismissed in 1720
Dauflise, Bonne	prompter	dismissed in 1720
Provenance: Wallonia or France		
Gouvillet, Carl	dance master at the University of Ingolstadt	
Piubelin, Johann Romedi	"Discantist"	maybe choir boy
Provenance: Italy		
Bartoli, Bartolomeo	soprano	see table 3
Brescianello, Giuseppe	violin	see table 3, 1717 in Stuttgart *Hofkapelle*
Cignoni, Francesco	tenor	see table 3
Corradi, Vincenzo	instrumentalist (later alto)	see table 3
Venturini, Francesco Maria	bass	see table 3

Provenance: Spain (Madrid)		
Thomas, Nikolaus Joseph	violin, oboe	sent to Madrid by Elector Max Emanuel, maybe relative of the court musician Ferdinand Matthias Thomas
Provenance: Klagenfurt/Graz (electoral princes's exile)		
Hindermair, Franz	double bass	
Le Comte, Johann Ferdinand	princes' dance master	from Vienna
Lauffensteiner, Wolff Jacob	music teacher (lute and other instruments)	from Graz
Provenance: "Hochstift" Regensburg		
Haveck, Anton Alexius	organ	former *Kapellmeister* of the "Hochstift" Ratisbon
Provenance: Bavarian/Austrian regiments		
Böhmer, Lorenz	trumpet	from count Arco's regiment
Leser, Johann Michael	trumpet	from count Arco's regiment
Leitenroth, Johann Georg	trumpet	from count of Taufkirchen's regiment
Kern, Lorenz Bruno	trumpet	from prince Löwenstein's occupation troupe
Taunickh, Elias Anton	trumpet	from prince Löwenstein's occupation troupe
Provenance: local		
Kerll, Johann Christoph	organ	Johann Caspar Kerll's son
Provenance: other		
Balatri, Filippo	soprano	passing through Munich

Panizza, Lucrezia	singer	1723 in Vienna *Hofkapelle*
Ganspöck, Johann Kaspar	horn	local musician?
Ganspöck, Matthias	horn	local musician?
Reininger, Paul	instrumentalist	local musician?
Augerneder, Veith	trumpet	local musician?

Letters

D-Mhsa, GHA, Obersthofmeisterstab 2164: Letter from the High Stewart ("Obersthofmeister") to Elector Max Emanuel from 13 April 1695

Most serene Elector,
most clement Lord.

Your electoral most serene court musician Gérard Sovve has asked me to grant him a journey to Antwerp for three or four months. But because it is beyond my power to grant for so a long time I therefore most humbly ask Your Electoral Highness for your most gracious order and in such a way as Your Electoral High Grace would like to command. Munich, 13 April in the year 1695.
Of Your Electoral Highness most humble and most obedient servant
[…]
the decision has already been made, signed Brussels, 11 May 1695.

Durchleüchtigister Churfürst,
Genedigister Herr.

Es hat Euer churfrt: drt: Hofmusicant, Gérard Sové mich gebetten, daß ich Ihme nach Antorf [Antwerpen] uf .3. oder .4. Monath Zuverraisen erlaubnus geben mechte; Weillen aber solche, uf solange Zeit Zuerthaillen in meinen Gwalt nicht stehet; Alß habe d[e]ss[e]thalben beÿ Eur churfrt: Drt: mich dero G[nä]digisten befelchs hierÿber, in Unnderthenigkheit erhollen „ unnd mithin solcher gestalten, Zu churfrt: hochen Gnaden befelchen wollen. München den .13. April anno .1695.
Euer Churfrt: Drt:

Unndterthenigist „ Gehorsambister
dienner.
[nonreadable signature, probably by the High Stewart]

[on the cover:] # die resolution ist schon ergang[en]. sign. Brüßel den 11. Maÿ 1695.

D-Mhsa, GHA, Obersthofmeisterstab 2164: Decree by Elector Max Emanuel from 18 June 1696

Maximilian Emanuel, by divine right Duke in Higher and Lower Bavaria and in the Higher Palatinate, Count Palatine of the Rhine, Arch-Seneschall and Elector of the Holy Roman Empire, Landgrave of Leuchtenberg

First our salutation, high- and well-born, dear abider,
We graciously decided to let come here in the Netherlands Simon Schuechpaur, musician and violinist in our *Hofkapelle*. We therefore tell you to properly command that my decision is imparted to Schuechpaur and that he shall either come with the women called to come here recently provided they did not leave yet or with the next opportunity.[98] Also our court chamber should be duly informed about the delivery of the boarding wages and the trip money. We are favourably disposed towards you with grace; given in the camp near Limale 18 June in the year 1696.
[...]

Von Gottesgnaden Maximilian Emanuel in ober und nidern Baÿrn, auch der obern Pfalz herzog Pfalzgraf bej Rhein des heil: Röm: Reichs Erztruchsess und Churfürst Landgraf zu Leüchtenberg

Unserm grues Zuvor, Hoch und wollgeborenner, lieber Getreuer.
Demnach Wür gn[ä]di[g]st resolvirt, den Simon Schuchbaur, Musicum und Violinisten beÿ Unser Hoff Capelln, anhero in Nid[er]landt ko[m]men zulass[en]; Alsbefohlen Wir Euch hiemit gn[ä]di[g]st, die behörige Verfügung Zuthuen, das ihme Schuchbaur solches bedeuttet werde, und Er entwed[er]s mit deren jüngst hieher berueffenen Weibs Persohnen, wann selbige noch nicht abgeraiset, od[er] mit negster gelegenheit herab ko[m]me; Warvon auch Unser HoffCammer[er] wegen Verreichung des benöthigten Kost- od[er] raisgeldts gebührendte nachricht zugeben; Seindt Euch anbej mit Gnad wolgewogen; dat: im feldtlager bej Limale

---

98 Only in 1697 a regular transport service for goods and people had been established. Cf. TRÖGER 1998, pp. 16 and 18.

den 18.t Junij a.o 1696.
Ex Comissione Ser.mi Dnj
Ducis Electoris

An Obristhoffmaistern   [clerk's signature?] P:F.Kempis [?]

[cover addressed to the High Stewart Paul Fugger, Graf zu Kirchberg und Weißenhorn]

Manuscript sources

Account books of Johann Paul Bombarda (D-Mhsa, MF 19581, 19582).
BALATRI, FILIPPO, Frutti del mondo. Esperimentàti da F.B. nativo dell['] Alfea in Toscana, 2 vols. (D-Mbs, Cod.ital.39).
Besoldungsbücher (D-Mhsa, Kurbayern, Hofzahlamt [KBH]).
Employment and other decrees (D-Mhsa, Fürstensachen 676-677; Kriegsarchiv, series F).
Chrfrl: Hoffstadt zu Brüssel (D-Mhsa, Geheimes Hausarchiv [GHA], Hofhaushaltsakten 461).
Decree of the Elector Max Emanuel from 18 June 1696 regarding Franz Simon Schuechpaur's delegation to Brussels (D-Mhsa, GHA, Obersthofmeisterstab 2164).
Letter of the High Stewart ("Obersthofmeister") to the Elector Max Emanuel from 13 April 1695 regarding Gerhard Sové's travel to Antwerp (D-Mhsa, GHA, Obersthofmeisterstab 2164).
Specification/Waß von Ihro Ch: Drl: do [?] Musicanti, so in der Königl: Capel zu Brüssel die dienste versech[en] gn[ä]di[g]st assignirt word[en], waß sie von den Königl: financen empfangen; und ihnen noch restirt [concerning staff costs between 1698 and 31 March 1701] (D-Mhsa, GHA, Hofhaushaltsakten 462).
Verzaichnuss./Der angschafften Hoch: und Nideren Bedienten zu Brissl, ... bsoldung beim Chrfr: Hofzahlambt München bezalt word[en]. (D-Mhsa, GHA, Hofhaushaltsakten 463).
Verzaichnuss/Der Churfrt: Hoch: und Nideren Bediente[n], welche beim Churfrt: Hofzahlambt alhier angeschafft: und sich dermahlen zu Brissl befundten, und auch, welche von hier hinundter ko[m]men, und ... aldort zu deren vorgehabten bsoldung, ainige besserung ad

adiuta seint bewilligt word[en]. (D-Mhsa, GHA, Hofhaushaltsakten 463).

Verzaichnuss./Was hernach folgent: und zu Brissl sich befindente chrfrt: bediente, an bsoldung für das 3. und .4.te Quartal, wie auch an den angeschaffte haus Zünz pro anno 1697 ybermacht [?] worden. (D-Mhsa, GHA, Hofhaushaltsakten 463).

Verzaig/aller Persohnen, welche der/mahlen bey der Churfrt: Hoff/haltung alhier abgespeiset:/oder mit dm monathlichem/adiuta berpflegt worden./... Brissl dm .12. July / 1698 (D-Mhsa, GHA, Hofhaushaltsakten 461).

Printed sources

Chur-cöllnischer Hof-Calender auff das Jahr [...] 1717. [...], [Bonn 1716].
[Kurkölnischer Hofkalender 1718], [s.l. 1717] (title page missing).
Almanach de la cour de S.A.S.E. de Cologne, &c. &c. pour l'année [...] 1719. [...], Liège [1718].
Chur-collnischer Hoff-Calender, für das Schalt-Jahr [...] 1720 [...], s.l. [1719].
Chur-collnischer Capelln- und Hoff-Calender, für das Jahr [...] MDCCXXI. [...], Cologne [1720].
Chur-cöllnischer Capelln- und Hoff-Calender, für das Jahr [...] MDCCXXII. [...], Cologne [1721].
Almanach de la cour de S.A.S.E. de Cologne &c. &c. pour l'année [...] MDCCXXII. [...], Cologne [1721].
Chur-cöllnischer Capelln- und Hoff-Calender, für das Jahr [...] MDCCXXIII. [...], Cologne [1722].
Chur-cöllnischer Capelln- und Hoff-Calender, für das Schalt-Jahr [...] MDCXXIV. [...], Cologne [1723].

Literature

ALBRECHT, DIETER, Staat und Gesellschaft. Zweiter Teil: 1500-1745, in: Handbuch der bayerischen Geschichte, vol. 2: Das alte Bayern. Der Territorialstaat vom Ausgang des 12. Jahrhunderts bis zum Ausgang des 18. Jahrhunderts, ed. by ANDREAS KRAUS, 2nd revised edition, Munich 1988, pp. 660-663.

ALTENBURG, DETLEF, Untersuchungen zur Geschichte der Trompete im Zeitalter der Clarinblaskunst (1500-1800) (Kölner Beiträge zur Musikforschung 75), 3 vols., Regensburg 1973.

ANTOINE, MICHEL, Note sur les violinistes Anet, in: "Recherches" sur la musique française classique 2 (1961-62) (La vie musicale en France sous les rois bourbons), Paris 1962, pp. 81-93.

ARETIN, ERWEIN VON, art. Arco, 4) Johann Baptist, in: Neue deutsche Biographie, vol. 1, Berlin 1953, pp. 338-339.

BOETTICHER, WOLFGANG, Handschriftlich überlieferte Lauten- und Gitarrentabulaturen des 15. bis 18. Jahrhunderts (Répertoire International des Sources Musicales B VII), Munich 1978.

BRAUBACH, MAX, Die Mitglieder der Hofmusik unter den vier letzten Kurfürsten von Köln, in: Colloquium amicorum. Joseph Schmidt-Görg zum 70. Geburtstag, ed. by SIEGFRIED KROSS/HANS SCHMIDT, Bonn 1967, pp. 26-63.

BRAUN, WERNER, Entwurf für eine Typologie der "Hautboisten", in: Der Sozialstatus des Berufsmusikers vom 17. zum 19. Jahrhundert, ed. by WALTER SALMEN, Kassel 1971, pp. 43-63.

CASADEMUNT I FIOL, SERGI, La capella reial de Carles III a Barcelona. Nova documentació sobre la música a la ciutat durant la Guerra de successió (1705-1713), in: Revista catalana de musicologia 4 (2011), pp. 81-100.

CESSAC, CATHERINE, Max Emanuel und seine französischen Musiker, in: Das Musikleben am Hof von Kurfürst Max Emanuel. Bericht über das internationale musikwissenschaftliche Symposium, veranstaltet von der Gesellschaft für Bayerische Musikgeschichte und dem Forschungsinstitut für Musiktheater der Universität Bayreuth, ed. by STEPHAN HÖRNER/SEBASTIAN WERR, Tutzing 2012, pp. 187-200.

CLERCX, SUZANNE, La chapelle royale de Bruxelles sous l'ancien régime, in: Annuaire du Conservatoire Royale de Musique de Bruxelles (1942), pp. 159-179.

ID., Le dix-septième et le dix-Huitième siècle, in: La musique en Belgique du moyen âge à nos jours, ed. by ERNEST CLOSSON/CHARLES VAN DEN BORREN, Brussels 1950, pp. 145-233.

COUVREUR, MANUEL/VAN AELBROUCK, JEAN-PHILIPPE, Gio Paolo Bombarda et la création du Grand Théâtre de Bruxelles, in: Le théâtre de la Monnaie au XVIIIe siècle, ed. by MANUEL COUVREUR, Brussels 1996, pp. 1-27.

COUVREUR, MANUEL, Pietro Antonio Fiocco, un musicien vénitien à Bruxelles (1682-1714), in: Revue belge de musicologie 55 (2001), pp. 147-163.

DUBOWY, NORBERT, Italienische Instrumentalisten in deutschen Hofkapellen, in: The Eighteenth-Century Diaspora of Italian Music and Musicians (Speculum Musicae 8), ed. by REINHARD STROHM, Turnhout 2001, pp. 61-120.

EINSTEIN, ALFRED, Italienische Musiker am Hofe der Neuburger Wittelsbacher. 1614-1716. Neue Beiträge zur Geschichte der Musik am Neuburg-Düsseldorfer Hof im 17. Jahrhundert, in: Sammelbände der Internationalen Musikgesellschaft 9 (1908), pp. 336-424.

ENGELBRECHT, JÖRG, Krone und Exil. Das Haus Wittelsbach in der deutschen und europäischen Politik (1679-1761), in: Im Wechselspiel der Kräfte. Politische Entwicklungen des 17. und 18. Jahrhunderts in Kurköln (Der Riss im Himmel. Clemens August und seine Epoche 2), ed. by FRANK GÜNTER ZEHNDER, Cologne 1999, pp. 9-22.

FLOTZINGER, RUDOLF, Rochus Berhandtzky und Wolff Jacob Lauffensteiner. Zum Leben und Schaffen zweier Lautenisten in kurbayerischen Diensten, in: Studien zur Musikwissenschaft 27 (1966), pp. 200-239.

GROOTE, INGA MAI, Pietro Torri. Un musicista veronese alla corte di Baviera. Con la prima edizione della musica per il torneo Già dall'Isser ameno (1718). In Appendice: BARBARA BROZ, I musicisti veneti in Europa ai tempi del Torri, Verona [2003].

HARRIS, C. DAVID/GIEBLER, ALBERT C., art. Kerll, Johann Caspar, in: Grove Music Online, 18.12.2014.

HENNAUT, ÉRIC/CAMPIOLI, MONICA, La construction du premier théâtre de la Monnaie par les Bezzi et ses transformations jusqu'à la fin du régime autrichien, in: Le théâtre de la Monnaie au XVIIIe siècle, ed. by MANUEL COUVREUR, Brussels 1996, pp. 33-109.

HÜTTL, LUDWIG, Max Emanuel. Der Blaue Kurfürst 1679-1726. Eine politische Biographie, 2nd ed., Munich 1976.

HUYS, JEAN-PHILIPPE, Le prince dans la ville. Les sorties de Maximilien-Emmanuel de Bavière à Bruxelles autour de 1700, in: Espaces et parcours dans la ville Bruxelles au XVIIIe siècle (XVIII. Études sur le 18e siècle 35), ed. by KIM BETHUME/JEAN-PHILIPPE HUYS, Brussels 2007, pp. 11-29.

ISER, ULRICH, "Wie du ein französisches lied vor meiner gesungen". Zur musikalischen Erziehung der Wittelsbacher Prinzen, in: Die Bühnen des Rokoko. Theater, Musik und Literatur im Rheinland des 18. Jahrhunderts (Der Riss im Himmel. Clemens August und seine Epoche 7), ed. by FRANK GÜNTHER ZEHNDER, Cologne 2000, pp. 86-112.

JAHRMÄRKER, MANUELA, Repräsentation im Wettstreit. Französische Stilzitate und musikalisch-theatralische Fest-Elemente in Torris Drammi per musica, in: Das Musikleben am Hof von Kurfürst Max Emanuel. Bericht über das internationale musikwissenschaftliche Symposium, veranstaltet von der Gesellschaft für Bayerische Musikgeschichte und dem Forschungsinstitut für Musiktheater der Universität Bayreuth, ed. by STEPHAN HÖRNER/SEBASTIAN WERR, Tutzing 2012, pp. 201-250.

KNAUS, HERWIG, Die Musiker im Archivbestand des Kaiserlichen Obersthofmeisteramtes (1637-1705), 3 Bde., Wien 1967-69 (Österreichische Akademie der Wissenschaften. Philosophisch-historische Klasse. Sitzungsberichte 254, 259, 264; Veröffentlichungen der Kommission für Musikforschung 7, 8, 10).

JAMBOU, LOUIS, Documentos relativos a los músicos de la segunda mitad del siglo XVII de las capillas reales y villa y corte de Madrid sacados de su archivo de protocolos, in: Revista de musicología 12 (1989), pp. 469-514.

JANZEN, ROSE-MARIE, The Loeillet Enigma, in: The Consort 39 (1983), pp. 502-506.

KÄGLER, BRITTA, Frauen am Münchener Hof (1651-1756) (Münchener historische Studien. Abteilung Bayerische Geschichte 18), Kallmünz 2011.

KENYON DE PASCUAL, BERYL, Instrumentos e instrumentistas españoles y extranjeros en la Real Capilla desde 1701 hasta 1749, in: España en la música de occidente. Actas del Congreso Internacional celebrado en Salamanca 29 de octubro-5 de noviembre de 1985, ed. by EMILIO CASARES RODICIO et. al., Madrid 1987, vol. 2, pp. 93-97.

ID., The Recorder Revival in Late Seventeenth-Century Spain, in: The Recorder in the 17th Century. Proceedings of the International Recorder Symposium Utrecht 1993, ed. by DAVID LASOCKI, Utrecht 1995, pp. 65-74.

KÖCHEL, LUDWIG VON, Die Kaiserliche Hof-Musikkapelle in Wien von 1543 bis 1867. Nach urkundlichen Forschungen, Vienna 1869, Reprint Hildesheim et al. 1976.

LIPOWSKY, FELIX JOSEPH, Des Churfürstens von Baiern Maximilian Emanuel Statthalterschaft in den spanischen Niederlanden und dessen Feldzüge. Historisch geschildert, und mit einem Anhange über die Schicksale der Jesuiten in Baiern, Tirol, Schwaben und der Schweiz, während dieser Zeit, begabt, Munich 1820.

METTENLEITER, DOMINICUS, Musikgeschichte der Stadt Regensburg. Aus Archivalien und sonstigen Quellen bearbeitet (Aus der musikalischen Vergangenheit bayrischer Städte [1]), Regensburg 1866.

MÜCKE, PANJA, "... liessen sich Trompeten und Paucken in dem Saal, neben dem TafelZimmer hören, auch wurden die Stücken von dem Walle an der Reith-Bahne darzu abgebrannt". Musik als zeremonielle Zeichengattung am Dresdner Hof, in: Zeichen und Raum. Ausstattung und höfisches Zeremoniell in den deutschen Schlössern der Frühen Neuzeit, ed. by PETER-MICHAEL HAHN/ULRICH SCHÜTTE, Munich et al. 2006 (Rudolstädter Forschungen zur Residenzkultur 3), pp. 65–82

MÜNSTER, ROBERT, Die Musik am Hofe Max Emanuels, in: Kurfürst Max Emanuel. Bayern und Europa um 1700, ed. by HUBERT GLASER, Munich 1976, vol. 1, pp. 295-316.

NIWA, SEISHIRŌ, "Madama" Margaret of Parma's Patronage of Music, in: Early Music 33 (2005), pp. 25-37.

OVER, BERTHOLD, Antonio Vivaldi und Therese Kunigunde von Bayern, in: Studi vivaldiani 4 (2004), pp. 3-8.

ID., "...sotto l'Ombra della Regina di Pennati". Antonio Vivaldi, Kurfürstin Therese Kunigunde von Bayern und andere Wittelsbacher, in: Italian Opera in Central Europe 1614-1780, vol. 3: Opera Subjects and European Relationships, ed. by NORBERT DUBOWY et. al., Berlin 2007 (Musical Life in Europe 1600-1900. Circulation, Institutions, Representation), pp. 251-297.

ID., Kurfürstin Therese Kunigunde von Bayern in Venedig (1705-1715), in: Das Musikleben am Hof von Kurfürst Max Emanuel. Bericht über das internationale musikwissenschaftliche Symposium, veranstaltet von der Gesellschaft für Bayerische Musikgeschichte und dem Forschungsinstitut für Musiktheater der Universität Bayreuth, ed. by STEPHAN HÖRNER/SEBASTIAN WERR, Tutzing 2012, pp. 85-117.

ID., Employee Turnover in *Hofkapellen* of the Wittelsbach Dynasty. Types of and Reasons for (Impeded) Migration (1715-1725), in: Music Migrations in the Early Modern Age. People, Markets, Patterns, Styles, ed. by VJERA KATALINIĆ, Zagreb i.pr.

OWENS, SAMANTHA, The Court of Württemberg-Stuttgart, in: Music at German Courts, 1715-1760. Changing Artistic Priorities, ed. by ID./BARBARA M. REUL/JANICE B. STOCKIGT, Woodbridge 2011, pp. 165-195.

PIANI, GIOVANNI ANTONIO, Sonatas for Violin Solo and Violoncello with Cembalo (Recent Researches in the Music of the Baroque Era 20), ed. by BARBARA GARVEY JACKSON, Madison 1975.

RAMPE, SIEGBERT/ROCKSTROH, ANDREAS, art. Kerll, Johann Caspar, in: Die Musik in Geschichte und Gegenwart. Allgemeine Enzyklopädie der Musik begründet von Friedrich Blume, 2nd revised edition ed. by LUDWIG FINSCHER, Personenteil 10, Kassel et al. 2003, col. 29-44.

RASCH, RUDOLF, A Venetian Goes North: Pietro Antonio Fiocco in Amsterdam, Hanover and Brussels, in: Revue belge de musicologie 56 (2002), pp. 177-207.

SÁNCHEZ-BELÉN, JUAN A., The Palace Royal Chapel at the End of the Seventeenth Century, in: The Royal Chapel in the Time of the Habsburgs. Music and Ceremony in the Early Modern European Court, ed. by JUAN JOSÉ CARRERAS et al., Woodbridge 2005, pp. 300-327.

ID./SAAVEDRA ZAPATER, JUAN C., La capilla real de Felipe V durante la Guerra de Sucesión, in: Homenaje a Antonio de Béthencourt Massieu, ed. by ISABEL GRIMALDI PEÑA, 3 vols., Las Palmas 1995, vol. 3, pp. 367-401.

SANHUESA FONSECA, MARÍA, Carlos II y las "Danzerías de la reyna": violones y danza en las postrimerías de la casa de Austria, in: Revista de musicología 20 (1997), pp. 261-274.

SARTORI, CLAUDIO, I libretti italiani a stampa dalle origini al 1800. Catalogo analitico con 16 indici, 7 vols., Cuneo 1990-1994.

SCHARRER, MARGRET, "pour le chant je suis du goust Italien, mais pour quelques instruments on exèle en france". Bayerisch-französische Musikerbeziehungen unter Kurfürst Max Emanuel, in: Das Musikleben am Hof von Kurfürst Max Emanuel. Bericht über das internationale musikwissenschaftliche Symposium, veranstaltet von der Gesellschaft für Bayerische Musikgeschichte und dem Forschungs-

Institut für Musiktheater der Universität Bayreuth, ed. by STEPHAN HÖRNER/SEBASTIAN WERR, Tutzing 2012, pp. 41-52.

SCHNETTGER, MATTHIAS, Der Spanische Erbfolgekrieg 1701-1713/14, Munich 2014.

SCHRYVER, REGINALD DE, Max II. Emanuel von Bayern und das spanische Erbe. Die europäischen Ambitionen des Hauses Wittelsbach 1665-1715 (Veröffentlichungen des Instituts für Europäische Geschichte Mainz. Abteilung Universalgeschichte 156), Mainz 1996.

SKEMPTON, ALEC/ROBINSON, LUCY, art. Loeillet, in: Grove Music Online, 09.01.2015.

SL/(BRIAN PRIESTMAN), art. Loeillet, in: Die Musik in Geschichte und Gegenwart. Allgemeine Enzyklopädie der Musik begründet von Friedrich Blume, 2nd revised edition ed. by LUDWIG FINSCHER, Personenteil 11, Kassel et al. 2004, col. 378-381.

SOMMER-MATHIS, ANDREA, Tu felix Austria nube. Hochzeitsfeste der Habsburger im 18. Jahrhundert (dramma per musica 4), Vienna 1994.

ID., Entre Nápoles, Barcelona y Viena. Nuevos documentos sobre la circulaciòn de músicos a principios del siglo xviii, in: Artigrama 12 (1996), pp. 45-77.

STAUDINGER, KARL, Geschichte des kurbayerischen Heeres unter Kurfürst Max II. Emanuel 1680-1726 (Geschichte des Bayerischen Heeres 2), 2 vols., Munich 1904.

STASZEWSKI, JACEK, August III. Kurfürst von Sachsen und König von Polen, Berlin 1996.

STELLFELD, CHRISTIANE, Les Fiocco. Une famille de musiciens belges aux XVIIe et XVIIIe siècles (Académie royale de Belgique. Classe des Beaux-Arts. Mémoires 7), Brussels 1941.

STRYCKERS, PIET, Music and Music Production in Seventeenth-Century Brussels, in: Embracing Brussels. Art and Culture in the Court City, 1600-1800, ed. by KATLIJNE VAN DER STIGHELEN et al., Turnhout 2013, pp. 59-79.

THIEFFRY, SANDRINE, La Chapelle royale de Bruxelles de 1612 à 1618 d'après les Libros de Razon de l'archiduc Albert, in: Revue belge de musicologie 55 (2001), pp. 103-125.

ID., L'archiduc Léopold-Guillaume à Bruxelles (1647-1656): le bon usage du mécénat musical en temps de guerre, in: Revue belge de musicologie 56 (2002), pp. 159-175.

TRÖGER, OTTO-KARL, Der bayerische Kurfürst Max Emanuel in Brüssel. Zu Politik und Kultur in Europa um 1700. Eine Ausstellung des Bayerischen Hauptstaatsarchivs für die Vertretung des Freistaates Bayern bei der Europäischen Union in Brüssel (Staatliche Archive Bayerns. Kleine Ausstellungen 10), Munich 1998.

VALDER-KNECHTGES, CLAUDIA, Die Musikgeschichte, in: Geschichte der Stadt Bonn, ed. by DIETRICH HÖROLDT/MANFRED VAN REY, vol. 3: Bonn als kurkölnische Haupt- und Residenzstadt 1597-1794, Bonn 1989, pp. 449-514.

VAN AELBROUCK, JEAN-PHILIPPE, Max Emanuels Aufenthalt in Brüssel und die Opéra du Quai au Foin (1682-1697), in: Das Musikleben am Hof von Kurfürst Max Emanuel. Bericht über das internationale musikwissenschaftliche Symposium, veranstaltet von der Gesellschaft für Bayerische Musikgeschichte und dem Forschungsinstitut für Musiktheater der Universität Bayreuth, ed. by STEPHAN HÖRNER/ SEBASTIAN WERR, Tutzing 2012, pp. 120-125.

WERR, SEBASTIAN, Politik mit sinnlichen Mitteln. Opern und Fest am Münchner Hof (1680-1745), Cologne et al. 2010.

ZEDLER, ANDREA, Alle Glückseligkeit seiner Education dem allermildesten Ertz-Hause Oesterreich zu dancken. Hofstaat, Bildung und musikalische Unterweisung des bayerischen Kurprinzen Karl Albrecht in Graz (1712-1716), in: Historisches Jahrbuch der Stadt Graz 42 (2012), pp. 337-366.

ZUBER, BARBARA, Pietro Torri und das Wittelsbacher Musiktheater im Exil. Neue Quellen und Erkenntnisse, in: Das Musikleben am Hof von Kurfürst Max Emanuel. Bericht über das internationale musikwissenschaftliche Symposium, veranstaltet von der Gesellschaft für Bayerische Musikgeschichte und dem Forschungsinstitut für Musiktheater der Universität Bayreuth, ed. by STEPHAN HÖRNER/SEBASTIAN WERR, Tutzing 2012, pp. 127-169.

ZUBER, KARL-HEINZ, art. Löwenstein-Wertheim-Rochefort, Maximilian Karl, in: Neue deutsche Biographie 15, Berlin 1987, pp. 98-99.

Migratory and Traveling Musicians at the Polish Royal Courts in the 17th Century
The Case of Kaspar Förster the Younger

BARBARA PRZYBYSZEWSKA-JARMIŃSKA

The period under research spans the reigns of five Polish kings, who were Grand Dukes of Lithuania at the same time. They were Zygmunt III Vasa (who reigned 1587-1632) followed by his sons Władysław IV (1632-48) and Jan II Kazimierz (1648-68), and also Michał Korybut Wiśniowiecki (1669-73) and Jan III Sobieski (1674-96). Towards the end of the 17th century, in 1697, the first of the two Polish kings from the Saxon Wettin dynasty ascended to the throne. These final years of the century are already within the chronological range researched in the MusMig project by Alina Żórawska-Witkowska.[1]

I decided to accept the year 1595 as the beginning of the period under scrutiny. It was in that year that Zygmunt III, an elected monarch born in Sweden, son of Johan III Vasa and the Polish princess Katarzyna Jagiellonka, reorganized the royal ensemble.[2] As a result of a recruitment action that took place in Rome and was inspired by the Polish king, more than 20 Italian musicians came to Poland, including two *Kapellmeister*: Annibale Stabile (who died in April 1595, probably during the journey or shortly after his arrival in Cracow/Krakau) and Luca Marenzio (whose

---

1   See her article on pp. 151-169 in the present volume.
2   SZWEYKOWSKA/SZWEYKOWSKI, 1997, pp. 22-53; PRZYBYSZEWSKA-JARMIŃSKA, 2007, pp. 15-27.

stay in Poland lasted from 1595 until 1597 or 1598).[3] From that time until the monarch's death, his court hosted a group of Italian musicians whose number remained stable. The group was managed by consecutive Italian *Kapellmeister*: Giulio Cesare Gabussi (1601-02) from Milan and two musicians recruited in Rome: Asprilio Pacelli (1602-23) and Giovanni Francesco Anerio (1624-30).[4] Following Anerio's death shortly after his departure from Warsaw, Zygmunt made efforts to employ other Italian *maestri di cappella*, Claudio Monteverdi and Vincenzo Ugolini, but neither of them agreed to leave Italy for Poland.[5]

The royal ensemble during the reign of Zygmunt III was characterized by a frequent turnover of the members. Some musicians returned to their homeland, others went there for a visit and returned to Poland in the company of new singers or instrumentalists recruited at the monarch's request; in other cases, they would return to Italy permanently, but upon their return would encourage other musicians to replace them; also, some of the members traveled to the royal courts of Central and Northern Europe. As Zygmunt's successive wives were Anna and Constanze of Habsburg of Inner Austria, particularly close bilateral relations existed between Zygmunt's court and that of his brother-in-law, Archduke Ferdinand, in Graz (musicians traveled between Graz and Cracow; from the second decade of the 17th century, journeys were made between Warsaw and Graz).[6] The exchange of musicians continued, although on a smaller scale, after 1619 when Ferdinand became emperor.[7] In addition, Italian musicians active at the court of Zygmunt III proved to be an attractive "catch" for King Christian IV of Denmark. In 1607, several members of the ensemble left Cracow for Copenhagen (by names there were

---

3   BIZZARINI, 1998, pp. 203-221; PRZYBYSZEWSKA-JARMIŃSKA, 1998, pp. 96-101; PRZYBYSZEWSKA-JARMIŃSKA, 2001, pp. 93-98.
4   More in: SZWEYKOWSKA/SZWEYKOWSKI, 1997; PRZYBYSZEWSKA-JARMIŃSKA, 2007.
5   SZWEYKOWSKA/SZWEYKOWSKI, 1997, pp. 80-82; PRZYBYSZEWSKA-JARMIŃSKA 2014a, p. 7.
6   Cf. FEDERHOFER, 1963, pp. 522-526; FEICHT, 1963, pp. 122-124; FEDERHOFER, 1967, pp. 50-60; SEIFERT, 2004, pp. 249f.; PRZYBYSZEWSKA-JARMIŃSKA, 2014b, pp. 188-190, 202f.
7   SEIFERT, 2004, pp. 250-255; PRZYBYSZEWSKA-JARMIŃSKA, 2014b, pp. 188-196, 202f.

listed Vincenzo Bertolusi and Jacobus Merlis).[8] It might be added that travels in this direction continued into the reign of Christian's follower, Frederick III.

It appears that taking these migrations into account in the MusMig database we are planning to develop will reveal a network of music-related connections that existed between the royal courts in cross-Alpine countries and expose the considerable impact of Italian musicians who, at various stages of their lives, pursued their activities in various centers, often in environments in which different religious creeds prevailed. Another noteworthy aspect is the links between the royal ensemble of the Polish king and musicians from Gdańsk (Danzig), which remained under Polish rule, but enjoyed considerable autonomy and possessed a specific culture, characterized by strong ties to Protestant Germany.

During the reign of Zygmunt III Vasa, the members of his ensemble included Andreas Hakenberger (born in Koszalin/Köslin in Pomerania). After leaving the royal court, he held the position of the *Kapellmeister* of St Mary's Church in Gdańsk (1608-27). Paul Siefert, born in that city, won a scholarship from the municipal council to study under Jan Pieterszoon Sweelinck in Amsterdam; after brief sojourns in Królewiec (Königsberg, now Kaliningrad) and Warsaw, he returned to Gdańsk and, in 1623, became organist in St Mary's Church (a position he held until his death, in 1666).[9] As early as in the 1620s, during his stay at court, Siefert criticized Italian musicians; in the 1640s, he entered into a dispute concerning the theory of music, in which his adversary was Marco Scacchi and which I shall discuss presently.[10]

When King Władysław IV Vasa ascended the throne after his father's death, he modified the music ensemble in a way that reflected his interest in theater and opera staged at his court. Another Italian employed as the new *Kapellmeister* was the above-mentioned composer and theorist Marco Scacchi (1632-49). He had already resided at court for eight years, employed as a violinist (in all probability, as a young man, he traveled to Poland in the company of Anerio, who had been his teacher in Rome and must have assisted him in perfecting his technique in Warsaw). It should be added, however that, before being appointed *Kapellmeister* at

---

8   HAMMERICH/ELLING, 1893, p. 75; CZAPLIŃSKI, 1968, pp. 95-97; PRZYBYSZEWSKA-JARMIŃSKA, 2007, pp. 156, 193.
9   PRZYBYSZEWSKA-JARMIŃSKA, 2002, pp. 114-116.
10 PATALAS, 2010, pp. 310-349 and the bibliography there.

the court of Władysław IV, Scacchi paid a visit to his homeland, during which he had opportunities to meet or become acquainted with Italian musicians and to learn about their views, the repertoire and performance practices prevailing in Rome in the early 1630s.[11]

Like his predecessor, King Władysław recruited Italian musicians either directly in Italy or via the imperial court. Vienna was also home to his first wife Cäcilia Renata of Habsburg, who arrived in Poland in 1637 (her entourage also included a small number of German musicians).[12] Following the marriage of Władysław and his second wife Marie Louise Gonzaga of Nevers, several musicians from France found employment at court. During the 1630s and 1640s, members of the royal ensemble included musicians from Gdańsk, who showed great willingness to travel during the period that followed. While we find relatively ample sources on Kaspar Förster the Younger, his activity at court and his travels (which I shall discuss below), in the currently known Polish sources there is no information about the stay of the young Christoph Bernhard at the court of Władysław IV. Bernhard was a musician and theorist of music born in Kołobrzeg (Kolberg) in Pomerania who, in his adult years, pursued his activities in Dresden (from where he made two journeys to Italy), Copenhagen, Hamburg and (again) Dresden. Information about the musical education Bernhard received in Gdańsk and in Warsaw (it can be conjectured that he was taught by Marco Scacchi during the 1640s) is included in an obituary poem written after his death by Constantin Christian Dedekind, who was related to him by marriage.[13] A similar case is that of Adam Drese who – according to sources known to Johann Gottfried Walther – visited Warsaw and collaborated with Scacchi for some time.[14] When returning, he took with him copies of instrumental music written by composers employed at the Polish royal court. According to my hypothesis, Drese may have visited Warsaw in 1647, directly after meeting Heinrich Schütz in Weimar in February of that year.[15] The Polish sources, however, contain no information whatsoever about Adam Drese's stay at court. More doubts arise about the information found in the sources preserved in Dresden, according to which

---

11   More in PATALAS, 2010.
12   SEIFERT, 2001, pp. 251-254; PRZYBYSZEWSKA-JARMIŃSKA, 2005, pp. 22-27.
13   SNYDER, 2001, p. 438.
14   WALTHER, 1732/2001, p. 199.
15   PRZYBYSZEWSKA-JARMIŃSKA, 2010, p. 24.

Marco Scacchi's students included Christoph Werner, singer of the St Catherine's Church in Gdańsk and participant in the dispute concerning music theory that occurred between the royal *maestro di cappella* and Paul Siefert, the organist at St Mary's Church in Gdańsk. Although it is confirmed in the sources that Werner and Scacchi maintained in contact, no evidence has been found of either Werner's stay in Warsaw or his receiving an education from Scacchi.[16]

Unfortunately, the political situation during the reign of Zygmunt III Vasa's second son, Jan II Kazimierz, did not favor the cultivation of musical life. The wars that started in 1648 caused the ensemble to reduce its membership. One of those leaving Poland for good was Marco Scacchi, replaced by the first *Kapellmeister* of non-Italian origin in the 17th century – Bartłomiej Pękiel. Other musicians also departed and were not replaced. Finally, in 1655, the muses became quiet. In the wake of the Swedish invasion, the royal castle in Warsaw had to be evacuated and the court dispersed. The *cappella* suspended its activities for two years. After reactivation, the *Kapelle*, now managed by Jacek Różycki, a Polish musician active at court since 1640s, never regained its former splendor. However, it still welcomed foreign musicians, and the regions from which new members were "imported" depended on matrimonial politics. Apart from the steady Italian presence, musicians from the imperial court arrived along with Eleonora Maria of Habsburg, the wife of King Michał Korybut Wiśniowiecki, or from other Austrian and Hungarian *Kapellen*, followed by Frenchmen (represented by an entire ensemble) when Jan III Sobieski married Marie Casimire de la Grange d'Arquien. This period in the history of the royal ensemble is also, if not predominantly, referred to in incidentally identified foreign sources, which mention musicians active at the Polish royal courts, who were not included in the continuously updated lists of musicians elaborated on the basis of Polish archives.[17] A good example is the organist and composer Orazio Pollarolo from Brescia (father of Carlo Francesco and Paolo). Had it not been for the research conducted by Italian historians, we would not be aware of the fact that Pollarolo and his disciple Paris Francesco Alghisi stayed at the court of Jan III Sobieski.[18]

This example and the cases quoted above testify to the poor state of preservation of the sources related to musical life at the courts of

---

16 PATALAS, 2010, p. 124f.
17 See PRZYBYSZEWSKA-JARMIŃSKA, 2002, pp. 71-80.
18 CROSATTI, 2009, p. 22; BIZZARINI, 2012, p. 208.

the Polish kings in the 17th century. Only vestigial sources produced by the ensemble itself have survived, including financial records (payroll documents listing musicians' names survive only for the years 1649-51). Apart from rare exceptions, musicians' letters, including official correspondence, have not been preserved. Neither is any musical material (like manuscript and printed scores and parts) used by the members of the ensemble available to researchers today. Musical prints from the royal library have been lost, including editions dedicated to the royalty. The repertoire of the *cappella* has been reconstructed mainly on the basis of copies produced in various circles, often foreign and of a different religious denomination. As for the publications of music composed by migratory royal musicians, editions which are known to have existed (but not all of them) are preserved in the form of (often unique and incomplete) volumes kept in various libraries throughout the world, only a small percentage of them in Poland.[19]

The list of foreign musicians[20] known to have been active at the Polish royal court (including over 150 names) has been compiled by "ferreting out" information from scattered sources of a very different nature. The list is dominated by musicians who were members of the ensemble during the first half of the 17th century. As for the later period (following the Swedish invasion, which is a watershed in the history of Polish culture), there is a need for comprehensive preliminary archival research.

Apart from foreign migratory musicians, one can distinguish a category of traveling musicians who arrived at the court (which resided mainly in Cracow, Vilnius or in Warsaw) from territories under Polish rule, but dominated by a religious creed and culture other than that of the royal circle. A representative of this group was Kaspar Förster the Younger from Gdańsk (1616-73), whose case is interesting because he changed his residence many times during his life, traveling from the north to the south and then back north, making sojourns somewhere in between or trips to the east and to the west. His experience included staying in environments which varied in terms of dominant languages and religious creeds, meeting musicians from various countries who

---

19 Cf. PRZYBYSZEWSKA-JARMIŃSKA, 2002, pp. 169-221 (chapter IV: Sources of Music Repertoire and Theoretical Writings).

20 I use the term "musicians" as an umbrella term referring not only to musicians as such (composers, singers and instrumentalists), but also to instrument-makers, copyists, music printers, librettists, dancers, and so forth.

composed stylistically diverse music and represented different performance styles. More than a century ago, the mark left by Förster's travels on his compositions was noticed by André Pirro[21] and Arnold Schering,[22] who pointed out the affinity of Förster's music to Giacomo Carissimi's compositions (especially to his Latin dialogues). In the late 1960s Søren Sørensen tried to identify Förster as a link that facilitated the reception of Claudio Monteverdi's style in the music of Dietrich Buxtehude,[23] while Jerrold Baab and Berthold Warnecke in their doctoral dissertations described the numerous ways in which Italian music influenced Förster's work.[24] Similar conclusions referring also to his instrumental compositions were reached by other researchers, including Lars Berglund[25] and myself.[26]

As regards the available information about the musician's life, only part of it can be reconstructed from archive sources. A biographical entry included by Johann Mattheson in his *Grundlage einer Ehren=Pforte*[27] gives us information, especially from the period after leaving the Polish royal court, but many of those data have never been verified in the sources. As we assume that Mattheson was able to use contemporaneous accounts and documents that are no longer available to us (as was the case with many other musicians), his information may be relied upon and perceived as a valid source. In recent years, however, archive research has been resumed in Gdańsk (Jerzy Michalak)[28] and in Copenhagen (Bjarke Moe).[29] Its results have partially challenged the reliability of the information on Förster given by Mattheson, Carl Thrane and Hermann Rauschning in their monographs about music culture at the Danish royal court and in Gdańsk respectively,[30] and in the outline of Förster's biography by myself.[31]

---

21   PIRRO, 1913, pp. 22-24, 69-85, 115-117, 245, 484.
22   SCHERING, 1911, pp. 158-161.
23   SØRENSEN, 1967.
24   BAAB, 1970; WARNECKE, 2004.
25   BERGLUND, 1994; BERGLUND, 1996.
26   PRZYBYSZEWSKA-JARMIŃSKA, 1992.
27   MATTHESON, 1740/1969, pp. 21, 73-76, 147.
28   MICHALAK, 2004; MICHALAK, 2009.
29   Most of the findings have not been published so far.
30   THRANE, 1908, pp. 16-28; RAUSCHNING, 1931, pp. 195-206.
31   PRZYBYSZEWSKA-JARMIŃSKA, 1987.

Kaspar Förster the Younger was born in Gdańsk, probably into a Lutheran family, on 22 February 1616 (he was baptized on the 28th of that month). His father, Kaspar Förster the Elder, had come to Gdańsk from Lower Lusatia (he was born in Zieckau, near Spreewald), his mother Maria Hintze was a citizen of Gdańsk and a daughter of Martin Hintze, a musician employed by the town council. It seems important to mention that Kaspar the Younger's godfather was the Gdańsk patrician Hans Czirenberg, father of Constantia, famous as a singer and keyboard player during the 1630s.[32]

Kaspar Förster the Younger spent his childhood in Gdańsk; following his father's conversion to Catholicism in 1623, he was no doubt raised a Catholic, but grew up in a Protestant environment; his first music preceptor was most likely his father, who at that time was cantor at the Gymnasium and at the Holy Trinity Church, later (from 1627) *Kapellmeister* at St Mary's church. As a boy, Förster sung in the choirs managed by his father, probably performing music in the Franco-Flemish style, in the tradition of Johannes Wanning and Nicolaus Zange but also Italian music which Kaspar the Elder stocked in his bookshop, including *Flores praestantissimorum virorum*, an anthology possibly ordered and sponsored by him, prepared by Filippo Lomazzo (Milan 1626), dedicated to the afore mentioned Constantia Czirenberg.[33]

It is probable, but not confirmed that the young Kaspar traveled to Warsaw to continue his music education in 1630. I assume that he joined (along with the new royal *Kapellmeister* Marco Scacchi) the entourage of Jerzy Ossoliński in the autumn of 1633, dispatched with an embassy of obedience to Pope Urban VIII; the ceremonial passage of the Polish envoy through the Eternal City took place on 28 November of the same year. In December of that year, Kaspar the Younger became a *convittore* at the Collegium Germanicum and joined the choir managed by Giacomo Carissimi at the St Apollinare church.[34]

According to the nuncio in Poland Mario Filonardi, after leaving Rome, probably in 1636, Kaspar visited the Medici court in Florence[35] and set off on his journey to Warsaw to attend the wedding of Władysław IV and Cäcilia Renata of Austria (in September 1637).

---

32   MICHALAK, 2004, pp. 195f., 205f.
33   On the anthology and different opinions about its context see: GROCHOWSKA, 2002; MICHALAK, 2004, p. 207.
34   CULLEY, 1970, pp. 40, 208.
35   LEWAŃSKI, 1973, p. 36.

During the years 1637-52, Förster served the kings Władysław IV and Jan II Kazimierz as an alto singer. During this time, the main royal residence was in Warsaw, where the musician married Ursula Wigboldt and where his three children were baptized. He traveled with the court around the Commonwealth of Poland and Lithuania (e.g. to Vilnius, Cracow and Gdańsk). In addition, he traveled to Italy in 1644.[36]

At the Polish royal court, he collaborated with composers from Italy (e.g. Marco Scacchi, Vincenzo Scapitta, Michelangelo Brunerio, Aldebrando Subissati) and from Poland (among others Adam Jarzębski, Marcin Mielczewski and Bartłomiej Pękiel, as well as musicians from Gdańsk: the young Christoph Bernhard, whom Förster was to meet in Germany many years later, and possibly Christoph Werner, another participant in the dispute between Scacchi and Siefert).

In 1652 – according to Mattheson – he traveled to Italy, from where he made a journey to Copenhagen. During the years 1652-57 and 1661-67, Förster served as *maestro di cappella* to King Frederick III of Denmark, but continued to travel. In Gdańsk, he served as the temporary *Kapellmeister* at St Mary's Basilica in 1654 and probably held this position during the years 1656-57, traveling between Copenhagen and Gdańsk[37]. (It seems that not by accident Crato Bütner, a cantor at the St Salvator church started copying music of Italian and other musicians active at the Polish royal court, when Kaspar Förster the Younger was present in Gdańsk, and that the first part of music copied in Gdańsk found its way to Stockholm, to the Düben Collection).

Förster spent the years 1658-60 in Venice (taking part in the war between Venice and Turkey) and in Rome (where he once again met Carissimi and resumed their collaboration in 1660).[38] Also, he visited German cities such as Hamburg (in 1667, encounters with Christoph Bernhard, Samuel Peter von Sidon, and probably with Matthias Weckmann), possibly Dresden and Weissenfels (it is hypothesized that he met Heinrich Schütz there). At the court of Frederick III, Förster entered into collaboration with musicians from Denmark (and from Scandinavia in general), from Gdańsk, Germany, France and Italy; he also supervised the musical education of Johann Krieger; however, in all probability, he did not meet Dietrich Buxtehude.

36 Przybyszewska-Jarmińska, 1987, pp. 8-12.
37 Archival research in these two cities is still in progress. I am grateful for all source information to Bjarke Moe and Jerzy Michalak.
38 Culley, 1970, p. 245.

It is possible that, after leaving the Danish court and a journey to Dresden in 1667, Förster made a trip to Cracow to attend in September of that year the funeral of Queen consort Marie Louise Gonzaga de Nevers, the wife of two Polish Vasa kings: Władysław IV and his successor, Jan II Kazimierz (according to an extant account former members of the royal ensemble arrived from various countries to attend the ceremony).[39]

He spent the last years in Gdańsk and nearby Oliwa (he lived with his widowed sister Barbara Helwig, but probably not in his own house – as wrote Mattheson – but as a guest of the Cistercians).[40] In Gdańsk, he could have been in contact with local musicians, such as Daniel Jacobi, Crato Bütner, Balthasar Erben, Thomas Strutius and Heinrich Döbel. He died on 2 February 1673 and was buried in the Cistercian convent in Oliwa.[41]

Kaspar Förster's preserved musical legacy consists of 48 compositions. They are mainly vocal-instrumental church concertos as well as Latin dialogues and instrumental sonatas, preserved in the form of manuscript copies made by Gustav Düben at the Swedish royal court in Stockholm and manuscripts from Gdańsk collected by him (most of them bearing the signature BEFASTRU whose meaning remains unexplained). Today, they are part of the Düben Collection in Uppsala.[42] A few compositions have another manuscript copies kept in the music collections of Berlin and Dresden.[43] The interest in Förster's life and work shown by researchers from many countries gives hope that new biographical data emerges or previously unverified data finds confirmation, and that we shall be able to enter new or confirmed information into the MusMig database.

---

39   PRZYBYSZEWSKA-JARMIŃSKA, 2007, p. 134.
40   MICHALAK, 2004, pp. 208, 213.
41   SNYDER/BERGLUND, 2001, p. 106.
42   PRZYBYSZEWSKA-JARMIŃSKA, 1987b; DCDC.
43   PRZYBYSZEWSKA-JARMIŃSKA, 1987b, pp. 21-23, 33-34, 44.

Figure 1: Part of a map of Europe in 1648 with the most important cities for Kaspar Förster the Younger's biography underlined

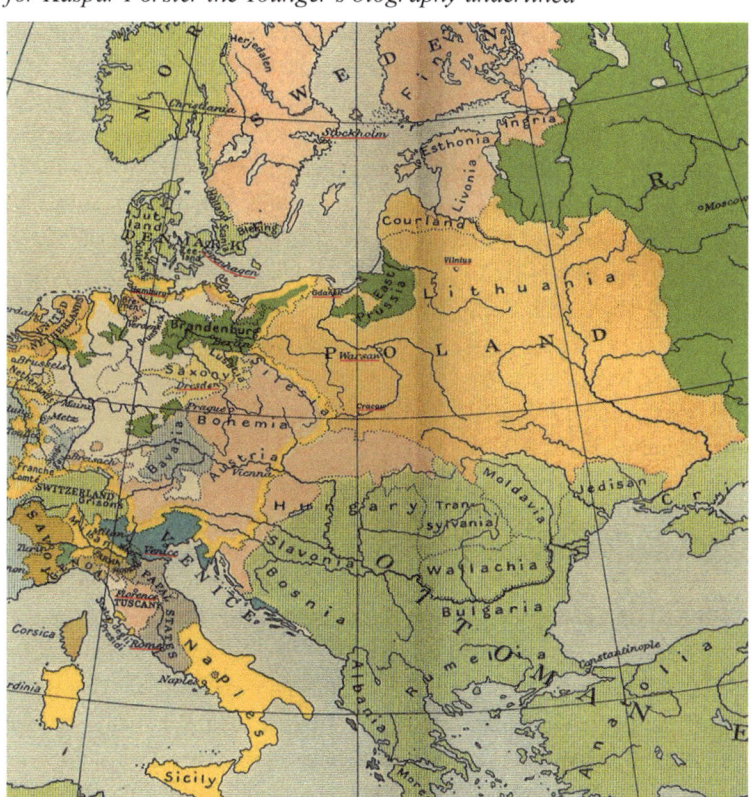

Literature

BAAB, JERROLD, The Sacred Latin Works of Kaspar Förster (1616-73), PhD University of North Carolina, Chapel Hill 1970.

BERGLUND, LARS, Kaspar Förster d.y. och 1600-talets sonata a 3 [Kaspar Förster the Youger and 17th century "sonata a 3"], Uppsala 1994.

ID., On Style and Tradition in the Sonatas by Kaspar Förster, in: Polish-Swedish Cultural Relations During the Vasa Dynasty, Stockholm,

February 10th-12th 1995 Conference Papers, ed. by TADEUSZ MACIEJEWSKI, Warsaw 1996, pp. 89-94.

BIZZARINI, MARCO, Marenzio. La carriera di un musicista tra Rinascimento e Controriforma, Rodengo Saiano 1998.

ID., Da Brescia a Varsavia. Le musiche policorali di Pietro Lappi con dedica a Sigismondo III (1605), in: La musica policorale in Italia e nell'Europa centro-orientale fra Cinque e Seicento/Polychoral Music in Italy and in Central-Eastern Europe at the Turn of the Seventeenth Century, ed. by ALEKSANDRA PATALAS/MARINA TOFFETTI, Venice 2012, pp. 199-213.

DCDC = The Düben Collection Database Catalogue, ed. by LARS BERGLUND et al., http://www2.musik.uu.se/duben/Duben.php, 08.07.2016.

CROSATTI, REMO, Musicam docet amor. Il musicista bresciano Paris Francesco Alghisi (1666-1733) e l'epistolario con madre Maria Arcangela Biondini, Brescia 2009.

CZAPLIŃSKI, WŁADYSŁAW, Przyczynki do dziejów mecenatu artystycznego Zygmunta III [Contributions to the history of the patronage of the arts bestowed by Zygmunt III], in: Sarmatia Artistica. Księga pamiątkowa ku czci prof. Władysława Tomkiewicza [Sarmatia artistica. A commemorative book in honor of Prof. Władysław Tomkiewicz], Warsaw 1968, pp. 95-100.

FEDERHOFER, HELLMUT, Musikalische Beziehungen zwischen den Höfen Erzherzog Ferdinands von Innerösterreich und König Sigismunds III. von Polen, in: The Book of the First International Musicological Congress Devoted to the Works of Frederick Chopin, Warsaw 1960, ed. by ZOFIA LISSA, Warsaw 1963, pp. 522-526.

ID., Musikpflege und Musiker am Grazer Habsburgerhof der Erzherzöge Karl und Ferdinand von Innerösterreich (1564-1619), Mainz 1967.

FEICHT, HIERONIM, Musikalische Beziehungen zwischen Österreich und Altpolen und Grazer Beiträge zur Polnischen Musikgeschichte, in: Festschrift der Akademie für Musik und darstellende Kunst in Graz, ed. by ERICH MRCKHL, Graz 1963, pp. 121-128.

GROCHOWSKA, KATARZYNA, From Milan to Gdansk: The Story of A Dedication, in: Polish Music Journal, 5/1 (2002), www.usc.edu/dept/polish_music/PMJ/issues.html, 08.07.2016.

HAMMERICH, ANGUL/ELLING, CATHARINUS, Die Musik am Hofe Christian's IV. von Dänemark, in: Vierteljahrsschrift für Musikwissenschaft 9 (1893), pp. 62-98.

Lewański, Julian, Świadkowie i świadectwa opery Władysławowskiej [Witnesses and accounts of the opera of Władysław IV], in: Opera w dawnej Polsce na dworze Władysława IV i królów saskich [Opera in Poland at the court of Władysław IV and the Saxon kings], ed. by Julian Lewański, Wrocław 1973, pp. 25-60.

Mattheson, Johann, Grundlage einer Ehren=Pforte, Hamburg 1740, new edition, ed. by Max Schneider, Kassel 1969.

Michalak, Jerzy M., Zwischen Kunst und Alltag. Caspar Förster der Ältere, seine Familie und Verwandtschaft, in: Musica Baltica. Im Umkreis des Wandels – von den "cori spezzati" zum konzertierenden Stil, ed. by Danuta Szlagowska, Gdańsk 2004, pp. 205-212.

Id., Od Förstera do Frühlinga. Przyczynki do dziejów życia muzycznego i teatralnego dawnego Gdańska [From Förster to Frühling. Contributions to the history of musical and theatrical life in old Gdansk] (Kultura Muzyczna Północnych Ziem Polski [The musical culture of the northern territories of Poland] 12), Gdańsk 2009.

Patalas, Aleksandra, W kościele, w komnacie i w teatrze. Marco Scacchi. Życie, muzyka, teoria [In church, chamber and theater. Marco Scacchi: his life, music and theory], Cracow 2010.

Pirro, André, Dietrich Buxtehude, Paris 1913.

Przybyszewska-Jarmińska, Barbara, Kacper Förster junior. Zarys biorafii [Kacper Förster Junior. A biographical sketch], in: Muzyka 32/3 (1987), pp. 3-19.

Id., Katalog tematyczny utworów Kacpra Förstera jun. [A thematic catalogue of the works of Kaspar Förster the Younger], in: Muzyka 32/3 (1987), insert, pp. 3-82.

Id., Sonaty Kaspra Förstera Juniora [The sonatas of Kaspar Förster junior], in: Muzyka w Gdańsku wczoraj i dziś, ii [Music in Gdańsk past and present] (Kultura muzyczna północnych ziem Polski [The musical culture of the northern territories of Poland] 6), Gdańsk 1992, pp. 135-150.

Id., W poszukiwaniu dawnej świetności. Glosy do książki Anny i Zygmunta Szweykowskich "Włosi w kapeli królewskiej polskich Wazów" [In search of former splendour. Comments on the book by Anna Szweykowska and Zygmunt Szweykowski 'Italians in the Royal Chapel of the Polish Vasa Kings' (Cracow 1997)], in: Muzyka 43/2 (1998), pp. 91-115.

Id., Annibale Stabile i początki włoskiej kapeli Zygmunta III Wazy

[Annibale Stabile and the beginnings of the Italian *cappella* of Zygmunt III Vasa], in: Muzyka 46/2 (2001), pp. 93-99.

ID., The History of Music in Poland, iii: The Baroque, part 1: 1595-1696, trans. John Comber, Warsaw 2002.

ID., Włoskie wesela arcyksiążąt z Grazu a początki opery w Polsce [The Italian weddings of the archdukes of Graz and the beginnings of opera in Poland], in: Muzyka, 50/3 (2005), pp. 3-27.

ID., Muzyczne dwory polskich Wazów [The musical courts of the Polish Vasas], Warsaw 2007.

ID., The Role of Heinrich Schütz and Silesian Musicians in the Dissemination of the Repertoire of the Polish Royal Chapel Led by Marco Scacchi in Silesia, Saxony and Thuringia, in: Schütz-Jahrbuch 2010, pp. 17-28.

ID., Marcin Mielczewski and Music Under the Patronage of the Polish Vasas, trans. John Comber (Eastern European Studies in Musicology 3), ed. by MACIEJ GOŁĄB, Frankfurt a.M. 2014.

ID., The Music-Related Contacts of Polish Vasas' Royal Courts with Rome and Vienna, in: Poland and Artistic Culture of Western Europe. 14th-20th Century, ed. by ID./LECH SOKÓŁ (Polish Studies – Transdisciplinary Perspectives 6), Frankfurt a.M. 2014, pp. 157-203.

RAUSCHING, HERMANN, Geschichte der Musik und Musikpflege in Danzig: von den Anfängen bis zur Auflösung der Kirchenkapellen (Quellen und Darstellungen zur Geschichte Westpreußens 15), Gdańsk 1931.

SCHERING, ARNOLD, Geschichte des Oratoriums, Leipzig 1911, reprint Wiesbaden 1966.

SEIFERT, HERBERT, Polonica – Austriaca. Schlaglichter auf polnisch-österreichische Musikbeziehungen vom 17. bis ins 19. Jahrhundert, in: Muzyka wobec tradycji. Idee – dzieło – recepcja [Music and tradition. Ideas – work – reception], ed. by SZYMON PACZKOWSKI, Warsaw 2004, pp. 249-258.

SNYDER, KERALA J., Bernhard, Christoph, in: The New Grove Dictionary of Music and Musicians, vol. 3, 2nd ed., ed. by STANLEY SADIE, London 2001, pp. 438-440.

ID./BERGLUND, LARS, Förster, Kaspar, in: The New Grove Dictionary of Music and Musicians, vol. 9, 2nd ed., ed. by STANLEY SADIE, London 2001, pp. 106-107.

SØRENSEN, SØREN, L'eredità monteverdiana nella musica sacra del Nord. Monteverdi – Foerster – Buxtehude, in: Rivista Italiana di Musicologia 2/2 (1967), pp. 341-355.

SZWEYKOWSKA, ANNA/SZWEYKOWSKI, ZYGMUNT M., Włosi w kapeli królewskiej polskich Wazów [Italians in the royal chapel of the Polish Vasas], Cracow 1997.

THRANE, CARL, Fra Hofviolonernes Tid: Skildringer af Det Kongelige Kapels Historie 1648-1848, væsentlig efter utrykte Kilder [From Hofviolonernes time. Sketch of the royal orchestra's history 1648-1848, significant for unprinted sources], Copenhagen 1908.

WALTHER, JOHANN GOTTFRIED, Musicalisches Lexicon oder Musicalische Bibliothek, Leipzig 1732, new edition, ed. by FRIEDERIKE RAMM, Kassel et al. 2001.

WARNECKE, BERTHOLD, Kaspar Förster der Jüngere (1616-1673) und die europäische Stilvielfalt im 17. Jahrhundert, Schneverdingen 2004.

Foreign Musicians at the Polish Court in the Eighteenth Century
The Case of Pietro Mira

ALINA ŻÓRAWSKA-WITKOWSKA

1. Foreign musicians at the Polish court

Let me begin with a clarification: the term "Polish court" refers to the royal court of Poland, and "musicians" denotes, according to the premise of our project (*Music Migrations*), all professions connected to music, with special regard to people commonly referred to as musicians: instrumentalists, composers and singers.

In the course of the eighteenth century three monarchs occupied the Polish throne, each ruling for roughly 30 years. They were two Saxon electors: Friedrich August I, who reigned over Poland as August II (1697-1704, 1709-33), and Friedrich August II, king of Poland under the name of August III (1734-63), as well as the Pole Stanisław August Poniatowski (reigned 1764-95). The organization of musical and theatrical personnel was similar for the two Saxon kings and consisted of concentrating the leading ensembles in Dresden: the *Königliche Capelle*, *la Danse*, *Hof-Trompeter und Pauker* and *Bockpfeifer*. In Warsaw the Saxon kings used ensembles selected *al fresco* from the Dresden ones, supplementing them with various Polish forces, predominantly the royal *Pohlnische Capelle* but also members of ensembles in the service of various churches and grandees, as well as the *comici italiani* and janissary band (in the case of August II) financed by the Polish exchequer.[1] Unlike the Saxon kings, Stanisław August Poniatowski had no need to share his artists with Saxony, but introduced in the 1770s a formal division of his personnel into ensembles financed by the royal treasury – orchestra and ballet – and those hired by impresarios in charge of the public theater, although the king remained a major sponsor of the latter.[2]

The musical patronage of each of those three monarchs was of course different – a fact linked to the significant political, economic and social upheavals in Europe at that time, as well as to major changes in the style of eighteenth-century music. The patronage of August II and August III was limited to courtly milieus, although the second king did in fact open his theater to citizens of the Commonwealth. Stanisław August Poniatowski, on the other hand, introduced a state patronage that encompassed the entire country. The reign of August II coincided with the twilight of the Baroque, and remained under the influence of the dominant French culture, whereas August III was fascinated by *opera seria* and by Italian music, which was witnessing an intense development of the *galant* style. Finally, Stanisław August Poniatowski's reign was contemporary with the emergence and maturity of the classical style, which originated in Vienna. Consequently, the choice of artists for the Polish court evolved over time, although it was consistently reliant on foreigners; it was only during the period of Stanisław August Poniatowski that Polish and "polonized" musicians also came into prominence.

August II

August II began his reign by directing his highest ambitions as a patron towards the Polish-Lithuanian Commonwealth. Hence his first Polish *Kapelle* was designed as an ensemble shared by Dresden and Warsaw, even though it primarily served the needs of the Polish court (1697-1703/04). At the height of its development it numbered over forty musicians of different nationalities and provenances, and was constituted after the French model. The dominant nationality was German, represented by instrumentalists from the former electoral *Kapelle* in Dresden; a dozen or so musicians, mostly Italian and Polish singers, had belonged to the *Ka-*

---

1 ŻÓRAWSKA-WITKOWSKA, 1997; ŻÓRAWSKA-WITKOWSKA, 2011b; ŻÓRAWSKA-WITKOWSKA, 2012b.
2 ŻÓRAWSKA-WITKOWSKA, 1995b.

pelle of the previous king of Poland, Jan III Sobieski; oboists came from Vienna, while several musicians migrated from the Wawel cathedral *Kapelle* in Cracow. August II's first *Pohlnische Kapelle* was headed by two kapellmeisters: the Pole Jacek Różycki and the German Johann Christoph Schmidt. In Warsaw it played during performances of French opera with an ensemble of sixty musicians assembled in Paris and led by Louis Deseschaliers (1700-03), as well as accompanying performances of French comedy given by the ensembles of Denis Nanteuil (1699) and Jean de Fonpré (1700-03) and by the *comici italiani* of Gennaro Sacco (1699). August II's second Polish *Kapelle*, active between 1716 and 1733, consisted of a mere 12-15 instrumentalists recruited from Germany. Its members later won great renown, examples being the flautist Johann Joachim Quantz and the violinists František (Franz) Benda and Jiří Čart. Depending on what repertoire was presented at any given time in Warsaw by the royal and electoral theatrical ensembles – i.e., either by Tommaso Ristori's *comici italiani* (1716-33) or by the French comedy and ballet (1715-33) – the *Kapelle* was directed alternately by two composers: Giovanni Alberto Ristori and Louis André. Through the activity of those artists Warsaw became one of the first centers outside Italy to cultivate the genre of comic intermezzi as early as 1716, as well as presenting *tragédies lyriques*, French cantatas and forward-looking ballets anticipating the genre known as the *ballet d'action*: these were performed in 1724-26 by leading dancers such as Jean Favier, Louis Dupré and Louise de Vaurenville under the musical direction of the Dresden *Kapellmeister* Jean-Baptiste Woulmier.

August II's *comici italiani* also left their mark on the court culture of Empress Anna Ivanovna in Moscow, where they were on loan for the year 1731. During that time they gave a number of *commedia dell'arte* performances, as well as staging the first-ever Italian opera in Russia: a *commedia in musica* entitled *Calandro*, which was on a libretto by Stefano Benedetto Pallavicini and with music by G.A. Ristori.

The Polish court of August II also retained a German-staffed ensemble of *Hoftrompeter und Paucker* and *Bockpfeiffer*, plus a janissary band modelled on Turkish ensembles, which was composed of musicians with Polish-sounding names, though these could well have included "polonized" (and converted) Turks.

In sum, my research to date has linked around 310 instrumentalists, singers, actors and dancers, originating primarily from Germany, France and Italy, to the Polish court of August II.

August III

This monarch's reign brought with it a major change of musical influence in the direction of the *opera seria*, which was dominant practically all over Europe. The one remaining area of French influence at the court of August III was the ballet, which for nearly twenty years was directed by the outstanding dancer and choreographer Antoine Pitrot. But even this dance company included an increasing number of Italian and German artists. Germans (mostly Saxons) continued to dominate the new *Pohlnische Capelle*, enlarged to around 30 musicians, which also at last included some actual Polish artists: the singers Stefan Jaroszewicz and Józef Sękowski (who did not perform in the theater), the organist Józef Czanczik, the oboist Dominik Jaziomski and the violinist Antoni Kossołowski or Kozłowski. On various occasions, members of the Dresden *Hofkapelle*, especially singers, helped out – Domenico Annibali, Ventura Rochetti, Pasquale Bruscolini, Bartolomeo Puttini, Teresa Albuzzi-Todeschini, and Caterina Pilaja – and, more rarely, also instrumentalists including the violinist Johann Georg Pisendel.[3]

In the years 1735-54 the presence in Warsaw of Italian singers and their far less numerous German colleagues was linked primarily to the performance at court of many "occasional" serenatas composed by Giovanni Alberto Ristori and Johann Michael Breunich, musicians who belonged to the Dresden-based *Königliche Capell- und Cammer-Musique*. Between 1754 and 1763 the royal and electoral singers, reinforced during the Seven Years' War by additional singers such as Elizabeth Teuber and Giuseppe Gallieni, gave a total of 124 operatic performances at the Warsaw theater, presenting eleven *drammi per musica* with music composed by the court's *Oberkapellmeister*, Johann Adolf Hasse. In order to prepare the Warsaw premieres of his works Hasse came to Poland at least five times from Dresden, Naples or Vienna.[4]

Until 1754 the *comici italiani* played a major role at the Warsaw theater, presenting the newest Venetian repertoire, mostly based on literary comedies, including plays by Carlo Goldoni. This ensemble boasted several talented vocalists, including Giovanna Casanova, who

---

3 Concerning the travels of musicians between Dresden and Warsaw, see also ŻÓRAWSKA-WITKOWSKA, 2009.
4 See ŻÓRAWSKA-WITKOWSKA, 1995a; ŻÓRAWSKA-WITKOWSKA, 2012a.

contributed to the performance in Warsaw of two works in a rare genre: *opera seria* parody.[5]

The *Pohlnische Capelle* of August III was closely linked to the *Kapelle* of his prime minister Heinrich von Brühl, which included German musicians, some of them outstanding: the *Kapellmeister* Gottlob Harrer and Georg Gebel, the violinist Christian Friedrich Horn, the harpsichordist Johann Gottlieb Goldberg and the oboist Johann Christian Fischer.[6]

The sojourns of August III in Warsaw continued to be accompanied by the royal-electoral ensembles of *Hof-Trompeter und Pauker* and *Bockpfeifer*.

In total, I have documented the presence at the Polish court of August III of around 320 artists active in music and the theater, the vast majority being foreigners.

Stanisław August Poniatowski

This monarch differed significantly from his Saxon predecessors. A leading exponent of the Enlightenment, he chose to exercise his cultural and social influence in the Commonwealth, a backward country in many aspects, through the Warsaw theater, which he made fully public, albeit, as already mentioned, heavily subsidized by the royal exchequer. Many important social reforms planned by Stanisław August were propagated from the stage, notably in the libretti of Polish operas (1778-94). Moreover, the theater also presented a wide spectrum of European operatic repertoire, hosting Italian, French, German and Polish ensembles. In the years of its operation, 1765-67 and 1774-94, it presented a number of Polish and international premieres of works that remain historically important. Italian singers active in Warsaw included such leading virtuosi as Caterina Ristorini, Caterina Bonafini, Anna Davia de Bernucci, Giovanni Battista Brocchi, Luigi Marchesi, Brigida Banti and Adriana Ferraresi Del Bene, as well as the first performers of the principal roles in Mozart's *Il dissoluto punito, ossia Il Don Giovanni* (Warsaw 1789): Antonio Baglioni, Luigi Bassi, Felice Ponziani and Caterina Micelli.[7] French singers included Victoire Clavareau and Antoinette Saint-Huber-

---

5   ŻÓRAWSKA-WITKOWSKA, 2007c.
6   KOLLMAR, 2006; ŻÓRAWSKA-WITKOWSKA, 2012b.
7   ŻÓRAWSKA-WITKOWSKA, 2011a.

ty, for whom Christoph Willibald Gluck created several operatic roles in *Orfeo ed Euridice* (Vienna 1762) and *Armide* (Paris 1787). Particular prominent was the presence in Warsaw of German singers, who, while lacking such stellar performers as those mentioned above, certainly presented a worthwhile repertoire that included the major singspiels of Mozart: *Die Entführung aus dem Serail* (Warsaw 1783) and *Die Zauberflöte* (Warsaw 1793).

Stanisław August Poniatowski was particularly fond of ballet, hence the staging at the Warsaw theater of numerous works of this kind, which were performed by over 90 foreign dancers, who included such leading virtuosi as Charles Picque (or Le Picq), Anna Binetti, Apollino Baldassare Vestris, Domenico Ricciardi and François Gabriel Le Doux. Significantly, these artists passed on their skills to around 30 native-born dancers active at the theater.

In the years 1765-94 (with an interruption between spring 1767 and spring 1774, when the theater was not in action for political reasons) the Warsaw theater presented around 260 Italian, French, German and Polish operas, the vast majority belonging to comic genres (*opera buffa, opéra comique, Singspiel*, Polish opera). Additionally, well over 200 ballets (mostly *ballets d'action*) were staged. The operas were predominantly Italian, performed by singers who usually originated from Venice. The second musical center that inspired Stanisław August's patronage was Vienna. Founding his royal orchestra in 1765, he based it on German musicians inherited from the *Pohlnische Capelle* of August III, but later, in 1779, he enlisted a group of Czech musicians coming from Vienna, which was the city of origin of many other singers and dancers active in Warsaw. It was likewise in Vienna that the founders of Polish national opera, the Slovak Maciej Kamieński and the Czech Jan Stefani, developed their careers.[8]

In Stanisław August's Warsaw public concerts were regularly held, with the participation of outstanding virtuosi such as the violinists Antonio Lolli, Ivan Jarnović (Giovanni Giornovichi), Gaetano Pugnani and Giovanni Battista Viotti, the bassist Joseph Kämpfer, the flautist Jan Křtitel Vaňhal, the oboist Carlo Besozzi, the clarinettist Anton Stadler and the pianists Jan Ladislav Dussek (Dusík) and Joseph Wölffl. Warsaw's royal court was also a favourite port of call for leading composers during their concert tours, as shown by Giovanni Paisiello (1784), Do-

---

8   ŻÓRAWSKA-WITKOWSKA, 2007b.

menico Cimarosa (1787 and 1791) and Vicente Martín y Soler (1788). Further artists, such as the German Johann David Holland and the Italian Gioacchino Albertini, were active in the city and made significant contributions to Polish culture; both men were associated in addition with the court of the *Voivode* of Vilnius, prince Karol Radziwiłł, in Nesivizh (Nieśwież, in present-day Belarus).

In total, the court of Stanisław August and the public theater in Warsaw witnessed the participation of around 570 Italian, German, French, Czech and Polish artists.

On the basis of the above-quoted numbers, it may be assumed that around a thousand foreign composers, instrumentalists, singers, dancers, copyists, impresarios and so forth were active at the Polish court in the course of the eighteenth century. Their migrations resulted not only from the inherent international mobility of artists, which increased in the second half of the century, but also from the court's alternation between Saxony and Poland and the consequent transit of personnel between Dresden and Warsaw. During the period of the Seven Years' War, which August III was forced to spend in Warsaw, many of his Dresden-based artists were granted leave of absence and spent that time developing their skills and careers in Venice, Naples, Vienna and Paris, except when summoned to Warsaw to serve the king. In contrast, during the reign of Stanisław August Poniatowski decisions made by artists increasingly became subject to the capitalist laws of the market. The presence of so many musicians, singers, dancers and composers in Warsaw suggests that the local court remained attractive with regard to both financial gain and prestige.

The above-quoted numbers place Warsaw amongst the leading eighteenth-century musical centers in Europe, a fact that has hitherto not been sufficiently emphasized in international musicology. Those statistics also produce an embarrassment of riches, bringing about a need to select for our projects those particular artists who merit inclusion in the developing database. The main criteria for such selection are the following: (1) the European significance of an artist: it will often prove possible to – at least partly – fill in the gaps in their biographies (gaps that persist even in the latest editions of the leading musical encyclopaedias); (2) the importance for Polish culture, in the case of "polonized" foreigners whose activity and art have contributed to the heritage of Polish music. Nonetheless, it may also prove worthwhile to include at least some artists known exclusively from their activity at the Polish court in the hope that the developing web of relationships will eventually allow us to augment their biographies with new facts. Of course, each name potentially harbors a more or less interesting biography that is today worth recounting to a varying extent (though sometimes perhaps not worth recounting at all).

For the time being, I have chosen Pietro Mira as the object of a case study, since he is a "special" character: certainly not the most prominent one, but one who is eminently interesting, possessing a number of musical and extra-musical talents – a person who functioned successfully in several countries and milieus, a fact that makes him a highly suitable artist to be featured in our *Music Migrations* project.

2. Pietro Mira, known as Petrillo (Pedrillo)

Pietro Mira was active in several areas of music: as a violinist, composer, singer, actor and impresario; but he was also successful outside the musical sphere as a jester, moneylender and innkeeper. Moreover, he appears to have undertaken various "special tasks", as suggested by the extraordinary favors granted to him by Central and Eastern European monarchs as well as by his intimacy with the leading artists of music and theater in Western Europe at that time.

Pietro Mira is hardly unknown to historians, but his life has been documented only partially and with many gaps. He has been particularly well regarded by students of Russian music, since it was in Russia that this "ruthless braggart" had a "stunning and particularly eventful career", according to Robert-Aloys Mooser.[9] It was Mooser who painted the most vivid pen-portrait of Mira – although one limited to the Russian court – rightly pointing out that his life would make an attractive biographical novel.[10] Also Leonid Mironovich Butir and Anna Leonidovna Porfireva devoted much attention to Mira, overestimating his role as a leading Italian violinist of his time,[11] although Jacob von Stählin, too, viewed him as an outstanding violinist during his Russian period.[12] Mira is also mentioned – to a limited extent and not always

---

9   Mooser, 1948, pp. 105-109.
10 Mooser, 1942, pp. 273-293; Mooser, 1948.
11 Butir/Porfireva, 1998, pp. 210-213.
12 Stählin, 1770, p. 84: "Petro [sic] Mira, Petrillo genannt, der […] sich

with factual accuracy – by some other authors, who include Ernst Ludwig Gerber, Moritz Fürstenau, Robert Eitner, Nikolai Findeizen, Ortrun Landmann, Marina Ritzarev and Anna Porfireva,[13] as well as some untrustworthy websites.[14] The Polish strands in Mira's career have been discussed in the writings of Karyna Wierzbicka-Michalska and myself.[15] The intention of the present case study is to assemble existing knowledge about Mira's career, paying special attention to facts that have not been presented before in an international context.

Pietro Mira is said to have been born the son of a poor sculptor in Monte Scaglioso near Naples at the turn of the 1710s and 1720s, and named Pietro or Adamo or Pietro Adamo Pedrillo. We do not know the circumstances in which he adopted his later surname, Mira. From December 1725 he was a member of the *Cappella palatina* in Lucca, from which he was dismissed in 1733, apparently on the grounds of promiscuity. Yet the Russian imperial court recorded his arrival from Italy in St Petersburg as early as summer 1732. Either Mira went to Russia without waiting for his official dismissal from Lucca in order to avoid the consequences of his immoral behavior, or he realized that Italy offered him no opportunity to rise above the many other talented musicians in that country. Whatever the circumstances, he took his chances and sought his fortune in a distant, exotic country in which Italian music was only just starting to gain ground. At that very time the young Empress Anna Ivanovna wished to deepen her links with Italian culture after playing host to the Polish King August II's *comici italiani* at the Moscow court in 1731. She was assisted significantly in that endeavor by Mira, who between 1733 and 1740 worked at the imperial court as a violinist, with an annual salary of 700 roubles. He additionally appeared as a singer in comic intermezzi and as an actor in the performances given in 1734 by

---

durch die erste Hofnarren-Stelle bekannter gemacht hat, als durch die erste Violin, die er sonst ungemein wol [sic] gespielt hatte."

13 GERBER, 1813 (Pedrillo); FÜRSTENAU, 1862, p. 246; EITNER, 1902; FINDEIZEN, 2008, pp. 16ff.; LANDMANN, 1972; RITZAREV/PORFIREVA, 2001, pp. 214-216; RITZAREV, 2006, p. 39.
14 htpp://aarticles.net/culture-art-history/12286-kak-italyanskij-komik-, 19.11.2015.
15 WIERZBICKA-MICHALSKA, 1975, pp. 119-121; ŻÓRAWSKA-WITKOWSKA, 2012b, pp. 330-337; other publications by ŻÓRAWSKA-WITKOWSKA listed below.

an Italian *commedia dell'arte* troupe. The empress soon recognized the extra-musical talents of Mira, sending him at the turn of 1734 and 1735 to Italy with the task of recruiting an Italian operatic ensemble, a company of *comici italiani* and an instrumental ensemble.

In performing that task Mira gave proof of his great understanding of the Italian musical market. He managed to engage over 30 outstanding singers, actors (including Giovanna Casanova, Antonio Costantini, Francesco Ermano, Antonio Piva and Bernardo and Isabella Vulcani, who later served August III), dancers, stage designers, technicians and musicians, led by their *maestro di cappella* Francesco Araja. The artists assembled in Venice before leaving for St Petersburg, where they arrived in summer 1735. From that moment the city emerged as one of Europe's leading musical centers, as Russian music historians emphasize. Mira earned Anna Ivanovna's particular recognition and in 1736 received the title of court jester (apparently, a promotion from his former position as a violinist); in that role he may have become the prototype for Petrushka, the Russian theatrical puppet. The empress, who enjoyed earthy humour, even established the mock order of San Benedetto, of which Mira was made a "knight". Jests attributed to Mira were published in Moscow in 1836, and in St Petersburg in 1871.[16]

Mira's talent for the violin is attested primarily by a manuscript collection of his violin compositions, *Zabavnaya shtuky dlya skripochki ssotchinenye issvestnovo shouta/Pedrillo* [Amusing pieces for violin composed by the famous jester Pedrillo], brought to light by Mooser. This is a series of brief, humorous variations full of technical intricacies such as double and triple stopping, abrupt shifts of position, left-hand pizzicato and so forth. Mira played such compositions in order to lighten the mood of the empress, embellishing them with comic visual effects.[17]

In the Russian documentation analyzed by Mooser Mira appears not only as a talented artist but also as a canny, enterprising, cynical, almost impertinent individual, resourceful in finding profit and greedy for both legal and illegal gains (via bribery, usury or pimping). As a favorite of Empress Anna Ivanovna of Russia and her fellow grandees, Mira is said to have amassed more than 20,000 roubles during the nine years of his activity at the imperial court! No wonder that after Anna Ivanovna's death on 28 October 1740 the universally loathed Mira asked to be re-

---

16 MOOSER, 1948, p. 110.
17 MOOSER, 1948, p. 106.

leased from imperial service on 28 December; his request was granted. He then went to Italy, where he lived for some time in Venice, appearing during the winter of 1745/46 at the Teatro San Moisè in comic intermezzi with music by Johann Adolf Hasse, the *Kapellmeister* of August III, king of Poland and elector of Saxony.[18]

Still in 1746, Mira found employment at August's court, perhaps thanks to a recommendation from Hasse or through his earlier links to the court of Anna Ivanovna, who had given military support to the Saxon Elector Friedrich August II in his claim to the Polish crown. At all events, at the Polish-Saxon court Mira served primarily as a jester, receiving the title – most likely facetious – of *Hof Commisario*.[19] He also appeared occasionally, as he had done earlier at the Russian court, as a singer and actor attached to the royal company of *comici italiani*. In 1746 and 1747 he appeared in Dresden in the performance of Johann Adolf Hasse's comic intermezzo *Don Tabarrano*.[20] On 7 October 1746 he sang in Warsaw, probably in the serenata *La liberalità di Numa Pompilio*, with music by Giovanni Alberto Ristori;[21] on 3 August 1748 he played in the *commedia dell'arte* piece *Gli torti imaginari*, which inaugurated the Warsaw opera house.[22] Later, on 4 November of that year, he could also be heard in the *dramma per musica* entitled *Le contese di Mestre e Malghera per il trono*, an *opera seria* parody staged by the *comici italiani* and based on a libretto by Antonio Gori adapted for the Polish court by Giovanna Casanova, with music by Salvatore Apollini.[23] The role of Bottenigo, which Mira took, is notated in the score in the tenor clef. By December 1748 Mira was back in Dresden.[24]

---

18 SELFRIDGE-FIELD, 2007, p. 592.
19 D-Dla, Geheimnis Cabinett, Loc. 907, vol. 3, 19 July 1747 notes that *Hof Commisario* Mira received a fee of 172 thalers.
20 FÜRSTENAU, 1862; SARTORI, 1990-94, nos. 8187, 8188.
21 D-Dla, OHMA I 114, k. 50, 103; ŻÓRAWSKA-WITKOWSKA, 2007a.
22 D-Dla, Nachlass Maria Antonia Nr. 16, letter of August III to Maria Antonia, Warsaw 7 August 1748.
23 D-Dla, OHMA I Nr. 120, k. 57, 90, Nachlass Maria Antonia Nr. 70a, letter of Heinrich von Brühl to Maria Antonia, Warsaw 30 October 1748; ŻÓRAWSKA-WITKOWSKA, 2007c.
24 D-Dla, Nachlass Friedrich Christian, Nr. 4c, letters of Maria Josepha to Friedrich Christian, Warsaw 28 December 1748 and Warsaw 15 January 1749.

In 1750 as well as in 1758-62 (i.e., during the Seven Years' War) Pietro Mira accompanied August III to Poland.[25] He took part in the king's hunts, and on the occasion of the monarch's name-day festivities (3 August 1758, 1759, 1760, 1761 and 1762) he performed comic scenes, reciting humorous poems and accompanying himself on the violin. A beautiful color illustration representing Mira during one of those shows (1759) has survived. The subject sits on a wooden donkey and plays a violin solo from a score held in front of him by Death depicted as a skeleton, while Mira also recites a satirical German-Italian poem.[26] Presumably, that performance and similar ones in Warsaw were inspired by Mira's jokes so warmly received at the Russian court.

In 1759, Mira was joined in Warsaw by his son, a top-tier physician in the Russian army.[27]

In mid-December 1762, thus just before the anticipated end of the Seven Years' War, Pietro Mira left Warsaw for Italy, where he attended to matters concerning inheritance arising from his wife's death and – as the prime minister of the Saxon court, Heinrich von Brühl, joked – looked for a new spouse.[28] In three letters sent at that time from Bologna, probably to Brühl, Mira reported on the preparations for the opening of the Nuovo Teatro Pubblico and the staging of Christoph Willibald Gluck's specially composed *opera seria* entitled *Il trionfo di Clelia*. On 17 April Mira wrote that Gluck "is fine, he studies, but he drinks like a devil, he stays with me, I had brought some boxes of wine from Florence, and he has drunken all of them".[29] Mira also reported that Farinelli, embarrassed by Brühl's benevolence, would continue to serve him (but we do

25   D-Dla: OHMA I Nr. 128, k. 32, 94, OHMA I Nr. 152, k. 212, 227, 232, OHMA I Nr. 163, k. nlb, OHMA II Nr. 1, *passim*, OHMA T III Nr. 35, k. 35, 60; Nachlass Maria Antonia Nr. 17, letter of queen Maria Josepha to Maria Antonia, Warsaw 8 July 1750.

26   D-Dla, OHMA I Nr. 152, fol. 226, reproduced in Żórawska-Witkowska, 2012b, pp. 331f, see there also for other depictions that are probably of Mira (OHMA I Nr. 152, fol. 175, 279, OHMA I Nr. 163).

27   D-Dla, Nachlass Friedrich Christian Nr. 240, Joseph Anton Gabaleon von Wackerbarth-Salmour to Friedrich Christian, Warsaw 14 April 1759.

28   D-Dla, Nachlass Maria Antonia Nr. 70 n, Heinrich von Brühl to Maria Antonia, Warsaw 15 December 1762.

29   "sta bene, studia, ma beve da diavolo, sta con me, ho fatto venire delle casse di vino da Firenze, e lui tutte mi le beve". D-Dla, Geheimnis Cabinett, Loc. 380, Mira à Bologna 1763.

not know in what capacity).³⁰ On 27 April, with reference to the premiere of the Gluck opera being prepared in Bologna, Mira assured the letter's recipient (probably expressing a generally held expectation): "you will see a spectacle that has never been seen in the whole world and that will leave the audience slack-jawed for its marvel".³¹ On 12 June 1763 Mira not only sent Brühl the poster for the opera's premiere, but also informed him that the work had met with disfavor in Bologna – even the replacement of Gluck's original arias with ones by composers better liked in Italy had not helped. He concluded: "here we do not want opere serie, but buffe", although he diplomatically added: "the Dresden opera will be at its peak".³² Mira also announced his imminent arrival in the Saxon capital, but after a short stay in Vienna, where he met Metastasio and handed him some messages from Farinelli,³³ he returned to Bologna.

Mira met Metastasio again in Vienna in January 1764, while *en route* for Dresden, where, following the end of the Seven Years' War and the deaths of August III and his all-powerful minister von Brühl, a substantial reorganization of the electoral court was underway. Metastasio reported on Mira's presence in Dresden to Farinelli: "After having been more than a spectator of the crowdy and tragic vicissitudes of poor Saxony, our amiable Pedrillo is passing our realms like a flash. He comes for breathing the air of bella Italia and for spending calmly the rest of his hitherto agitated days."³⁴ In February 1764 Mira was once more in Dresden (or perhaps he had never left the city?), following which he acted as an intermediary to deliver to Padre Martini, resident in Bologna, presents from the Saxon elector's widow, Maria Antonia Walpurgis: a china coffee and chocolate set plus a china inkwell.³⁵

---

30 IBID.
31 "si vedrà uno spettacolo mai più veduto al mondo, che farà restare a bocca aperta per meraviglia." IBID.
32 "non ci vogliamo qui opere serie, ma buffe [...] l'opera di Dresda sarà al non plus ultra." IBID.
33 METASTASIO, 1954, p. 296, Pietro Metastasio to Farinelli, Vienna 11 June 1763.
34 "Passa come un lampo per queste nostre contrade il nostro amabile Petrillo dopo essere stato più che spettatore delle affollate, tragiche peripezie della povera Sassonia. Ei viene a respirar l'aria della bella Italia, e a passar tranquillamente il resto de' sinora agitati suoi giorni". IBID., pp. 338f., Pietro Metastasio to Farinelli, Vienna 1 February 1764.
35 I-Bc, *Carteggio Giovanni Battista Martini*, I. 019.21.058, letter of Giovanni Lorenzo Bianconi to Giovanni Battista Martini, Dresden 13 February 1764.

Nonetheless, Mira did not lose his influence in Warsaw despite the anticipated change of occupant of the Polish throne. In early August 1764 – i.e., before his pending election as king of Poland (with military support from Empress Catherine II) – Stanisław August Poniatowski contacted Mira in Bologna. Initially when acting as secretary of the British ambassador, and subsequently as August III's ambassador in Russia (1755-58) and afterwards the lover of the future Empress Catherine, Poniatowski was well aware of the bygone meritorious services of Mira at the Russian court. Consequently, via the mediation of Gaetano Ghigiotti (who in 1760-62 was secretary of the Polish nuncio Antonio Eugenio Visconti, and from autumn 1764, royal secretary and head of the Italian chancellery), the future king entrusted Mira with the task of organizing, in view of his forthcoming coronation (which duly took place on 25 November 1764), an *opera buffa* company in Italy, the singer being earmarked as its director. Correspondence related to that project carried on from early August to late October 1764.[36] The company was eventually not formed, most likely because Mira's financial expectations and Stanisław August's limited resources at that time did not coincide, or perhaps there was simply not enough time to complete the task.

In May 1765 Mira and his young, newly wed wife passed again through Vienna (on their way to Dresden?), where he again met Metastasio. The latter wrote to Farinelli: "I saw passing like a flash our aged Petrillo with his juvenile wife and I admired this union."[37] On his return journey (from Dresden?), Mira once more profited from his presence in Vienna to meet Metastasio, who reported the fact to Farinelli on 31 October 1765.[38]

Another man named Pietro Mira, perhaps a child from Mira senior's second marriage, worked as a bass singer at the Teatro de' Fiorentini in Naples in the 1793-94 season.[39]

---

36 Pl-Wagad, Archivio Ghigiotti, 451, four letters of Pietro Mira to Gaetano Ghigiotti, Bologna 1764; see WIERZBICKA-MICHALSKA, 1975, pp. 119-121.

37 "Vidi come un lampo passaggiero il nostro annoso Petrillo con la sua giovanetta consorte ed ammirai l'innesto." METASTASIO, 1954, p. 392, letter of Pietro Metastasio to Farinelli, Vienna 31 May 1765.

38 IBID., p. 425, letter of Pietro Metastasio to Farinelli, Vienna, Vienna 31 October 1765.

39 YAMADA, 2012, p. 161.

Pietro Mira's last two, or maybe even three, decades were spent in Venice, where he was the proprietor of the "tavern at the Ponte dei Dai" ("locanda al Ponte dei Dai"). On 20 September 1775 a diplomatic dispatch to the imperial court mentioned "the tavern of Petrillo, small, but very clean" ("l'auberge de Petrillo, petite, mais très propre").[40] Mira lived in Venice and worked there as an innkeeper for what seems to have been another 30 years. In 1782 the fact was noted with surprise by the librarian of the Russian Grand Duke Pavel Petrovich (the later Tsar Paul I) who undertook a Grand Tour of Europe with his wife Maria Fyodorovna.[41] Mira was still running the locanda in 1788, as indicated by a brief report in the press: "Since the inn of Signor Petrillo at San Giovanni Grisostomo was not sufficient for the accomodation of the foreigners who came to him, he placed some in private houses."[42] Moreover, a press announcement in 1794 of the loss of a thoroughbred dog asked the founder to bring the pet "to the inn of Mr Petrillo and he will receive two sequins as a gratuity".[43] In the last-mentioned case, however, the expression "locanda di M. Petrillo" could perhaps have been used after the owner's death, which is not documented.

At all events, Mira's vitality is breathtaking, as are his readiness to undertake travel to distant locations (Lucca; St Petersburg; Venice; Warsaw to Dresden and back several times; Bologna; Dresden via Vienna; Bologna via Vienna; Dresden via Vienna; Venice via Vienna) and his ability to display different talents in different circumstances. He was an artist (violinist, singer and actor), impresario and *éminence grise* of the Russian and Saxon courts, whose expertise within the Italian operatic market was trusted by Stanisław August Poniatowski – a globe-trotter who maintained close ties with Gluck, Farinelli, Metastasio and perhaps also Padre Martini.

Nonetheless, Pietro Mira remains a mysterious and intriguing character. We must hope that new information emerges from the researches of

---

40 Mooser, 1942, p. 290.
41 Mooser, 1948, p. 109.
42 "Non essendo stata sufficiente la Locanda del signor Petrillo a S. Giovanni Grisostomo all'alloggio de' forastieri, che giunti sono da lui, egli ne dispose alcuni in abitazioni particolari". *Gazzetta urbana veneta*, 1788 no. 36, 3 May, 288.
43 "alla Locanda di M. Petrillo che gli saranno dati due zecchini di cortesia". *Gazzetta urbana veneta*, 1794 no. 47, 11 June, 376.

historians in their various sub-disciplines who are currently exploring a wealth of European archives with renewed zeal. Will their findings possibly change our general view of Mira as a person? Not necessarily.

Sources

D-Dla, Geheimnis Cabinett, Loc. 380, Mira à Bologna 1763.
D-Dla, Nachlass Maria Antonia Nr. 16, letter of Augustus III to Maria Antonia, Warsaw 7 August 1748.
D-Dla, OHMA I Nr. 114, k. 50, 103.
D-Dla, OHMA I Nr. 128, k. 32, 94, OHMA I Nr. 152, k. 212, 227, 232, OHMA I Nr. 163, k. nlb, OHMA II Nr. 1, passim, OHMA T III Nr. 35, k. 35, 60.
D-Dla, OHMA I Nr. 120, k. 57, 90, Nachlass Maria Antonia Nr. 70a, letter of Heinrich von Brühl to Maria Antonia, Warsaw 30 October 1748.
D-Dla, OHMA I Nr. 152, fol. 226.
D-Dla, Nachlass Friedrich Christian, Nr. 4c, letters of Maria Josepha to Frederick Christian, Warsaw, 28 December 1748, and Warsaw 15 January 1749.
D-Dla, Nachlass Friedrich Christian Nr. 240, Joseph Anton Gabaleon von Wackerbarth-Salmour to Frederick Christian, Warsaw 14 April 1759.
D-Dla, Nachlass Maria Antonia Nr. 17, letter of queen Maria Josepha to Maria Antonia, Warsaw 8 July 1750.
D-Dla, Nachlass Maria Antonia Nr. 70 n, Heinrich von Brühl to Maria Antonia, Warsaw 15 December 1762.
Gazzetta urbana veneta, 1788 no. 36, 3 May, 288.
Gazzetta urbana veneta, 1794 no. 47, 11 June, 376.
I-Bc, Carteggio Giovanni Battista Martini, I. 019.21.058.
Pl-Wagad, Archivio Ghigiotti, 451, four letters of Pietro Mira to Gaetano Ghigiotti, Bologna 1764.

Literature

Butir, Leonid Mironivich/Porfireva, Anna Leonidovna, Mira Pietro, in: Muzykalnyi Peterburg, Entsiklopedicheskyi slovar, XVIII vek [Musical St Petersburg, Encyclopedic Dictionary, 18th Century], vol. 2, ed. by Anna Leonidovna Porfireva, St Petersburg 1998, pp. 210-13.

Eitner, Robert, Biographisch-bibliografisches Quellen-Lexikon, vol. 7, Leipzig 1902.

Findeizen, Nicolai, History of Music in Russia from Antiquity to 1800, vol. 2: The Eighteenth Century, transl. by Samuel William Pring, ed. by Miloš Velimirović/Claudia R. Jensen, Bloomington – Indianapolis 2008, pp. 16-17 (Russian original, Moscow 1929).

Fürstenau, Moritz, Zur Geschichte der Musik und des Theaters am Hofe zu Dresden, 2. Teil, Dresden 1862.

Gerber, Ernst Ludwig, Neues historisch-biographisches Lexicon der Tonkünstler, vol. 3, Leipzig 1813.

Kollmar, Ulrike, Gottlob Harrer (1703-1755), Kapellmeister des Grafen Heinrich von Brühl am sächsisch-polnischen Hof und Thomaskantor in Leipzig, Beeskow 2006.

Landmann, Ortrun, Quellenstudien zum Intermezzo comico per musica und zu seiner Geschichte, 2 vols., PhD University of Rostock 1972 (manuscript in D-Dl).

Metastasio, Pietro, Tutte le opere, ed. by Bruno Brunelli, vol. 4: Lettere, Milan 1954.

Mooser, Robert-Aloys, Annales de la musique et des musiciens en Russie au XVIIIe siècle, vol. 1, Geneva 1948.

Id., Violinistes-compositeurs italiens en Russie au XVIIIe siècle, in: Rivista Musicale Italiana 46 (1942), fasc. 4, pp. 273-93.

Ritzarev, Marina/Porfireva, Anna, The Italian Diaspora in Eighteenth-Century Russia, in: The Eighteenth-Century Diaspora of Italian Music and Musicians (Speculum musicae 8), ed. by Reinhard Strohm, Turnhout 2001, pp. 214-16.

Ritzarev, Marina, Eighteenth-Century Russian Music, Aldershot/Burlington, Vermont 2006.

Sartori, Claudio, I libretti italiani a stampa dalle origini al 1800. Catalogo analitico con 16 indici, 7 vols., Cuneo 1990-94.

Selfridge-Field, Eleanor, A New Chronology of Venetian Opera and Related Genres, 1660-1760, Stanford 2007.

STÄHLIN, JACOB VON, Nachrichten von der Musik in Rußland, in: JOHANN JOSEPH HAIGOLD, Beylagen zum Neuveränderten Rußland, Riga/ Leipzig 1770, reprint Leipzig 1982.

WIERZBICKA-MICHALSKA, KARYNA, Aktorzy cudzoziemscy w Warszawie w XVIII wieku [Foreign actors in Warsaw in the eighteenth century], Wrocław 1975.

YAMADA, TAKASHI, La versione napoletana de 'Il matrimonio segreto' (Napoli 1793): una partitura ritrovata all'Università di musica Kunitachi di Tokio. Con annotazioni sulle condizioni di esecuzione attraverso i mandati di pagamento dell'Archivio del Banco di Napoli, in: Da Napoli a Napoli. Musica e musicologia senza confini. Contributi sul patrimonio musicale italiano presentati alla IAML Annual Conference Napoli 20-25 luglio 2008, ed. by MAURO AMATO et al., Lucca 2012, pp. 131-62.

ŻÓRAWSKA-WITKOWSKA, ALINA, Johann Adolf Hasse und die Musik am polnischen Hof Augusts III. (1734-1763), in: Hasse-Studien 7, ed. by WOLFGANG HOCHSTEIN/REINHARD WIESEND, Stuttgart 2012a, pp. 54-68.

ID., Muzyka na polskim dworze Augusta III, Part I [Music at the Polish court of August III. Part 1], Lublin 2012b.

ID., Domenico Guardasoni a Varsavia: due episodi polacchi dalla sua carriera operistica (1774-1776, 1789-1791), in: Böhmische Aspekte des Lebens und des Werkes von W. A. Mozart, ed. by MILADA JONAŠOVÁ/ TOMISLAV VOLEK, Prague 2011a, pp. 213-238.

ID., The Saxon Court of the Kingdom of Poland, in: Music at German Courts, 1715-1760. Changing Artistic Priorities, ed. by SAMANTHA OWENS et al., Woodbridge 2011b, pp. 51-77.

ID., Between Dresden and Warsaw. The Travels of the Court of August III of Poland (Friedrich August II of Saxony), in: Musicology Today. Polish Studies on Baroque Music, Warsaw 2009, pp. 7-25.

ID., Giovanni Alberto Ristori and His Serenate at the Polish Court of Augustus III, 1735-1746, in: Music as Social and Cultural Practice. Essays in Honour of Reinhard Strohm, ed. by MELANIA BUCCIARELLI/ BERTA JONCUS, Woodbridge 2007a, 139-158.

ID., Mozart „a sprawa polska" czyli o muzycznych koneksjach Warszawy i Wiednia w drugiej połowie XVIII wieku [Mozart and Poland. The musical links between Warsaw and Vienna in the second half of the eighteenth century], in: Mozart i współcześni. Muzyka w Europie Środkowej w XVIII wieku [Mozart and his contemporaries. Music in

Central Europe in the eighteenth century], ed. by DANIEL GOLIANEK/ BEATA STRÓŻYŃSKA, Łódź 2007b, pp. 139-154.

ID., Parodies of 'Dramma per Musica' at the Warsaw Theater of August III, in: Italian Opera in Central Europe 1614-1780, vol. 3: Opera Subjects and European Relationships, ed. by NORBERT DUBOWY et al., Berlin 2007c, pp. 125-145.

ID., Muzyka na dworze Augusta II w Warszawie [Music at the court of August II], Warsaw 1997.

ID., I drammi per musica di Johann Adolf Hasse rappresentati a Varsavia negli anni 1754-1763, in: Johann Adolf Hasse und Polen. Materialien der Konferenz Warszawa, 10-12 Dezember 1993, ed. by I. PONIATOWSKA/ID., Warsaw 1995a, pp. 123-48.

ID., Muzyka na dworze i w teatrze Stanisława Augusta [Music at the court and theater of Stanisław August Poniatowski], Warsaw 1995b.

Luka Sorgo – a Nobleman and Composer from Dubrovnik

VJERA KATALINIĆ

The education of young noblemen in the Republic of Dubrovnik (Ragusa) during the second half of the 18th century was organized within the Jesuit College until 1773, when their order was dissolved and their school taken over by the Piarists. The *Ratio studiorum* included the acquaintance with the general foundations of natural sciences, philosophy, culture and arts, including music. This type of education was obligatory and, from 1779 onwards, young aristocrats could not become members of the *Consilio major* – at the age of 18 – without completing it. Their further training was completed by private teachers in Dubrovnik or at foreign, mostly Italian, universities in Naples, Rome, Bologna or Padua. They visited more distant centers only sporadically as, for example, Luka's nephew Toma (Tommaso) Basseglì, who studied in Switzerland, organized and supported by the Italian Abbot Alberto Fortis. It was also quite common for young students to obtain a fine general cultural overview not only in order to take part in learned discussions, but also to promote the culture of their Republic during foreign missions on diplomatic and business trips throughout the continent. Even though the primary education of noblewomen of Dubrovnik was entirely and exclusively oriented towards private lectures – later, some of them were sent to Italy as well – many of them made their names as intellectuals, poets and musicians, on equal terms with their male compatriots of the same status.

The educational path of Luka Sorgo (or, Luka Sorkočević, as his name is to be found in contemporary lexica,[1] 1734-1789), following his

---
1 For example in BUJIĆ, 2001, p. 747.

initiation into the ruling structures of the Republic of Dubrovnik, at first consisted of private lessons in music, which he continued when he went to the university in Rome. Thus, this article focuses on the presentation of his musical achievements and intends to answer questions concerning the cultural transfer of patterns related to the music migrations and musical encounters of a noble musician from Dubrovnik with the renowned musicians from abroad of his time.

1. Music encounters with Italian teachers

Dubrovnik was a center that imported culture: composers, performers, teachers and even entire groups (touring theater companies)[2] mostly went there during the 18th century, although some local musicians were active there, too, and some went to seek supplementary music study in Italy. Music education books (tutors for composition, playing instruments and singing)[3] and music material for private and public performances[4] were also imported from Italian publishers or obtained as manuscript copies. Music was in demand as a part of sacred and secular representation, as well as for the entertainment of the numerous local nobility and bourgeoisie.[5] It seems that a number of Luka's teachers among the Jesuits had also been of Italian origin.[6] Following the termination of this school,

---

2 The Dubrovnik Republic officials never allowed the existence of a permanent opera company in the town. It was easier to control the touring troupes from the Venetian Republic, Papal State or Neapolitan Kingdom.

3 For example, *L'Armonico pratico al cimbalo* by Francesco Gasparini (second edition, 1715) was still in use in Dubrovnik at the end of the 18th century.

4 Several hundreds of symphonies, chamber music and church pieces, mostly by Italian, German and French as well as by some local authors, are kept in the Franciscan monastery music archives and in the local cathedral archives today.

5 The theater code was quite strict. The offices of the Republic issued orders about the reserved places for the higher and lower nobility (the so-called "salamanchesi" and "sorbonesi"), as well as for the citizens ("antunini" and "lazzarini"). An intended theater reform at the end of the 18th century by the Italian undertaker and impresario Antonio Brambilla included plans to designate seats for the Jewish audience as well.

6 For example, VANINO (1987, pp. 68f) mentions public academies, as well as names by some *magistri* as Aloisio Valsisi from Livorno (in 1741), Carlo Menghini (in 1754), Morcelli, or just *Magister Pietro* etc.

his father engaged Giuseppe Antonio Valente/Valenti, active since 1749 as *maestro di cappella* in the Dubrovnik cathedral, probably originating from Naples, to give private lessons to Luka, the most promising musical talent of the family. It is possible that his older sister Kata, his younger brother Miho and his sister Marija joined this programme as well, at least for a while. This private education started in 1754, as noted in Luka's music booklet *Lezioni di contrapunto date del Sig. Giuseppe Ant.o Valenti M.ro di Capella al sig.r Luca Ant.o di Sorgo* preserved in the Dubrovnik Franciscan monastery (according to RISM sigla: HR-Dsmb, 78/2020). Although the studies written there start with the simplest practices, they progress very rapidly, so that it is possible that Luka had previously had another teacher and that Valente only briefly revised and checked his skills. Namely, the first among Luka's symphony-overtures was dated as early as in July of the same year (HR-Dsmb, 77/1995), soon followed by two others (HR-Dsmb, 9/220 and 77/1994). According to his rare preserved compositions, Valente was musically well-trained, but of modest invention.

There are no precise indications of how long these lessons lasted. After a dispute with Luka's father in 1757, which ended in the court of justice, Valente was banned from Dubrovnik and left permanently for Italy in 1761. However, it seems that already in 1756, Luka was probably sent to Rome for studies that included not only university education but also becoming acquainted with "cultural education" *in situ*. Luka continued with his duties in the offices of the Dubrovnik Republic in 1763, so it seems that the six- or seven-year period included the stay in Rome and his educational journey. During his sojourn there, he also took music lessons from the well-known opera composer Rinaldo di Capua.[7]

According to a few dozen compositions by Giuseppe Antonio Valente preserved in Dubrovnik and abroad (Italy, Great Britain), this composer was a skilful musician who could provide Luka with solid basic knowledge in the art of composing. Nevertheless, the Roman episode supplied him with new musical experiences – visiting the theater, hearing representative church music as well as good musical training. Rinaldo di Capua was known to contemporaries in and outside of Italy. Charles Burney met him in Rome in 1770 and described him as an excellent Neapolitan composer, intelligent and sensible in conversation who had,

---

[7] The notice in his second booklet with exercises is entitled „Roma a 20 Giugno. Seguitano Fugi fatti sotto la scola del Sig. Rinaldo di Capua" (HR-Dsmb, 78/2021, p. 25).

at that time, already fallen somewhat out of fashion, but was still achieving some success with his theater works.[8] However, there is not much preserved from his œuvre. It is said, that his son (allegedly Marcello di Capua/Marcello Bernardini) sold or destroyed his legacy. Rinaldo's most important works are the *opera seria Vologeso, re de'Parti* (1739) and the *opera buffa La libertà nociva* (1740). Burney referred to Rinaldo's music as passionate and to an aria from *Vologeso* as "a specimen of the perfection to which dramatic music was brought in Italy".[9] Furthermore, his surviving arias range "from farcical caricature to lyrical and sentimental expression"[10] and the text is clearly articulated, while the ensembles are skilfully composed: "The score reveals Rinaldo's favourite setting – three parts, generally for strings: the first violin doubles the vocal line, sometimes varying it; the second violin either doubles the first or follows it at a 3rd or 6th (it is rarely independent); the bass, doubled by the viola (which rarely has an independent part), provides an accompaniment, often in fast repeated notes."[11]

These qualifications of Rinaldo's style are quoted here because it was Luka Sorgo who applied a similar style in his eleven preserved symphonies and two separately found movements.[12] The only date marked on the material in the Franciscan monastery in Dubrovnik is 1754 on the first three, all preserved as autograph scores (as well as another symphony without a date, and the two separate movements) and the first two among them still bearing the title "overtura". The formal scheme follows contemporary works in their three movements pattern (fast-slow-fast), already emancipated from the opera overture type, sometimes shifting away from the Baroque binary forms, and with foretelling of the contrasting motives or, in the vocabulary of Heinrich Christoph Koch, the "cantabler Satz".[13] The first theme (or, rather, a thematic group) usually starts with broken chords. The setting of the composition is distinctively

---

8   BURNEY, 1974, p. 154.
9   HOGARTH, 1838, p. 374; GALLICO, 2001, p. 426.
10 GALLICO, 2001, p. 426.
11 IBID., p. 425.
12 They are all in HR-Dsmb: the already mentioned two overtures (77/1995, 9/220), two *sinfonie* (77/1994, 77/1993) and two movements (77/1994) in scores, and seven of them preserved in parts (77/1991, 9/221, 77/1988, 77/1990, 77/1987, 77/1989 and 77/1992).
13 KOCH, 1793, vol. III, p. 333.

individual: phrases sometimes cover one or two, three or even four bars, searching for a new balance between the melody, (simple) progression of the harmony (to the dominant, and the return through subdominant keys), rhythm and transparent instrumentation, generally following the pattern of his, especially Roman, teachers. The last seven symphonies seem to be of later origin, possibly created during Luka's stay in Rome; they have been preserved in parts, copied by a professional copyist, and are ready to be played.

2. Music encounters with famous composers and musicians of his time

After completing his studies in Rome, Luka Sorgo most probably continued his education by traveling to some Italian towns, taking care of family business as well. After his return to Dubrovnik in 1763, he continued with his official duties for the Republic. These various administrative tasks lasted from a few months to a year or more. He was active as councillor, senator, lawyer, supervisor of institutions, representative, judge, and so on.[14] Amongst others, he was named envoy to the court of France in 1765, but declined the appointment. Another diplomatic mission offered to him was in Vienna. The Dubrovnik Republic did not have a permanent envoy there, but only the trustworthy advocate Sebastiano d'Ayala, a Jesuit from Sicily, who promoted Dubrovnik's interests for almost 30 years. It was only at crucial junctures that the Republic sent its own reliable officer. Such a moment occurred after the death of Empress Maria Theresa in November 1780, and Luka Sorgo obtained that appointment in January 1781.[15] He travelled to Rijeka (Fiume) by ship and then by coach to Vienna, probably in August of the same year. His diary with notes on his contacts and activities has been preserved, covering the period from the beginning of September to the end of January 1782.[16] Although Sorgo's Viennese diary primarily concentrated on the descrip-

---

14   For the list of his duties, see KATALINIĆ, 2014, pp. 31-35.
15   Cf. *Libro Officiali Pubblici o Specchio del Maggior Consiglio*, preserved in the Historical Archives in Dubrovnik, DAD, ser. 21.1 (Specchio, 1700-1799), p. 311.
16   The diary, entitled *Memoriae* – written in Italian – is preserved in the Historical Archives in Dubrovnik, but the initial pages are missing (HR-Dha, 21-2/145).

tion of his political and diplomatic contacts, it also provided plenty of information about his encounters with people from the cultural/musical sphere.[17] He went to the opera and declared himself to be an admirer of Christoph Willibald Gluck on several occasions, whom he visited in Vienna a few months after serious health problems. Sorgo praised Gluck's compositions, above all his revolutionary changes in music which he used to express great passions with the simplest means. He was acquainted with Gluck's opera performances in Paris and of the "querelle" they had caused there. He probably also brought to Dubrovnik some copies of Gluck's works, partially preserved in the archives of the Franciscan monastery in Dubrovnik.[18] The librettist Pietro Metastasio was one of the court employees who helped Sorgo to establish contact with important people.[19] The old poet was well known and highly esteemed also in Dubrovnik. In his Viennese house, Luka also met Marianne von Martínez, Metastasio's pupil and protégée, and heard her performing her own new cantata.[20]

Joseph Haydn visited Luka, brought with him his newly composed six quartets,[21] and complained about the Emperor Joseph II, who did not like him at all. Haydn's music was already known in Dubrovnik through some manuscript copies coming from Italy. A series of his works has been preserved in the private collection of the Gozze family, close friends and relatives of the Sorgos.[22]

Luka attended private and public academies where he could hear and meet amateur and professional musicians. He was invited to court feasts and balls of various types. On a chamber gathering (his diary entry on

17 On that topic, see KATALINIĆ, 2004, pp. 187-196.
18 For example, there is the aria "Che farò senza Euridice" from Gluck's *Orfeo ed Euridice*, copied for Luka's daughter Marina (HR-Dsmb, 61/1692) as well as the entire opera (61/1693).
19 Metastasio reported on Sorgo's activities and the good impressions he made in Vienna in his letter to Abbé Rugiero Boscovich, a friend of Luka Sorgo, on 18 August 1781, published in: METASTASIO, vol. 3, pp. 277-279.
20 Cf. the diary entry for 14 October 1781.
21 They are the op. 33 quartets, also called *Russian*, dedicated to the Russian Prince Paul, who was on a "secret" visit to the Viennese court at the same time as Luka Sorgo, who also met him at the court.
22 There are twenty pieces by Joseph Haydn listed in the catalog of music materials in the possession of the Gozze family, partly preserved in the Dubrovnik Franciscan monastery: cf. KATALINIĆ, 2015.

18 December 1781) he testifies that the minuet was danced as well as the round dance and the quadrille, even the waltz, which was not danced by the princesses, only by nobles of the lower rank (see figure 1). In Vienna, Luka was not only able to communicate with well-known musicians and acquire music material, but also hear new and previously unknown compositions; he also had the opportunity to compare Viennese performances with those he knew from Italy.

Figure 1: A page from Sorgo's Viennese diary, describing the dances at the court

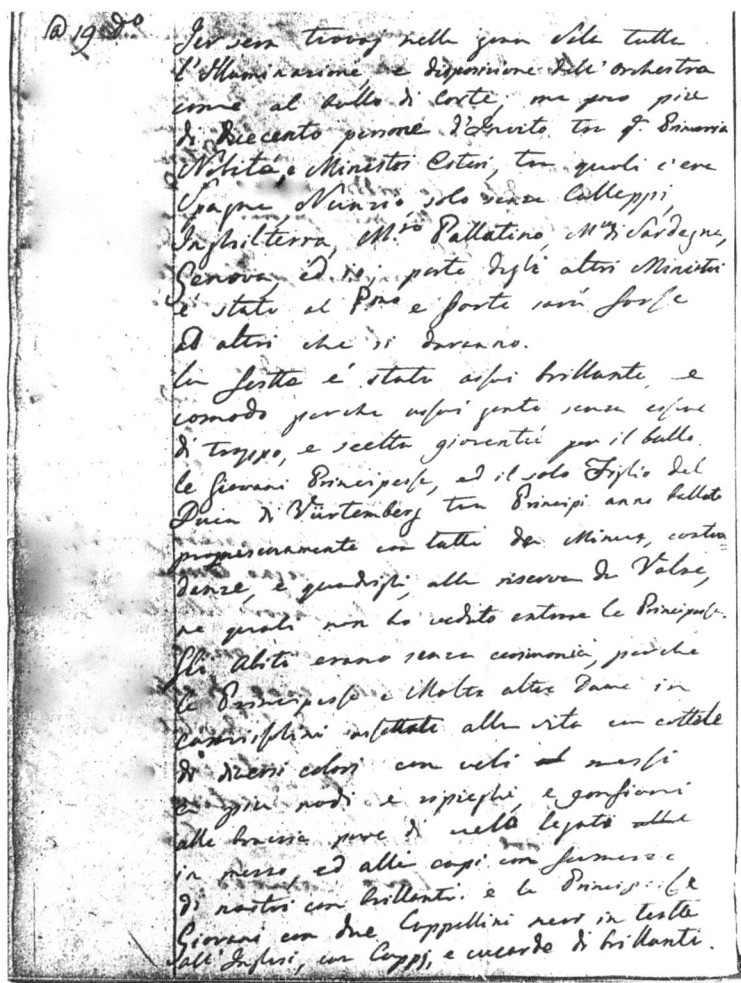

When and where Luka became acquainted with Julije/Giulio Bajamonti (1744-1800) is not known;[23] we only know that he met him through his brother Miho, probably during the late 1770s.[24] Bajamonti was a physician by profession but also had excellent training in music – first in his native Split, and later probably in Padua or Venice. Bajamonti also visited Italy very often after his graduation, and some of his compositions were written in Venice. His work, especially his vocal-instrumental œuvre, was strongly influenced by the contemporary Venetian operatic style. As a polymath, he also dealt with medical, historical, ethnological and other issues and wrote essays, some of which were published in Italy. Beside inevitable discussions on music in his letters with Luka and (later) with Luka's son Antun/Antonio, Bajamonti borrowed literature from his friends from Dubrovnik as, for example, Rousseau's *Dictionnaire de musique* from Miho Sorgo, when working on his own music dictionary.[25] After Luka's death, Bajamonti supported his son Antun with suggestions and advice on his compositions.[26] Luka held in high esteem Bajamonti's "mixed style",[27] a combination of the style of the Venetian opera in his vocal music and early classicistic clear shapes in instrumental pieces. Therefore, he ordered suitable music for the funeral mass for the Dubrovnik scientist Ruđer Bošković/Ruggero Boscovich, who had died in 1787.[28]

---

23 Bajamonti was in Dubrovnik for the first time in 1781 (cf. MILČETIĆ, 1912, p. 245).

24 Although the first of Miho's preserved letters to Bajamonti dates from 1778, they may have met earlier, during their studies in Italy: Bajamonti in Padua (where he graduated in medicine in 1773) and Miho Sorgo in Bologna. These letters are mostly preserved among Bajamonti's legacy in the Archaeological Museum in Split.

25 Cf. TOMIĆ FERIĆ, 2013.

26 On that topic, see the article TOMIĆ FERIĆ, 2014, pp. 230-255.

27 The combination of the elements of the Venetian opera, some layers of the baroque and early classical style is obvious in all Bajamonti's compositions, above all in his vocal pieces (cf. KOS, 2004).

28 Bajamonti composed a *Requiem* for Bošković, but it arrived too late to be used for that occasion. Therefore, it was probably performed at a private *academia* in the Dubrovnik house of the Sorgos.

3. Implementation of musical style and patterns

As a young man, Luka Sorgo traveled throughout the Italian lands, gathering his cultural and musical experiences. He regularly visited the theater,[29] accumulated music material,[30] and both his diary and his correspondence reveal his lasting preoccupation with music. For example, a letter by Giulio Bajamonti to Luka Sorgo in 1785 provides information on their playing together and studying Gluck's *Alceste* (see figure 2).[31]

However, the only date occurring in Luka's musical œuvre – at least that of his 11 symphonies – is 1754, i.e. before his educational years in Rome. Still, one can be sure that his teacher Rinaldo not only asked him to compose "fughe a 2 e a 3" (as written on the title page of his second booklet of practices), but also some more complex works. Therefore, it is most likely that he was also active as a composer, at least during his stay in Rome until the early 1760s. Following his return to Dubrovnik, where he married in 1764 and became more deeply involved in the administration of the Republic (from 1763), there are no indications of his compositional activity whatsoever. And yet, seven of his symphonies have been preserved in parts, copied for a small ensemble. In the majority of them there are two parts copied for *violino primo*, two for *violino secondo*, sometimes two for *viola*, and in two symphonies even for *contrabasso*, i.e. *violoncello*. Usually, the oboe parts are written separately for the first and for the second, while both horns are notated together. All of them have titles, as in his first symphony (among those preserved in parts) in D: *Sinfonia | Con V.V., obue, corni da Caccia | Violetta, e Basso | Dell'Ill.*

---

29 In his diary he assessed some performances and performance styles, showing great experience in music.
30 There is not much left of his general and music library, because his son Antun sold his legacy at the beginning of the 19th century, before permanently moving to Paris. Still, a score of Pergolesi's *Stabat mater* (preserved at present in the Dubrovnik cathedral (HR-Dk, without shelf no.) and one manuscript – instrumental music by Baldassare Galuppi – preserved in the Franciscan Monastery (HR-Dsmb, 19/663) bear witness to his interests, much more evident in the list of music materials from the Gozze legacy, another noble and learned family, also related to the Sorgos. For the Gozze music material, see KATALINIĆ, 2015.
31 The letter is preserved in the Archaeological Museum in Split, and the score of the overture is preserved in Dubrovnik (HR-Dsmb, 62/1695).

Figure 2: Giulio Bajamonti's letter to Luka Sorgo with the notice of studying Gluck's Alceste

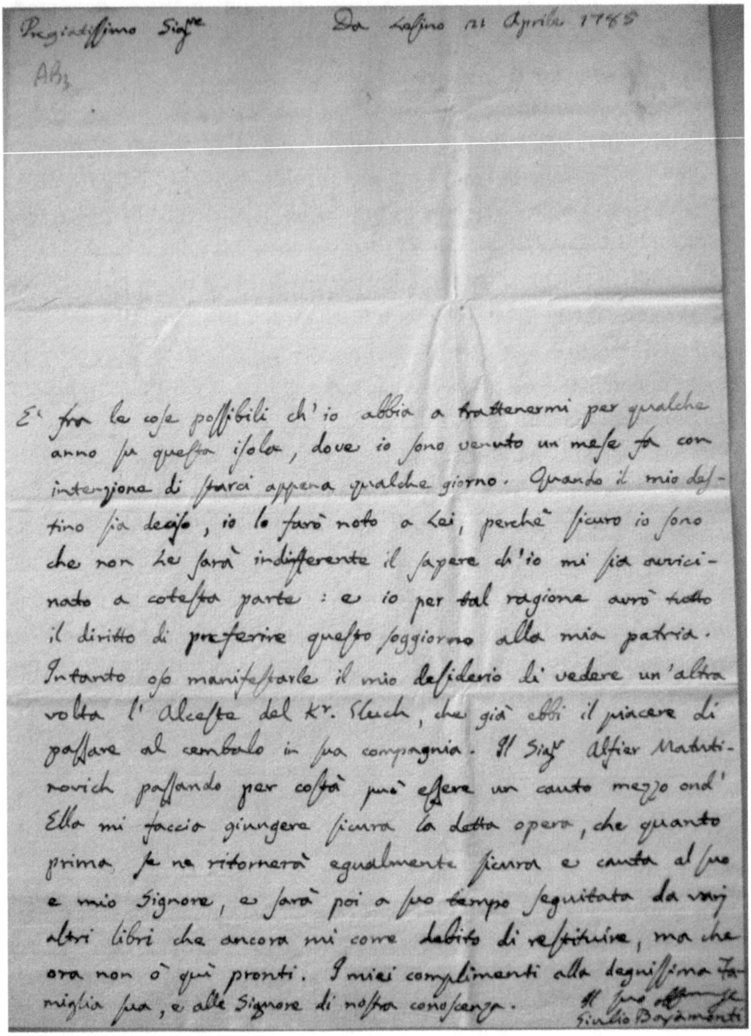

Pregiatissimo Sig.re Da Lesina 21 Aprile 1785

E' fra le cose possibili ch'io abbia a trattenermi per qualche anno su questa isola, dove io sono venuto un mese fa con intenzione di starci appena qualche giorno. Quando il mio destino sia deciso, io lo farò noto a Lei, perchè sicuro io sono che non Le sarà indifferente il sapere ch'io mi sia avvicinato a cotesta parte: e io per tal ragione avrò tutto il diritto di preferire questo soggiorno alla mia patria. Intanto oso manifestarle il mio desiderio di vedere un'altra volta l'Alceste del Kr. Gluch, che già ebbi il piacere di passare al cembalo in sua compagnia. Il Sig.r Alfier Matutinovich passando per costà può essere un cauto mezzo ond'Ella mi faccia giungere sicura la detta opera, che quanto prima se ne ritornerà egualmente sicura e cauta al suo e mio Signore, e sarà poi a suo tempo seguitata da varj altri libri che ancora mi corre debito di restituire, ma che ora non ò qui pronti. I miei complimenti alla degnissima Famiglia sua, e alle Signore di nostra conoscenza.

Il suo obblig.mo
Giulio Bajamonti

Sig. D. Luca d'Antonio | Sorgo. Therefore, the new "mixed" sound of the early classical orchestra, unlike his first four symphonies or overtures,[32] has been established. Consequently, they seem to be more mature, and intended for performance. As a nobleman, he considered it inappropriate to participate in a public performance. On the other hand he could do so in a private circle, with musically trained members from other noble families (as, for example, with the previously mentioned Gozze family, although there are other marked family names as former owners on the sheet music), or supported by professional musicians. The other possibility is that the professionals, i.e. the members of the duke's orchestra,[33] presented them in public at concerts or even in private at special occasions.[34]

In the Franciscan monastery, where – beside the standard liturgical compositions – a significant amount of the music repertoire of the Dubrovnik Republic has been preserved, one can find various imported works by contemporary musicians, mostly from Italy and Austria, later also from France, with numerous symphonies among them.[35] Miho Demović, a researcher of the Dubrovnik musical history, has identified a list of names of musicians active there – members of the local orchestras, organists, music teachers, even composers – some from abroad, and a few locals. Still, beside their compositional output for the church (masses, simple motets and church songs), most of their secular compositions did not advance beyond short chamber works and dance music. There-

---

32 There the instruments vary, between only two of them (*violino* and *basso* in the second and the third one) and strings with only one wind instrument (oboe with strings in the first and flute with violin and basso in the fourth symphony), while the two orchestral movements are composed for strings and flutes or oboes (*a due*).

33 The members of the representative orchestra of the duke of the Republic merged with the orchestra of the cathedral during the mid-18th century. That ensemble performed at festive events in connection with the Republic and its duke, as well as for the church festivities. Its musicians were sufficiently trained to perform Sorgo's symphonies as well.

34 For example, for birthdays and other family feasts or learned gatherings. On the other hand, more festive occasions, like marriages, required a more representative music programme.

35 There are names/authors of symphonies such as Ignace Pleyel, Johann Stamitz, Pasquale Anfossi, Giuseppe Sarti, etc.; a score of a symphony by Frederick the Great is also preserved there. Cf. also: KATALINIĆ, 1993; TUKSAR, 1997; TUKSAR, 1999.

fore, Luka was the only local musician during the 1760s and 1770s who composed symphonies and his son Antun was the only person whom he musically influenced in that aspect (setting), who – besides chamber music – also composed four symphonies at the end of the 18th and the very beginning of the 19th century. It seems that it was only during the 1810s and 1820s that there were some orchestral works composed by local composers (of Italian origin) such as Angiolo Maria Frezza from Rome or Tommaso Resti from Lecce, both active in Dubrovnik.[36]

In mid-18th century Dubrovnik, when Luka Sorgo/Sorkočević, a local nobleman, was trained for his diplomatic service and in music – both, in his home town and abroad – the local audience could enjoy the musicians from the cathedral orchestra and the duke's orchestra playing imported music as well as some domestic creations in church, in the theater and in concerts, in public and privately.[37] Luka also composed for such occasions, thus participating in the implementation of the new early classical style and the symphony, as instructed by his Italian teachers in Dubrovnik and Rome. After focusing entirely on his public service activities for the Republic, especially after traveling to Italy and Vienna, he applied his experiences in the organization of music life and education in his role as superintendent of the home for girls (in 1785) or the public theater (1787). Although he probably no longer composed, he undoubtedly stayed in touch with music: attending music performances, playing in private and studying music as well as taking care of the music education of his children and supplying them with music material. In that aspect, he was a typical representative of his educated class which included poets, philosophers and other polymaths. During his Viennese mission, his contemporaries described him as a learned person with exquisite manners and a fine soul, who had well represented the interests of his small fatherland.

---

36   Cf. DEMOVIĆ, 1989, pp. 228f.
37   Only by the 1770s, the Senate had allowed that the hall in the city customs office (Dogana/Palazzo Sponsa), besides the local theater building, might also serve for concert performances.

Literature

Bujić, Bojan, Sorkočević, Luka, in: The New Grove dictionary of music and musicians, ed. by Stanley Sadie, London et al. 2001, vol. 23, pp. 747.

Burney, Charles, Music, Men and Manners in France and Italy 1770, ed. by H. Edmund Poole, London 1974.

Id., A General History of Music from the Earliest Ages to the Present Period, 4 vols., London 1776-1789.

Demović, Miho, Glazba i glazbenici u Dubrovačkoj Republici od kraja XVII. do prvog desetljeća XIX. stoljeća [Music and musicians in the Republic of Dubrovnik from the end of the 17th to the first decade of the 19th century], Zagreb 1982.

Gallico, Claudio, Rinaldo di Capua, in: The New Grove dictionary of music and musicians, ed. by Stanley Sadie, London et al. 2001, vol. 21, pp. 425f.

Gasparini, Francesco, L'armonico pratico al cimbalo, Venice 1715.

Hogarth, George, Memoires of the Musical Drama, London 1838.

Katalinić, Vjera, Die Werke W.A. Mozarts und einiger seiner Zeitgenossen in kroatischen Sammlungen bis ca. 1820, in: Internationaler musikwissenschaftlicher Kongress zum Mozartjahr 1991, Baden – Wien, ed. by Ingrid Fuchs, Tutzing 1993, vol. 2, pp. 685-691.

Id., Luka Sorkočevićs Wiener Tagebuch, in: Muzikološki zbornik, XL/1-2 (2004), pp. 187-196.

Id., The Sorkočevićes – Aristocratic Musicians from Dubrovnik, Zagreb 2014.

Id., Imported Music Scores in the Possession of the Gozze Family in Dubrovnik, in: De musica disserenda, XI/1-2 (2015), pp. 199-211.

Koch, Heinrich Christoph, Versuch einer Anleitung zur Composition, 3 vols., Leipzig 1782-1793.

Kos, Koraljka, *La Traslazione di San Doimo* von Julije Bajamonti. Ein Werk des Übergangs, in: Musical Culture on the Adriatic in the Period of Classicism, ed. by Vjera Katalinić/Stanislav Tuksar, Zagreb 2004, pp. 75-90.

Metastasio, Pietro, Opere postume del Signor Abate Pietro Metastasio date alla luce dall'Abate Conte d'Ayala, 3 vols., Vienna 1795.

Milčetić, Ivan, Dr. Julije Bajamonti i njegova djela [Dr Julije Bajamonti and his works], in: Rad JAZU, 192 (1912), pp. 97-250.

Tomić Ferić, Ivana, Julije Bajamonti: Glazbeni rječnik [Julije Bajamonti: Music Dictionary], Zagreb 2013.

Id., Suradnja s Julijem Bajamontijem [Collaboration with Julije Bajamonti], in: Luka & Antun Sorkočević: diplomati i skladatelji [Diplomats and composers], ed. by Pavica Vilać, Dubrovnik 2014, pp. 230-255.

Tuksar, Stanislav, Music by Eighteenth-Century German and Austrian Composers Preserved in Venetian Dalmatia and Dubrovnik. Differences and Similarities, in: Relazioni musicali tra Italia e Germania nell'età barocca. Atti del VI Convegno internazionale sulla musica italiana nei secoli XVII-XVIII, ed. by Alberto Colzani et al., Loveno di Menaggio/Como 1997, pp. 447-461.

Id., Late 18th and Early 19th Century Diffusion of the First Viennese School Music in Croatian Lands. Factography and Some Socio-Cultural Aspects, in: Music, Words and Images. Essays in honour of Koraljka Kos, ed. by Vjera Katalinić/Zdravko Blažeković, Zagreb 1999, pp. 195-209.

Vanino, Miroslav, Isusovci i hrvatski narod [The Jesuits and the Croatian people], vol. 2, Zagreb 1987.

MUSICI and MusMig
Continuities and Discontinuities

BERTHOLD OVER, TORSTEN ROEDER

1. Introduction

Today migration is often perceived as a phenomenon of the last 150 years; one thinks of those who left their country as a result of recruitment activities, due to wars, or to escape modern economical misery in search for a better life in other parts of the world. Such an example of migration from recent times is the large waves of immigration into the USA caused by the Nazi era in Germany. Yet migration was a natural part of life in the Early Modern Age. People took astonishing paths similar to those from recent history or current times. Even back then migration was a global phenomenon, bridging countries and continents as well as taking place locally, from one city to another. For example merchants traveled for months or even years and would often settle down for a longer time to do business. Journeymen, that is persons who just finished their apprenticeship, were on the road for training purposes and possibly never returned to their native homes. Religious communities emigrated and settled down in other regions.

Musicians have always been a highly mobile professional group. In the Early Modern Age particularly many musicians are known to have left their native places or places of activity either permanently or for a certain period of time. Their migration movements were not limited to single regions and countries but included all of Europe and the regions beyond.¹ Currently, this phenomenon and its consequences are being investigated by interdisciplinary and international research groups. Up until 2012 the project "MUSICI. Musicisti europei a Venezia, Roma e Napoli" focussed on musicians who traveled to Venice, Rome and Naples between 1650 and 1750 with a wide variety of objectives and active in vastly different positions.² Now the project "MusMig. Music Migrations in the Early Modern Age: the Meeting of the European East, West and South", launched in autumn 2013, continues to research migration movements of musicians, but has expanded the focus to the entire 17th and 18th centuries, revolving mainly around Northern and Eastern Europe.³

In this project the meaning of "migration" is not restricted to emigration or immigration, but embraces every movement in a territorial space. This provides, in contrast to topographic or cultural approaches, a perspective closer to historical facts oriented to dominions. Therefore musicians or opera companies that traveled to represent their musical work, Grand Tours in which musicians would take part, or musicians traveling for professional training purposes, are all part of the investigation for this project. The term "musician" is defined broadly as well. It comprises instrumentalists, singers, composers etc. as well as librettists, instrument makers and theorists of music.⁴ It is expected to be shown that music migrations have contributed considerably to the dynamics and synergy of the European cultural scene at large, stimulating innovations, changes of styles and patterns of musical and social behavior, and contributing to the cohesive forces in the common European cultural identity.

---

1   See for example the anthologies GOULET/ZUR NIEDEN, 2015; EHRMANN-HERFORT, 2013; OTTENBERG/ZIMMERMANN, 2012; MAHLING, 2011; MÜNS, 2005; MEYER, 2003; STROHM, 2001; BRUSNIAK/KOCH, 2000.
2   GOULET/ZUR NIEDEN, 2015. The project has been financed by Deutsche Forschungsgemeinschaft (DFG) and Agence nationale de la recherche (ANR) and was headed by Anne-Madeleine Goulet (Paris) and Gesa zur Nieden (Mainz).
3   The project, financed by the European research initiative HERA (Humanities in the European Research Area), is headed by Vjera Katalinić (Zagreb) and unites researchers from Croatia, Poland, Slovenia and Germany.
4   This musician concept implies, of course, also female personnel, especially singers.

2. MUSICI and MusMig

MusMig is in a certain sense a continuation of MUSICI and therefore is in the fortunate position to benefit from the experiences of the former project. But the projects are by no means identical; thus MusMig modified certain parameters in order to fit with the project's modified questions. MUSICI concentrated for example on three Italian cities (Venice, Rome, Naples) and their musical institutions, which supported the travel and work of "foreign" musicians.[5] However, it should be noted that "foreign" musicians included those who came from the other cities studied in the project (that is, a musician from Venice was considered "foreign" in Rome). In addition the institutions could be broken down in a very detailed manner in the database structure. Yet due to MusMig's broader conception this detailed structure could not be replicated. MusMig must be able to systematize every institution in every local context: from a residence over an imperial city to a rural monastery. Whereas before MUSICI created a relatively detailed breakdown of the three cities' institutional employers, this is no longer possible because of the abundance of institutions to be considered in the territories investigated by MusMig. On a systematic level, a more general structure must enable the study of a broader range of places and institutions. Moreover in view of varied political frameworks, a further differentiation in the MusMig project is necessary to assure that different types of governments are also accounted for. Although Venice was a republic, Rome an ecclesiastical elective monarchy and Naples a territory dominated by a foreign power based on hereditary monarchy (Spain, France or Austria), the spectrum of MusMig is still much broader: from the Holy Roman Empire to electorates, duchies, prince bishoprics, imperial cities and other unique metropolises (like Leipzig, a city belonging to the electorate of Saxony, but having a special status as a trade fair town).

3. The data schemas of MUSICI and MusMig

Based on the experiences of the MUSICI project, the follow-up project MusMig started with the development of a data scheme in order to document information on migrating musicians. It is based on the Person

---

5 See also the database documentation in BERTI et al., 2013, and BERTI/ ROEDER, 2015.

Data Repository (PDR) of the Berlin Brandenburg Academy of Sciences and Humanities, a project started in 2009 and financed by the German Research Foundation.[6] PDR aims at creating a digital infrastructure for prosopographical research. It provides a flexible data scheme, a server environment, the client program "Archiv-Editor"[7] and a selection of web services.

Figure 1: The data model of the Person Data Repository (image: Torsten Roeder, 2014).

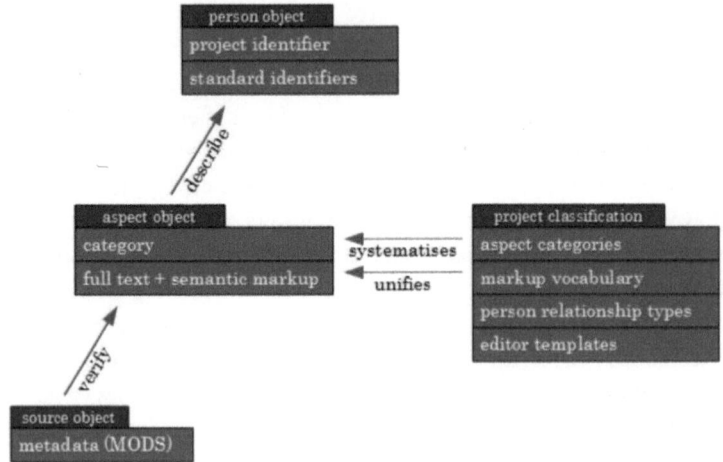

The data model provided by the Person Data Repository (see figure 1) intentionally follows a very general concept, as it aims to be implemented by a number of greatly different projects. The cornerstone of the data model is the person object, to which any number of information can be correlated. A single piece of information is called an "aspect" and can, for example, consist of a name, a profession or a place of sojourn. Each aspect has to be verified by at least one source.[8] Considering musicians, it could cover teacher and pupil relations, networks of patronage, partici-

---

6 Personendaten-Repositorium, http://pdr.bbaw.de, 19.03.2015.
7 Archiv-Editor, http://pdr.bbaw.de/software/ae, 19.03.2015, see also PLUTTE, 2011.
8 For bibliographic description of sources, the Person Data Resository uses the Metadata Object Description Schema (MODS). See http://www.loc.gov/standards/mods, 19.03.2015.

pation in concerts, composed works and more. Thus each person-object consists of an arbitrary amount of small bits of separate information. This means a person is less constituted by a classical data sheet, and more in a dynamic form, which is defined by all the information correlated to that person.[9] Following this principle, the MUSICI project gathered 2,200 aspects on over 300 individualized persons. In the MusMig project this amount will be at least two times as high, due to the larger scale of the project.

In order to maintain the sometimes very helpful character of the classical data sheet, it is possible to assign each aspect to a biographical category. Categories are groups of semantically comparable information, like date of birth and death, education, employments, journeys, compositions, etc. (as displayed by the example in figure 2). The categories can later be used to construct a data sheet or a systematic biography. Fitting to the generic approach of the Person Data Repository, the categories can be defined by the project itself. Furthermore, the system allows not only the definition of project-specific categories, but also a general mapping

Figure 2: Example of aspects for George Frideric Handel. The dark boxes display the respective categories (image: Torsten Roeder, 2014).

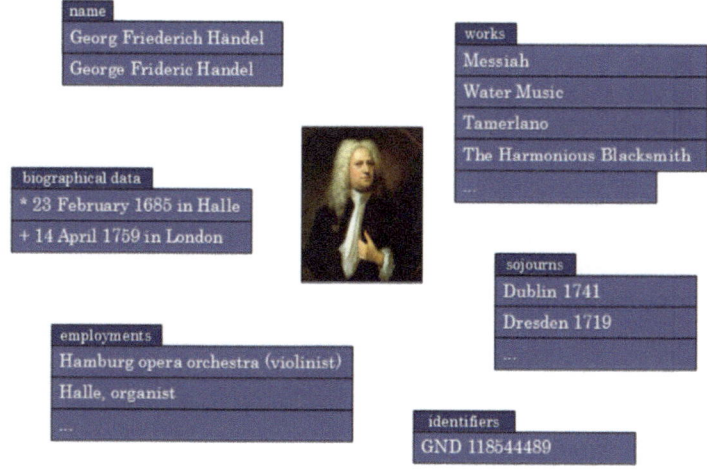

---

9   See also WALKOWSKI, 2009, p. 3, http://nbn-resolving.de/urn:nbn:de:kobv: b4-opus-9221, 19.03.2015.

to standard categories (e.g. CIDOC CRM),[10] thus creating comparable data amongst different projects. Usually, the perspective of the individual research project is priority, so the choice of categories – excepting those most basic such as "name" – will primarily support the single project's approach.

The category scheme that has been composed for the MusMig project is similar to the scheme for the MUSICI project, which is publicly available and documented at the database website[11] and is also presented and discussed in the final volume of the MUSICI project.[12] The categories of both projects contain on the one side very general basic categories, like biographical data, names and genealogical information. On the other side they are extended and designed in a way that allows examination of the more specific structures of the migrating musicians' biographies, and thus supports the investigation of typical careers of education and employment, production of compositions, relationship-networks and reception. Despite the similar approaches of MUSICI and MusMig, there are some different usage practices, due to the very different scopes of the projects. Consequently, on the technical level as well there are continuities and changes in this move from MUSICI to MusMig.

A key to database supported research is semantic enrichment of data. In the Person Data Repository, every single aspect consists of freely composed text, usually a small number of words or a phrase, which is then enriched by semantic information. Figure 3 shows an example of an aspect: "In 1698 he played for the prince-elector in Berlin" (this describes an event in the life of George Frideric Handel). The information found within such a phrase, such as names, dates, places and organizations, is recorded with XML markup, which forms the basis for systematic research. The XML, although still human-readable for anyone familiar with its structure, is for usability purposes hidden by the Archiv-Editor. Instead the various information types are simply highlighted with different colors. In the above example one finds a date, a place name and a person name, which are tagged respectively as "persName", "placeName" and "date". Additional information, such as the specification that a placeName is a country, is represented in XML with attributes.

---

10   CIDOC CRM (Comité international pour la documentation/Conceptual Reference Model), http://www.cidoc-crm.org, 19.03.2015.
11   BERTI et al., 2013, http://www.musici.eu/database, 19.03.2015.
12   See BERTI/ROEDER, 2015.

Figure 3: Semantic markup in XML. The complex, semantically enriched XML format is simplified in the editor view (image: Torsten Roeder, 2014).

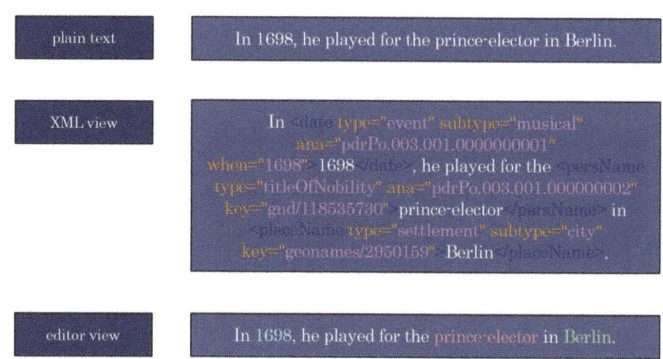

In addition to the already described categories, the MusMig classification also comprises a hierarchic vocabulary which helps to specify the information recorded (such as with the attributes "type", "subtype" and "role"). In this way the place name "Berlin" from the example can be attributed as "settlement / city", the date ("1698") can be attributed as a musical performance: "event / musical", and the "prince-elector" can be tagged as person. In addition the "prince-elector" – without him being named explicitly – can be connected to an existing entry in the database with the *ana* (analysis) attribute. Alternatively, persons can be identified with a standard identifier provided by a library, such as GND, VIAF or LCNAF,[13] in the *key* attribute. As the semantic XML markup is embedded directly in the source text, it is also possible to record more than one person (or places, dates, organizations) within one aspect (the identities would be distinguished by appropriate *ana* or *key* attributes). This is important for migration processes between places and for relationships between persons or organizations.

If a researcher later wished to compose a systematic list of all performances in 1698, or all performances in Berlin, or all performances with the prince-elector, the data could be retrieved easily by filtering (supported by appropriate search masks in the database interface). This method can also be used

---

13   GND = Gemeinsame Normdatei, see http://www.dnb.de/gnd, 19.03.2015; VIAF = Virtual International Authority File, see http://viaf.org, 19.03.2015; LCNAF = Library of Congress Name Authority File, see http://id.loc.gov/authorities/names, 19.03.2015.

in order to generate chronological views, geographical displays or statistical evaluations.

The following example (figure 4) demonstrates how this was implemented in the MUSICI database. The structure of the aspects indicates that the researchers followed different practices in collecting the data (the aspect of Johann Adolf Hasse contains more than one sojourn, while the other four aspects contain exactly one), and thus the format is not always consistent. To avoid similar situations in the MusMig database, it is planned to utilize templates with predefined text patterns and basic data sheets with predefined categories.

Figure 4: Research example from the MUSICI database (extract), displaying search results for "place = Rome, time = 1725, category = sojourn". The relevant aspect is displayed below the name of the musician (image: BERTI et al., 2013).

```
8
Nome:       Antonio Dankey
Risultato:  Roma, 1709-1732, almeno.
Categoria:  Permanenza


9
Nome:       Urbano Fraus
Risultato:  Roma, 1715-1729, almeno.
Categoria:  Permanenza


10
Nome:       Michele Surignach
Risultato:  Roma, 1722-1759.
Categoria:  Permanenza


11
Nome:       Euberto Ignazio Loyselet
Risultato:  Roma, prima del 1720 - dopo 1735.
Categoria:  Permanenza


12
Nome:       Johann Adolf Hasse
Risultato:  Venezia:1) Carnevale - luglio 1730.2)Primavera 1731.3) Carnevale -
            maggio 1732.4)Probabilmente 1733.5) 1734 - 1736.6) Autunno
            1738 - carnevale 1739.7) Estate 1744 - estate 1745.8) Autunno
            1746.9)Probabilmente inverno 1748 - primavera 1749.10)
            Probabilmente estate 1753.11) 1756 - estate 1758.12) Autunno
            1764.13) 1773 - 1783. Napoli:1) 1722/ 1724 - 1733.2) Autunno
            1732.3) Autunno 1758. Roma:1) Gennaio 1732.
Categoria:  Permanenza
```

The following examples will demonstrate in which way persons and places are relevant for the MusMig project and its database.

4. Music and dynasty. Migration of musicians in dynastic contexts

This subproject will investigate a group of German royal households or "courts" unified by a dynastic tie and merged over time due to dynastic successions: these are the courts of the Wittelsbachs in Munich and the Wittelsbach branches Pfalz-Neuburg, Pfalz-Sulzbach and Pfalz-Zweibrücken.[14] These courts to some extent cooperated closely in terms of politics and their militaries, due to the so called "Wittelsbachische Hausunion" (union of the houses of Wittelsbach) from 1724.[15] The research regarding these courts will focus on three aspects:

1. Did the very close dynastic ties and the political and military cooperations facilitate the migration of musicians and, in connection with the latter, cultural exchange?
2. Were music migrations caused by the various successions, for instance through dismissals of musicians or dislocations of the court?
3. How did musicians with different local origins manage to fit to specific courtly profiles, as seemed to be the case in Mannheim (with Bohemian musicians) and in Munich (with Italian musicians)?

While the first and second aspects investigate possible inland migrations produced by the exchange of musicians and by the relocation of residences, the third aspect focuses on questions regarding the recruitment of musicians. The sources for this research are mostly account and

---

14 In 1716 Karl Philip of Pfalz-Neuburg succeeded his brother Johann Wilhelm; in 1742 Karl Theodor of Pfalz-Sulzbach succeeded Karl Philipp. In 1777 Karl Theodor became, as the successor of the Bavarian Wittelsbach, Elector of Bavaria. After his death in 1799 the Electorate of Bavaria went to Maximilian Joseph of Pfalz-Zweibrücken.

15 Cf. KRAUS/SCHMID 1988, p. 517. Cf. the house treaties (Hausverträge) of 1724, 1728, 1734, 1746, 1747, 1761, 1766 and 1774 in D-Mhsa, Geheimes Hausarchiv, Hausurkunden 1773, 1774, 1787-1790, 1841, 1843-1850, 1852-1853, 1855-1856, 1856-1859, 1872. Documents regarding the house treaties and succession agreements between Pfalz-Sulzbach and Pfalz-Zweibrücken can be found in D-Mhsa, Geheimes Hausarchiv, Korrespondenzakten 504, 746, 1281-1282, 1689.

salary books preserved for the courts. These documents primarily provide data on employment periods and the amount of salary received, although sometimes more information can be found. Moreover court calendars, which began to be published in the early 18th century, offer valuable data, often giving a complete overview of the courtly household.

The following examples present three migratory musicians within the Wittelsbach dynasty: the composer Johann Christoph Pez (1664-1716), the castrato Valeriano Pellegrini (ca. 1663-1746) and the well-known flutist Johann Baptist Wendling (1723-1797).

Johann Christoph Pez received his musical training in Munich and began to work for the Munich court in 1688, before being sent to Rome shortly after by Elector Max Emanuel for further studies.[16] Between 1692 and 1694 he resided again at the court in Munich where, however, musical life had been reduced to a minimum. This was due to Max Emanuel's function as governor of the Spanish Netherlands which caused the relocation of his residence to Brussels. This development was certainly the crucial factor behind Pez's employment in Bonn at the court of the Elector of Cologne, Joseph Clemens, who was Max Emanuel's brother.[17] During the War of the Spanish Succession Pez left Bonn and returned to the Munich court in 1702. At this time the court had increased in importance because Max Emanuel had returned from the Spanish Netherlands to his former residence. In Munich Pez received a waiting salary until a suitable position in the court chapel should become vacant.[18] After Max Emanuel fled from Bavaria in 1704, he undertook the task of instructing the princes in music during the Austrian occupation[19] and remained in

---

16   On Pez's biography, here with additional information, cf. RAMPE/BERBEN, 2005; ROCHE, 2001.

17   D-Mhsa, Hofzahlamt 732, Besoldungsbuch 1694, fol. 61v: „Vermög Sig[nat] aus Brüssl [...] dato 18. Martj 1695. ist dem Pöze[n] d[a]ß 4. quartal diss iahrs, weil Er hernach in Chur Cöllnische dienst kome[n], [ver]wiligt word[en]."

18   D-Mhsa, Hofzahlamt 741, Besoldungsbuch 1702, fol. 77v: „gewest Chur= Cöllnischer Capellmaister, ist vermög ordonanz, in die Churfürstl: dienst aufgenom[m]men = und ihn in dessen Zum Warthgelt, bis er völlige installirt wirde, vom .1. [Septem]b[e]r diss iahrs angeschafft worden".

19   D-Mhsa, Hofzahlamt 745, Besoldungsbuch 6 June-31 December 1705, fol. 75v: „musico so Ihro d[u]r[chlauch]t: den Churprinzen instruirt"; Hofzahlamt 746, Besoldungsbuch 1706, fol. 59r: „Instructore bei denen ältern duchleichtigen .3. Prinzen". Cf. also ISER, 2000, p. 97.

Munich until the boys were exiled in 1706 to Klagenfurt and Graz.[20] Subsequently, Pez found employment at the Duke of Wurttemberg's court in Stuttgart. Pez left the Catholic dynasty of the Wittelsbach in order to serve a Protestant employer, a shift of focus which from a confessional point of view created numerous problems.[21]

Valeriano Pellegrini is an example of the classical type of a traveling singer (castrato) holding permanent positions at courts in addition to temporary opera engagements in various cities. Pellegrini was probably born in Bologna and was at times a member of the Papal chapel in Rome.[22] After opera engagements in Vienna (1699), Mantua (1700), Genoa and Piacenza (1701), Max Emanuel employed him at his court, just after returning from Brussels in 1702. Pellegrini remained in Munich until 1705/06, when he left the city because of the War of the Spanish Succession and entered the service of Elector Palatine Johann Wilhelm von der Pfalz in Düsseldorf, a member of the Wittelsbach branch Pfalz-Neuburg.[23] Pellegrini remained in his service until Johann Wilhelm's death in 1716, functioning as his agent (he bought a collection of medals and paintings) and was additionally engaged by opera houses in Venice (1709) and London (1712-1713), mainly performing works by George Frideric Handel.[24] In 1716 he entered the service of Johann Wilhelm's successor, his brother Karl Philipp, and moved with the latter to his new residence, Mannheim. Pellegrini spent the latter years of his life again in Rome.

The flutist Johann Baptist Wendling switched from being of service to the court of Duke Christian IV von Pfalz-Zweibrücken to that of Elector Karl Theodor von der Pfalz in 1752, apparently due to the former's pedagogical competence and his reputation. Wendling had been Duke Christian IV's flute teacher and fulfilled the same duties during his new employment at the Mannheim court of the Wittelsbach branch Pfalz-

---

20 On the princes' sojourn in Klagenfurt and Graz cf. ZEDLER, 2012.
21 Cf. OWENS, 2011, pp. 167-172.
22 On Pellegrini's biography cf. MARX, 2008; DEAN/ROSSELLI, 2001.
23 On the employment in Munich, not mentioned in the *New Grove* cf. D-Mhsa, Hofzahlamt 741, Besoldungsbuch 1702, fol. 77r, and Hofzahlamt 744, Besoldungsbuch 1705, fol. 75r, and OVER, 2007, p. 274. On his employment in Düsseldorf cf. EINSTEIN, 1908, p. 409.
24 *Agrippina* (Venice 1709/10), *Il pastor fido*, *Teseo*, maybe *Lucio Cornelio Silla* (London 1712-13).

Sulzbach.[25] While being in the service of Duke Christian and Elector Karl Theodor he did numerous concert tours, for example to Paris, London and Berlin. When Karl Theodor succeeded Max III Joseph of the Wittelsbach and became Elector of Bavaria, thus relocating to Munich, Wendling moved along with the Mannheim court to Munich and continued his service there.[26]

5. Visualization

As demonstrated in chapter 3, the data model of the MusMig database allows filtering, grouping and sorting of information using different parameters. Usually, a search is performed as a full text search, and the output of the results is displayed as a linear list. Yet there are different and more sophisticated methods available. Through semantic filters which determine the type of information that is actually searched for and by appropriatly choosing a visualization method, the selection and the output of the material can be refined to serve specific research interests.

Some visualization methods are fairly common and are able to give a general overview of the available data or its distribution in the database corpus. Some examples are: timelines order information by the proportion of their chronological distance. Maps spread the information (presuming it has been enriched with geospatial data) on a two-dimensional spherical projection. Tables order data chessboard-like using two independent parameters. Tree diagrams allow the visualization of hierarchic relationship structures. Such visualizations can be created dynamically and generically, as the method is mostly independent from the semantic details within the data.

In the MUSICI database this was realized with the help of a relatively simple visualization programming interface provided by Google.[27] With this tool, it is possible to process filtered sets of aspects from the database automatically, and return a pie chart, a bar chart, a geographical chart or

---

25 PELKER, 2007; GUNSON, 2001. Also PELKER, 2011; PELKER, 2002; GUNSON, 2002.
26 Wendling and his wife received a reimbursement of their relocation expenses in 1780. D-Mhsa, Hofzahlamt 192 (Jahresrechnung 1780); Hofzahlamt 2153 (receipts).
27 Google Charts, https://developers.google.com/chart, 19.03.2015.

even a timeline.[28] The following example (figure 5) shows the distribution of all aspects related to sojourns in Venice over the decades from 1650 to 1750. It is easy to see that there was a peak in the 1740s, and that there was apparently no data for the 1660s in the database. This kind of result reveals possible areas of investigation for researchers, that is, specifically to find reasons for these phenomena. It should be mentioned that the database does not necessarily reflect the historical reality one-to-one – it reflects simply the data in the database, which is but an extract from a vast amount of available sources. Although the corpus is composed to be as representative as possible, it is still a selection.

Figure 5: Temporal distribution of all data concerning sojourns in Venice in the MUSICI database. The information above the bar shows the number of available data on the peak in the 1740s (image: BERTI et al., 2013).

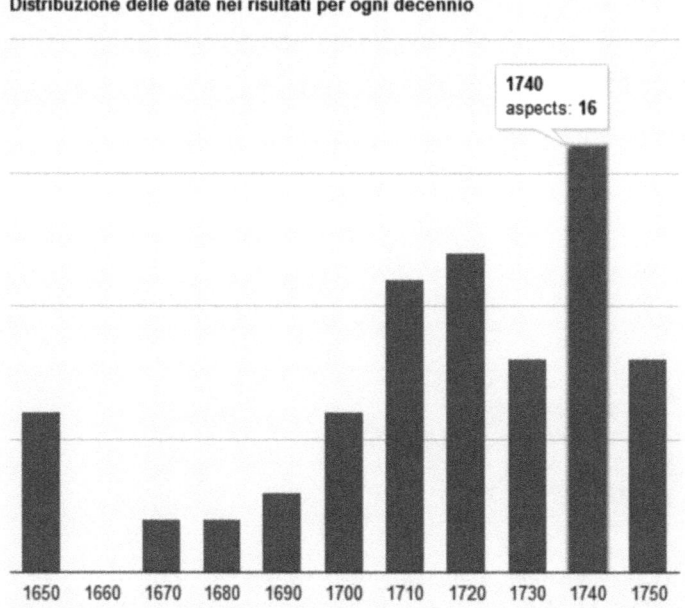

---

28 By including the SIMILE timeline widget by the MIT, see http://www.simile-widgets.org/timeline, 19.03.2015.

This visualization approach aims to provide a variety of views from the same set of data, thus opening up more perspectives on the material. The next example (figure 6) displays exactly the same information as above (all sojourns in Venice), but with a geographical display. Every dot on the map represents an aspect which contains both information on Venice and on another city outside of Venice, which implies relationships between Venice and those other places, e.g. migration movements of musicians. The researcher's attention could especially be attracted by the dots outside of Italy (Bergedorf, Grenoble and Sibenik/Sebenico).

Figure 6: Spatial distribution of all aspects related to Venice in the MUSICI database. The information in the box (above the most northern dot) shows that there is one database entry concerning Bergedorf (the birthplace of Johann Adolf Hasse), while the majority of locations related to Venice are gathered around northern Italy (image: BERTI et al., 2013).

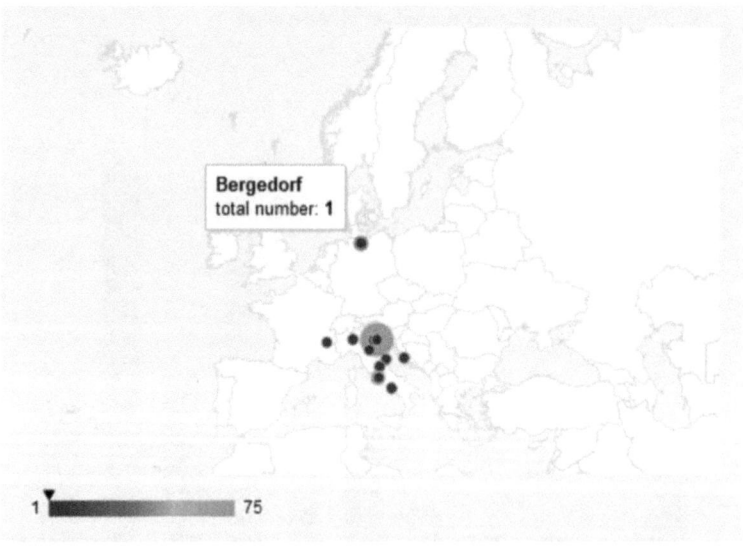

After implementing rather generic visualizations in the MUSICI database, the MusMig project aims to develop more individual visualizations which support the work of single researchers. Such visualizations, which deviate from the usual patterns and combine aspects of a greater variety as well as dimensions in parallel views, are less common but potentially very effective.[29] They allow focus on very specific questions, but they also require more elaboration and are highly complex in their implementation. The following two examples are drafts which are oriented on the historical examples given above.

Figure 7: Parallel visualization of succession and migration movements (image: Torsten Roeder, 2014).

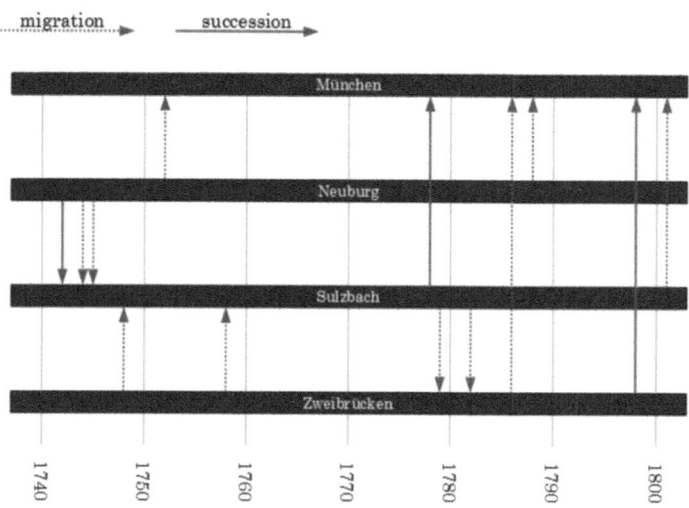

The basic scheme of the first draft (figure 7) corresponds to a simple time line. Above, the places of four courts are displayed as horizontal bars. Their geographical quality is converted to a line in order to support a parallel chronological view. These lines that represent places are connected by arrows, each of which depicts a moving person or a change of court. Each dotted line describes a musician who migrated from place A to place B, and each solid line represents the succession of a ruler. Thus it is possible at a glance to discover successions that probably involved immigration or emigration movements. It can also give an impression of the comparative attractiveness of the four courts over the decades. It is again up to the researcher to investigate further the phenomena revealed by the visualization.

---

29   This is soundly demonstrated in ROSENBERG/GRAFTON, 2012.

Figure 8: Compared itineraries of Pez and Pellegrini (image: Torsten Roeder, 2014).

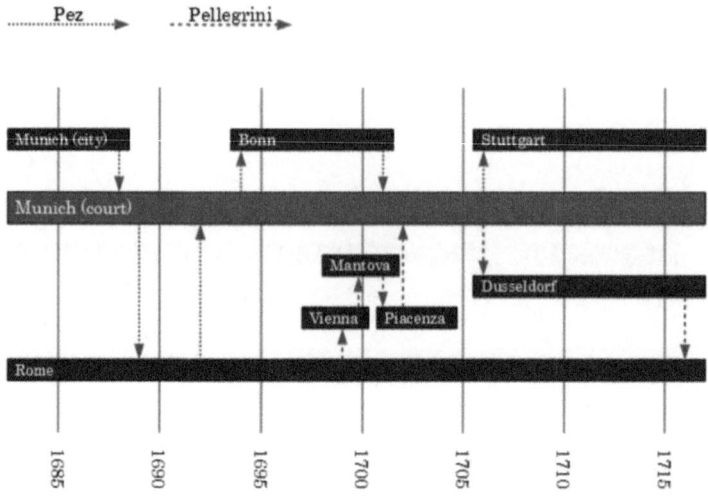

With a very similar method it is possible to compare the biographies of musicians and their individual relationship to a certain court. This draft (figure 8) focuses on the court of Munich and on the two biographies of Johann Christoph Pez and Valeriano Pellegrini. Migration movements are again displayed as arrows, the dotted line representing Pez and the dashed line representing Pellegrini. It becomes visible that the court of Munich played an important role in both biographies during the early 1700s: Both were engaged at nearly the same time by Max Emanuel (1701 and 1702) and left the court after he fled (1706). It would be of great interest to include other musicians' biographies in this comparison and to conduct further musicological research on the period during the War of the Spanish Succession.

Given these examples, it is planned to develop a set of inspiring visualizations that are able to support the specific approaches of the individual projects. This would give the researchers and all potential database users a unique and focused view on the one side, and more exploratory perspectives on the other side.

6. Summary

Despite all similarities that seem to place MUSICI and MusMig on the same level, significant differences can be observed. MusMig can thus be seen not only as a mere extension of MUSICI and neither MUSICI as a preliminary study of the extensive MusMig, but they are two projects with independent research approaches, which touch each other in essential, both methodological and substantive points and relate to each other. The continuities and discontinuities are also reflected in the digital representations of the two closely related projects which are based on a common data model, but pursue individual classification and implementation approaches.[30]

Literature

BERTI, MICHELA/ZUR NIEDEN, GESA/ROEDER, TORSTEN (eds.), Musicisti europei a Venezia, Roma e Napoli (1650-1750), Berlin/Rome 2013, http://www.musici.eu/database, 19.03.2015.

BERTI, MICHELA/ROEDER, TORSTEN, The "Musici" Database. An Interdisciplinary Cooperation, in: Europäische Musiker in Venedig, Rom und Neapel (1650-1750). Les musiciens européens à Venise, Rome et Naples (1650-1750). Musicisti europei a Venezia, Roma e Napoli (1650-1750) (Analecta musicologica 52), ed. by ANNE-MADELEINE GOULET/GESA ZUR NIEDEN, Kassel et al. 2015, pp. 633-645.

BRUSNIAK, FRIEDHELM/KOCH, KLAUS-PETER (Eds.), Probleme der Migration von Musik und Musikern in Europa im Zeitalter des Barock – Tagungsbericht der 15. Arolser Barock-Festspiele 2000 (Arolser Beiträge zur Musikforschung 9), Sinzig 2000.

DEAN, WINTON/ROSSELLI, JOHN, art. Pellegrini, Valeriano, in: The New Grove dictionary of music and musicians, vol. 19, ed. by STANLEY SADIE, London 2001, p. 299.

---

30 A German version of this article has been published in *Grenzen und Möglichkeiten der Digital Humanities*, ed. by CONSTANZE BAUM and THOMAS STÄCKER (Sonderband 1 [2015] der *Zeitschrift für Digital Humanities*), www.zfdh.de, 19.03.2015.

EHRMANN-HERFORT, SABINE (ed.), Migration und Identität. Wanderbewegungen und Kulturkontakte in der Musikgeschichte (Analecta musicologica 49), Kassel et al. 2013.

EINSTEIN, ALFRED, Italienische Musiker am Hofe der Neuburger Wittelsbacher. 1614-1716. Neue Beiträge zur Geschichte der Musik am Neuburg-Düsseldorfer Hof im 17. Jahrhundert, in: Sammelbände der Internationalen Musikgesellschaft 9 (1908), pp. 336-424.

GOULET, ANNE-MADELEINE/ZUR NIEDEN, GESA (eds.), Europäische Musiker in Venedig, Rom und Neapel (1650-1750). Les musiciens européens à Venise, Rome et Naples (1650-1750). Musicisti europei a Venezia, Roma e Napoli (1650-1750) (= Analecta musicologica 52), Kassel et al. 2015.

GUNSON, EMILY JILL, art. Wendling, in: The New Grove dictionary of music and musicians, ed. by STANLEY SADIE, London 2001, vol. 27, pp. 280-282.

ID., The Court of Carl Theodor: "A Paradise for Flautists", in: Mannheim – Ein Paradies der Tonkünstler? (Quellen und Studien zur Geschichte der Mannheimer Hofkapelle 8), ed. by LUDWIG FINSCHER et al., Frankfurt a.M. et al. 2002, pp. 263-283.

ISER, ULRICH, "Wie du ein französisches lied vor meiner gesungen". Zur musikalischen Erziehung der Wittelsbacher Prinzen, in: Die Bühnen des Rokoko. Theater, Musik und Literatur im Rheinland des 18. Jahrhunderts (Der Riß im Himmel. Clemens August und seine Epoche 7), ed. by FRANK GÜNTHER ZEHNDER, Cologne 2000, pp. 86-112.

KRAUS, ANDREAS et al. (eds.), Handbuch der bayerischen Geschichte, begr. von Max Spindler, vol. 2: Das alte Bayern. Der Territorialstaat vom Ausgang des 12. Jahrhunderts bis zum Ausgang des 18. Jahrhunderts, 2nd ed., Munich 1988.

MAHLING, CHRISTOPH-HELLMUT (ed.), Musiker auf Reisen. Beiträge zum Kulturtransfer im 18. und 19. Jahrhundert, Augsburg 2009.

MARX, HANS JOACHIM, Händel und seine Zeitgenossen. Eine biographische Enzyklopädie, vol. 2, Laaber 2008, pp. 762-764.

MEYER, CHRISTIAN (ed.), Le musicien et ses voyages. Pratiques, réseaux et représentations (Musical Life in Europe 1600-1900. Circulation, Institutions, Representation), Berlin 2003.

MÜNS, HEIKE (ed.), Musik und Migration in Ostmitteleuropa (Schriften des Bundesinstituts für Kultur und Geschichte der Deutschen im Östlichen Europa 23), München 2005.

OTTENBERG, HANS-GÜNTER/ZIMMERMANN, REINER (eds.), Musiker-Migration und Musik-Transfer zwischen Böhmen und Sachsen im 18. Jahrhundert. Bericht über das Internationale Symposium vom 7. bis 9. November 2008, Dresden [2012], http://nbn-resolving.de/urn:nbn:de:bsz:14-qucosa-88008, 19.03.2015.

OVER, BERTHOLD, "... sotto l'ombra della Regina de' Pennati". Antonio Vivaldi, Kurfürstin Therese Kunigunde von Bayern und andere Wittelsbacher, in: Italian Opera in Central Europe 1614-1780 (Musical Life in Europe 1600-1900. Circulation, Institutions, Representation), vol. 3: Opera Subjects and European Relationships, ed. by NORBERT DUBOWY et al. in collaboration with DOROTHEA SCHRÖDER, Berlin 2007, pp. 251-297.

OWENS, SAMANTHA, The Court of Württemberg-Stuttgart, in: Music at German Courts, 1715-1760. Changing Artistic Priorities, ed. by SAMANTHA OWENS et al., Woodbridge 2011, pp. 165-195.

PELKER, BÄRBEL, Ein "Paradies der Tonkünstler"? Die Mannheimer Hofkapelle des Kurfürsten Carl Theodor, in: Mannheim – Ein Paradies der Tonkünstler? (Quellen und Studien zur Geschichte der Mannheimer Hofkapelle 8), ed. by LUDWIG FINSCHER et al., Frankfurt a.M. et al. 2002, pp. 9-33.

ID., art. Wendling, in: Die Musik in Geschichte und Gegenwart. Allgemeine Enzyklopädie der Musik begründet von Friedrich Blume, 2nd revised ed., ed. by LUDWIG FINSCHER, Personenteil 17, Kassel et al. 2007, col. 765-769.

ID., The Palatine Court in Mannheim, in: Music at German Courts, 1715-1760. Changing Artistic Priorities, ed. by SAMANTHA OWENS et al., Woodbridge 2011, pp. 131-162.

PLUTTE, CHRISTOPH, Archiv-Editor – Software for Personal Data, in: Lecture Notes in Computer Science 6966 (2011), pp. 446-448.

RAMPE, SIEGBERT/BERBEN, LÉON, art. Pez, Johann Christoph, in: Die Musik in Geschichte und Gegenwart. Allgemeine Enzyklopädie der Musik begründet von Friedrich Blume, 2nd revised ed., ed. by LUDWIG FINSCHER, Personenteil 13, Kassel et al. 2005, col. 454-456.

ROCHE, ELIZABETH, art. Pez, Johann Christoph, in: The New Grove Dictionary of Music and Musicians, vol. 19, ed. by STANLEY SADIE, London 2001, pp. 533-534.

ROSENBERG, DANIEL/GRAFTON, ANTHONY, Cartographies of Time, Princeton 2012.

STROHM, REINHARD (ed.), The Eighteenth-Century Diaspora of Italian Music and Musicians (Speculum Musicae 8), Turnhout 2001.

WALKOWSKI, NIELS-OLIVER, Zur Problematik der Strukturierung und Abbildung von Personendaten in digitalen Systemen, http://edoc.bbaw.de/volltexte/2009/922/, 19.03.2015.

ZEDLER, ANDREA, Alle Glückseligkeit seiner Education dem allermildesten Ertz-Hause Oesterreich zu dancken. Hofstaat, Bildung und musikalische Unterweisung des bayerischen Kurprizen Karl Albrecht in Graz (1712-1715), in: Historisches Jahrbuch der Stadt Graz 42 (2012), pp. 337-366.

Sources of Musicians' Migrations Between Court and City

Musical Travels
Sources of Musicians' Tours and Migrations in the Seventeenth and Eighteenth Century

NORBERT DUBOWY

In modern times, everyone who practices the lifestyle of Western civilization leaves rich traces of data behind that allow his or her movements or travels to be tracked. Before the watershed of the digital revolution occurred, research into the movements, travels and tours of individuals relied upon basic methods, official as well as unofficial records, most of them in the form of easily perishable paper records. Despite the relatively huge amount of "testimonies", let's say, in the 20th century and the increasing loss of documents the further we go back in time, most of the types of sources we use for research in the digital era already existed in the 17th and 18th century albeit sometimes in a different format.

Sources for tracing the movements and travels of musicians are as manifold as the cases themselves. Everyone who undertakes biographic or prosopographic research on musicians is confronted with sources and documents that are peculiar to each individual case. Even though there are recurring kinds of sources, such as records from courtly employment, it seems hazardous to give a complete list or categorization of sources as scholars should always be aware that uncommon sources might be detected along the way. The sources presented here – most from personal research – are chosen as much for their exemplarity as for their uniqueness. A guiding principle when looking at them is the question of the perspective they offer on the traveling and touring done, and their informational value, i.e. the kind of information that can be gained from them.

Before entering into detail, it should be emphasized that no distinction has been made here between (a) "traveling" as touring and (b) "traveling" as migrating, emigrating and immigrating. The first may be defined as moving from place to place, sometimes in a loop, with the return to the place of departure, possibly with relatively short single trips, frequent stops and temporary stays. The second one, "traveling" as migrating, is more like moving from A to B with the goal of setting up a household, i.e. of making the destination the new center of life. However, one has to keep in mind that it is not always possible to draw a clear-cut line between touring and migrating. Therefore, migration is used here as a generic term covering both types of traveling.

This also is not the place to consider the different goals and motivations behind these types of movements, trips, and journeys, as important and interesting as that might be. Tourist activities, to gain some savoir-vivre by getting to know distant towns, artistic monuments and foreign cultures (motivating factors and educational goals for the upper class Grand Tour) are only a side effect for musicians who usually belong to the middle class. Socializing – as important as it may be judging from the large amount of space that is given to the description of encounters with family, colleagues, and patrons in many travelers' reports – was rarely the goal either. Legal affairs and health issues are among the strictly personal reasons musicians invoke when seeking leave of absence from their employer. For the most part, however, the true motivations are found in the profession of the musician itself. Next to seeking musical education or recruiting other musicians,[1] migrating was about seeking employment in a stable position and about practicing the profession as a traveling virtuoso. The latter became more and more of an option in the 18th century. The goal was to make a monetary surplus, i.e. to make money, as Johann Christian Bach bluntly stated in a letter to his brother Carl Philipp Emanuel when he asked him to support the traveling Davies family.[2] In many cases, however, given the social and professional dependency of the musician on a patron, the decision to go on a trip and, even less, the

---

1   George Frideric Handel's trips to Italy to recruit singers for his opera companies in London are well-known.
2   According to Johann Christian Bach's letter, the Davies' were "making this tour in order to earn a little money, and for that reason you would oblige me very much if you would help her [Miss Davies] to achieve this aim." See MATTHEWS, 1975, p. 154.

choice of the destination was not within the musician's power. Trips were often ordered by the patron,[3] or musicians traveled with their patron as part of the latter's entourage whether it was on a military expedition or a stay at a health spa.[4]

Research into the topic is often the art of connecting dots, dots that are geographically and chronologically often quite far apart. First and foremost it is in our interest to increase the frequency or number of these dots or, more precisely, the pieces of information that allow us to locate a person in a place. An often-overlooked aspect, however, regards the kind of "dots", their nature and quality: in other words, we have to ask what kind of information we can obtain, as the sources vary greatly in their "informational value". It might be useful, therefore, to start with a rough distinction between – what can be called – "records of presence" and "records of movement". In the first case, the record serves as evidence of someone being somewhere, in the second case for them getting there.

Among the variety of sources to be dealt with, there are recurring types that allow them to be grouped and organized into certain categories. The following remarks discuss some of these categories. It is tempting to place the criteria of presence vs. motion in relation to the factual types and classes of sources. Both ordering principles, however, will never match totally, even though, by the very nature of the source types, one category may contain predominantly information on presence while another may present more data on motion. This does not preclude that individual sources may not follow this pattern and the ratio between informa-

---

[3] See the case of the concert master Franz Joseph Pirker sent to Italy by the duke of Württemberg (MAHLING, 1973) and Berthold Over's contribution to the present volume, pp. 91-133.

[4] Claudio Monteverdi accompanied Duke Vincenzo Gonzaga on an expedition to Hungary in 1595 and to the Flemish city of Spa in 1599 (FABBRI, 1985, pp. 44f. and 47f.). Johann Sebastian Bach, too, traveled with his patron, Prince Leopold of Cöthen, to the health spa of Carlsbad in 1718 and 1720 (WOLFF, 2000, pp. 210f.). While the knowledge of Monteverdi's and Bach's trips are based on archival documents (in the case of Bach also on the *Necrolog* written by his son Carl Philipp Emanuel), travels to health spas may be documented in a special type of source, the *Kurlisten*, handwritten or printed listings of visitors to the spas that may also contain names of musicians. Some *Kurlisten* are accessible online (see http://www.portafontium.eu/contents/kurliste/?language=de); I would like to thank Berthold Over for drawing my attention to this phenomenon.

tion on presence or motion may be different. In this sense, the distinction between records of presence and records of motion is meant as a first guiding principle for our investigation and as a way of looking at the sources for musicians' migration.

Along the same lines it is necessary to ask some questions that are part of the critical assessment of the source (or of any source). These may be summarized with criteria such as precision, liability, objectivity, intentionality, function, and perspective. Needless to say that we are dealing, in most cases, with written text documents; sometimes a musical composition may be signed, dated, and "geo-tagged", and there may be iconographic sources as well, but I will not consider them here.

Records of presence

"Records of presence" may be defined as sources that show or imply the presence of someone in a certain place without reference to the act of traveling. It is just a point in time or a time-span, but does not give a precise date of arrival or departure. A record of this kind can be as simple as a name on a list, in a libretto or in a score. A single signature on a payment record can act as a witness. Such is the case with the violinist Jean Baptiste Farinel (1655-c. 1725) signing a receipt on behalf of Marc'Antonio Ziani (c. 1653-1715) for the latter's participation in three serenades for the duke of Hanover in Venice in 1686. This testifies to Farinel's presence in the city 28 years before he permanently settled in Venice.[5]

In contrast to the single item, there are "bulk" sources that offer a lot of names of musicians at one time. Listings of this kind may be documents showing musicians who were hired for a particular performance; very often there are administrative documents from the institution the

---

5   The record is preserved in a stack of material related to the duke of Hanover's visits to Venice in 1685 and 1686; D-Hs, Cal. Br. 22 No. 1077, f. 256: "Jay recu de Monsieur Korfei six sequins pour les trois serenade que le Signeur Marc Antoine Ziani a servi pour le Sigre Gianetini par ordre de Son altesse Serenissime fait a Venise le trentiesme juillet mil six cent quatre vint et six / Jean Baptiste Farinelli." On the serenades see DUBOWY, 1998, p. 186. Farinel was violinist and concertmaster in the service of the duke from 1680 on. He moved to Venice in 1714; see TIMMS, 2003, p. 46.

musician belongs to,[6] courtly account books, the payroll, or an evaluation of the chapel members by the *Kapellmeister*.

A common type of document in 18th-century Central Europe is found in the *Hof- und Adresskalender*, printed booklets that mirror the complete structure of the administration and the personnel of a court or sovereignty. As an example, we may look at lists found in the *Chur-Cölnischer Capellen- und Hof-Calender* for the year 1718,[7] that is the *Hofkalender* for the court of the archbishop and elector of Cologne, who normally resided in Bonn. Here, among kitchen aids and grooms, we also find three groups of musicians or organizational units within the musical establishment of the court, the *Hof-Musicanten*, the trumpeters and kettledrum player, and the oboe players, often called the *Oboistenbande*, altogether totaling not less than 40 people.

It would be naïve to assume that all of them came from Cologne or Bonn; a large portion of the musicians probably came from elsewhere. There are plenty of musicians with non-German, mostly French, Flemish, or Italian sounding names. Already this simple fact points towards some kind of migration, as some movement to the place of employment must have occurred.

If we place several years of *Hof-Calender* issues next to one another – here for the years 1717 to 1719 –,[8] changes or fluctuations that hint at migration also become apparent (see table 1).[9]

When we consider the group of oboe players, we note that Pürfüscht (Purfürst) listed in 1717 is not listed again in 1718 and 1719, but the name of Jamet appears instead. One of the other player's names is Biarelle, a name that does not seem to be German, but rather French or Walloon.

If we stay with the source type of the *Hofkalender*, the same name, Biarelle, shows up in a similar document albeit from a different geographic area, the *Hofkalender* of Salzburg for the year 1735.[10] There, a certain Johann Franz Biarelle is mentioned as "Zwerchflautenist," i.e. a transverse flute player. Could this be the same Biarelle from Bonn, who has moved south? The switch from oboe to flute – one treated as a secondary instrument to the other – would not be unusual, as we know from

---

6   See for example KNAUS, 1967-1969.
7   Court Calendar Bonn, 1718.
8   Court Calendar Bonn, 1717-1719.
9   Other reasons for fluctuation include retirement or death.
10 SCHNÜRER, 1735.

the case of Johann Joachim Quantz who was hired as an oboe player in Dresden, but became one of the most famous flute virtuosos of his time.

While the *Hofkalender* give us a basic framework for migration, other types of data may integrate the information. Braubach, who lists the court musicians of the last four electors of Cologne, gives 1700 as Biarelle's entry date and 1724 as the last time Biarelle was documented in Bonn.[11] Curiously, there is also a Giovanni Francesco Biarelle listed in Kirsch's *Lexikon Würzburger Hofmusiker*, who was present in Würzburg from May to October 1724, when he was dismissed due to the death of his patron.[12] While the employment of Giovanni Francesco (or Johann Franz) fits the date of Biarelle's departure from Bonn, the Würzburg Biarelle shares the names with the Salzburg one. If it is the same person in all three cases, Biarelle may have moved from Bonn to Würzburg and later to Salzburg. According to Hintermaier's study of the Salzburg Hofkapelle Johann Franz Biarelle entered the service of the Archbishop of Salzburg in 1731.[13]

It is unlikely that Biarelle was Italian, as Kirsch reports, even though he was listed as an Italian in the Würzburg documents.[14] Maybe Biarelle used the Italian form of his name as a fashionable variant. It is also possible that the label "Italian" was used as a synonym for "foreigner". There are two more artists named Biarelle, the painter Johann Adolph Biarelle (†1750), active in Bonn and Ansbach, and his brother, the sculptor Paul Amadé Biarelle (1704-1751).[15] The latter was born in Namur in the Walloon Region (today's Belgium), and this may well be the area where our musician is from. He could even be a relative of the two artists, who happened to work at some point in the same area, the court of the archbishop of Cologne. The Salzburg sources call Franz Anton "Leodicensis", i.e. from the Liège area,[16] not far from Namur.

---

11 BRAUBACH, 1967, p. 33.
12 KIRSCH, 2002, p. 60; see also *Bayerisches Musiker-Lexikon Online*, ed. by JOSEF FOCHT, http://bmlo.de/b2508.
13 HINTERMAIER, 1972, p. 17; based on court records Biarelle died on 30 Oktober 1743. In 1731 he had married Maria Josepha Theresia Boussier, the daughter of the Innsbruck court musician Franz Anton Boussier. I would like to thank Dr. Eva Neumayer for providing me with information from Hintermaier's study.
14 I would like to thank Rashid-Sascha Pegah for this information.
15 BOSL, 1983, p. 71; BEYER, 1995, p. 457.
16 HINTERMAIER, loc. cit.

A *Hofkalender* is a very basic type of source, which contains information that varies in its amount and quality. The problem with the *Hofkalender* in particular is its limited precision and the occasional inconsistency of its data.[17] It is like a snapshot, but it is hard to say when the snapshot was taken and who was responsible; in addition, there is no guarantee of its completeness. It is an interesting phenomenon to find similar listings of musical establishments comparable to the *Hofkalender* that appeared after the middle of the 18th century. These are the *Hofmusik* listings in musical periodicals such as Friedrich Wilhelm Marpurg's *Historisch-kritische Beyträge zur Aufnahme der Musik* or Johann Adam Hiller's *Wöchentliche Nachrichten und Anmerkungen die Musik betreffend*.[18] The publication of the listings in periodicals hint at the changing perceptions of *Hofmusik* as a performing body and at a heightened awareness of the individual musician as a performing artist.

One other type of source that provides a "record of presence" deserves attention, i.e. printed opera librettos that often give the names of the singers. It is a common practice followed by music historians to use the information from the librettos for tracing the chronological and geographical trajectory of a singer's career, but there are some caveats. The practice of printing the names of the performers in the libretto was not consistently followed. Librettos often lack exact information about the date of the performance; in many cases only generic terms are used to indicate the season (autumn, spring, summer, carnival, fair, etc.), while the only exact albeit optional date to be found, the date of the dedication, needs to be taken with a grain of salt as well. As librettos were printed some time ahead of the performance, we cannot even say with certainty whether the singer was actually in town, or whether he or she was replaced by someone else, not to mention when he or she arrived, left, or moved to another place.[19]

---

17 Some issues of *Hofkalender* give more information than others (e.g. Salzburg 1768). The *Chur-Cöllnischer Hof-Calender* does not give first names for most of the musicians; the "Sing-" and "Concert-Meister" are not always listed.

18 See MARPURG, 1754-1762, 1778; HILLER, 1766-1770; FORKEL, 1782-1784; CRAMER, 1783-1787.

19 In some cases, printed librettos bear handwritten marks that testify to the replacement of a singer with another one. See for instance the printed li-

Collecting information from all of the sources mentioned so far can already provide a large amount of prosopographic data, which either by itself or in combination with similar sources, reveals basic information on the movements, and migration of musicians.

Records of movement

The latter kind of information, data about the actual movement of musicians such as arrival, departure, and route (start date, end date, path, destination) – which I have labeled "records of movement" –, are gained primarily from other types of sources, ranging from administrative records to news and memoires. Sorted in some way by their degree of formalization and officiality, the following grouping is possible: a. official administrative documents, b. printed newsletters, handwritten newssheets, *avvisi*, dispatches from ambassadors and agents, chronicles and diaries (by someone other than the traveler), and c. personal documents such as letters (like personal letters of the traveler), including letters of introduction or recommendation, i.e. letters in support of the traveler written by someone else, and diaries, travel accounts or itineraries, and (auto-)biographical accounts.

It is not a problem that is peculiar to these kinds of documents, but the cases to be considered are particularly apt to illustrate inherent problems. These are the problems of precision and reliability, as well as scope and intentionality, which are all connected to the question of the perspective and role of the writer. The second group of sources, i.e. all kinds of news media available for the distribution and dissemination of information in Early Modern Europe, illustrates this point quite well.

In the 17th and 18th centuries – and not so different from today –, the decision of a news agent to mention a musician in a news record depends on its newsworthiness: is it interesting enough to appeal to the reader, i.e. is the case itself extraordinary and curious enough or is the person to be reported on important, interesting or famous? Whether the information finds its way into the newssheet depends on the writer's judgment as well as on his reader's interests. One factor that determines newsworthiness is surely the social rank of the traveler.

---

bretto to *Giannina e Bernardone*, Novara 1784 (printed at Milan), copy at US-CHH, (298livi); the singer's name for the female title role, Barbara Sassi, has been crossed out and replaced with Clementina Clossé.

In the *avvisi* – the kind of newssheet (bulletin) scholars of Italian music are familiar with – information on high-ranking travelers abounds as in the issue of a Venetian newssheet from 1700 quoted below. It records the departure of the Prince of Hesse and the arrival of two Polish noblemen of the Sobieski family. It is not only the destination or route (Milan via Padua; Rome) that is revealed, but even the place of sojourn in the town (the Lion Bianco inn) is mentioned:

> "Yesterday morning the Prince of Hesse mentioned earlier left for Padua, and it is said he wanted to go to Milan thinking that he would enjoy the carnival there [...].
> Some grandees from Poland have arrived who took lodgings with the nobleman Delfino at S. Apollinare, and some say that it is Prince Lubomirski; but several people think that it is Prince Alexander Sobieski, son of the late King John of Poland, on his way to Rome to visit the queen his mother.
> --
> Finally the two Princes and brothers Sobieski arrived and took lodgings in the Lion bianco (White Lion) hotel."[20]

Ordinary people (and musicians are just ordinary people) are much less represented in the newssheets. The following note about singers at the Venetian opera houses is rather the exception than the rule:

> "As reported, the singer Margarita Salicola left for Bologna on Monday; now they say she will not go to Genoa, but will return to Venice, which is already stipulated in her contract with the theater at S. Giovanni Grisostomo. Mr Girolamo, nicknamed 'Il Napolitano', will however leave for Vienna in the service of the Emperor; Mr Gioseppe

---

20 "Hieri mattina lo scritto Principe d'Hassia hà preso le poste per Padova e dicono vaddi à Milano con opinione vogli colà godere il Carnovale, [...]. Sono qui capitati alcuni Grandi di Polonia loggiati in Casa del nobile Delfino à S. Apollinare, et dicono sia il Principe di Lubomirschj; ma diversi sono d'opinione che sia il Principe Alessandro Sobieski figlio del fù Rè Gioanni di Polonia, e che vaddi à Roma à trovare la Regina sua Madre.
--
Finalmente sono arrivati li due Principi fratelli Sobieski; et alloggiati al Lion bianco." Mercurio 1700, I-Vnm, It.VI-477 (= 12121), entry of 16 January 1700 (1699 more veneto).

also left for Parma, being a singer of his Highness; and with him went Mrs Maddalena, known as 'La Francesina di Rio Marin'; she is said to be evangelized and planning to enter the monastery, but no one believes it; various [people], the Chevalier Peruzzino, a famous painter of Rome, and other foreigners accompanied her to Padua, where they made the waters of the Brenta river, drained by drought, rise with the tears shed over the separation."[21]

The singers are leaving town following the end of the operatic season; one of them is accompanied by her fans who shed so many tears that they make the dried out Brenta river rise. Despite the quizzical tone there is quite a bit of information in this note. Some of the singers are mentioned by their nicknames, which testifies to a certain reputation. As a record of the performers of Venetian opera at that time, the note is first of all a record of presence in that city but it also helps to narrow down the date of departure. For almost all of the musicians the destination is named which is always in conjunction with professional employment – e.g. the service of the emperor – and the engagement.

Handwritten newssheets that serve a rather limited clientele and the closely related printed newsletters, which have wider readership, both share an important characteristic as they appear on a regular basis and at fixed intervals and more or less on precise dates (a certain day of the week). Printed newsletters, with their wider range of distribution, rather than reporting the presence of the musician, serve the purpose of advertising. It is in this context that more detailed information on a musician's travel is communicated.[22]

21 "È partita, come si disse, per Bologna lunedì la Signora Margarita Saligola Cantatrice, non per incaminarsi à Genova, mà per ritornare à Venetia, già pattuita per l'Anno venturo per il Teatro di S. Giovanni Grisostomo. Partirà bensì per Vienna al servitio dell'Imperatore il Signor Girolamo detto il Napolitano, si come è partito per Parma il Signor Gioseppe del Resto Musico di quell'Altezza, e seco è partita ancora la Signora Maddalena, detta la francesina di Rio Marino, dicesi convertita per monacarsi colà, mà non si crede; è stata accompagnata sino à Padova da diversi [? indecipherable] dal Cavaliere Peruzzino celebre Pittore Romano, e da altri Signori forastieri, che nella separatione con le lacrime loro hanno cresciuto l'acque per la siccità scemate della Brenta." Mercurio 1682, I-Vnm, It.VI-459 (= 12103), entry of 21 February 1682.

22 See for example the case of the singer [Giovanni Battista] Palmerini (one

While the newssheets help to narrow down the range of dates for the arrival or departure of a person, there are other documents that provide more exact information thanks to the different scope they have.

One of the most fascinating sources (in my opinion) are the records of the Venetian health department (Magistrato alla Sanità) found and described by Paolo Rigoli. The Venetian health department held a quarantine office, the *lazaretto*, in Verona, an important gateway for trips from Germany to Italy.[23] To some extent, these records may be comparable to the registration slips one has to fill out today upon arriving at a hotel. Travelers from the north were required to stay at the *lazaretto* up to a full month after entering the Venetian territory in order to assure they did not carry any contagious diseases.[24] Among the musicians mentioned in the documents are Georg Muffat, Johann Adolf Hasse, Faustina Bordoni, and Johann Georg Pisendel. The latter, described in the document as "chamber musician of His Majesty the King of Poland who came from Dresden" (Musico di Camera di S.M. il Rè di Polonia, venuto da Dresda), entered the territory (at Ossenigo) together with other travelers on March 16 1716.[25] He was placed into quarantine in Verona while he was on his way to Venice to join the Saxon Prince Friedrich August who had already arrived on February 9.[26] The note about Pisendel's stop in Verona may seem insignificant – just a glimpse of the traveling conditions in Early Modern Europe – since Pisendel's trip to Venice is well known through other sources: One of these is his biographical account already published in the 18th century by Hiller,[27] who states that Pisendel's stay in Venice lasted nine months beginning in late April. Diana Blichmanns's

---

  of Handel's singers), stopping in Frankfurt on a trip from London in July 1730; ISRAEL, 1876, p. 25.

23 RIGOLI, 1996, pp. 139-150.

24 A different treatment was probably reserved for high-ranking travelers, who stayed on the San Lazaro island in the Venetian lagoon; see I-Vnm, It.VI-464 (=12108), f. 106v, *avviso* of January 4, 1687: "Il Prencipe d'Hannover si trova nell'Isoletta di San Lazaro con suo seguito a far una breve contumacia."

25 RIGOLI, 1996, p. 146.

26 BLICHMANN, 2010, p. 1.

27 HILLER, 1766-1770: Sechs und dreyßigstes Stück. Leipzig den 3ten März. 1767, pp. 277-281, Sieben und dreyßigstes Stück. Leipzig den 10ten März. 1767, pp. 285-292. The information is on p. 281; also HILLER, 1784, p. 188.

assertion (based on Venetian *avvisi*) that Pisendel arrived in Venice on April 20 together with the delegation from Dresden, however, needs correction, since according to the data from Verona, Pisendel did not leave until April 25! He was accompanied by the oboe player Johann Christian Richter from Dresden who is mentioned in Hiller's account as well – and the trumpet player Johann Greber whose destination may also have been Venice. He was in the service of the governor of Tyrol, Count Charles III Philip of Neuburg,[28] who was also the patron of Faustina Bordoni who gave her Venetian debut later that year.

Records like the one from the Venetian health office are either not very common, or there are more documents of this particular type but we have not paid enough attention to them. These documents are among the most objective records one could imagine. Unless personal negligence on the side of the official at the gateway station is involved, the information must be correct, as the records are taken by someone with no personal interests in the traveler who is entering the territory.

Still left for consideration is the huge group of personal documents. The importance of personal letters for the reconstruction of trips and tours is well known, if we just think of Wolfgang Amadé Mozart and his family. We are not always in the comfortable position of having so many letters as in the case of Mozart, but there are letters by many musicians even from periods prior to Mozart, some of them in considerable quantity. One may think in particular of the letters exchanged between Johann Adolf Hasse and Giammaria Ortes,[29] or the rich holdings of the Museo internazionale e biblioteca della musica in Bologna preserving the collection of Padre Martini or letters addressed to Giacomo Antonio Perti among others.[30] Letters do not necessarily talk about travels but if they do, they are often particularly instructive about the circumstances of traveling. It depends on the eagerness of the traveling writer as a chronicler of him or herself whether they inform about precise dates or whether

---

28 He was governor of Tyrol from 1712 to 1716, when he became Elector Palatine, succeeding his brother Johann Wilhelm.

29 The significance of those letters as testimonies of Hasse's travels is emphasized in DEGRADA, 1997, pp. 93-98. The letters are published by Livia Pancino (PANCINO, 1998).

30 According to the catalog of the Martini letters by Anne Schnoebelen (SCHNOEBELEN, 1979), information on traveling seems limited, but the letters addressed to Perti are rich in information.

they serve more as records of presence rather than motion that need to be organized in order to reconstruct the traveling route.

A group of letters that deserves special attention are letters of introduction or recommendation, which travelers requested from friends, colleagues and patrons to ease access to relevant people and circles at their destinations. I already mentioned one of those letters briefly at the beginning, Johann Christian Bach's letter for the Davies family, preserved as a whole set of letters of this kind.[31] These letters are important as they highlight what kind of social network was needed to plan and carry out a Grand Tour and possibly any, even a shorter trip, to a new place. As these letters had to be requested well ahead of the trip, there is no guarantee that they were actually used, i.e. that the musician really traveled to the place where the addressee of the letter lived.

Along with these letters, early biographies and autobiographical accounts place themselves in close connection to the category of the letters. Here, the case of Marietta Barbieri deserves attention as the records of her personal and artistic life represent one of the most fascinating documents of the late 17th century.[32] Marietta Barbieri was not a diva, but one of the mostly nameless secondary ranked singers of the time. Raised as an orphan on the Venetian mainland, she received musical training and made a modest career as an opera singer and composer (even though no composition of hers has ever been identified).

In Claudio Sartori's catalog of Italian opera librettos, the name of Maria (Marietta) Barbieri shows up only once: as a singer and composer in the oratorio *L'alloro trionfato*, an oratorio sponsored by the Accademia degli Unanimi in 1672 in Bologna.[33] A much richer picture becomes visible thanks to a unique source, the *Serie virtuose*, the biography written by her husband, Faustino Barbieri, published in Venice in 1692. A second, enlarged edition appeared in 1694.[34] The biography is written in verse, with more passion than skill. One of the copies preserves handwritten additions probably for a third edition most likely by Faustino Barbieri himself.

Like her husband, Marietta was probably from the Brescia area, where she may have had her debut as a singer. At some point in their life

---

31   See MATTHEWS, 1975, and THOMSEN-FÜRST, 2003, pp. 349-369.
32   See DUBOWY, 2002, pp. 181-208.
33   SARTORI, 1990-1994, vol. 1, no. 928.
34   BARBIERI, 1692.

the Barbieri moved to Venice. This is migration in the stricter sense as they moved the center of their life permanently to another location. In addition, the synopsis of her career as it is described in her biography shows that they made several trips through the peninsula, some to major centers such as Bologna and Naples, but also to many minor places such as Portomaggiore and Forlì.

In addition to the documentation of the professional trips of the Barbieris (who seemed to always travel as a couple, by the way), the *Serie virtuose* is also a document of the receptivity of people of their social class and background in the face of the arts and attractions they found at their destination.

On the other hand, they also reveal the problems of this kind of a source: the lack of precision, the possible mix-up of dates and places, as memories may be blurred, and the loss of information.

This brings us to the issue of intentionality and perspective raised earlier. The sources of this last group have their origin with the musician or someone in his or her immediate surroundings. We hold these documents in high esteem for their closeness to the person we are interested in, and they provide, without a doubt, valuable first hand information. On the other hand, together with the factors just mentioned, i.e. the risk of in-accurate information, there is also the risk of intentionally altered information since the writers may have a personal interest in presenting a particular picture of themselves or the situation they are describing. Thus, a simple date in an administrative record may be much more reliable as the writer has no personal interest in changing it. This quality of being un-intentional, having no personal interest in the face of the facts, belongs also to eyewitness accounts, such as diaries[35] or chronicles. Needless to say: asking about the precision, reliability, objectivity, intention, function, and perspective of the sources is a fundamental step in the critical assessment of any source (and sources for migration are no exception).

---

35 See for example John Evelyn remembering in his diary the performance of the Italian singer Siface (by Evelyn called Cifacca) at Samuel Pepys's house in London (Tower Hill) in 1687 (April 19) – a record of presence for the singer Giovanni Francesco Grossi (see http://data.open.ac.uk/page/led/lexp/1408487781292, 15.7.2015).

Conclusion

If the goal is to investigate the phenomenon of migration on a large scale, it is legitimate and practical to organize the data in a data base like in the MUSICI project.[36] It is the nature of a database that it operates at a certain level of abstraction to make the data comparable, but it is also desirable that it reflects the peculiarities of the individual case. Two final ideas are left for consideration with regard to the collection and presentation of data on traveling musicians. For one, one might suggest that it includes not only a reference to the source (a primary source, of course), but to the type of source, preferably even the presentation and display of the source itself in a digital image or transcript. This would be preferable to limiting the information (or what the compiler of the data file thinks the information is) to a reduced token that has to fit the template of the database. This would help decrease the array of potential subjective interpretations. In substance, this has to be a relational database consisting of two components, the personnel file database and the source storage database where the sources themselves have to be appropriately encoded. The second suggestion relates to the contents of the data base. As traveling and information about travelers is often influenced by human relationships and interests, it should be possible to link the personal data file to the tagged items of the source data base in order to reflect the "human factor", the network of human relationships. The MUSICI database does this (and the growing MusMig database will do it) – occasionally listing colleagues and patrons –, but it could be done on a more comprehensive scale. An intelligent database should be able to represent – possibly visualized in a topic map or word cloud – the social networks (which are also networks of information) of personal relationships, friendships (among people of the same social rank), obligations (between people of different rank), or relationships between colleagues (based on common experience) that are behind and accompany people's movements, travels and migration.

---

36   See http://www.musici.eu, 08.07.2016.

Table 1: Musicians in Bonn Hofkalender *1717-1719*

1717	1718	1719
		Le Teneur, erster Singmeister
		Brogniez, zweiter Singmeister
		Lambert, erster Concertmeister
		Donnini, zweiter Concertmeister
Vokalisten		
		Corbisier
		Montée
		Degrimon
Fagniani	X	X
Kircher	X	X
Delvincour	X	X
Chastelin	X	X
Ambrosini	X	X
Marquier	X	X
du Croux	X	X
Colbeaut	X	X
le Petit	X	X
Rissack	X	X
le Long	X	X
Rault	X	X
	Schwöller	X
		Barez
Instrumentisten		
Haveck	X	X
Deridder	X	X
Canda	X	X
M. Autgartten	X	X
Le Cerf	X	X
Van der Haque	X	X
Cornillor (Cornillio)	X	X

Thirreur	X	X
F. Autgartten	X	X
	Graeb	X
Rubini	X	X
Sommereis	X	X
Stumpff (2x)	X	X
Meuris (2x)	X	X
		Piva
		Bar

Trompeter/Pauker		
Poll		
Lüttgenhausen	X	X
Wastizky	X	X
Cron (Krenn)	X	X
von der Horst	X	X
Comans	X	X
	Ball	X
Penzenauer (Pientzenauer)	X	X

Oboisten		
Fabri	X	X
Flemment	X	X
Pürfüscht		
Klain	X	X
Biarelle	X	X
Reling (Röhling)	X	X
	Jamet	X

Kalkant		
Wilhelm Eschwiller		X
		Franciscus Philippus Rees

Printed sources

BARBIERI, FAUSTINO, Serie virtuose delle operationi esercitate in diversi tempi, e luochi dalla Signora Marietta Barbieri, descritte in quaderni da Faustino Barbieri suo consorte, Venice 1692 (second edition Venice 1694).

Chur-Cölnischer Capellen- und Hof-Calender [...], Bonn 1718; preserved in Göttingen, Niedersächsische Staats- und Universitätsbibliothek, 8 H Rhen 4205:2. Digital copy http://resolver.sub.uni-goettingen.de/purl?PPN678797455.

Chur-Cöllnischer Hof-Calender [...], Bonn 1717; preserved in Munich, Bayerische Staatsbibliothek, Asc. 3552c. Digital copy http://www.mdz-nbn-resolving.de/urn/resolver.pl?urn=urn:nbn:de:bvb:12-bsb10315060-5.

Chur-Cölnischer Hof-Calender [...], Bonn 1719; preserved in Munich, Bayerische Staatsbibliothek, Germ. Sp. 59-1719. Digital copy http://www.mdz-nbn-resolving.de/urn/resolver.pl?urn=urn:nbn:de:bvb:12-bsb10018624-7.

CRAMER, CARL FRIEDRICH, Magazin der Musik, Hamburg 1783-1787.

FORKEL, JOHANN NICOLAUS, Musikalischer Almanach für Deutschland, Leipzig 1782-1784.

HILLER, JOHANN ADAM, Wöchentliche Nachrichten und Anmerkungen die Musik betreffend, Leipzig 1766-1770.

ID., Lebensbeschreibungen berühmter Musikgelehrter und Tonkünstler neuerer Zeit, Leipzig 1784.

MARPURG, FRIEDRICH WILHELM, Historisch-kritische Beyträge zur Aufnahme der Musik, Berlin 1754-1762, 1778.

SCHNÜRER, JOHANN GEORG, Hochfürstlich-Salzburgischer Kirchen- und Hof-Calender [...], [Salzburg 1735]; preserved in Munich, Bayerische Staatsbibliothek, Germ. Sp. 252m-1735. Digital copy http://www.mdz-nbn-resolving.de/urn/resolver.pl?urn=urn:nbn:de:bvb:12-bsb10019907-8.

Literature

BEYER, ANDREAS et al. (eds.), Saur allgemeines Künstlerlexikon. Die bildenden Künstler aller Zeiten und Völker, vol. 10, Munich 1995.

BLICHMANN, DIANA, Der Venedig-Aufenthalt Pisendels (1716-1717). Erlebnisse im Gefolge des sächsischen Kurprinzen Friedrich August als Auslöser eines Kulturtransfers von Venedig nach Dresden, in: Johann Georg Pisendel. Studien zu Leben und Werk, ed. by ORTRUN LANDMANN/HANS-GÜNTER OTTENBERG, Hildesheim 2010, pp. 1-57.

BOSL, KARL (ed.), Bosls Bayerische Biographie: 8000 Persönlichkeiten aus 15 Jahrhunderten, Regensburg 1983.

BRAUBACH, MAX, Die Mitglieder der Hofmusik unter den vier letzten Kurfürsten von Köln, in: Colloquium amicorum. Joseph Schmidt-Görg zum 70. Geburtstag, ed. by SIEGFRIED KROSS/HANS SCHMIDT, Bonn 1967.

DEGRADA, FRANCESCO, Voyages et lettres de Hasse, de Vienne à Venise, in: Mozart. Les chemins de l'Europe, Actes du Congrès de Strasbourg, 14-16 octobre 1991, ed. by BRIGITTE MASSIN, Strasbourg 1997, pp. 93-98.

DUBOWY, NORBERT, 'L'amor coniugale nel Seicento'. Das Leben der Sängerin und Komponistin Marietta Barbieri erzählt von Faustino Barbieri aus Brescia, in: Barocco padano 1, Atti del XI Convegno internazionale sulla musica sacra nei secoli XVII-XVIII, Brescia 1999, ed. by ALBERTO COLZANI et al., Como 2002, pp. 181-208.

ID., Ernst August, Giannettini und die Serenata in Venedig (1685/86), in: Studien zur italienischen Musikgeschichte XV/Analecta musicologica 30 (1998), pp. 167-235.

FABBRI, PAOLO, Monteverdi, Turin 1985.

FOCHT, JOSEF, Bayerisches Musiker-Lexikon Online, http://bmlo.de, 20.07.2016.

HINTERMAIER, ERNST, Die Salzburger Hofkapelle von 1700 bis 1806. Organisation und Personal, Phil. Diss. Salzburg 1972.

ISRAEL, CARL, Frankfurter Concert-Chronik: 1713-1780, Frankfurt a.M. 1876.

KIRSCH, DIETER, Lexikon Würzburger Hofmusiker vom 16. bis zum 19. Jahrhundert, Würzburg 2002.

KNAUS, HERWIG, Die Musiker im Archivbestand des kaiserlichen Obersthofmeisteramtes (1637-1705), 3 vols., Wien 1967-1969.

MAHLING, CHRISTOPH-HELLMUT, "Zur anherobringung einiger italienischer Virtuosen". Ein Beispiel aus den Akten des württembergischen Hofes für die Beziehungen Deutschland-Italien im 18. Jahrhundert, in: Studien zur italienischen Musikgeschichte VIII/Analecta musicologica 12 (1973), pp. 193-208.

MATTHEWS, BETTY, The Davies Sisters, J.C. Bach and the Glass Harmonica, in: Music and Letters 56 (1975), pp. 150-169.

PANCINO, LIVIA, Johann Adolf Hasse e Giammaria Ortes: Lettere (1760-1783), Turnhout 1998.

RIGOLI, PAOLO, Il virtuoso in gabbia. Musicisti in quarantena al lazzaretto di Verona (1655-1740), in: Musica, scienza e idee nella Serenissima durante il Seicento. Atti del convegno internazionale di studi, Venezia – Palazzo Giustinian Lolin, 13-15 dicembre 1993, ed. by FRANCESCO PASSADORE/FRANCO ROSSI, Venice 1996, pp. 139-150.

SARTORI, CLAUDIO, I libretti italiani a stampa dalle origini al 1800. Catalogo analitico con 16 indici, 7 vols., Cuneo 1990-1994.

SCHNOEBELEN, ANNE, Padre Martini's Collection of Letters in the Civico Museo Bibliografico Musicale in Bologna (Annotated Reference Tools in Music 2), New York 1979.

THOMSEN-FÜRST, RÜDIGER, "This will be delivered to you by Mr. & Mrs. Davies & Charming Daughters." Die Konzertreise der Familie Davies 1767/68-1773, in: Le musicien et ses voyages. Pratiques, réseaux et représentations (Musical Life in Europe 1600-1900. Circulation, Institutions, Representation), ed. by CHRISTIAN MEYER, Berlin 2003, pp. 349-369.

TIMMS, COLIN, Polymath of the Baroque. Agostino Steffani and His Music, Oxford 2003.

WOLFF, CHRISTOPH, Johann Sebastian Bach. The Learned Musician, New York 2000.

"... und bißhero mein Glück in der Welt zu suchen ..." – Notes on the Biography of Jonas Friederich Boenicke[1]

RASHID-S. PEGAH

Researching and studying 17th- and 18th-centuries musicians seems to be an easy task, especially when the individual in question was a member of a *Hofkapelle*. That is: when it is known at which court he (rather more seldom: she) belonged to the musical forces. The simplest way would be to go looking at the relevant archive for the accounts of the court and period of time and the relevant archival records of that *Hofkapelle*. In addition, one could look for the parish records to expand the picture with information from the family and social life of the musician. Yet, some of these musicians used to travel around extensively – even when they had a stable position in a court or civic musical ensemble. Thus, it can become a more difficult task to trace their whereabouts.

If account ledgers are extant, normally it seems to be sufficient to look up exclusively the *Hofkapelle* section or sections of each ledger. Although, increasingly, it seems to be reasonable to also examine other

---

[1] For their generous help with my research and writing this article I am gratefully indebted to the following: the staffs of the Thüringisches Staatsarchiv Gotha (especially to Frau Archivamtsrätin Rosemarie Barthel who facilitated my studies most kindly) and of the Landeshauptarchiv Sachsen-Anhalt, Abteilung Dessau; Herr Stadtarchivar Christoph Engelhard (Stadtarchiv und Wissenschaftliche Stadtbibliothek Memmingen); the staff of the Staatsbibliothek zu Berlin SPK. Brian Clark, M. A. (Arbroath, UK), kindly shaped my English. Dipl.-Desig. Rainer Nowak (Regensburg) visualized Boenickes travels and I am grateful for his efforts.

sections of courtly (or civic) account ledgers. More recent experiences have revealed the section "Auff Verehrungen und gnädigsten Befehl" ("for honorarium and on most gracious order") as a frequently rewarding and interesting source. Whoever is searching for traveling or itinerant musicians might find traces of the individual in question in that very section. Also other itinerant individuals normally turn up there, as the rulers at Early Modern German courts commonly showed their grace and munificence by giving them some money to continue their travel or itinerary, if the ruler himself had no interest in employing the person offering his or her services. Currently, it seems that entries in this section for some musicians are the only documentation of their existence. One such example comes from the time of Johann Sebastian Bach's (1685-1750) tenure as *Hofkapellmeister* to Prince Leopold of Anhalt-Köthen (1694-1728, since 1704 ruling under the regency of his mother, since 1713 independently). In the *Kammerrechnung* (chamber [of finances] accounts) Johannis 1718/19 it says:

> "March 21, 1719
> To the castrato Ginacini, on his departure, who sang here, too,
> [receipt] nr. 320   20 Thaler."[2]

As far as I have been able to discover, nothing else is known on the castrato Ginacini[3] so far.

---

2   "21 *Mart*[iis]: [1719]. Den *Castraten Ginacini* Zur Abfertigung[,] welcher sich alhier auch höhre[n] laßen., N. 320 – 20 [Thaler]." D-DElsa, Z 73 Kammer Köthen, Kammerrechnung Johannis 1718/19, fol. 43v [olim Ausgabe, pag. 35]; Wäschke, 1907, p. 36; Smend, [1951], p. 19, n. 29 (p. 153); Hoppe, 2000, p. 43; Richter, 2010 [2008], p. 58.

3   Rudolf Rasch suggested in the discussion which followed this paper to identify "Ginacini" with (Francesco Bernardi detto) Senesino. More likely seems his identity with Pietro Guaccini (Guazzini), probably born in or around Cremona. Guaccini came to London, in March 1713. In about 1718 he was as a virtuoso and chamber-musician at the ducal court of Wolfenbüttel. On November 14, 1718, he was praised in a poem for his performance in the opera *Teodosio* at Hamburg, yet he left soon after in disgust. During carnival 1726 he performed in two *drammi musicali* at Genoa (*Adelaide* by unknown authors, and *Partenope* with a libretto by Silvio Stampiglia and music by Pietro Vincenzo C[h]iocchetti); see Burrows et al., 2013, p. 265; Merbach, 1924, p. 355; Marx/Schröder, 1995, pp. 366f. and 446; Sartori, 1990-1994, vol. 1, p. 26, no. 286; vol. 4, p. 359, no. 17831.

Köthen is also the place where the main subject of this brief contribution is clearly documented for the first time. And apart from an important note elsewhere – which I shall quote in the following chronological turn – Jonas Friederich Boenicke's biography can mostly be reconstructed, thanks to diverse entries in the section "for honorarium and on most gracious order" and to recently discovered letters of recommendation. "Johann [erroneous for Jonas] Friedrich Bohnako who sang" ("Joh[ann]: Friedrich *Bohnako*, so sich *vocaliter* höhren laßen") received five thaler on his departure from Köthen on 8 August 1723.[4] Sometimes, instead of Jonas Boenicke, he is called Johann by the accountants and Bohnako may be a misspelling of his surname. During the second half of October 1727, Boenicke visited the court of Landgrave Friedrich III Jacob of Hesse-Homburg (1673-1746, ruling since 1708) and in early November the court of the duke of Saxe-Eisenach. The latter recommended him to Duke Friedrich II of Saxe-Gotha-Altenburg (1676-1732, ruling since 1691/93), describing the singer as "born at Halberstadt" ("von Halberstadt gebürtig"). By mid-November 1727, Duke Friedrich II gave Boenicke a letter of recommendation to Duke Christian of Saxe-Weißenfels (1682-1736, ruling since 1712).[5] Again at the princely court of Köthen, Boenicke can be found twice more. Both times, he appears under the section "expenditure, for the princely *Kapelle*" ("Außgabe Geld, Zur Fürstl[ichen] Capelle"). "To a musician Bönigken of Halberstadt on departure" ("Einen *Musico* Bönigken Von Halberstadt Zur abf[ertigung]") two thaler were paid on May 1st, 1728.[6] As a letter of recommendation cited above states, he was born in (or in the vicinity of) Halberstadt.

---

4   D-DElsa, Z 73 Kammer Köthen, Kammerrechnung Johannis 1723/24, Ausgabe, p. 48, receipt no. 593; SMEND, [1951], p. 20, n. 30 (pp. 153-155, here p. 153), reads "Bohnando"; HOPPE 1998, p. 33, n. 78 (p. 47, corrects Smend and identifies "Bohnako" erroneously as the "schwarzburg-sondershäusischen Vocalisten Friedrich Johann Bonan").
5   Duke Johann Wilhelm of Saxe-Eisenach to Duke Friedrich II of Saxe-Gotha-Altenburg, *Datum* Eisenach den 5. *Novembr*[is] 1727. [only *courtoisie* and signature autograph] (D-GOtsa, Geheimes Archiv, AAA IV, nos. 36-39, no. 37, not foliated; on the lower end of the page, left, the note: "Jst den 15 9br(is) [1727] | nach Weißen-|felß *recom*[m]*en-|diret* worde[n]." ("Was recommended to Weißenfels, on November 15 [1727]").
6   D-DElsa, Z 73 Kammer Köthen, Kammerrechnung Johannis 1727/28, p. 110, receipt no. 287; SMEND, [1951], p. 20, n. 30 (pp. 153-155, here 155).

More concrete information about his place of birth shall be discovered presently.

By the end of July 1728, he again visited the Weißenfels court from where Duke Christian sent him to Gotha, while Duke Friedrich II of Saxe-Gotha-Altenburg provided him with a recommendation to the younger ruling Duke Ernst August (I) of Saxe-Weimar (1688-1748, ruled as co-regent since 1707, independently since 1728).[7] Jonas Friederich Boenicke is recorded once more in Gotha between 12 May 1729 and 3 January 1730. The first date is that of the letter of recommendation given to him by Landgrave Friedrich III Jacob of Hesse-Homburg at Homburg vor der Höhe (near to Frankfurt am Main). This letter is one of the most interesting documents about the singer in question, due to the wealth of information included:

> "The bearer of this [letter], a virtuoso, called Jonas Friederich Boenicke, born at Gröningen near Halberstadt, asked most subserviently to enter Our services. Yet, We presently don't know how to employ him, even though he was found very able and skillful in musical matters when he performed more than once. Thus he asked Us most subserviently for a most gracious letter of recommendation to Your Dear Grace, which We didn't want to deny him, none the less in view of his ability – rather We wanted to entreat Your Dear Grace hereby to assoil the above mentioned Boenicke, if a vacant post is available, at Your *Kapelle* or elsewhere, as according to his own statement he his versed too in law studies. He will recognize the high grace shown herein with most subservient gratitude […]."[8]

---

7   Duke Christian of Saxe-Weißenfels to Duke Friedrich II of Saxe-Gotha-Altenburg, *Datum* auf Unserm Schloße Neü Augustusburg zu Weißenfelß den 29. *Iul*[ii]: 1728. [only *courtoisie* and signature autograph] (D-GOtsa, Geheimes Archiv, AAA IV, nos. 36-39, no. 38, not foliated; a note: "An | den jüngern H[errn]. | hertzog Zu weimar." ("To the younger Sir Duke at Weimar").

8   Der "[…] überbringer Dießes[,] ein *Virtuosus*, Nahmens *Joh*: [recte: Jonas] *Friederich Boenicke*, aus Grüningen beÿ Halberstadt gelegen, gebürtig, [hat,] umb in Unßere Dienste zu gelangen, unterthänigste Ansuchung gethan; Wir aber selbigen, obwohlen er, *in Musicalibus*, beÿ mehrmahliger Ablegung seiner *Proben* sehr *habil* und geschickt befunde[n] worden, Dermahlen nicht gar wohl Zu *emploÿren* wißen; So hat er beÿ Unß umb ein

The most important information included in this exceptionally detailed letter of recommendation is the name of Jonas Friederich Boenicke's place of birth: Gröningen, situated immediately to the north-east of Halberstadt. Furthermore Boenicke mentioned during his sojourn at Homburg vor der Höhe his earlier law studies. This letter also reveals an impression of Boenicke's vocal abilities for the first time. After the Landgrave of Hesse-Homburg heard him sing several times – Boenicke had been there already in October 1727 (see above) – he found the singer "very able and skillful". Surprisingly, it seems that Boenicke did not immediately travel to Gotha once he had received the letter of 12 May 1729, at Homburg vor der Höhe. Did he make detours on his way, or stay longer at other places in the meantime, or did he spend the following months up to the beginning of the new year at Friedenstein palace? From there, he was recommended just once more to the Köthen princely court, on 3 January 1730.[9]

Thus, the third entry from the Köthen chamber accounts regarding Boenicke dates from 27 February 1730. On this day, the "Musicus Börnicke" received "on departure" four thaler.[10] This seems to have been Boenicke's last musical visit to the princely court of Anhalt-Köthen.

At Weimar he receives "on departure" 4 fl 12 groschen, on 1 April 1730.[11]

    Gnädigstes *Recom*[m]*endations*-Schreiben an Ew[er]: l[ie]bd[en]: unterthänigst angehalten, welches Wir ihm auch, in Ansehung Seiner Geschickligkeit, umdoweniger [lies: um desto weniger] abschlagen – Vielmehr Ew[er]: l[ie]bd[en]: hiedurch FreundVetterl[ich]: ersuchen wollen, obgedachter *Boenicke*, wo anderst beÿ *Deroselben Capelle* oder sonsten, da er seinem Angeben nach *in Studio Juris* auch *versiret*, ein- oder ander *vacante* Stelle Vorhanden seÿn solte, mit denselben zu begnadigen. Er wird dieße ihm hierunter bezeügende hohe Gnade mit allem unterthänigsten Danck erkennen [...]". Friedrich III. Jacob L[andgraf] Z[u] Hessen[-Homburg] to Duke Friedrich II. of Saxe-Gotha-Altenburg, Dat[um]: *Homburg* Vor der höhe den 12.ten *Maÿ* 1729 [only *courtoisie* and signature autograph], D-GOtsa, Geheimes Archiv, AAA IV, no. 40, not foliated; on the first page a note: "an | AnhaltCöth[en] d[en] 3. Jan[uarii]. 1730" ("to Anhalt-Köthen, January 3, 1730").

9   See note 8.
10   D-DElsa, Z 73 Kammer Köthen, Kammerrechnung Johannis 1729/30, p. 118, receipt no. 433.
11   D-WRl, Rechnung Nr. 253, fol. 273r, no. 4204-5.

After that date, Jonas Friederich Boenicke once again pays repeated visits to the ducal court of Saxe-Gotha, at Friedenstein palace. His next documented appearance there dates from 8-12 November 1731. Boenicke introduced himself with a letter addressed to the ducal heir.[12] The ruling duke must have been either absent or already ill, as he died only four months later, in March 1732. In his letter, Boenicke refers to his earlier occupation at another Central German court. And he mentions being on his journey home, unfortunately without specifying the place where home is:

> "[…] it has now been some years since I as a musician left the service of the prince [duke] of [Saxe-Merseburg-]Spremberg, and hitherto I was forced to try my luck in the world, and now I am intended to travel to my home. As, Most Serene Hereditary Prince, most gracious Prince and Sir, I lack the means necessary for it, I beg You most submissively, most humbly, to condescend most graciously by letting me have something to cover the traveling expenses, as a particular sign of Your Highness's exceeding graciousness […]"[13]

Jonas Friederich Boenicke dated his letter – currently the only one by him which is known – "Gotha, 8 November 1731".[14] Four days later, he attested with his signature the receipt of three thaler. Where his home place was then (Gröningen or Halberstadt?) or how long Boenicke stayed there, is impossible to say. However, at the end of the following year, he was – perhaps albeit briefly – at the ducal court of Saxe-Hildburghausen.

---

12 This was not an unusual procedure as the example of Filippo Balatri shows. Cf. the article by Berthold Over in the present volume, pp. 109-133.

13 "[…] welchergestalt ich als ein *Music*[us] einige Jahr her außer Hochfürstl[ichen]: *Sprem*bergische[n] Dienste[n] gewese[n], und bißhero mein Glück in der Welt Zu suche[n,] genöthiget worde[n], und nunmehro nacher meine Heÿmath Zu reise[n] willens bin; da nun[,] Durchlauchtigster Erb=Printz, gnädigster Fürst und Herr, mir die da zu gehörige[n] Mittel fehle[n]; Alß ergehet an *Dieselbe*[n] mein unterthänigst demüthigstes bitte[n,] *Dieselben* wolle[n] aus besondere[n] Hochfürstl[ichen]. hohe[n] Gnade[n] mir ein *Viaticum* | darreiche[n] Zu laße[n,] gnädigst geruhe[n.]"

14 D-GOtsa, Friedensteinische Kammerrechnungen, Belege, 1731/32, vol. V (Nr. 400 - 530b), no. 410. See also D-GOtsa, Friedensteinische Kammerrechnungen Vol. 94 Michaelis 1731/32, fol. 222r, receipt no. 410.

Indeed, another letter of recommendation for Jonas Friederich Boenicke from Hildburghausen was dated, 27 November 1732. From that letter, one learns more about his voice type and gets another impression of his skill in singing. The Duke of Saxe-Hildburghausen calls "Jonas Friedrich *Bænick* a tenor [who] knows his profession well" ("Jonas Friedrich *Bænick, ein Tenorist* [der] auch sein *metier* wohl verstehet").[15] Boenicke presented himself with this letter again to the Gotha Duke, now Friedrich III (i.e. the former princely heir who had shown his gracious benevolence to the singer one year before). Duke Friedrich III of Saxe-Gotha-Altenburg (1699-1772, ruling since 1732) let Boenicke have a letter of recommendation to the Duke of Württemberg-Bernstadt-Oels (Oleśnica in Silesia, which is part of Poland today). Together with that letter, the "*Musicus* Jonas Friedrich Bönicke" received 4 florins (gulden) and 12 groschen "on his departure", by "most gracious" order of the Gotha duke[16] on 2 January 1733. The 4 florins and 12 groschen were paid to Boenicke by Johann Valentin Schneider,[17] a trumpeter and ration noncommissioned officer (*fourier*) of the Gotha court, whose son, Ludwig Michael Schneider, painted the most appealing portrait of Georg Philipp Telemann (1681-1767).[18]

During winter 1733/34, Jonas Friederich Boenicke visited a court where a friend of Telemann acted as *Hofkapellmeister*.[19] From 1722 until

---

15 Duke Ernst Friedrich II of Saxe-Hildburghausen to Duke Friedrich III of Saxe-Gotha-Altenburg, *Dat*[um]: Hildburghauße[n,] d[en]. 27: *Novembr*[is]: 1732; a note: "Ist de[n] 2. *Jan*[uarii]: nach Oelß *recom*[m]*endiret* word[en] […]" (D-GOtsa, Geheimes Archiv, AAA IV, no. 43, not foliated).
16 D-GOtsa, Friedensteinische Kammerrechnungen Vol. 95 Michaelis 1732/33, fol. 182v, receipt no. 215.
17 D-GOtsa, Friedensteinische Kammerrechnungen, Belege, 1732/33, vol. II (Nr. 151 - 289), no. 215.
18 Cf. Portraits.
19 D-DElsa, Z 92 Kammer Zerbst, Kammerrechnung 1733/34[I], pag. 218, 1. no. 1788; Kammerrechnung 1733/34[II], pag. 218, 1. Nr. 1788: "10. [Reichsthaler]. Einem Sänger Nahmens Böhnig, welcher sich unterschiedene mahlen hören laßen" ("a singer called Böhnig who sang at several times") [undated entry (after December 1st, 1733)]; WÄSCHKE, 1906, p. 54: "Die Wintersaison 1733/34 brachte die Gastspiele des Sängers B ö h n i g , der wiederholt seine Kunst zu zeigen Gelegenheit erhielt […]." ("The winter season 1733/34 brought guest performances of the singer B ö h n i g [Boenicke] who had repeated opportunities to display his artfulness […]").

his death, Johann Friedrich Fasch (1688-1758) directed the court music of the princes of Anhalt-Zerbst (Zerbst is situated midway between Magdeburg and Dessau, and southwest of Berlin).

While the documents quoted so far placed Jonas Friederich Boenicke exclusively in a Central German and Hessian context, a brief description of a concert appearance places him at a South German trading town and makes his inclusion in an article devoted to itinerant musicians crucial. But before considering that Bavarian source, some short remarks are necessary about its origin. It belongs to another category than the account entries so far quoted. The small town in South Germany where Boenicke is recorded is called Memmingen. Memmingen is situated midway between Ulm and Kempten, southwest of the better known city of Augsburg. Especially during the 18th century, Memmingen was an important trading place, as it belonged to the Electorate of Bavaria since 1702, and the Elector bestowed the monopoly for the Bavarian salt trade on the municipality of Memmingen. As the town grew richer, the arts flourished. Yet, already by the middle of the 17th century, an art-loving medical doctor had initiated a *collegium musicum*.[20] It became a flourishing musical institution, and professional musicians or competent amateurs on their way to or from Italy sometimes took part in the concert assemblies of the Memmingen *collegium musicum*. The activities of this important civil musical circle were noted in minutes or records, of which two volumes are still extant – originally there were three. According to an entry in the second volume of the Memmingen minutes, the third assembly in the year 1735 was caused by the unexpected arrival of a musician not from this area of the Roman-German Empire. It sounds as if that foreign musician was in need of a performance occasion. Thus, the third assembly of the members of the Memmingen *collegium musicum* took place on 5 February 1735:

> "[...] a most noble private council [...] had sent Herr organist Ellmer to my insignificant self, to arrange an extraordinary [assembly of the] *collegium musicum*, as a foreign musician was here, called Johann [Jonas] Friederich Boenicke from Merseburg in Saxony, who came

---

20 Cf. on musical life in Memmingen HOYER, 2001. My source studies in Memmingen took place in July 2007, as part of the research project "Expedition Bach", organized by the Bach-Archiv Leipzig and sponsored by the Alfried Krupp von Bohlen und Halbach Foundation.

from Italy, along with his wife. And to the remarkable pleasure of the numerous assemblies of members [of the *collegium musicum*] he sang [with] a tenor voice in a fine manner. They were his own pieces, foreign Italian ones, and other agreeable fine pieces were performed too. Honorary guests paid their honor to the *collegium musicum* [...]. For the musicians who played on *corni da selva*, trumpets [and], oboes, an extra glass of wine was procured."[21]

Most interesting is the first part of that description. Johann Conrad Ellmer the elder (1701-1779), the mentioned organist, belonged to a local dynasty of civic musicians who also had some connections to Central Germany, as one of Johann Conrad Ellmer's sons studied at Leipzig university.[22] Jonas Friederich Boenicke was on his way back from Italy, in February 1735. Where exactly and since when he had been there remain open questions. There is virtually no documentation of German or other northern musicians in Italy itself other than later biographical or autobiographical accounts. More intriguing is the fact that Boenicke was married. Had he married his wife prior to traveling in Germany or did he come to know and marry her during his Italian sojourn? The listener who wrote down what happened in the extraordinary *collegium musicum* assembly of 5 February 1735 qualified Boenicke's manner of singing as "fine". When it comes to the content of the performance by Boenicke,

---

21 "[...] hath Ein hoch Edler Geheimbder Rath [...] H[err]en *organist* Ellmer Zu meiner wenigkeit gesant, um[m] Ein *Extra Colleg*[ium]: *Music*[um]: Zu halten, weilen Ein Frembder *Musicus* Sich allhier befand, Nahmens, Johan[n] [recte: Jonas] Friderich *BenicKe* von Mörßeburg in Saxen, welcher aus Welschland kam, nebst Seyner Frau, und Zu der in Zahl reicher h[err]en *Collegiaten*, Ihrem sonderbahren vergnügen, Einen *Tenor* mitt Schöner *Manier* sang, Es waren Seyne Eygene Stück, Welsch, worbey noch andere angenehme Schöne Stück *Music*[ire]t. wurden, Ehren Gäste beEhrten das *Colleg*[ium]: *Music*[um]:, H[erre]n *Baron BucKhamer* Preüßischer haubtma[n], Ihro wohlweish[ei]t, der Geheimbde H[er]r *Schelhorn*, und noch andere hießige h[er]ren. Denen h[er]ren *Musici*, so die Wald horn= *Trompeten*= *hopoy*, geblaßen, ist ein Glas Wein *Extra* angeschafft worden." *Pars II*da | *Continuatio* | Des *Protocolls* von E[einem]. | Lo[e]bl[ichen]. *Collegio Musico.* | Von *A*[nn]*o*: 1731. Biß d[en] 23. August | 1763, p. 68 (D-MMa, A 396/4).

22 Kirchenbuch St. Martin Memmingen, Beerdigungen, p. 107 (D-MMa, 156-37); HOYER, 2001, pp. 29f.

the pieces are described as "his own pieces, foreign Italian ones". Were they his own compositions perhaps on (more recent) Italian poetry? Or did he simply just own them? And to what extent did Boenicke require the accompaniment of horns and trumpets and oboes? Or did they just contribute some purely instrumental interludes – early samples of *Harmoniemusik*? Boenicke's presence at Memmingen called forth a second extraordinary assembly of the *collegium musicum* members:

> "[…] on 8 February 1735, again an extraordinary *collegium* was held, before the departure of the above mentioned virtuoso Boenicke of Merseburg in Saxony, during which he sang fine and rare pieces again, but mostly foreign Italian ones. For the rest fine and agreeable music was performed. At the same time it was agreed to let circulate a plate at the table, on behalf of the aforementioned Boenicke. Then a sum of 6 florins and 15 kreutzer came together, to which 1 florin and 15 kreutzer were given from the cash-box, and a present of one doubloon which he accepted with great thanks. There were honorary guests present at this *collegium* […] and the younger daughter of Herr mayor Herrman who sang a little song 'Sometimes a little funny, sometimes a little thirsty' etc., for the pleasure of all the gentlemen."[23]

The two performances at the Memmingen *collegium musicum* seem to have been rewarding for the tenor virtuoso Jonas Friederich Boenicke, on his way back from Italy to Central Germany. He must have arrived in

---

23 "[…] den 8ten Febr[uarii]: [A(nno): 1735.] ist wiederum ein *Extra Colleg*[ium]: gehalten worden, vor der abReyße des obbemelten *virtuosen BenicKe* von Mörßeburg in Saxen, in welchem Er widerum Schöne u[nd]: *rare* Stuck gesungen, aber mehrentheils Welsche, ist auch übrigens Schöne u[nd]: angenehme *Music* gemacht worden, Zu gleich hath man[n] beliebt, einen Deller an der Tafel | herum gehen Zu laßen, *p*[ro] bemeltem *BenicKe*, da dan[n] fl 6 x 15. gefallen seyn, worauf noch fl 1 : 15. aus der *Cassa* gegeben worden, u[nd]: man[n] Ihme ein *præsent* von einer *Duplonen* gemacht, so Er mitt großem danck angenom[m]en. Ehren Gäst waren in dießem *Colleg*[ium]: herr *Consulent* Wegelin von Lindau, Geheimbder herr Schelhorn, und *Tit*[uli]: herr Burger Meister herrman jüngere J[un]gf[er]: Tochter[,] die Zu aller herren vergnüegen gesungen, ein Liedel, [']Alle weil ein wenig Lustig, alle weil ein wenig durstig['], et[cetera]:". D-MMa, A 396/4 *Pars II*^{da} | *Continuatio* | Des *Protocolls* von E[einem]. | Lo[e]bl[ichen]. *Collegio Musico.* | Von *A*[nn]o: 1731. Biß d[en] 23. August | 1763, pp. 68f.

Hesse at the latest during September of the same year of 1735 because the penultimate signs of his life date from about this time. In the end, they lead back to Gotha and to the by now well-known section "Auff Verehrungen ...".

According to yet one more letter of recommendation to the Gotha court, Jonas Friederich Boenicke made an appearance before a Count of Stolberg-Gedern.[24] The small court of Gedern was situated approx. 50 km to the north-east of Frankfurt am Main. With a recommendation from the Count of Stolberg-Gedern, the singer presented himself to the Prince of Schwarzburg-Sondershausen who was then at Gehren, a small town where the Prince had a remarkable palace. At the end of September 1735, he sent Boenicke from Gehren to Gotha, several kilometers to the north-west. At the ducal Friedenstein palace, Jonas (erroneously: Johann) Friederich Boenicke received 4 thaler "on his departure"[25] on 8 October 1735. The last sign of life (presently known) of Jonas Friederich Boenicke also dates from Gotha; it is another receipt written in his hand:

> "3 rl. that is three imperial thaler have been paid to me
> the undersigned, as a sum to cover traveling expenses, from
> the high princely chamber, with all thanks,
> Gotha,
> 21 November 1737   Jonas Friederich Bönicke
>   musician."[26]

The case of Jonas Friederich Boenicke shows the relevance of more detailed research of historical account ledgers and letters of recommenda-

---

24 Prince Günther I (XLIII) of Schwarzburg-Sondershausen to Duke Friedrich III of Saxe-Gotha-Altenburg, Gehren den 30[te[n]] *Sept*[embris]: 1735 [only *courtoisie* and signature autograph] (D-GOtsa, Geheimes Archiv, AAA IV, no. 45, not foliated).

25 D-GOtsa, Friedensteinische Kammerrechnungen Vol. 98 Michaelis 1735/36, fol. 129v, receipt no. 158.

26 "3 rl. sage dreÿ Reichs[thaler] sind mir Endes / unterschriebe[nem] Zu eine[m] *Viatico* aus / Hochfürstl[icher]. Cam[m]er mit allem Dancke / geZahlet worde[n], / *Gotha* / d[en] 21te[n] / *Novembr*[is] 1737: *Jonas* Fried[erich]: *BönicKe / Musicus.*" D-GOtsa, Friedensteinische Kammerrechnungen, Belege, 1737/38, vol. II (Nr. 117 - 255b), no. 139; cf. D-GOtsa, Friedensteinische Kammerrechnungen Vol. 100 Michaelis 1737/38, fol. 120r, receipt no. 139.

tion from Central German courts for the reconstruction of the biography and itinerary of (traveling) musicians. The relevant entries are valuable sources for chronologies and to obtain an idea of the extent of the contribution of itinerant musicians and other artists or persons to 17th- and 18th-century court culture. The letters of recommendation help to refine such chronologies; they sometimes contain important and vital further information which can be invaluable for the reconstruction of biographies. They also provide an idea of princely networks which enabled itinerant musicians to search for (and in some cases find) their individual happiness in Early Modern Europe.

Figure 1: Jonas Friederich Boenicke's itinerary (1727-1737)

Literature

BURROWS, DONALD et al., George Frideric Handel. Collected Documents, vol. 1: 1609-1725, Cambridge 2013.

HOPPE, GÜNTHER, Zu musikalisch-kulturellen Befindlichkeiten des anhalt-köthnischen Hofes zwischen 1710 und 1730, in: Beiträge zum Kolloquium "Kammermusik und Orgel im höfischen Umkreis – Das Pedalcembalo" am 19. September 1997 im Johanngeorgsbau des Schlosses Köthen, ed. by ID. (Cöthener Bach-Hefte 8 / Veröffentlichungen der Bachgedenkstätte Schloß Köthen/Anhalt XXI), Köthen 1998, pp. 9-51.

ID., Die Hofkapelle in Köthen, in: Bachs Orchestermusik. Entstehung – Klangwelt – Interpretation. Ein Handbuch, ed. by SIEGBERT RAMPE/ DOMINIK SACKMANN, Kassel et al. 2000, pp. 39-46.

HOYER, JOHANNES, "Wo man die Musik pflanzet". Aus der Memminger Musikgeschichte vom Mittelalter bis zum Ende der Reichsstadt (Materialien zur Memminger Stadtgeschichte, Reihe B: Forschungen, Heft 7), Memmingen 2001.

RICHTER, MAIK, Die Hofmusik in Köthen. Von den Anfängen (um 1690) bis zum Tod Fürst Leopolds von Anhalt-Köthen (1728), 2nd ed., Saarbrücken 2010 [first published: 2008] (likewise: Halle, Univ., master thesis, 2007).

MARX, HANS JOACHIM/SCHRÖDER, DOROTHEA, Die Hamburger Gänsemarkt-Oper. Katalog der Textbücher (1678-1748), Laaber 1995.

MERBACH, PAUL ALFRED, Das Repertoire der Hamburger Oper von 1718 bis 1750, in: Archiv für Musikwissenschaft 6 (1924), pp. 354-372.

Portraits von denen jetzt=lebenden Herren Capellmeistern, [Nuremberg] 1750.

SARTORI, CLAUDIO, I libretti italiani a stampa dalle origini al 1800. Catalogo analitico con 16 indici, 7 vols., Cuneo 1990-1994.

SMEND, FRIEDRICH, Bach in Köthen, Berlin [1951].

WÄSCHKE, [HERMANN], Die Zerbster Hofkapelle unter Fasch, in: Zerbster Jahrbuch 2 (1906), pp. 47-63.

ID., Die Hofkapelle in Cöthen unter Joh. Seb. Bach, in: Zerbster Jahrbuch 3 (1907), pp. 31-40.

The Russian Experience
The Example of Filippo Balatri

JAN KUSBER, MATTHIAS SCHNETTGER

When in the fall of 1698 Prince Petr Alexeyevich Golitsyn, one of the chamberlains of Tsar Peter I who were sent to Venice to study navigation, left Florence for his Muscovite home, he was accompanied by the fourteen-year-old castrato Filippo Balatri. Balatri, called "Filippushka" by the Russians, stayed in Moscow until 1701 when Golitsyn was named ambassador of the tsar at the imperial court of Vienna.[1]

Balatri has left a couple of writings giving a rich report of his experiences in Muscovy and elsewhere. While his original journal, kept by the order of Grand Duke Cosimo III of Tuscany, has been lost, his *Vita e viaggi*, written in Munich in 1725-1732, provides a detailed account of his life up to 1732. Finally he put his tales into verse in 1735. The 343 pages of the *Frutti del Mondo, esperimentati da F.B. nativo dell'Alfea in Toscana* contain the shortest and most distant summary of his Russian adventures. While Balatri for these "sacrificed [the] spontaneity and richness of detail while straining for rhyme, meter, and what he thought was the proper poetic tone"[2] the first part of the *Frutti del Mondo* contains the most thoroughly composed image of Moscow and Muscovia delivered by the Tuscan castrato. Written over more than thirty years when Balatri was in the service of the Prince-Bishop Johann Theodor of Freising and Regensburg, the *Frutti del Mondo* are an important source not as much for the "real" Russia of Peter the Great

---
1   For Filippo Balatri and his biography cf. ZAPPERI, 1963; SCHLAFLY, 1997; DI SALVO, 1999/2001.
2   SCHLAFLY, 1997, p. 183.

than for the image of Russia that persisted in Balatri and was recreated by him in the *Frutti del Mondo*. This is, of course, always the case with such sources we call ego-documents. But the writings of Balatri are special to all those who are studying Muscovy in the Early Petrine empire at the turn from the 17th to the 18th century with reference to encounter and cultural transfer.[3]

For historians, Balatri's texts are somehow unique. The castrato did not know all the "classical" writings hitherto on Russia, such as Sigismund von Herberstein, Adam Olearius or that of contemporaries such as Johann Georg Korb, the envoy of the Habsburg Emperor, when he wrote his memoires, in which he did not follow any conventions of composition or style of the first half of the 18th century. He was in no way touched by the written traditions of perception that ruled diplomatic contact and transfer since the 16th century.[4] It remains unclear to whom he actually appeals with his sketches.

And unlike professional foreign observers, he did not pay much attention to politics at all. Balatri saw the cruel punishment of those who were the losers of Tsar Peter's ground gaining reform program. They tried to take advantage of the Tsar's absence during his Great Ambassade and had started quarreling against the social decline. The turmoil was oppressed before Peter I returned.[5] Thus, whereas Korb gives a detailed account of the shooting of the streltsy, those elite regiments who revolted against Peter I in 1698 (for the second time), Balatri believes that he witnessed the hanging of catholic heretics.[6]

What set him apart from other observers is his involvement in daily life of a family of the high aristocracy, the Golitsyns, who in persona underwent the change from old to new within the so called "petrine revolution".[7] Thus, it is somewhat surprising how little historians turned to his writings as a persistently valuable source. There is still no full reliable and complete translation of his writings into Russian. The only two Western experts on Balatri, Maria di Salvo and Daniel Schlafly, did not manage to complete a critical edition of his writings in Italian either.[8]

3 KUSBER, 2010.
4 On that: SCHEIDEGGER, 1987; POE, 2000.
5 MOUTCHNIK, 2006.
6 BOECK/MARTIN/RUSSEL, 2012.
7 In depth discussed in: CRACRAFT, 2004.
8 Apart from the mentioned literature: DI SALVO, 2010.

The following paper also has a rather limited aim; it analyzes the image of Muscovia and its inhabitants as it is presented in *Frutti del Mondo*. It concentrates less on the specific adventures of Balatri than on the more general information given by him in his writing. There are two fields that shall be investigated in particular: the image of the tsar, of Moscow and the Muscovites, and the relations between Moscow and Western Europe. We are integrating in these two topics some remarks on Balatri's mentioning of music, because that is the reason he was brought to Russia: to entertain the aristocratic high society of Moscow, at least Petr Golitsyn, in a new fashion.

1. Tsar Peter I, Moscow and the Muscovites

Peter I became Tsar in 1682 as a boy, together with his elder ill-minded half-brother Ivan V, one too young, the other incapable to govern. So, up to 1689, a half-sister of Tsar Peter, Sophia Alekseyevna, was the leader of state affairs trying to ascend the Muscovite throne herself. However, in 1689, Peter, at the age of 17 took over power and forced Sophia to retire from the public and retreat to a monastery. Taking a deep interest in western technique and military warfare, cultural practices, especially in the Nemetskaya Sloboda in Moscow, Peter gradually implemented sweeping reforms aimed at modernizing Russia. Heavily influenced by his advisors from Western Europe, Peter reorganized the Russian army along modern lines and dreamed of making Russia a maritime power. He faced much opposition to these policies at home, but brutally suppressed any rebellion against his authority: the streltsy mentioned above, Bashkirs, Astrakhan, and the greatest civil uprising of his reign, the Bulavin Rebellion. Peter implemented social modernization in an absolute manner by requiring courtiers, state officials, and the military to shave their beards and adopt modern clothing styles. One means of achieving this end was the introduction of taxes for long beards and robes in September 1698.[9] During this time, Balatri had his first encounters with Peter.

Tsar Peter is described in favorable, even emotional terms when Balatri claims to have been called "son" by the monarch.[10] He is affable and

---

9   KUSBER, 2012.
10 BALATRI, vol. 1, fol. 14.

makes friendly jokes about the castrato.[11] Peter is not depicted as tyrant, but as legitimate monarch ("monarca") with the title "Zar" or even "Gran Zar".[12] Although Balatri writes in the 1730s, he never attributes the title "Emperor" to Peter. His reign is classified as "Regno" (kingdom).[13] It is most likely, that the young Italian, when he came to Moscow, was fully unaware of the diplomatic struggles over precedence rivalries between the Habsburg Emperors and the tsars at least since the times of Ivan III (reg. 1462-1505), when Emperor Maximilian I offered the Muscovite Grand Duke the title "King". Ivan III refused based on his own dignity, as did Ivan IV (reg. 1547-1584), the first ruler to be crowned tsar of all Russia.[14] Whether he became familiar with these ever worsening disputes when Peter I assumed the title "Emperor" in 1722 after the treaty of Nystad, is not known.

The Muscovite court is called "grand"[15] by Balatri and, according to him, the tsar at least tries to keep it in good order.[16] He is described as severe with a heart like Caesar. On the other hand he is pious and Balatri is hopeful he will prove to be merciful, too.[17] Obviously, Peter was very generous towards him.[18]

Balatri also acknowledges the tsar's openness for the inhabitants of the above mentioned *sloboda*,[19] the foreign quarter of the capital founded about three decades before by Peter's father Aleksei, and praises him as a very learned monarch who managed to turn the Russian plums into roses.[20] Right at the beginning of the *Frutti del Mondo,* Balatri praises Tsar Peter for his efforts to fertilize Muscovy with sciences and arts by sending his nobles to Western Europe.[21] Balatri had the opportunity to

---

11   IBID., fol. 55r.
12   IBID., fol. 58r.
13   IBID., fol. 57r.
14   NITSCHE, 1991.
15   BALATRI, vol. 1, fol. 16r.
16   This stands in some contradiction to his critical assumptions of the other pages and chamberlains ("spàlnicchi") of the court. See below.
17   BALATRI, vol. 1, fol. 86v-87r.
18   IBID., fol. 184v.
19   IBID., fol. 96v-97v.
20   IBID., fol. 185r-186v. Obviously, this characterization of Peter is influenced by the knowledge of later events.
21   "Pietro gran' Zar, che regna sullo Scita,/la Moscovia s'invoglia fecondare/di Scienze e di bell'Arti, e fa cercare/Gente ch'in quelle bene sij instruita." IBID., fol. 8v.

meet Peter in the informal way the Tsar liked so much: Not only during assemblies and other occasions in the palace of the Golitsyns at the Tverskaya street near the Kremlin, one of the first buildings in a western style, but, more important, in the *sloboda*. Here, as a nice exception from the usual, Balatri gained access to the house of Anna Mons, the daughter of a wine-entrepreneur and influential mistress of the tsar. It was in the wealthy houses of the *sloboda* that Russian nobles and the tsar himself came in contact with western European music and it was here and in the Golitsyn-palace, where Balatri performed his singing, Italian Arias, but also Russian (folk) songs in an Italian style.[22] The most striking characteristic of Russia being expressed in the *Frutti del Mondo* is the vastness of the country. Balatri seldom uses the term "Russia"/"Russian" but obviously prefers "Moscovia". While Balatri does not describe his way to Moscow in a detailed manner,[23] he catches up later when he gives an account of his journey to the Kalmyk Chan in 1699. On his disastrous way ("viaggio disastroso") he describes a desert without churches and houses and suffers much from the heat first, while he is confronted with the effects of the Russian winter on his way back to Moscow.[24] Of course, it is the icy cold that shocks the young Italian most.[25] Moscow itself is described as a huge city, but very vulnerable to fires because of the wooden construction of the houses. Furthermore, there are hardly any outstanding buildings.[26]

Near to the tsar, Prince Petr Alekseyevich Golitsyn[27] and his wife are depicted most favorably in Balatri's writing. The nobles ("i Grandi") in general appreciated him. Much more hostile was the attitude of the common people ("Popol' subalterno")[28] – predominately because of religious reasons.

For Filippo Balatri, who entered the Cistercian monastery of Fürstenfeldbruck about four years after the writing of the *Frutti del Mondo,* it seems to be very important that he had not only the possibility to practice his Cath-

---

22 DI SALVO, 2010, p. 104.
23 He only speaks of "un viaggio lungo e disastroso". BALATRI, vol. 1, fol. 12v.
24 BALATRI, vol. 1, fol. 19v-44r, quotation at fol. 19v.
25 "Li freddi in quel' Paese san' far sassi / quegl'Uomini ch'à lor' troppo s'espongono". IBID., fol. 101r.
26 IBID., fol. 138v-139r.
27 On his position at the court: BUSHKOVITCH, 2002, pp. 115, 118.
28 BALATRI, vol. 1, fol. 15r, 139r.

olic faith in Moscow but was also encouraged by the Tsar to do so.[29] This should not be misunderstood as a general "tolerance", because the Catholic clergies are not allowed to wear their habits, and Filippo Balatri himself is insulted several times because of his Catholic faith.[30] When he uses the term "tollerati" in this respect, the most appropriate translation seems to be "toleration" rather than "tolerance" in the sense Benjamin Kaplan has pointed out recently.[31] Religion seems to have been a most important field of conflict. Balatri could not have been aware of the fierce struggle on "foreign" influences on orthodoxy, which went on until the abolition of the Patriarchy of Muscovy. Not only clergymen were suspicious of Protestant influences of foreigners and foreign advisors and of "Catholic" intrusions through the Ukraine.[32] That Balatri evoked the impression that most Muscovites regarded the western churches with enmity was his own experience. For Russians, Balatri wrote, the Catholic castrato is not a Christian, but a pagan, a Muslim or an idolizer of the Golden Calf, and he is called "dog" several times. A lot of people do not even want to touch him, at all.[33] It is merely of religious reasons that a lot of Muscovites show a mere animosity against strangers.[34] Balatri, for his part, is naturally confident to confess the true faith also and accuses the Muscovites of being superstitious.[35] Nevertheless, he appreciates the extraordinary fear of God in Muscovia.[36]

There is a certain group of people, the "Spàlnicchi" (*spalniki*), pages at Muscovite court, who seem to have developed a marked hatred against Balatri for religious reasons, too, but also because of the arrogant attitude developed by the young castrato when he was favored by the tsar and his nobles, as he admits himself. The hostility went so far that Tsar Peter decided to remove Balatri from the court to avoid further quarrels.[37] Arriving in Moscow, Balatri had to stay with the *spalniki* without any privacy before he changed to the Golitsyn-palace in Moscow.

---

29   IBID., fol. 13v.
30   IBID.
31   KAPLAN, 2007.
32   On this in detail CRACRAFT, 1972.
33   BALATRI, vol. 1, fol. 14v, 53r-53v.
34   BALATRI, vol. 1, fol. 138v.
35   IBID., fol. 139v.
36   IBID., fol. 137v-138r. His approval of the Muscovite piety might be a censure of the increasing irreligion Balatri had to observe in Western Europe.
37   IBID., fol. 16v-18r, 57r-57v.

Another hostile and perhaps even more perilous group was the "Baàrina", old women who looked after the young virgins in the palace and, according to Balatri, masked their predator-like attitudes with an enormous zeal against sin. They, too, reject him because of his Roman faith, but also because he was (almost) a young man.[38] Actually, this term was a misunderstanding for the word "boyarin", the female form of "Boyar". But these "old women" had to protect the young noble girls from boyar or even tsarist families living in the secluded *terem*, the closed quarter for women in the Kremlin, and were generally suspicious of every foreigner and especially those who frequented the *sloboda*.[39] A time of transition began for Russian noble women. One of Balatri's first impressions when he entered Russia in Smolensk was that women did not appear in the same room as men. In Moscow, segregation of sexes was not that strongly observed and Balatri, as a chamberlain, had the opportunity of switching between the spheres of men and women in the Kremlin palaces. Peter approached the problem in a characteristic manner. Balatri remembers how some Muscovite ladies were invited to a ball in the house of François Lefort, a Suisse favorite of Peter. There, the ladies were greeted by the Tsar and he tried to dance with them. Guards were posted at the doors to stop the guests from leaving early. But there were also court events, concerts and plays for example where the noble women had to hide behind a curtain and were merely allowed to listen.[40]

For Balatri, ordinary Muscovites seemed to be rather rude people, but they were not described as savages. This becomes most obvious when Balatri gives an account of his travel to the Kalmyk in the entourage of Boris Golitsyn,[41] appointed ambassador to the khan in 1699.

The Kalmyks (Oirats) at that time were a borderland power, often allying themselves with the tsarist government against the neighboring Muslim population. During the era of Ayuka Khan, whom Golitsyn (and Balatri) visited, the Kalmyks rose to political and military prominence as the tsarist government sought the increased use of their cavalry in support of its military campaigns against the Muslim powers in the south, such as Persia, the Ottoman Empire, the Nogays and the Kuban Tatars and Crimean Khanate. Ayuka Khan also waged wars against the Ka-

---

38 IBID., fol. 59r-59v, 61v.
39 DAHLMANN, 2004.
40 HUGHES, 1998, pp. 187f.
41 BUSHKOVITCH, 2002, pp. 68f., 85-87.

zakhs, subjugated the Turkmens, and undertook expeditions against the highlanders of the North Caucasus.[42] These campaigns highlighted the strategic importance of the Kalmyk Khanate which functioned as a buffer zone, separating Russia and the Muslim world, as Peter concentrated fully on Europe to establish himself as a European power.

Although, in his description of this journey, the castrato laments that Golitsyn with his military strength would not have taken in account that Italians were more sensitive than the Muscovite,[43] when they arrived at the khan's residence, the assortment of "we" and "they" suddenly changed. Ayuka Khan is interested in Balatri and unsuccessfully asks Golitsyn to leave the young Italian to him. It is now the Kalmyk who are depicted as "strange" with their infernal music ("infernal canzone"), their impropriate clothes and disgusting manners, while good order prevails in the Muscovite camp. But Muscovites and Kalmyk have one thing in common: their passion of "l'Acquavita".[44]

Despite his rather critical comments on Muscovia – "a land full of misunderstanding"[45] – and the Muscovite people at the very beginning of his tale when he deals with his arrival at Moscow, Balatri calls it "Patria".[46] He claims to have learned the Russian language within 18 months.[47] The mentioned Anna Mons asked him to write a letter for her "in Muscovite". However, receiving the chance to leave Russia in the entourage of Prince Golitsyn and to go to Vienna where Golitsyn was appointed ambassador was obviously happy news for Balatri.[48]

---

42   KHODARKOVSKY, 1992, pp. 134-169.
43   BALATRI, vol. 1, fol. 22v.
44   IBID., fol. 24v-41v, quotations at fol. 25r, 28v. The following sequence (fol. 28v) is meaningful, too: "Almen' nel nostro Campo v'è buon'ordine / et ognun'è vestito dà Signore, / si balla in Simetrìa, in buon' tenòre / si canta, e intutto non v'è gran' disordine." Nevertheless the khan of the "Tartari" is depicted as a kind of noble savage who appreciates Balatri's singing very much (fol. 29v-31v, 34v-38r).
45   "Paese pien d'errore". BALATRI, vol. 1, fol. 71r.
46   IBID., fol. 13r. Cf. also fol. 142: "Ammè piace la Scitia".
47   IBID., fol. 17r.
48   IBID., fol. 126v.

2. "Muscovia" and Western Europe

When, as has been pointed out, Tsar Peter's efforts to cultivate Muscovy by importing scientists and artists from Western Europe are praised by Balatri, he implicitly expressed a certain inferiority of Muscovy at the same time. In order to fulfill the designs of the tsar, the principal nobles of the country were sent to the most important cities of Italy, Germany, France and England.[49] According to Balatri, their task was to learn the western languages, to get to know the places of interest, the customs, the laws etc. so that they would return to Moscow as equals of the people of their host countries.[50] Furthermore, they should take learned men with them – a fate that happened to Balatri himself.

Balatri was *nota bene* not the only expert who traveled back from Italy to Moscow with Petr Golitsyn. Golitsyn extensively recruited craftsmen, scientists, artists and musicians for the Tsar's service.[51] Peter I developed a deeper interest for western European music during his "Great Ambassade" in 1697/1698, when he attended the courts of Brunswick, Königsberg, The Hague, Dresden, and Vienna.[52] We have no recordings whether he was impressed by the music he heard. However, he was impressed by the way women and men came in contact through music – by dancing. It is noteworthy that Peter was keen to acquire musicians from abroad after his journey.

Around 1700, Peter's interest in secular music began to develop. The use of musical instruments, including the organ, was still banned in church, but sacred music for human voices was adapted in the new era.[53] Thus, Balatri and the other "imported" musicians were also welcome here. Peter showed greater preference of parades, celebrating military victories with fanfares and also choirs singing panegyric verses and chants. In this way, the Muscovite seventeenth century choral tradition was harnessed for the needs of the state. The richness of the Russian unaccompanied

---

49 See apart from the Golitsyns the most prominent example of Boris Kurakin: ZITSER, 2011.
50 "Ci vuol' insomma, che si faccin' uomini / e ch'al ritorno si dimostrin' tali, / che piucche ponno rendansi coeguali / al Gallo, all'Anglo, All'Italo, ò a cui nomini." BALATRI, vol. 1, fol. 9v. Cf. IBID., fol. 10v; the best study on the *sloboda* is the rich and thorough account of KOVRIGINA, 1998.
51 SCHLAFLY, 1997, p. 182.
52 In detail studied in: GUSKOV, 2005.
53 A brilliant overview is provided by JENSEN, 2009.

choral music in church continued into a new age under the influence of both Russian native composers and foreigners, as did folksong. The ruling elite, as Peter's favorite Alexandr Menshikov and the Golitsyns, maintained a choir of Russian and Ukrainian singers, for example, and started to hire foreign instrumentalists to play alongside the choir. Balatri may have seen the beginning of these developments, which came into full swing after the move of the court to St. Petersburg after 1712.[54] Balatri may also have heard the first modern chants in the churches of Moscow around 1700. But it was not until the 1730's that a complete opera production from an Italian troop was to be seen in St. Petersburg.[55]

It is interesting that Balatri qualifies his singing as mere "passable" at that time but satisfactory to please Peter's wish to hear "our" music at Moscow.[56] Thereby he underlines the differences between the western countries and a strange, obviously culturally inferior Russia. Also the descriptions of the *sloboda* suggest a cultural inferiority of the Muscovites because western artists have lived there for hundred years, now, and Moscow does not seem to have become independent of this foreign aid, so far.[57] Only in *sloboda* one can find "the rarest things which the Russians do not know".[58] Obviously, the level of education is very low, books are a scarce commodity.

Another point of criticism is the situation of the women whom the tsar wants to be released from their "imprisonment" of the above mentioned *terem*.[59] In the palace of Peter Golitsyn, Balatri became the trustee of the lady of the house, Darya Golitsyna, a conservative religious woman who ruled the house through the *terem*. This was not a weak position, but for Balatri, who had access to the women's chambers, it was strange enough. Although Darya seemed to be charmed by the castrato who was no threat for the women in the *terem*, she had strong reservations about the new style of events taking place in the *sloboda*. She only changed her attitude when she accompanied her husband (and Balatri) to Vienna.[60]

---

54 HUGHES, 2006, pp. 72f.
55 HUGHES, 1998, pp. 243-248.
56 BALATRI, vol. 1, fol. 11r.
57 IBID., fol. 13v.
58 "La si trovan' le cose le piu rare / delle quali li Russi so' ignoranti". IBID., fol. 96v.
59 BALATRI, vol. 1, fol. 97v-98r, 125v; for the situation of the women cf. IBID., fol. 139r, too.
60 SCHLAFLY, 1997, pp. 193-195.

On the other hand, there can be no doubt that also in Balatri's view there had been an exchange between Moscow and the western countries even before Peter. Balatri by no means evokes the image of an isolated, self-content Russia. But, he obviously thinks that the Muscovites have to be enlightened and he himself tries to do his best in this respect.[61]

As has been pointed out earlier, another difference was clearly marked by the confession. In this respect, Balatri alludes to a difference between Tsar Peter, the high nobility and the ordinary people: When Peter or the Golitsyn exercised severity against one of his persecutors, they were accused of injustice and protection of heresy.[62] Even among the entourage of Prince Golitsyn in 1701, there are people who are afraid of the lands of the infidels they expect to enter.[63]

Conclusion

Balatri, who was to become famous following his Russian experience, was neither the first nor the last to come to Russia and to make a specific contribution on the westernization of court culture. It is not easy to estimate their impact in a longer perspective, because transfer and influence of people, practices and habits in Russian elite culture were severe and led to new forms of hybrid fashioning in Russian high nobility as well as the new court in St. Petersburg. The patterns of his travels are similar to later examples in as far as most of these travelers just stayed for a short period of time. This is especially true for musicians, actors and artists. What renders Balatri's case singular are the ego-documents left by him presenting and digesting his various and capricious experiences within – and not only on the periphery of – the Muscovite court. Furthermore, his observations illuminate a crucial period of change from Muscovia to the Petrine Russian Empire, a period that has not at least been shaped by the re-definition of relations to Western Europe, and Balatri's writings provide an insight into this from a point of view which is, at the same time, internal and "western". Of course, this is just one reason why they should be examined more closely and in greater detail.

---

61   IBID., fol. 140r. He uses the verb "illuminare"/enlighten here.
62   IBID., fol. 61v.
63   IBID., fol. 127r-127v.

Manuscript sources

BALATRI, [DIONISIO] FILIPPO, Frutti del Mondo, esperimentati da F.B., nativo dell'Alfea in Toscana. Bayerische Staatsbibliothek München, Cod.ital. 39(2), http: http://daten.digitale-sammlungen.de/~db/0004/ bsb00045469/images/index.html?seite=00005&l=en, 30.03. 2014.

Literature

BOECK, BRIAN J. et al., Pictures at an Execution: Johann Georg Korbs Execution of the Streltsy, in: Dubitando. Studies in History and Culture in Honor of Donald Ostrowski, ed. by DANIEL ROWLAND, Bloomington 2012, pp. 399-408.

BUSHKOVITCH, PAUL, Peter the Great. The Struggle for Power, 1671-1725 (New Studies in European History), Cambridge 2002.

CRACRAFT, JAMES, The Church Reform of Peter the Great, Stanford 1972.

ID., The Petrine Revolution in Russian Culture, Cambridge et al. 2004.

DAHLMANN, DITTMAR, Die Frauen des russischen Hochadels im 16. und 17. Jahrhundert. Der lange Weg aus der Isolation, in: DAMALS 36 (2004), Nr. 2, pp. 22-28.

DI SALVO, MARIA, Vita e viaggi di Filippo Balatri, in: Russica Romana 6 (1999/2001), pp. 37-57.

ID., The 'Italian' Nemetskaya Sloboda, in: Personality and Place in Russian Culture. Essays in Memory of Lindsey Hughes, ed. by SIMON DIXON, (Slavonic and East European Review 88,1-2), London 2010, pp. 96-108.

GUSKOV, A. G., Velikoe posol'stvo Petra I. Istoričeskoe issledovanie [The Great Embassy of Peter I. A historical study], Moscow 2005.

HUGHES, LINDSEY, Russia in the Age of Peter the Great, New Haven 1998.

ID., Russian Culture in the 18th Century, in: The Cambridge History of Russia, Vol. II, ed. by DOMINIC LIEVEN, Cambridge 2006, pp. 67-91.

JENSEN, CLAUDIA, Musical Cultures in Seventeenth-Century Russia, Bloomington 2009.

KAPLAN, BENJAMIN, Divided by Faith. Religious Conflict and the Practice of Toleration in Early Modern Europe, Cambridge, Mass./London 2007.

KHODARKOVSKY, MICHAEL, Where Two Worlds Met: The Russian State and the Kalmyk Nomads 1600-1771, Ithaca et al. 1992.

KOVRIGINA, VERA A., Nemeckaja sloboda Moskvy i ee žiteli v konce XVII-pervoj četverti XVIII vv [The Muscovite German Quarter and its inhabitants in the end of the 17th and the first third of the 18th century], Moscow 1998.

KUSBER, JAN, Kulturtransfer als Beobachtungsfeld historischer Kulturwissenschaft. Das Beispiel des neuzeitlichen Russland, in: Historische Kulturwissenschaften. Positionen, Praktiken und Perspektiven, ed. by ID. et al. (Mainzer Historische Kulturwissenschaften 1), Bielefeld 2010, pp. 261-285.

ID., Beschleunigung, Bruch und Dauer. Die Veränderung der Zeiten im Russland Peters I., in: Frühe neue Zeiten. Zeitwissen zwischen Reformation und Revolution, ed. by ACHIM LANDWEHR (Mainzer Historische Kulturwissenschaften 11), Bielefeld 2012, pp. 179-197.

MOUTCHNIK, ALEXANDER, Der "Strelitzen-Aufstand" von 1698, in: Volksaufstände in Russland. Von der Zeit der Wirren bis zur "Grünen Revolution" gegen die Sowjetherrschaft (Forschungen zur osteuropäischen Geschichte 65), ed. by HEINZ DIETRICH LÖWE, Wiesbaden 2006, pp. 197-222.

NITSCHE, PETER, Moskau – das Dritte Rom?, in: Geschichte in Wissenschaft und Unterricht 42 (1991), pp. 341-354.

POE, MARSHALL T., A People Born to Slavery. Russia in Early Modern European Ethnography, 1476-1748, Ithaca, N.Y. 2000.

SCHEIDEGGER, GABRIELE, Das Eigene im Bild vom Anderen. Quellenkritische Beobachtungen zu den russisch-abendländischen Begegnungen im 16. und 17. Jahrhundert, in: Jahrbücher für Geschichte Osteuropas 35 (1987), pp. 339-355.

SCHLAFLY, DANIEL L., Filippo Balatri in Peter the Great's Russia, in: Jahrbücher für Geschichte Osteuropas N.F. 45 (1997), pp. 181-198.

ZAPPERI, ADA, Balatri, Filippo, in: Dizionario Biografico degli Italiani 5 (1963), Online-Version: http://www.treccani.it/enciclopedia/filippo-balatri_%28Dizionario-Biografico%29/, 31.03.2014.

ZITSER, ERNEST A., The Vita of Prince Boris Ivanovich "Korybut"-Kurakin. Personal Life-Writing and Aristocratic Self-Fashioning at the Court of Peter the Great, in: Jahrbücher für Geschichte Osteuropas 59 (2011), pp. 163-194.

Soloists of the Opera Productions in Brno, Holešov, Kroměříž and Vyškov
Italian Opera Singers in Moravian Sources c. 1720-1740 (Part I)

JANA SPÁČILOVÁ

The years of approx. 1720-1740 saw an unprecedented number of *opera seria* productions being staged in the region of Moravia, which was then part of the Austro-Hungarian monarchy.[1] The earliest sources recording productions of Italian operas come from Johann Adam Questenberg's castle in Jaroměřice (Jarmeritz, see Jana Perutková in Part II of this study).[2]

Another renowned patron of Italian music in Moravia was Wolfgang Hannibal Schrattenbach (1660-1738, from 1711 bishop in Olomouc/Olmütz), who spent several years in Italy at various places and posts, the viceroy of Naples among others (1719-1721). Having moved from Italy to Moravia in 1722, he became an ardent promoter of Italian culture at his own court, where Italians played an important part as musicians and singers. Productions of opera at his *château* in Kroměříž (Kremsier) are documented from 1727 to 1734, when they were moved to another of the bishop's castles, that in Vyškov (Wischau). Operas were staged at both of the bishop's residences twice a year on the occasion of the bishop's

---

1 The study is an output of a research project financially supported by the Faculty of Arts, Palacký University Olomouc (FPVC 2015/15).
2 For music performances in Jaroměřice, see the recent book PERUTKOVÁ, 2011.

birthday (12 September) and his name day (31 October).³ The productions stopped following the bishop's death in 1738.

Productions of opera in Holešov (Holleschau) are known from 1733, the date presumably coinciding with the promotion of Franz Anton Rottal (1690-1742), the owner of the estate, to count in 1728. The productions took place twice a year – on the occasion of the birthday of countess Maria Caecilia (26 July) and the count's birthday (12 October).⁴ The last records of opera productions in Holešov originate from the year 1740.

As well as the above-mentioned private aristocratic productions, Italian opera also flourished in form of *teatro impresariale* as produced in the Municipal Opera House in Brno (Brünn), the capital of Moravia.⁵ First opera productions documented there fall into the carnival season in 1732/33; they are connected with the Italian impresario Angelo Mingotti who performed with his group at the temporary wooden stage in the town's *manège* (*Teatro alla Cavalleriza*). The opening performance of the season took place on some day after 19 November 1732.⁶ Just one year later, however, the productions were moved to the newly adapted *Teatro della Taverna*, founded and operated by the municipal council and financially supported by patrons-aristocrats mentioned explicitly on the front pages of the libretti of the given operas. Mingotti's troup performed in Brno until 1736, when the *impresa* was taken over by Filippo Neri del Fantasia (1736/37, and from autumn 1738 to the end of 1740) and later by Alessandro Manfredi (1737/38). A regular season in Brno saw up to four opera productions being staged, one in "autumn", i.e. at the beginning of the Advent (official permission allowed opera to be staged during that season) and three others during the carnival season (from 26 December to the Tuesday before Ash Wednesday).

The focus of this paper is going to be especially on the Italian singers performing in the mentioned locations, although singers of Moravian origin would also be of interest in this respect, as some of them gained

---

3   For opera productions at the court of bishop Schrattenbach cf. esp. SPÁČILOVÁ, 2006; SPÁČILOVÁ, 2013b, pp. 75-88.
4   SPÁČILOVÁ, 2012, pp. 27-35.
5   For the beginnings of the Brno opera see the recent book by HAVLÍČKOVÁ, 2009.
6   HAVLÍČKOVÁ, 2009, p. 126. Similarly to the following years, the impresario opened the season of 1732 shortly before the start of the Advent (the first Advent Sunday fell on 30 November this year).

acceptance not only in their native country but also abroad. One example of the latter is Rosalia Andreides, an Olomouc native, who played in Holešov from 1733, and after marrying Ignaz Holzbauer (April 30, 1737), left Moravia with him, making appearance all around Europe (Vienna, Hamburg, Stuttgart, Mannheim, Munich).[7]

One of the most important sources of information concerning Italian musicians in Moravia are, similarly to other locations, the libretti of the operas. These have been currently processed as part of a wider research project, the outcome of which is going to be a printed catalog of the extant items.[8] Up to now, 78 libretti of Italian operas staged in Moravia before 1750 have been discovered, 17 coming from Jaroměřice, 24 from Kroměříž and Vyškov, 14 from Holešov and 23 from Brno. The lists of *personaggi* provide the names of the singers (the names are not stated for the Schrattenbach productions, though), the place of their origin, and – for the German versions – also the family state of the singers.[9] This detail can be of considerable importance – for instance, the real identity of a certain "Frau Laura Bambini" was revealed as the first wife of the composer and impresario Eustachio Bambini, not his daughter as considered by previous scholars.[10] Besides this, the names of employers are given with some of the artists, who, in fact, served on more or less formal terms as patrons and sponsors of the singers; an example of such a relationship is Ottavio Albuzzi, who was named "Virtuoso [di] S. E. il Sig. Conte Leopoldo di Dietrichstein" on the list from 1739.[11] Occasional mutilations of a name due to poor knowledge of the Italian orthography on the part of the scribe do not pose such problems as the typographical

---

7   SEHNAL, 1974, pp. 55-77.
8   Catalog of the Italian Opera Libretti in Central Europe in the 1st Half of the 18th Century, I: Moravia. Project supported by Grant Agency of Czech Republic, P409/12/P940 (Association for Central European Cultural Studies, Prague).
9   While in Brno the extant libretti were printed bilingually, in Italian and German on the facing pages, the different language variants of libretti from other localities were printed in separate volumes.
10 The last known performance starring Laura Bambini took place in 1742. The singer Anna Tonelli was mentioned as Bambini's wife in summer 1755, collaborating with him from 1745. SARTORI, 1990-1994.
11 Libretto *Penelope la casta*, CZ-Pnm, B 4126. For more about Albuzzi see PERUTKOVÁ in Part II of this study.

errors; an example of the latter is, for instance, the libretto of *Argippo* (1733) that gives different names of the intermezzo singers in the two extant versions: Italian and German.[12] No sufficient explanation of this inconsistency has been offered by now and, unfortunately, the scope of this paper prevents me from exploring in detail the – otherwise extremely absorbing – topic of German versions of the libretti.

The table in the appendix shows 45 different names of Italian singers discovered in 37 libretti from Brno and Holešov by now. Several conclusions can be drawn from the material. For instance, we know that Mingotti performed his first season 1732/33 with singers hired mostly from the Prague impresario Antonio Denzio, who found himself in a pressing financial situation at that time.[13] These included Giovanni Michaeli, Margarita Flora, Cecilia Ramis and Giacinta Spinola Costantini with her husband Antonio Costantini. Rosalia Fantasia, whose husband Filippo Neri del Fantasia took over the Brno impresa in 1736, came to Mingotti's troupe from Prague in 1734, as well as Anna Cosimi, who first became one of the big names of Denzio's ensemble, went through the critical years with him until the dissolution of his troupe, and then left for Brno to join Mingotti in the same year. The close connection of Denzio and Mingotti's *stagioni* is apparent from the Brno municipal deeds, where Mingotti is mentioned as "ein Prager Operist", although his only other previous place of activity was Vicenza during the carnival season in 1731.[14] Mingotti continued with Denzio's work in terms of repertoire, too; at least eight out of eleven known operas staged in Brno during Mingotti's era were taken from Prague, though usually with newly-composed music.[15] The German translations of the original libretti, the texts of which

---

12 "Gli Intermezzi saranno rapresentati dalla: La Sig. Laura Bambini di Pesaro, Il Sig. Mateo Luchini / Die Zwischen-Spiele werden von der Frau Caecilia Monti, und von dem Herrn Bartholomeo Cajo repraesentiret werden." Libretto SI-Ls, Z/VII 6/3.
13 FREEMAN, 1992.
14 HAVLÍČKOVÁ, 2009, p. 121.
15 *Argippo* (1730 Prague/Vivaldi, 1733 Brno/pasticcio by Costantini), *Gli amori amari* (1732 Prague, 1733 Brno, pasticcio by Costantini), *Armida abbandonata* (1725 Prague/Bioni, 1733 Brno/Bambini), *Lucio Vero* (1725 Prague/Albinoni, 1733 Brno/Bambini), *La pravità castigata* (1730 Prague/ Caldara, 1734 Brno/Bambini), *Didone* (1731 Prague/Albinoni, 1734 Brno/ Sarri), *Orlando furioso* (1724 Prague/Bioni, 1735 Brno/pasticcio with

did not always correspond with the Italian versions due to changes in solo parts, were also taken over from Denzio.[16]

Notes in the Brno municipal protocols prove that Mingotti regularly traveled to Venice during the summer to recruit new singers and search for up-to-date musical pieces for his repertoire.[17] Domenico Battaglini, together with Laura Bambini, came from Venice to Brno in the 1732/33 season and Rosa Cardini, together with Teresa Peruzzi detta "La Denzia" for 1733/34. As far as we know, two operas were brought from Venice to Brno, besides a number of individual arias that were grouped in pasticci, i.e. *Argenide* by Baldassare Galuppi (Venezia 1733, Brno 1734) and *Didone* by Domenico Sarri (Venezia 1730, Brno 1734).[18]

Some of the singers who stayed in Moravia in summer took part in the productions staged in Holešov: between 1733 and 1740, in total, thirteen singers from Italian troups active in Brno played there together with five more foreign artists who had no connections to Brno (Catarina Mayerin, Ignaz Finsterbusch, Catarina Zane and Domenico Negri in October 1737 and Dario Luca Cattani in 1738 and 1739).[19] The most important of the Brno Italian singers was Giuseppe Nicola Alberti, who held the post of "maestro di musica dell'Illustrissimo Sign. Conte / Directore der Gräffl. Operen und Music" in Holešov in 1734-1735.[20]

Besides the names and whereabouts of the singers, the libretti from Brno offer invaluable information about three Italian musicians who worked there (and in the entire region) as composers. Since their lives and careers have been sufficiently examined elsewhere, the following text concentrates solely on the Central European engagement of the three

---

Vivaldi's music), *Tullo Ostilio* (1727 Prague, 1725 Brno/pasticcio with Vivaldi's music).

16 The topic has been partially treated in Spáčilová, 2013a, pp. 6-21.
17 Havlíčková, 2009, p. 157.
18 The opera *Didone*, staged in Brno in 1734, combined the Prague libretto from 1731 (adapted by Antonio Denzio, music by Tomaso Albinoni) and Sarri's second version for Venice from 1730 (score I-Nc Rari, 7.2.5, RISM ID no. 850009015). See Spáčilová, 2014, pp. 18-30.
19 Dario Luca Cattani was later employed with Domenico Tasselli in Pressburg (today Bratislava) in the 1740s. See Kačic, 2014.
20 According to the libretti of the operas *Astianatte* (Holešov 1734, CZ-Bm, B 383, I-Mb, Racc. dram. 3496) and *Venere placata* (Holešov 1735, I-Mb, Racc. dram. 2720).

personalities, the first of whom is Antonio Costantini (often misspelled Constantini). He is first mentioned in the Prague records for the 1731/32 season as the author of two operas and two intermezzos; rather than a composer, he was only a compiler of pasticci, though, which is apparent from frequent references to borrowed arias in "his" librettos.[21] He married Giacinta Spinola in Prague in autumn 1731, and they both left for Brno with the greater part of Denzio's troup, joining Mingotti for the 1732/33 season. Costantini is specified as the composer of two operas from the carnival season of 1733 there, *Gli amori amari* and *Argippo*, with the exception of several arias inserted according to the preferences of the singers.[22] Further information about Costantini comes from as late as 1738/39, when he worked as a composer in Brno again, this time in the services of impresario Filippo Neri del Fantasia. He produced two operas there, *Elisa regina di Tiro* and *Costantino riconosciuto*, both of them once again with the exception of several inserted arias ("eccetto alcune arie"). It remains unclear if he accompanied his wife on her tour around Moravia in 1752, when she performed in Brno, too.[23]

Another Italian composer to stay in Moravia temporarily was Eustachio Bambini (1697-1770). He probably arrived there as early as the end of 1732, since his wife Laura was engaged by Mingotti for the 1732/33 season. They both stayed in Holešov over the summer of 1733, where Bambini staged his operas *Partenope* and *Artaserse*, collaborating with the local composers Georg Orschler and Ferdinand Seidl.[24] He was employed in Brno as a composer in the 1733/34 season, where his pasticci *Armida abbandonata* (28 November 1733) and *La pravità castigata* (carnival season in 1734, "à riserva d'alcune

---

21 He was the composer of the intermezzo and the greater part of the opera *Ipermestra* ("degli intermezzi è la musica del Antonio Costantini, come pure la maggior parte di quella del Drama"), while the score for *Gli amori amari* contained arias by different composers according to the preferences of the singers ("a riserva d'alcune arie messe al piacere de Virtuosi"). FREEMAN, 1992, pp. 265-267.
22 "a riserva d'alcune Arie poste al piacere de virtuosi". Libretto *Gli amori amari* (CZ-Bu, ST1-0500.998), *Argippo* (SI-Lsk Z/VII 6/3).
23 SEHNAL, 1974, p. 65.
24 Orschler composed some of the arias in *Partenope*; Seidl wrote the ballet numbers in *Artaserse*, apart from several arias in *Partenope*.

arie")[25] were produced; he also seems to have participated in the adaptation of *Argenide* by Galuppi and the pasticcio *Lucio Vero* with music by the same composer. Bambini most probably left Brno for Vienna, as revealed by the letter Georg Adam Hoffmann wrote to count Questenberg in August 1735 in which he states Laura was engaged in the Kärntnertortheater during the 1734/35 and 1735/36 seasons.[26] He may have shortly come back to Holešov in July 1736, as Laura starred in *L'Olimpiade* and *Cesare in Egitto* staged there at that time.[27]

The third of the composers, Giovanni Matteo Lucchini, is actually better known as a tenor singer. He stayed in Central Europe from 1725 (Dresden), working with Denzio as a singer and composer in Prague in 1726 and 1728-1730. An interesting account survived of an argument Lucchini had had with the singer Margherita Gualandi (later married to Lorenzo Moretti, both engaged in Brno in 1735/36) over the pay for twelve arias he composed for her in summer 1729. He asked renowned European composers to express their opinions on the matter, and the letters they sent to him have fortunately survived.[28] Later, he became a member of the Italian opera company in Wrocław (Breslau) – his performance in eight operas has been recorded for the period from the end of 1731 to September 1733.[29] After the Wrocław company dissolved, he went back to Prague and tried to operate an opera business with a group of Italian artists in the theater in Malá Strana (Lesser Town of Prague); they staged his *Alessandro nell'Indie* there in autumn 1734.[30] Lucchini is mentioned as a singer of the Lesser Town company for the last time in spring 1735.[31]

---

25 The Brno version of the opera corresponds with the Prague one (premiered with the libretto by Antonio Denzio, and pasticcio music of Antonio Caldara in 1730) in nine arias out of 27. The reconstruction of the opera is the subject of further enquiry.

26 See PERUTKOVÁ in Part II of this study.

27 The music for both operas was allegedly written by Johann Adolf Hasse. While his participation on the composition of the latter was convincingly denied, this is not possible to state about the former, since its libretto is lost today.

28 FREEMAN, 1992, pp. 96-98, Appendix II, pp. 291-292.

29 Opera in Wrocław is subject to on-going research; at present, we have 25 libretti at our disposal.

30 He received permission to stage the Italian operas in the Malá Strana ball house in September 1734, see FREEMAN, 1992, p. 67.

31 IBID., pp. 274-275.

In the Brno records, he is mentioned in the Italian version of the libretto for *Argippo* in the carnival season of 1733 as a singer of the intermezzo for the first time, but the account is impossible to verify according to the current state of knowledge (however, no opera productions were staged in Wrocław during this carnival season). He was, beyond all doubt, employed in Brno as a singer in the 1736/37 season, and his negotiation with the *Kärntnertortheater* in Vienna is recorded from autumn 1737, as well as his engagement at count Heissler's estate.[32] In the following season of 1737/38, Lucchini is already recorded as the author of music for all operas premiered in Brno in the similar way as the other two above-mentioned composers "with the exception of several added arias" ("eccetto alcune arie").[33] He was listed as a composer in the following season (1739/40) too, and the last known opera produced by him in Brno was *Alessandro Severo* in autumn 1740.

The presence of Italian singers in Moravia is documented also by the records in civic registers, although the occurrence of such data is, in fact, scarcer than one would expect. By now, only the records from Holešov were available, having been published by Jiří Sehnal in 1974.[34] Three accounts connected to Giuseppe Nicola Alberti can be found there: the record from July 1735 mentions him and Anna Cosimi as godparents of an illegitimate child; the baptism of his daughter Amalie Antonie in August 1735; and the death of the child in October 1736.[35] Especially the second record provides interesting details about Alberti's life, e.g. the previously unknown name of his wife, Anna Maria, his position at

---

32   Cf. PERUTKOVÁ in Part II of this study.
33   Autumn 1737: *Teodorico*; carnival 1737: *Argene*, *Arsace* and *Gli veri amici*; autumn 1739: *Vincislao*; carnival 1740: *Cleonice e Demetrio*; autumn 1740: *Alessandro Severo*.
34   SEHNAL, 1974, pp. 65f.
35   15 July 1735: "Josephus spurius" [illegitimate son], "pater ignotus, mater Susanna Folin Holleschov.", godparents: "Josephus Nicolaus A[l]berti Comes Palatinus, Anna Cosmi, ex Italia oriundi", Register of births, Holešov, Moravský zemský archiv (MZA) Brno, call mark 7534, p. 502. 6 August 1735: Amalia Antonia, parents: "Josephus Nicolaus Alberti Eques Italicus, Comes Palatinus, p. t. operista Domini Holles. Anna Maria, ambo Itali", godparents: dean Franz Karl Wagner, countess Marie Cecilie von Rottal, Register of births, Holešov, p. 504. 7 October 1736: "Amal[ia] Anton[ia] filia Josephi Alberti, Holleschov." (died in the age of 1 year and 2 months), Register of deaths, Holešov, MZA Brno, call mark 7629, p. 153.

the Rottal's court ("operista Domini Holleschoviensis"), and the fact that he was *Eques Italicus*, i.e. the holder of a minor aristocratic title, *Comes Palatinus* (it was a knightly title granted to a single person, not transferrable to his progeny).

The fourth record from April 1738 makes note of a Venetian citizen, Giacobbo Casarini and his wife Maria – it is the baptism of their twins, named aptly after their godparents, count and countess Rottal.[36] Incidentally, a female singer of the same name, Domenica Casarini, was employed in Brno and Holešov at the same time (1737/38 and 1738/39 engaged in Brno, in October 1738 she sang in Holešov). She is called "Jungfrau" (virgin) in the extant libretti; it seems plausible that she was actually Casarini's sister.

One of the most amazing recent discoveries was the record of Cecilia Ramis' son having been baptized in the church of St. James in Brno on March 23, 1733.[37] It is worth noting in this respect that Ramis performed at the carnival of the same year in *Gli amori amari*, impersonating the male character of Flavio, while she is not to be found on the list of *personaggi* of the next opera in the season, *Argippo*, apparently due to the advanced level of pregnancy. The civic register also gives her maiden name, Delfini, which allows the positive identification of the singer, whose name was falsely considered to represent two different people until now. Further research also brought insight into her dwellings before the arrival to Moravia. She made her debut in the opera *Venceslao*, produced at Theodor Constantin Lubomirsky's court in Kraków (Cracow) in 1725, later starring there in *La Mariane* (1726) and *La Griselda* (1727).[38]

---

36 "Franciscus Antonius Simon et Maria Caecilia gemini", parents: "Jacobus Cassarini, Maria Venetijs", godparents: count and countess von Rottal, Register of births, Holešov (see previous note), p. 596.

37 Joannes Antonius Raphael, parents: "D[omi]no Josepho Romis Italo Venetijs, Matri Caeciliae natae Delphin", godparents: Johann Matthias Thurn-Valsassina and Antonia Rodenin de Hirzenau, born Salawin de Lippa. Register of births, Brno – St. James, MZA Brno, call mark 16863, p. 418.

38 From the period of Italian opera in Kraków only four libretti from 1725-1727 were discovered by now. However, the issue is currently being subject to further research, which has revealed names of the artists present at Lubomirsky's court in the given span of time: Veneranda Bernina (later married as Pendisich), Francesco Bianchi, Giuseppe Giorgio, Cecilia Grepaldi, Marc'Antonio Mareschi, Camilla Poli, Bartolomeo Straparappa. Cecilia Delfini's name was being distorted in the local versions of libretti (e.g. Dolfini, Delfhini, Delflini).

That is why she is later called Lubomirsky's *virtuosa di camera* in the libretti of *La Silvia* and *Romilda*, staged in the 1730/31 season at the Teatro S. Moisè in Venice.[39] She must have married Giuseppe Ramis soon after the end of the carnival season 1731, as she is found to be employed under the new surname in Prague as early as in autumn of the same year.[40] Her trace is lost at the moment of the birth of her son in 1733; attempts to find a record of her death in the Brno registers were equally fruitless.

As a matter of fact, on the one hand, quite a lot of information is available concerning the singers who performed in Brno and Holešov in the given period. On the other hand, our attempts to describe the lives of opera singers at the court of the Olomouc bishop Schrattenbach faced several complications. First of all, Italian singers were full members of Schrattenbach's court, often executing other functions – usually taking religious posts. Second, the extant libretti from Kroměříž and Vyškov do not mention names of particular singers. As a result, the Italian singers at Schrattenbach's court are still more or less *terra incognita* to us with only a few names having been confirmed recently. As for the sources available to us, they vary from musical scores to financial accounts, official letters and records in the archive of the cathedral church in Olomouc.

The starting point for our research was the accounts for the production of an opera *Nitrocri* staged in 1735 in Vyškov.[41] The accounts provide seven names of singers involved in the productions: Santo, Antonio, Mauro, Wegschmitt, John, Rosalia and Teresa.[42] With a high level of certainty, we succeeded in determining the identity of native singers (Rosalia Bees-Majerin, Teresia Majerin, Anton John and Anton Weckschmidt) with other sources, namely the civic registers and records of the Piarists in Kroměříž.[43]

---

39   SARTORI, 1990-1994, no. 22031, 20116.
40   FREEMAN, 1992, p. 355.
41   MZA Brno, fund G 76, family archive Kálnoky Letovice, inv. n. 83, cart. 16; inv. n. 144, cart. 18.
42   The account of the tailor Ignatius Polsator: "H. [= Herr] Santo, H. Antoni, H. Wegschmitt, H. John, Don Mauro and Jungfrau Rosalia" (sign. 144, cart. 18, fol. 8). The account of Jacob Joseph Cžada (ibid., fol. 1-2): "Jungfr. Rosalia, Jungfr. Theresa, Herr P. Wegschmidt, Herr Santo, Herr Antonio, Herr Jonn."
43   SPÁČILOVÁ, 2010, pp. 198-206.

Another score of the *Stabat Mater* by Girolamo Pera deposited in Vienna, helped us determine the voice register of the given singers.[44] Girolamo Pera was Schrattenbach's *maestro di capella* in 1738, as is recorded on the title page of the oratorio *Il giusto aflitto nella persona di Giobbe*, performed in Brno during Lent in the same year.[45] His composition was apparently produced at the bishop's court in 1737, as the solo parts bear the names of the singers corresponding to those recorded in the Moravian sources. According to these notes, Antonio and Santo were, most probably, castrati; both female singers were sopranos; Weckschmidt tenor and John bass. Besides these, a certain Italian singer, Don Domenico, is mentioned in the score, who seems to have been a baritone, since he sang both tenor and bass parts.

"Don Mauro" could represent the bishop's curate and musician Mauro Fanti, whose discharge record from August 1738 is to be found in the documents of the Olomouc consistory.[46] As for Don Domenico, his true identity has not yet been determined, although it is highly probable that he – like Fanti – favored a religious position at the bishop's court; according to my hypothesis, Domenico could be identical with the noted Italian bass singer who is said to have participated in the first opera productions in Kroměříž at the end of the 1720s.[47]

On the contrary, the said "Signor Antonio" is doubtless Antonio Fornarini, whose discharge papers from July 1738 are deposited in the Olomouc archive.[48] According to the document, Fornarini entered Schrattenbach's service as a chamber musician in May 1734. Sartori's catalog makes note of this singer only once, in connection with *Alessan-*

---

44 Score: A-Wgm, I 2761.
45 "La Musica è del Sig. Don Girolamo Pera, Maestro di Cappella di Sua Altezza Em." Libretto: I-Mb, Racc. dram. 5510.
46 "Presbyter Ecclicus. et Quonda. Em. Cels. B. B. Eppi. Olomucen. Capellanus Aulicus & musicus Maurus Fanti supplicat pro testimonialibus vitae apud dictam aulam actae literis, ut his provisus ad Italiam redire valeat." Zemský archiv Opava, pobočka Olomouc [Provincial Archives Opava, Branch Olomouc] (ZAO-Ol), fund ACO – Arcibiskupská konsistoř [Archbishop consistory] Olomouc, cart. 9, 21.8.1738.
47 BOMBERA, 1979, pp. 326–348.
48 "Dominus Antonius Fornarini de Urbino, apud altem fatam Eminentissimam Suam Celsitudinem, quatuor annis, et tribus mensibus, pro Camerae Musico serviverit." ZAO-Ol, fund AO, Arcibiskupství [Archbishopric] Olomouc, sign. F IV a 49/4c.

dro nell'Indie by Leonardo Vinci (Urbino 1734).[49] The same piece was staged in Vyškov in October 1734;[50] the later production is well documented in the letters between Schrattenbach and his brother Felix, bishop of Ljubljana (Laibach), which I discovered in November 2013 in the archive of the Ljubljana archdiocese.[51] Several of these letters from the end of October and November 1734, written by Wolfgang Hannibal Schrattenbach, mention two Italian singers who had recently arrived in Vyškov and, thanks to their artistry, made the production of the last opera a great success.[52] Bishop Felix was, in fact, so generous as to lend his brother 25 ducats (100 fl.) to cover the expenses of the singers' trip to Moravia.[53]

One of these singers must have been Fornarini himself (the lapse of time between May and October is of no importance here, as singers were usually contracted in advance). The more important question is: who was his counterpart? It may have been Carlo Tessarini from Urbino, mentioned as the "direttore della musica stromentale" at Schrattenbach's court in 1737.[54] Tessarini was employed as a musician in the Urbino cathedral in the 1730s, his name being mentioned in the cathedral records for the last time in 1733, and then only one more time on 27 December 1738; that is already after the bishop's death (July 23). However, the formulation in the bishop's letter rather suggests that the "two virtuosos" were, in fact, two singers, which brings us to the identification of the second virtuoso with Sante Lorenzini. He performed together with Fornarini in the above-mentioned opera by Vinci in Urbino; moreover,

---

49 SARTORI, 1990-1994, no. 724.
50 Libretto: Cz-OP, STA 250.
51 Si-Lna, fund Škofijski arhiv, ser. Škofje, sign. Šal/Šk., fasc. 5, Sigmund Schrattenbach 1728-1742.
52 Letter from 27 October 1734: "Morgen wird meine anderte Opera anfang, welche gewisslich um so mehr zu jedermannes approbation reusiren muss, als die zwey aus Wällischland neuangekommene Musici in Wahrheit rechte Virtuosi seynd, ob welchen ich eine besondere Vergneigung habe [...]."
Letter from 3 November 1734: "die opera ist bey denen neuangekommenen zwey virtuosn so gutt reusirt, dass alle insgesambt hierob ein besonderes wohlgefallen gehabt haben [...]."
53 Letter from 3 November 1734: "[...] e. E. belieben hier 25 stuck dukaten zuempfangen welche vor die meinen zwey Musicis vorgestreckte 100 fl. Seyn sollen und bedanke mich hiemit nochmahls vor die Ihnen gethane vorschiessung [...]."
54 On the title page of his collection *La Stragavanza*, Amsterdam c. 1737.

his not very common first name, Sante, corresponds with "Herr Santo" from the bishop's accounts. Last but not least, he is further recorded to perform in Italy only in 1740, which gives him enough time to move to Moravia for some years.[55]

Other Italian singers connected to Schrattenbach's court were the castrato Andrea Devoti, whose presence at the court is documented in 1732, and "ecclesiasticus Aulae, Capellanus et Musicus Cremsirii" Filippo Regini, who died in Kroměříž in 1731.[56]

The libretti and other Moravian sources presented in this study include a wide range of information about more than 50 Italian singers performing in Brno, Holešov, Kroměříž and Vyškov in the 1730s. The ways in which the Italians participated in the Moravian opera productions were manifold: in Jaroměřice, the cast was completely local,[57] while in Holešov and in bishop Schrattenbach's ensembles, Italian musicians mixed with the locals, the bishop employing his own court artists, and count Rottal hiring singers from Brno; the vocalists of the municipal opera in Brno were exclusively Italian.

A considerable amount of Italian artists known from Moravian sources was also related to other transalpine centers of Italian opera (Prague, Wrocław, Kraków, Vienna, Graz, Klagenfurt, Ljubljana) as well as with the later *imprese* of the Mingotti brothers in Germany. To put it simply: if an Italian singer grew bold enough to cross the Alps, he usually stayed there for a longer period of time, or returned back later. The traces of the movement of opera singers and other *operisti* all over Europe, together with their professional and personal relationships, a large intertwined network, create the separate threads which can be found and interpreted on the basis of careful research of the local sources.

Speaking from the point of cultural studies, the fact that they provide information not only about the professional engagement and family relationships of the concrete people, but also about their position and relationships within the society is the most important aspect about these sources. The Moravian civic registers are especially telling when it comes to the dichotomic position of the *operisti* in the microcosm of Moravian towns, which oscillate between respect and distrust (as Reinhard Strohm

---

55 In Vinci's *Artaserse*, Macerata, carnival 1740. SARTORI, 1990-1994, no. 2966.
56 BOMBERA, 1979, p. 329; SEHNAL, 1974, p. 63.
57 See PERUTKOVÁ in Part II of this study.

indicated in his study *Italian Operisti North of the Alps*).[58] For instance, godparents of the *operisti's* children are usually the aristocrats; this is surprising, since the aristocratic presence at such events in the role of godparents was considered a great honor reserved only to the members of the same estate, important members of the family household, and for special occasions, such as baptisms of Jewish children, etc. The crossing of social boundaries is traceable also in the opposite direction, although under certain restrictions: if *operisti* became godparents at all, they were – as a foreign and floating element to the home society – invited only to the private environment of the lesser courts (such as count Rottal's Holešov estate), and the illegitimate children's baptisms.

Since the local civic registers paid great attention to the presence of Italian singers, they sometimes reveal their personal circumstances which otherwise would have remained unknown. Good examples of such instances are the already mentioned Cecilia Delfini Ramis and Giuseppe Alberti.

The network of locations and relationships also enables us to identify and follow the communication channels through which the Italian opera repertoire was transferred across Europe not only in the form of the frequently quoted "arie di baule" (baggage arias), but also as libretti and entire operas, for instance Vinci's *Alessandro nell'Indie* produced in Kroměříž by Italian artists, who had arrived from Urbino shortly before.

The presented examples were designed to show the ways local sources can be helpful in providing and specifying somewhat discontinuous information about the movement of artists and the repertoire of Italian opera throughout Europe during the 18th century. A necessary precondition of further research is an international cooperation of researchers dealing with the particular nodal points on the map of the Italian opera's realm in Europe, which would bring together the scattered pieces of information to create a comprehensive picture. First steps in this field have already been taken with respect to the informal grounds between Moravia, Ljubljana and Vienna that instantly bore fruits.[59] However, a profound extension of such manners of cooperative research will need to be established in future to allow us to grasp and understand the complexity of Italian opera in transalpine countries.

---

58 STROHM, 2001, pp. 1-59.
59 Many thanks to Metoda Kokole from Ljubljana and Andrea Sommer-Mattis from Vienna for the fruitful information exchange.

Appendix

Italian opera libretti from Brno and Holešov

Brno – Angelo Mingotti:
1733/1 *Argippo* (carnival),
1733/2 *Gli amori amari* (carnival),
1733/5 *Armida abbandonata* (28 November),
1734/1 *Lucio Vero* (1st January),
1734/2 *Argenide* (26 January),
1734/3 *La pravità castigata* (20 February),
1734/6 *Arianna e Teseo* (25 November, lost),
1734/7 *Didone* (26 December),
1735/1 *Orlando furioso* (18 January),
1735/2 *Tullo Ostilio* (carnival),
1736/1 *Antigona in Tebe* (carnival, lost).

Brno – Filipo Neri del Fantasia:
1736/4 *Cambise sacrilego* (fall),
1737/1 *Anagilda* (carnival),
1738/5 *Elisa regina di Tiro* (fall),
1739/1 *Penelope la casta* (carnival),
1739/2 *Costantino riconosciuto* (carnival),
1739/6 *Vincislao* (fall, lost),
1740/1 *Cleonice e Demetrio* (carnival),
1740/2 *Alessandro severo* (fall, lost).

Brno – Alessandro Manfredi:
1737/3 *Teodorico* (fall),
1738/1 *Argene* (carnival),
1738/2 *Arsace* (carnival),
1738/3 *Gli veri amici* (carnival, lost).

Holešov:
1733/3 *Partenope* (July),
1733/4 *Artaserse* (15 October),
1734/4 *Amore e pace* (26 July),
1734/5 *Il Matrimonio per forza*, intermezzo (fall),

1735/3 *Astianatte* (26 July),
1735/4 *La Contadina*, intermezzo (summer),
1735/5 *Venere placata* (12 October),
1736/2 *Cesare in Egitto* (26 July),
1736/3 *L'Olimpiade* (?26 July, lost),
1737/2 *Lucio Papirio dittatore* (12 October),
1738/4 *Sesostri rè d'Egitto* (12 October),
1739/3 *Amore e fortuna* (summer),
1739/4 *Nel perdono la vendetta* (fall),
1739/5 *Vologeso re di Parti* (fall).

Italian singers and characters in libretti from Brno and Holešov
Fr. = Frau (Mrs); Jfr. = Jungfrau (Miss); interm. = intermezzo

Alberti, Giuseppe Nicola, di Padova: 1733/5 *Rambaldo*, 1734/1 *Lucio Vero*, 1734/2 *Idomeneo*, 1734/3 *Don Alvaro*, 1734/6 *Minosse*, 1734/7 *Iarba*, 1735/1 *Orlando*, 1735/2 *Tullo Ostilio*, 1735/3 *Pirro*, 1736/1 *Creonte*. Composer: 1734/4, 1735/3 ("maestro di musica dell'illustrissimo Sign. Conte"), 1735/5.

Albuzzi, Ottavio, di Milano: 1738/4 *Amasi*, 1738/5 *Fenicio*, 1739/1 *Ulisse* ("virtuoso di S. E. il Sign. Conte Leopoldo di Dietrichstein"), 1739/2 *Foca*.

Andreides Holzbauer, Rosalia: 1733/3 *Partenope*, 1733/4 *Mandane*, 1734/4 *Diana*, 1735/3 *Ermione* ("virtuosa del Sign. Conte di Rottal"), 1735/5 *Aminta*, 1736/2 *Cornelia*, 1736/3 *Aristea*, 1737/2 *Quinto Fabio*, 1738/4 *Artenice*, 1739/3 *Arnea*, 1739/5 *Berenice*.

Bambini, Laura, di Pesaro (Fr.): 1733/1 *Osira,* ?interm., 1733/2 *Lotario*, 1733/3 *Rosmira*, 1733/4 *Artabano*, 1733/5 *Tancredi*, 1734/1 *Aniceto*, 1734/2 *Telemaco*, 1734/3 *Manfredi*, 1736/2 *Tolomeo*, 1736/3 *Megacle*.

Battaglini, Domenico, di Pesaro: 1733/1 *Silvero*, 1733/2 *Lamberto*, 1733/3 *Arsace*, 1733/4 *Arbace*, 1733/5 *Ubaldo*, 1734/1 *Claudio*, 1734/2 *Aristo*, 1734/3 *Don Ottavio*, 1736/2 *Giulio Cesare*, 1736/3 *Licida*.

Cajo, Bartolomeo, di Venezia: ?1733/1 interm., 1733/5 interm., 1734/1 interm., 1734/2 interm., 1734/3 *Mallorco*, 1734/5 *Gerondo*, 1735/4 *Don Tabarano*, 1736/1 *Ormindo,* interm.

Cardini, Rosa, di Venezia: 1733/5 *Rinaldo*, 1734/1 *Vologeso*, 1734/2 *Climero*, 1734/3 *Don Giovanni*.

Soloists of the Opera Productions (Italian Opera Singers, Part I)

Casarini, Domenica (Jfr.): 1737/3 *Leone*, 1738/1 *Cambice*, 1738/2 *Megabise*, 1738/3 *Tilamè*, 1738/4 *Sesostri*, 1738/5 *Nino*, 1739/1 *Eurimaco*, 1739/2 *Alessandro*.
Cattani, Dario Luca, di Pistoia: 1738/4 *Orgonte*, 1739/3 *Creonte*, 1739/5 *Anicetto*.
Cosimi, Anna, di Roma (Jfr.): 1734/6 *Carilda*, 1734/7 *Selene*, 1735/1 *Alcina*, 1735/2 *Sabina*, 1735/3 *Andromaca*, 1735/5 *Adria*, 1736/1 *Giocaste*.
Danese Pischlin, Teresia: 1737/2 *Rutilia*, 1738/4 *Nitocri*, 1738/5 *Cirene*, 1739/1 *Antiope*, 1739/2 *Fausta*, 1739/3 *Ormonda*, 1739/5 *Lucilla*.
Danese, Veneranda (Jfr.): 1737/3 *Antigono*, 1738/1 *Zamiro*, 1738/2 *Artabano*, 1738/3 *Lagide*, 1740/1 *Alceste*, 1740/2 *Alessandro*.
Dardozzi, Carlo, di Faenza: 1734/6 *Alceste*, 1734/7 *Araspe*, 1735/1 *Medoro*, 1735/2 *Curazio*, 1735/3 *Pillade*, 1735/5 *Tirsi*, 1736/2 *Achilla*, 1736/3 *Clistene*.
Delfini Ramis, Cecilia (Fr.): 1733/2 *Flavio*.
Della Parte, Anna Caterina (Fr.): 1740/1 *Cleonice*, 1740/2 *Giulia*.
Della Stella, Giovanna (Jfr.): 1740/1 *Barsene*, 1740/2 *Sallustia*.
Fantasia, Rosalia, di Mantova (Jfr.): 1734/6 interm., 1734/7 interm., 1735/1 interm., 1735/2 interm.
Finsterbusch, Ignaz: 1737/2 *Marco Fabio*.
Flora, Margarita, di Venezia (Jfr.): 1733/1 *Argippo*, 1733/2 *Emilia*, 1734/6 *Tauride*, 1734/7 *Osmida*, 1735/1 *Ruggero*, 1735/2 *Silvio*.
Gabbiati, Giuseppe, di Venezia: 1738/4 *Fanete*, 1738/5 *Agenore*, 1739/1 *Medone*, 1739/2 *Argiro*, 1739/3 *Aristeo*, 1739/5 *Lucio Vero*.
Gaggiotti, Pellegrino: 1739/6 interm., 1740/1 interm., 1740/2 *Claudio*, interm.
Galetti, Filippo, di Cortona: 1736/1 *Evalco*.
Giusti, Maria (Fr.): 1737/1 *Anagilda*.
Isola, Anna: 1739/6 interm., 1740/1 interm., 1740/2 interm.
Lucchini, Matteo: ?1733/1 interm., 1737/1 *Rodrigo*, 1737/3 *Odoacre*, 1738/2 *Arsace*, 1738/3 *Amasi*. Composer: 1737/3, 1738/1, 1738/2, 1738/3, 1739/6, 1740/1, 1740/2.
Madonis, Girolama (Fr.): 1737/3 *Ostilia*, 1738/1 *Barsene*, 1738/2 *Statira*, 1738/3 *Candace*, 1738/5 *Elisa*, 1739/1 *Penelope*, 1739/2 *Zoe*.
Mareschi, Marc'Antonio: 1740/1 *Fenicio*, 1740/2 *Marziano*.
Marini, Francesca (Fr.): 1739/1 *Aquilio*.
Mayerin, Catarina: 1737/2 *Cominio*.

Mazzioli, Giuseppe: 1737/1 *Fernando*.
Michaeli, Giovanni, di Padova: 1733/1 *Tisifaro*, 1733/2 *Ugone*, 1734/6 interm., 1734/7 interm., 1735/1 interm., 1735/2 interm.
Monteviali Rubini, Angelica (Fr.): 1737/1 *Dantea*, 1737/2 *Papiria*.
Monti, Cecilia, di Roma (Fr.): ?1733/1 interm., 1733/5 interm., 1734/1 interm., 1734/2 interm., 1734/3 *Rosalba*, 1734/4 *Adone*, 1734/5 *Rosmene*, 1735/4 *Scintilla*, 1736/1 interm.
Moretti, Lorenzo, di Venezia: 1736/1 *Ceraste*.
Moretti, Margarita, di Bologna: 1736/1 *Osmene*.
Negri, Domenico: 1737/2 *Lucio Papirio*.
Orlandi, Chiara, di Mantova (Jfr.): 1733/5 *Erminia*, 1734/1 *Lucilla*, 1734/2 *Ercena*, 1734/3 *Donna Beatrice*, 1734/4 *Venere*, 1734/6 *Teseo*, 1734/7 *Enea*, 1735/1 *Bradamante*, 1735/2 *Silvio*.
Pampini, Teresa (Jfr.): 1737/1 *Sancio*.
Personè, Catterina (Jfr.): 1737/3 *Clotilde*, 1738/1 *Mitrena*, 1738/2 *Rosmiri*, 1738/3 *Niceta*.
Peruzzi, Teresa, detta La Denzia, di Venezia (Jfr.): 1733/5 *Armida*, 1734/1 *Berenice*, 1734/2 *Argenide*, 1734/3 *Donna Isabella*, 1734/6 *Arianna*, 1734/7 *Didone*, 1735/1 *Angelica*, 1735/2 *Marzia*, 1736/1 *Antigona*.
Sosue, Teresa: 1740/1 *Mitrane*, 1740/2 *Albina*.
Spinola Costantini, Giacinta (Fr.): 1733/1 *Zanaida*, 1733/2 *Guido*, 1738/5 *Clearco*, 1739/1 *Telemaco*, 1739/2 *Eraclio*, 1739/3 *Ismero*, 1739/5 *Vologeso*, 1740/1 *Olinto*.
Susanni, Antonia (Jfr.): 1737/1 *Florindo*.
Tasseli, Domenico: 1737/3 *Teodorico*, 1738/1 *Argene*, 1738/2 *Mitrane*, 1738/3 *Evergete*.
Zane, Cattarina: 1737/2 *Servilio*.

Literature

BOMBERA, JAN, K významu Liechtenštejnova zpěváckého semináře v Kroměříži [On the importance of Liechtenstein's vocalist seminar in Kroměříž], in: Hudební věda [Musicology] 16 (1979), pp. 326–348.
FREEMAN, DANIEL E., The Opera Theater of Count Franz Anton von Sporck in Prague (Studies in Czech Music 2), Stuyvesant/N.Y. 1992.

HAVLÍČKOVÁ, MARGITA, Profesionální divadlo v královském městě Brně 1668-1733, Brno 2009 (German version: Berufstheater in Brünn 1668-1733, Brno 2012).

KAČIC, LADISLAV, Kapela Imricha Esterházyho v rokoch 1725-1745 [The music ensemble of Bishop Imrich Esterházy in 1725-1745], in: Musicologica slovaca 5, 2 (2014), pp. 189–254.

PERUTKOVÁ, JANA, František Antonín Míča ve službách hraběte Questenberga a italská opera v Jaroměřicích [František Antonín Míča in the service of Count Questenberg, and the Italian opera in Jaroměřice], Praha 2011.

SARTORI, CLAUDIO, I libretti italiani a stampa dalle origini al 1800. Catalogo analitico con 16 indici, 7 vols., Cuneo 1990-1994.

SEHNAL, JIŘÍ, Počátky opery na Moravě. Současný stav vědomostí [The beginnings of opera in Moravia – the current state of knowledge], in: O divadle na Moravě [Theater in Moravia], Praha 1974, pp. 55-77.

SPÁČILOVÁ, JANA, Hudba na dvoře olomouckého biskupa Schrattenbacha (1711-1738). Příspěvek k libretistice barokní opery a oratoria [Music at the court of Olomouc bishop Schrattenbach (1711-1738). A contribution to the analysis of the libretti of baroque opera and oratorio], PhD, Brno 2006.

ID., Nové poznatky k hudbě na dvoře olomouckého biskupa Schrattenbacha [New findings on music performances at the court of Olomouc bishop Schrattenbach], in: Musicologica Brunensia 45, 1-2 (2010), pp. 198-206.

ID., K repertoáru italské opery v Holešově ve 30. letech 18. století [The repertoire of Italian opera in Holešov in the 1730s], in: Opus musicum 44, 6 (2012), pp. 27-35.

ID., Brněnská opera Argippo z roku 1733 ve světle nových výzkumů [The Brno opera Argippo from 1733 in the light of new research], in: Opus musicum 45, 2 (2013), pp. 6-21.

ID., Die Rezeption der italienischen Oper am Hofe des Olmützer Bischofs Schrattenbach, in: The Eighteenth-Century Italian Opera Seria: Metamorphoses of the Opera in the Imperial Age, ed. by PETR MACEK/JANA PERUTKOVÁ, Praha 2013, pp. 75-88.

ID., Sarriho opera Didone v Brně (1734) a její rekonstrukce pro novodobé provedení [Sarri's Didone in Brno (1734) and its reconstruction], in: Opus musicum 46, 1 (2014), pp. 18-30.

STROHM, REINHARD, Italian Operisti North of the Alps, c. 1700-c. 1750, in: The Eighteenth-Century Diaspora of Italian Music and Musicians (Speculum musicae 8), ed. by ID., Turnhout 2001, pp. 1-59.

Vienna Kärntnertortheater Singers in the Letters from Georg Adam Hoffmann to Count Johann Adam von Questenberg
Italian Opera Singers in Moravian Sources c. 1720-1740 (Part II)

JANA PERUTKOVÁ

During the first half of the 18th century, count Johann Adam von Questenberg (1678-1752) was a major promoter of Italian *dramma per musica* in Moravia. The owner of the Jaroměřice (Jarmeritz) *château* in south-west Moravia was not only a connoisseur and patron of music, but also a skilled lute player.[1] Music had a very special meaning for him. In 1722, he established a private theater in the Jaroměřice *château*, which hosted up to 20 opera performances per year. Composers he commissioned included domestic authors such as Franz Anton Mitscha (Míča) and Carl Müller, but also Antonio Caldara, Ignazio Maria Conti or Domenico Natale Sarro. Unlike other Moravian centers, he continued staging Italian opera until his death in 1752. He acquired operatic works primarily through his friends among the nobility or through various artists, both from within the Habsburg Empire and from Italy (Rome, Venice, Naples, Pesaro, Lucca), but also from Lis-

---
1 In 1724 the Count appeared as a player on the theorbo in *Euristeo*, an opera composed by Antonio Caldara, performed solely by members of noble families. The *Wienerisches Diarium* magazine reported on the event on May 17, 1724. The performing singers are listed in the libretto cited by Sartori under number 9417 (SARTORI, 1990-1994).

bon, London, Paris or some German cities (Munich, Berlin, probably Leipzig und Mannheim).[2]

Count Questenberg significantly contributed to the fact that Moravia became a very important center for opera staging during the first half of the 18th century, and he therefore ranks amongst the music-loving European aristocratic elite. He easily measures up not only to the Bishop of Olomouc (Olmütz) Wolfgang Hannibal Cardinal Schrattenbach and Count Franz Anton von Rottal, who also staged musical dramas at their Moravian estates, but also against the Salzburg Archbishop Franz Anton Harrach. The Saxe-Meiningen duke Anton Ulrich procured operatic works with similar passion as Count Questenberg, but he was just a collector – unlike Questenberg; he did not have an ensemble at his court to perform extended musico-dramatic works. Moreover, the aristocrats with whom Questenberg compares were disproportionately richer than him. The frequency of music and dramatic performances staged by the count in Jaroměřice, but also at his other estates and in some towns in Moravia (Brno/Brünn, Olomouc), is even comparable to Vienna, and more reminiscent of a professional opera company. The most recent discoveries include the identification of more than forty opera and oratorio scores from Questenberg's possession, located mainly in Viennese libraries and archives.[3] Extremely interesting are the stage designs for the *château* theater found recently in Vienna by Andrea Sommer-Mathis.[4]

As far as the amount of sources is concerned, Jaroměřice is an especially blessed location. Nevertheless, musical productions in Jaroměřice hosted solely home singers as performers, although some of them studied

---

[2] A lot of information on this topic is in the Moravský zemský archiv (MZA, Moravian Provincial Archive) in Brno: fund F 459: Velkostatek Jaroměřice nad Rokytnou (Jaroměřice nad Rokytnou Estate, especially revenue accounts in Jaroměřice coffers), fund F 460: Ústřední správa a ústřední účtárna Kouniců Slavkov (Central administration and central accounting department of the Kounic family in Slavkov, mainly accounts from Questenberg's Vienna coffers) and fund G 436: Rodinný archiv Kouniců (Kounic family archive, namely various correspondence), as well as identified scores from the property of Count Questenberg stored mainly in A-Wgm and A-Wn. For details cf. PERUTKOVÁ 2011 and 2015.

[3] Cf. PERUTKOVÁ, 2011.

[4] Cf. upcoming set of studies of ANDREA SOMMER-MATHIS, JANA PERUTKOVÁ, MARTINA FRANK and JANA SPÁČILOVÁ.

with renowned music teachers in Vienna. However, the documents from count Questenberg's estate also contain invaluable information about opera productions in other musical centers in Europe, especially Vienna. The most important source for this topic is the letters of Questenberg's *Hofmeister* Hoffmann that he sent to his master between 1729 and 1740, which are today deposited in the Moravian Provincial Archives in Brno.[5] Georg Adam Hoffmann, the father of the distinguished Austrian *Wiener Klassik* composer Leopold Hoffmann (1738-1793), was of paramount importance for the count. His reports reveal that he had good taste and was well versed in all kinds of art, especially in music. His judgements about music and musical theater are always very insightful and show that their author was a musician.[6] In one of his letters, we found his statement expressing his musical preferences. It is dated November 7, 1735 and in it he writes: "I am a great lover of well-composed music, except perhaps pastorale, and I am not a lover of *gaudéen* and dances that are contrary to my spirit, and I am their enemy."[7]

Hoffmann was the count's confidant and – to some extent – an advisor in matters of art; for instance, he provided and sent him libretti of most musical and dramatic pieces staged in Vienna, either at the Court Theater or the municipal Kärntnertortheater; he also regularly informed him about the latest news of the social and musical life in Vienna.

Of all of Hoffmann's dispatches, those concerned with the Kärntnertortheater are probably of the greatest importance, since very little is known about this prominent center of transalpine opera culture today. For opera productions in the Kärntnertortheater, hiring artists such as Francesco Borosini and Joseph Carl Selliers in 1728 was a milestone. According to an imperial regulation, they were allowed to stage only

---

5   MZA, fund G 436, cartons 747-748, Inv. no. 6133, total approx. 1500 folios. In this paper, reference is made only to the individual data from Hoffmann's letters to Questenberg.

6   In a letter of January 3, 1731, for example, he writes: "Happily, the first act has finally arrived from Venice which, at first glance, seems to be well composed." ("Der erste Act von Venedig ist endlich glücklich ankommen, welcher mir, so viel primo intuitu sehen kann, wohl componiret vorkombt.")

7   „Ich meines orths, so grosser liebhaber ich von rechtschaffener Music bin, so wenig außer dergleichen pastorellen, und bin, aller orthen bekannter masser, kein liebhaber von gaudéen, und tantzen, welches wider meinen genie ist, und dauon ein abgesagter feind bin, [...]."

„comedies with some integrated sung intermedia and nothing else" ("Comödien mit einigen untermischt gesungenen Intermedien, und nichts anders zu präsentieren").[8] The two famous artists – tenor and ballet master – made great and successful efforts to perform opera series in the Kärntnertortheater after 1730, although they initially focused primarily on pasticcio and abbridged opera versions (*intermezzi musicali*), although it meant a certain – apparently tolerated – circumvention of the emperor's decree. The famous Italian tenor Francesco Borosini undoubtedly had the decisive influence on the operatic operations in the Kärntnertortheater. He was active as a singer at the imperial court between 1712 and 1731.[9] During this time, he also performed in Italy and England; Handel hired him for the Queen's Theatre in the Haymarket for the season 1724/1725. Borosini scored major success.[10]

During his time in the Kärntnertortheater, Francesco Borosini was in lively contact with Count Questenberg, not only in terms of art, but also personally. Their relationship seems to have somewhat exceeded the usual limits of the aristocrat – musician relationship, because Hoffmann's correspondence shows that Borosini even helped to choose a husband for Countess Carolina. Borosini and Questenberg engaged in a lively exchange of repertoire, but the issue cannot be presented in the context of the present study due to its volume.

Questenberg negotiated with Borosini to secure a performance or engagement of Matteo Lucchini in the Kärntnertortheater in Vienna. On October 26, 1737 Hoffmann writes:

> "Mr Borosini regrets the fact that he has not heard from Mr Lucchini, he was now equipped with everything, however, considering Your Excellency, he wanted to accept him anyway in case he intended to comply with the conditions, as evident."[11]

---

8 HADAMOWSKY, 1994, p. 195. Cf. also SCHENCK, 1969, p. 125.
9 Reinhard Strohm comments on his influence on the shape of Vienna carnival operas in: GRONDA, 1990, p. 93.
10 On F. Borosini cf. MICHELS, 2012, pp. 113-130.
11 "H.n Borosini ist leyd, daß er vom H: Lucchini nichts ehender gehört er wäre nunmehro schon mit allen versehen, in ansehung Ewer Excellenz aber wolte er ihn gleichwohl annehmen, im fall er die conditiones, wie beÿschlüssig zu ersehen, eingehen wollte."

A few days later, on November 6, 1737, Hoffmann reported to the count:

> "[I] have not been able to find Mr Borosini at home all day, then been able to relay the answer of Luchini on another day; particularly since he has been engaged at count von Heissler until 1 September, thus there is nothing to be done in this matter in any case, if anything changes in the local theater he would think about him; which is why he could report from time to time."[12]

It turns out that, in addition to his contract in Brno opera companies between 1736 and 1740, Lucchini was engaged with the Imperial Privy Councilor and Chief Justice of the Provincial Court in Brno, Franz Joseph von Heissler Heitersheim, owner of the Uherčice (Ungarschitz) estate. The situation was therefore similar to Ottavio Albuzzi.[13] He worked in Graz in 1738, in Brno during the season 1738/39, while in autumn 1738 he also performed in Holešov (Holleschau) for Count Rottal. In June 1739, at the end of the season, Albuzzi performed in the Kärntnertortheater, where Hoffmann documented his presence also during the following season in November 1739/40. In the libretto of the opera *Penelope la casta* staged in Brno during the 1739 carnival, he is named as "Virtuoso S. E. il Sig. Conte Leopoldo di Dietrichstein".[14]

In addition to productions of German-speaking comedy with music, the Kärntnertortheater staged six to eight new operas every year.[15] A current research project of the Austrian Academy of Science aims at reconstructing the theater's repertoire based on the catalog of libretti to operas produced there over the years (Das Wiener Kärntnertortheater in der Zeit von 1728-1748: Vom städtisch-bürgerlichen Schauspielhaus zum höfischen Opernbetrieb / The Wiener Kärntnertortheater during the time of 1728-1748: from civic theater to court opera operation). Unfortunately,

---

12 "[Hn. Borosini] den ganzen tag nicht mehr zu haus antreffen kommen, denn des anderten tags den antworth von Luchini ausgerichtet habe; und zumahlen dieser bies 1. Sept: bei Herrn grafen von Heissler engagieret, so wäre dermahlen in der sache ohne deme nichts zu thuen, solte sich inmittelst bei hiesigen theatro was änderen, wolte er auf ihn schon reflexion machen; wessentwegen er dann, und wann von sich was hören lassen kann."
13 Cf. SPÁČILOVÁ, pp. 255-273, in the present volume.
14 More on that in PERUTKOVÁ, 2015.
15 SEIFERT, 2011, pp. 208f.

the extant libretti from the Kärntnertortheater, unlike those retrieved in other transalpine municipal theaters, do not record the names of solo singers involved in the productions. Information available to us concerning the conditions of the singers' ensemble before 1740 are equally scarce, since the only relevant sources had long been just the four opera scores from the years 1730-1732, one manuscript libretto of the opera *Girita* 1738, and one opera score from 1741 (see Sources).

The five scores are archived in the Anton-Ulrich-Musiksammlung in Meiningen and do not mention seasons, only the year of staging (*Eumene* – 1730, *Giulio Cesare in Egitto* – 1731, *Arminio* and *Il Contrasto delle due Regine in Persia* – 1732, *Hypermnestra* – 1741). *Giulio Cesare in Egitto* is a pasticcio based on George Frideric Handel's homonymous opera,[16] *Girita* was created by the Italian composer Antonio Bioni, *Hypermnestra* with the libretto by Johann Leopold van Ghelen was composed by Ignaz Holzbauer;[17] the remaining three operas were composed by Francesco Rinaldi, of whom very little information has been found to date.[18]

Six Italian female solo singers are mentioned in these six sources:

- Maria Camati Brambilla, detta la Farinella (soprano, 1730-1732)
- Teresa Zanardi di Bologna (soprano, 1730)
- Maria Maddalena Salvai (soprano, 1732)
- Dorotea Loli (alto, 1732)
- Catarina Zane (?, 1738)
- Marianne Im[m]er (?, 1738)[19]

Three other singers are listed only by their first names, only the first was Italian:

- Vittoria (alto, 1730, probably Peruzzi)
- Catherl (soprano, 1731-1732, Catharina Mayerin)
- Gioseffa (soprano, 1731, Josepha Pircker)

The last two mentioned artists shall be discussed later. Two prominent artists performing in the Kärntnertortheater in 1741 were also local for-

---

16 For more on the same see PERUTKOVÁ, 2012, pp. 95-122.
17 BENNETT, 2006, pp. 63-90, and STROHM, 2014, pp. 133-170.
18 IBID.
19 Daughter of the impresario, singer and librettist Giuseppe Imer, cf. GOLDONI, 2008, p. 462.

ces: Maria Anna Eckardt[20] and Rosalia Holzbauer, originally from Moravia.[21] Rosa Pasquali, born Schwarzmann, also referred to as "la Bavarese", was German (soprano, 1738).

We have not yet been able to identify two more female Italian singers, namely Signora Galeta and Signora Giulia (both 1738).

The above sources list only two Italian singers:

- Toselli (tenor, 1732), probably Giuseppe Toselli, certainly other than the castrato Domenico Taselli, performed between 1737-1740 in Moravia, Prague and Bratislava (Pressburg)[22]
- Francesco Arrigoni (tenor, 1738)[23]

The other singers were of local origin:

- Christoph Hager (tenor, 1730–1732)
- Maxmilian Miller (baritone, 1731–1732)
- Anton Lehner (bass, 1741)
- Hauer (bass, 1741), cannot be further identified.

In total, of the six sources, we only know 19 singers' names, 11 of them Italian.

Hoffmann's letters provide additional information about six of these aforementioned artists, and 15 new names.[24] His letters offer a significantly broader picture of the Kärntnertortheater at that time. He not only records the names of solo singers participating during entire theater seasons and singular productions, but also presents surprisingly detailed information about theater funding and contracting of specific singers together with frequent remarks on their voice, acting dispositions, and so on.

The earliest notes date back to 1730, concerning singers referred to as Josepha, Capuona and Cöllnerin, and the composer Francesco Rinaldi.[25] Again, Hoffmann often adds his own remarks concerning

---

20 † Wien 1743, at the age of 25, in the civic register as "Singerin im Komödienhaus", cf. GUGITZ, 1958.
21 Cf. SPÁČILOVÁ, pp. 255-273, in the present volume.
22 Cf. KAČIC, 2014, p. 196.
23 Cf. STROHM, 2001, p. 30.
24 An article with an alphabetical list of the known artists performing in the Kärntnertortheater from 1730 until 1742 is under preparation.
25 The first mention dates from June 14, 1730: "The operetta has not been well received, because the singers, with the exception of one female singer, were

the quality of productions which prove that he was a skilled musician. In September, Hoffmann records the successful staging of an opera by Rinaldi featuring "Josepha and Faranelli",[26] while in January 1731, he writes about a production of the other piece, which was a flop because of the unfortunate indisposition of the same Josepha.[27]

This Josepha, mentioned also in the score to *Giulio Cesare* in the role of Cleopatra, seems to be Josepha (Gioseffa) Susanna Pircker, born Gayarek, whose employment in Vienna falls between her engagement in Prague (two seasons, 1726-1728) and Venice. She is referred to as "di Praga" in the Prague libretti, but, more likely, she came from Graz.[28] In Vienna, she spent at least two seasons of 1729/1731. According to Gerber, she died in Milan in January 1734.[29] Hoffmann even mentioned her once in a non-musical context; the quotation does

> by no means extraordinary, the bass singer does not deserve any hearing at all, the music, with respect to the composition, was not bad; this is neither due to Josepha nor Capuona, nor the so-called Cöllnerin. [...] The music of the initially mentioned operetta is by the so-called Francesco, who is supposed to be a Neapolitan." ("operetta nicht gar zu viel approbation gefunden, dann die singer, eine aussgenohmen haben nit viel extraordinaires an sich, der Bassist meritiret gar kein gehör, die Music gienge endlich quod compositionem schon an; es hat weder die Josepha noch Capuona, noch die so genannte Cöllnerin hierauf einen part. [...] Die Music von eingangs erwehnter opereta ist wiederumb von so genanten Francesco einem seyn sollenden Neapolitaner.")

26 September 20, 1730: "I humbly attach the textbooks of the new operetta produced on the 17th of this month; it was quite successful and was well received, the singers Josepha and Faranelli; the music, in turn, was once again by Francesco." ("Von der am 17. hujus producirten neuen operetta schlüsse die büchl in unterthännigkeit bey; welche gar wohl reussiret hat, und findet zimliche approbation, worauf Josepha und Faranelli singen; die music ist wiederumb von Francesco.")

27 January 3, 1731: "The new operetta will not be to the liking, the author or composer is once again Mr Francesco, and Josepha did not seem to be well disposed; the reason may be that the others were applauded instead of her." ("Die neue operetta will nicht viel approbation finden, dessen Author, oder Compositor noch H. Francesco ist, und ist mir die Josepha nicht wohl disponiret vorkomen vielleicht auss ursachen, weilen man denen anderen, ihr aber nicht mit denen händen geglitschet.")

28 Cf. KOKOLE, 2013, mainly p. 152. See also FREEMAN, 1992, *passim*.

29 Cf. GERBER, 1792, col. 149. See also FREEMAN, 1992, passim.

not make it clear to which precise affair it refers. On May 28, 1729 he writes: "The past case with Josepha should have already been solved in the administration, shall also sing in the operetta tomorrow".[30] "Capuona" is in fact Angela Capuano, who sang during the 1726/1727 season in Venice, including two Vivaldi operas. Sartori has no more record of her, but she sang for two more seasons, until 1729, in Prague under the *impresa* of Antonio Denzio.[31] "Faranelli" is the nickname "Farinella" of the soprano Maria Camati. She performed in various Italian cities from 1729 to the mid-1750s, except for the years 1730-1733, when Sartori fails to mention her – she apparently spent the period in Vienna.[32]

The true identity of the last singer, whom Hoffmann refers to as "the so-called Cöllnerin", has not yet been revealed. However, a singer of this name performed for Count Thomas Vinciguerra of Collalto in 1764 and 1765, as evidenced by accounts.[33]

In his letter of October 1733, Hoffmann offers his opinion on the new singer of the Kärntnertortheater, Cecilia Bellisani Buini, the wife of the impresario and composer Giuseppe Maria Buini. She traveled to the transalpine area for the 1733/1734 season, when Sartori has her documented in only one role in Italy. Hoffmann compares Buini with Maddalena Salvai; on October 10, 1733 he writes about the staging of an unspecified opera: "The Hager has gotten a bright and clear voice, the new singer equals Salvai in person, but has a better voice; however, the action is not so good, and is to be called Buina."[34] Cecilia Buini performed again in Vienna in August 1735. Subsequently, she left for Bologna for certain; hence her – otherwise undocumented – further employment in Vienna claimed by Hoffmann does not seem plausible.[35]

---

30 "Der vorbeygegangene casus mit der Josepha solle bey der Regierung schon vergleichen worden seyn, wirdt auch morgen auff der operetta singen."
31 Cf. FREEMAN, 1992, passim.
32 After 1750 she sang in European countries outside Italy, her activity is detectable until 1775 (SARTORI, vol. 7, 1994, p. 136). See also STROHM, 2008, pp. 111-126.
33 STRAKOVÁ, 1966, pp. 231-268, especially p. 250.
34 "der Hager hat eine heller, und reiner Stimm bekommen, die neue singerin gleichet in der person der Salvai, hat aber eine bessere stimm, jedoch die action nit so gut, undt solle Buina heissen."
35 On August 31, 1735 Hoffmann reports to Questenberg: "The performances of the operetta are supposed to [...] start on Saturday; also Buina shall be

Hager is mentioned several times in the Hoffmann letters. This is the tenor Christoph Hager, documented in the Kärntnertortheater sources in the years 1730-1741. In Vienna, he was still active as a singer during the early 1740s, his son died in Vienna in 1742. His application for admission to the Viennese imperial court from 1738 was published by Köchel.[36] Under the name Cristofero D'Hager or De Hagen he is documented by Sartori as a singer in the years 1748-1759 in Hamburg and Stuttgart, but it could also have been his son or other close relative.[37]

In another letter, Hoffmann enlists all singers contracted in the forthcoming 1735/36 season; five of them remain the same as in the previous season. In a letter dated August 17, 1735 he informs count Questenberg: "Here, most of the previous shall sing, that is: Bambina, Castrat, Catherl, Joseph, and Bassist Baczek, and shall only introduce only a single Babiera with her husband of that name, called from Italy, as a new person, namely prima donna."[38]

The first in the list, Bambina, is Laura Bambini, who was active in the transalpine area during the years 1733-1737.[39] In Vienna, she was probably active in the 1734/35, 1735/36 and perhaps 1736/37 seasons; in the 1732/33 and 1733/34 seasons in Brno and during summer 1733 and 1736 in Holešov.[40] "Catherl" is, in fact, Catharina Mayerin, documented to have performed in Vienna in the pasticcio *Giulio Cesare in Egitto* in 1731 and in 1732, both Rinaldi's operas; autumn 1737 together with other artists performing in Vienna in Holešov, 1737-1739 in Graz.[41]

    singing in it." ("die operetta soll [...] am samstag seinen Anfang nehmen, worauf auch die Buina singen wird".) On March 28, 1736 he informs: "From what I hear, the local operettas are not supposed to start before June; it is also not certain yet whether Buina, who has long left here for Bologna, will return." ("Die hiesige operetten sollen dem verlauth nach vor Junio ihrer anfang nicht nehmen, auch noch nicht gewiess seyn, ob die schon längst von hier nach Bologna abgereissete Buina retournieren dörffte.")

36 Cf. GUGITZ, 1958, p. 125; KÖCHEL, 1872, p. 450; SARTORI, vol. 7, 1994, p. 349.
37 SARTORI, vol. 7, 1994, p. 349.
38 "Hierauf werden die vorige meistens singen, das ist: die Bambina, Castrat, Catherl, Joseph, u. Bassist Baczek, und wird nur ein eintzige Babiera mit ihren Mann dieses nahmens, so aus Italien beruffen worden, eine neue persohn, und zwar prima donna vorstellen."
39 SARTORI, vol. 7, 1994, p. 45.
40 Cf. SPÁČILOVÁ, pp. 255-273, in the present volume.
41 IBID. See also SARTORI, vol. 7, 1994, p. 430.

Information about her latest role comes from Vienna in 1741;[42] she often played male roles.

The name of the castrato mentioned in Hoffmann's list was impossible to identify; however, it is the first known remark of a castrato being employed in the Kärntnertortheater. The singer (tenor?) named Joseph and the bass singer surnamed Baczek could not be identified so far, but they are most likely local, not Italian singers.

The most important name on the list is Livia Barbieri, summoned to Vienna from Italy. Her husband, singer Antonio Barbieri, probably performed with his wife at the Kärntnertortheater, as is apparent from Hoffmann's letter quoted above. Three of his performances are documented in Florence in 1735; then, the Italian sources are missing until 1737. Thus, the couple must have spent at least the 1735/36 season and possibly also the next, in Vienna.

On June 20, 1739, Hoffmann informs the count about the casting for the opera *L'inganno tradito dall'amore*: "Mireno, contr'alto, Sig.ra Pentemora. Solinda, Soprano, Sig.ra Gasparina, Ramige, Soprano, Sig.ra Angela Romana. Zittane, Tenore, Sig. Albuzio. Tivame, Soprano, Sig.ra Catterl. Trasone, Basso, Löhner."

"Signora Pentemora" is the Italian singer Elisabetta Moro. This can also be inferred from the fact that she has been referred to as "Moro" by Hoffmann in the autumn of the same year (see below). The singer ventured beyond the Alps for the first time in 1732, when she sang in Wrocław (Breslau).[43] In 1738/1739, she performed in Graz, so her employment in the Kärntnertortheater took place concurrently in spring 1739 and fall of the same year, i.e. during the next 1739/1740 season in Vienna.[44] The singer referred to by Hoffmann as "Gasparina" is Maria Giovanna Gasparini, who spent the 1738/39 season in Prague. She moved to Vienna at the end of the season, and performed in Graz in spring 1740.[45] From 1741 onward, she worked as a *prima donna* at the Berlin court, where she performed alongside the aforementioned Maria Camati for some time.[46] Angela Romana is Angela Romani Bartoli. During the 1738/39 season, she sang in Klagenfurt, from where she probably left for Vienna. Then,

---

42 IBID.
43 BORCHERT, 1910, p. 47.
44 SARTORI, vol. 7, 1994, p. 459.
45 MÜLLER VON ASOW, 1917, p. 14.
46 SCHNEIDER, 1852, p. 65.

in 1741, she was with Pietro Mingotti in Bratislava, and subsequently, inter alia, in Graz, her last engagement in 1748 in Prague.[47] "Albuzio" is the tenor Ottavio Albuzzi, (see above). The case of Anton Lehner, bass, is outstanding in at least one respect: he is the only recorded singer from the Jaroměřice estate to get contracted for the Kärntnertortheater, as far as we know. A testimonial by the Kapellmeister Franz Anton Mitscha regarding Lehner's admission to Questenberg's services in 1728 was preserved in a letter from the administrator (*Hauptmann*) to the count stating, among other things, that Lehner has a superb voice and that he can also play wind instruments. During the years of 1735-1736, he is registered in the count's services as a lackey. At the Kärntnertortheater 1739, he sang in the operas *L'inganno tradito dall'amore* and *Arsace*, in 1741 in *Hypermnestra*; however, at that time he was still in the service of Questenberg.[48]

Furthermore, Hoffmann's letter from November 1739 enlists the complete cast for the opera *Arsace*. The *prima donna* part introduces a new person, Francesca Cuzzoni. She apparently stopped in Vienna on her way from Turin to Hamburg where she was to perform from September 1740. This opera star – whose fame had somewhat faded away, though – received great attention in Vienna, as is clear from Hoffmann's letters.[49] We are informed that the expenses for hosting Cuzzoni would be extremely high and, consequently, shared between the theater and Vienna aristocracy. Hoffmann comes up with this highly interesting testimony in a letter dated November 5, 1739: "It is no small feat that the *Cavaliers* have generated 3000 fl and the *Theatrum* 1000 fl for Cozzona, who shall sing here until Lent, starting with the operetta *Arbace* [sic! = *Arsace*]."[50] Although not much is known about financial business of the Kärntner-

---

47   SARTORI, vol. 7, 1994, p. 567.
48   Cf. PERUTKOVÁ, 2011, passim.
49   Hoffmann mentions Cuzzoni alongside other singers in a letter dated November 14, 1739: "The following persons shall act during the next operetta *Arsace*, which shall be performed on Thursday or Saturday: Cozzona, Gasparina, Hager, Albuzzi, Moro and Lehner." ("auf künfftiger operetta Arsace, welche am donnerstag, oder sambstag wird produziert werden, werden agieren: Cozzona, Gasparina, Hager, Albuzzi, Moro und Lehner.")
50   "es ist nicht ohne, daß die Cavalliers 3000 fl und das Theatrum 1000 fl. zusammen geschaffen vor die Cozzona, welche hievor bies auf die fasten singen wird, und zwar den anfang nehmen mit der operetta Arbace genant."

tortheater in general, this financial support from home "cavaliers" was surely unprecedented and corresponded to the unique event. Cuzzoni was expected to stay in Vienna for the entire carnival season, and another letter reveals she made her debut there on November 19, 1739.[51] Hoffmann himself attended the performance a few days later; his verdict was that although Cuzzoni's voice was still clear and beautiful, her acting skills had deteriorated due to her age, which made her colleague Gasparini the star of the night.[52]

After 1740, when Hoffmann left count Questenberg's service, another Vienna agent, Franz Haymerle, took over the duty to send information about the Kärntnertortheater to his master. His notes on the musical life in Vienna are much rarer. So far, only one note about the Kärntnertortheater singers has been found, dated February 10, 1742. Haymerle writes to Questenberg that the recently performed operas included *Didone abbandonata*, *Hypermnestra* and *Merope* starring "[...] Holzbauer, la Bavarese [= Rosa Pasquali], Drexler, Catherle, Hager another tenor and a buffo-singer".[53] Most of the singers were presented in the preceding text; the artist with the surname Drexler has not yet been identified.

Based on our present knowledge, it seems that local artists began to prevail in the Kärntnertortheater after 1740. This is probably also related to the fact that serious German operas, such as *Hypermnestra* by Ignaz Holzbauer, staged in 1741, or the still unnoticed opera from the same

---

51 Hoffmann in a letter of November 21, 1739: "The day before yesterday the new operetta has been produced where the new famous singer Cuzzoni performed." ("Vorgestern ist die neue operetta produciret worden, worauf agierte die neue famose singerin Cuzzoni.")

52 Hoffmann reports to Questenberg on November 26, 1739: "Today, I have seen and heard the opera *Arsace* myself and your Excellency are right; the voice is good, clear and beautiful, but her acting is not particularly good; she does not receive any great acclamation which may be due to her age; and Gasparina receives more applause." ("heut habe die opera Arsace selbst gesehen, und gehöret, und haben Ewer Excellenz recht, daß die stimm gut, rein und schön, aber ohne besondere action, keine extra approbation findet sie nicht, welches vielleicht ihr alter verhindern mag, und bekommt die Gasparina mehr approbation.")

53 "[...] Holzbauer, die la Bavarese, die Drexler, die Catherle, der Hager, weiters ein Tenor und ein Buffo-Sänger". MZA, fund G 436, carton 777, Inv. no. 6265.

year titled *Die glückliche Vorbedeutung*, with music composed by Ignazio Maria Conti[54] became more popular during this period.

The above stated facts confirm the hypothesis mentioned by Reinhard Strohm[55] and Jana Spáčilová[56] that numerous Italian artists performing in the transalpine area stayed longer or returned repeatedly. The available data suggest that some artists performed during certain seasons, parallel in Vienna and Graz, or in Vienna and Moravia.

In Hoffmann's correspondence, there is only one Italian female singer with no relationship to the Kärntnertortheater, but directly to the court of Count Questenberg. Letters about Anna Caterina della Parte detta di Portogalo provide an interesting insight into Count Questenberg's relation with Italian female singers. Hoffmann calls della Parte by her artistic pseudonym, Nina di Portugal, in his letters. She is known to have sung at the 1738 carnival in Turin in Brivio's *Demofoonte*, which was also staged in Jaroměřice in the fall of the same year. It is plausible that della Parte herself acquired the copy of the score for the count in the very same way as Anna Mazzoni obtained a copy of *Salustia* for him in Venice.[57] Questenberg, probably in return for the score, arranged della Parte's performance before the Emperor. Her performance should have been mediated by *Musikgraf* Ferdinand von Lamberg. On June 17, 1739, Hoffmann informed Count Questenberg: "I had the opportunity to speak with Count Lamberg of the singer, under the name della Parte, whom he knows and whom he heard sing, regrets that he cannot serve Your Excellence in this matter and let her sing before the Emperor."[58]

He even paid for a couch to take della Parte from Vienna to the emperor's summer residence Laxenburg.[59]

---

54 A study of the newly discovered libretto is under preparation.
55 STROHM, 2001, pp. 1-60.
56 Cf. pp. 255-273, in the present volume.
57 On the lengthy procurement of the opera *Salustia* by Questenberg see KAPSA et al., 2012, pp. 313-341.
58 "Mit H: Gr: v. Lamberg habe bey gelegenheit dessen auch geredet wegen der Cantatricin, mit dem nahmen Dela Parte hat er sie nicht, wohl aber, als er hörte, dass es Nina di Portugal seye, wohl gekennet, und schon hören singen, bedauret, dass er Ewer Excellenz hereinfalls nicht dienen könte, und sie vor dem Kayser singen lassen."
59 Invoice dated June 6, 1739: "Einem Lehengutscher nach Laxenburg wegen der Cantatricin Nina di Portugal. 2 fl. 30 kr." (MZA, fund F 460, carton 2430, inv. no. 9748, f. 21r.).

In any case, della Parte did not return to Italy, but remained in the Habsburg monarchy for some time. Hoffmann, in his letters from October 31, informs the count that "Signora Nina herself does not know yet due to her time possibility whether and when she will come to Jaroměřice".[60] On November 5, he writes: "To date, Signor Abbate Fabris cannot determine the date of his departure, as the Portuguese secretary has to dispatch a courier from here to Portugal beforehand; so Signora Nina can make her way via Jaroměřice, as he shall inform her."[61] Finally, on November 21, 1739, Hoffmann wrote to his employer: "Signora Nina di Portugal has already parted from here to Brno in order to sing at the theater there."[62] In 1740, della Parte is documented in two librettos of Brno provenance, during the carnival and in the fall season.[63] She spent a long time in Moravia and therefore, her performing in Jaroměřice cannot be ruled out.

Circulation of Italian singers in Central Europe, which is also closely related to migration of repertoire, is among the most interesting phenomena in the field of opera during the first half of the 18th century. Processing it is one of the most demanding research tasks. The situation is complicated by incomplete primary sources (librettos, scores), a lot of relevant information is often missing in the sources (printed librettos of the Kärntnertortheater, for example, do not list the names of performers). In addition, it is necessary to examine the issue not only in the environment of opera companies that operated in Central Europe, but also in the context of music performed in aristocratic palaces and musical preferences of some members of the nobility. The purpose of this paper was therefore to point out the importance of secondary sources; especially the aristocratic correspondence, in the research of repertoire and musician migration in Central Europe (not only) during the first half of the 18th century cannot be emphasized enough.

---

60   "Sign.ra Nina selbst noch nicht weiß wegen ihrem impegno, ob oder wann sie wird nach Jaromeritz kommen".
61   "Sig: Abbate Fabris kann den Tag seiner abreiß dato nicht determinieren, massen der Portugesische Secretarius bevor einen Courier von hier nach Portugal abfördern muss; damit Sig.ra Nina ihren weeg über Jaromeritz nehme, wird er ihr ausrichten."
62   "die Sign.ra Nina di Portugal bereits auch von hier nach Brünn abgereyset, umb auf dasigen theatro zu singen."
63   It was the pasticcio titled *Cleonice e Demetrio* and *Alessandro Severo*, compiled by the composer/singer Giovanni Matteo Lucchini. More on the subject in SPÁČILOVÁ, 2006, no paging.

Sources

HANDEL, GEORGE FRIDERIC, Giulio Cesare, D-MEIr, Ed 129n.
HOLZBAUER, IGNAZ, Hypermnestra, D-MEIr, Ed 130d.
RINALDI, FRANCESCO, Arminio, D-MEIr, Ed 147q.
RINALDI, FRANCESCO, Il contrasto delle due regine in Persia, D-MEIr, Ed 147r.
RINALDI, FRANCESCO, Eumene, D-MEIr, Ed 147p.
Girita, A-Whh (Haus-, Hof- und Staatsarchiv), Staatskanzlei: Interiora, 86, fol. 3r-23v.
Moravský zemský archiv (MZA) [Moravian Provincial Archive], Brno, fund F 460, carton 2430, inv. no. 9748.
Moravský zemský archiv (MZA) [Moravian Provincial Archive], Brno, fund G 436, cartons 747-748, inv. no. 6133.
Moravský zemský archiv (MZA) [Moravian Provincial Archive], Brno, fund G 436, carton 764, inv. no. 6186.
Moravský zemský archiv (MZA) [Moravian Provincial Archive], Brno, fund G 436, carton 766, inv. no. 6187.
Moravský zemský archiv (MZA) [Moravian Provincial Archive], Brno, fund G 436, carton 767, inv. no. 6187.
Moravský zemský archiv (MZA) [Moravian Provincial Archive], Brno, fund G 436, carton 777, inv. no. 6265.

Literature

BATCHVAROVA-SCHWEITZER, RADMILA, The Mingotti Opera Company in Brno, Graz, Prague, and Copenhagen, Diploma thesis, UK, Prague 1994.
BENNETT, LAWRENCE, Ignaz Holzbauer and the Origins of German Opera in Vienna, in: Eighteenth-Century Music 3,1 (2006), pp. 63-90.
BORCHERT, HANS HEINRICH, Geschichte der italienischen Oper in Breslau, in: Zeitschrift des Vereins für Geschichte Schlesiens 44 (1910), pp. 18-51.
FREEMAN, DANIEL E., The Opera Theater of Count Franz Anton von Sporck in Prague, New York 1992.
GERBER, ERNST LUDWIG, Pirckerin (Josepha), in: Neues historisch-biographisches Lexicon der Tonkünstler, vol. 2, Leipzig 1792, col. 149.
GOLDONI, CARLO, Memorie italiane, vol. 3: Prefazioni e polemiche, Venice 2008.

GRONDA, GIOVANNA ET AL., La carriera di un librettista: Pietro Pariati da Reggio di Lombardia, Bologna 1990.

GUGITZ, GUSTAV, Die Totenprotokolle der Stadt Wien als Quelle zur Wiener Theatergeschichte des 18. Jahrhunderts, in: Jahrbuch der Gesellschaft für Wiener Theaterforschung 9 (1953/54), Vienna 1958, pp. 114-145.

HADAMOWSKY, FRANZ, Wien – Theatergeschichte. Von den Anfängen bis zum Ende des Ersten Weltkrieges (Geschichte der Stadt Wien 3), Vienna 1994.

KAČIC, LADISLAV, Kapela Imricha Esterhazyho v rokoch 1725-1745 [Imrich Esterhazy's Kapelle in the years 1725-1745], in: Musicologica Slovaca 5 (31), 2014, no. 2, pp. 189–254.

KAPSA, VÁCLAV ET AL., Some Remarks on the Relationship of Bohemian Aristocracy to Italian Music at the Time of Pergolesi, in: Studi Pergolesiani 1,8 (2012), pp. 313-341.

MICHELS, CLAUDIA, Francesco Borosini – Tenor und Impresario, in: Musicologica Brunensia 47,1 (2012), pp. 113-130.

KOKOLE, METODA, The Mingotti Opera Company in Ljubljana in the Early 1740s, in: The Eighteenth-Century Italian Opera Seria. Metamorphoses of the Opera in the Imperial Age, ed. by PETR MACEK/ JANA PERUTKOVÁ, Prague 2013, pp. 138-163.

MÜLLER VON ASOW, ERICH HERMANN, Angelo und Pietro Mingotti. Ein Beitrag zur Geschichte der Oper im XVIII. Jahrhundert, Dresden 1917.

PERUTKOVÁ, JANA, František Antonín Míča ve službách hraběte Questenberga a italská opera v Jaroměřicích [František Antonín Míča in the service of Count Questenberg and Italian Opera in Jaroměřice] (Clavis monumentorum musicorum regni bohemiae IV), Prague 2011.

ID., Giulio Cesare in Egitto am Wiener Kärntnertortheater im Jahre 1731. Ein Beitrag zur Rezeption der Werke von G.F. Händel in der Habsburgermonarchie in der 1. Hälfte des 18. Jahrhunderts, in: Hudební věda [Musicology Journal] 49,1-2 (2012), pp. 95-122.

ID., "Der glorreiche Nahmen Adami". Johann Adam Graf von Questenberg (1678-1752) als Förderer der italienischen Oper in Mähren (Specula Spectacula 4), Vienna 2015.

SARTORI, CLAUDIO, I libretti italiani a stampa dalle origini al 1800. Catalogo analitico con 16 indici, 7 vols., Cuneo 1990-1994.

SCHENK, ELEONORE, Die Anfänge des Wiener Kärntnertortheaters (1710 bis 1748), Vienna 1969.

SCHNEIDER, LOUIS, Geschichte der Oper und des königlichen Opernhauses in Berlin, Berlin 1852.

SEIFERT, HERBERT, Barock (circa 1618 bis 1740), in: Wien Musikgeschichte. Von der Prähistorie bis zur Gegenwart (Geschichte der Stadt Wien 7), ed. by ELISABETH TH. FRITZ-HILSCHER/HELMUT KRETSCHMER, Vienna/Berlin 2011, pp. 142-212.

SEHNAL, JIŘÍ, Počátky opery na Moravě. Současný stav vědomostí [The beginnings of opera in Moravia. Current state of knowledge], Prague 1974, pp. 55-77.

SPÁČILOVÁ, JANA, Současný stav libret italské opery na Moravě v 1. polovině 18. století [The current state of Italian opera librettos in Moravia in the first half of the 18th century], in: Acta musicologica 3, 2 (2006), no foliation, http://acta.musicologica.cz/, 27.9.2014.

ID., Die Rezeption der italienischen Oper am Hofe des Olmützer Bischofs Schrattenbach, in: The Eighteenth-Century Italian Opera Seria. Metamorphoses of the Opera in the Imperial Age, ed. by PETR MACEK/ JANA PERUTKOVÁ, Prague 2013, pp. 75-88.

ID., Catalogue of the Italian Opera Libretti in Central Europe in the 1st Half of the 18th Century, I: Moravia, in preparation.

STRAKOVÁ, THEODORA, Hudebníci na collaltovském panství v 18. století [Musicians at the Collalto estate in the 18th century], in: Časopis Moravského Musea [Moravian Museum Journal] 51 (1966), pp. 231-268.

STROHM, REINHARD, Italian Operisti North of the Alps, c. 1700-c. 1750, in: The Eighteenth-Century Diaspora of Italian Music and Musicians (Speculum musicae 8), Turnhout 2001, pp. 1-60.

ID., Argippo in "Germania", in: Studi Vivaldiani 8 (2008), pp. 111-126.

ID., Ignaz Holzbauers Hypermnestra (1741). Zur Geschichte und Interpretation des Librettos, in: Studien zur Musikwissenschaft 58, 2014, pp. 133–170.

Dissemination and Transfer of Music and Music Theory Between Copies, Adaptations and References

Estienne Roger's Foreign Composers

RUDOLF RASCH

In the history of music publishing, Estienne Roger takes a very special place.[1] This Huguenot, born in Caen in France, who settled in Holland after the Revocation of the Edict of Nantes in 1685, started a publishing firm in Amsterdam with another Huguenot, Jean-Louis de Lorme, in 1696. From 1697, he worked on his own. He published "conventional" books as well as music books. It was in the latter field that he earned his renown. He can be said to have been the first publisher with a truly international catalog and also with a truly international market. He sold his music not only in Holland, but also in the Low Countries, France, the German-speaking areas, Scandinavia and England. Roger died in 1722, but had transferred the music business nominally to his younger daughter Jeanne Roger prior to his death. Her name is mentioned in the imprint of all editions from some point in 1716 onwards, but it is unclear if she was actually involved in the management of the firm. She died later in 1722, and after her death the music publishing enterprise came into the hand of Roger's son-in-law, Michel-Charles Le Cène, who had married

---

[1] The basic study about the music publishing firm of Roger and Le Cène is still LESURE, 1969. The author of this article is developing a web-based catalog: *The Music Publishing House of Estienne Roger and Michel-Charles Le Cène (My Work on the Internet, Volume Four)*, especially *Part Four: The Catalogue*. Roger's editions are undated but the first issuing normally can be determined or estimated from advertisements or from the catalogs. All publication years mentioned in this article were established that way. See http://www.let.uu.nl/~Rudolf.Rasch/personal/Roger/Roger.htm.

Roger's elder daughter, Françoise Roger. After Le Cène's death in 1743, the business was continued by two minor figures, first Emanuel-Jean de La Coste (1743-1746), followed by Antoine Chareau (1746-1748), but all stock and plates of the firm were sold at auction and dispersed among a large number of buyers in 1749. *Sic transit gloria mundi.*

Roger's reprints

Roger's publishing output is well known to us due to the catalogs he either inserted in his music editions or published as separate booklets. At the end of the enterprise in 1743, some 750 music editions had been published. Many of these are reprints of foreign editions first published mainly in Italy or in France and these reprints must all be considered unauthorized or pirated, published without consent of the composer or the original publisher. The lack of international copyright made it very easy to do so.

The list of Italian composers whose works were reprinted by Roger is long. Most of them lived in Italy, and Roger always reprinted an edition published previously in Italy. The following composers fall in this first group of "Roger's foreign composers": Giuseppe Matteo Alberti, Tomaso Albinoni, Giuseppe Aldrovandini, Lorenzo Balbi, Antonio Luigi Baldassini, Giovanni Battista Bassani, Giacomo Battistini, Bartolomeo Bernardi, Giovanni Bianchi, Francesco Antonio Bonporti, Antonio Caldara, Arcangelo Corelli, Mauro D'Alay, Pietro Degli Antonii, Giovanni De Zotti, Andrea Fadini, Andrea Fiorè, Angelo Maria Fiorè, Giovanni Pietro Franchi, Gasparo Gaspardini, Giorgio Gentili, Alessandro Grandi, Andrea Grossi, Francesco Manfredini, Benedetto Marcello, Carlo Antonio Marini, Artemio Motta, Aurelio Paolini, Giovanni Reali, Giovanni Maria Ruggieri, Giulio Taglietti, Luigi Taglietti, Giovanni Battista Tibaldi, Bernardo Tonini, Giuseppe Torelli, Giuseppe Valentini, Antonio Veracini and Antonio Vivaldi.

The Italian editions reprinted by Roger were normally produced by letterpress method, which was the most common way to print music in Italy but produces – at least in our modern eyes – a rather unsatisfactory result. Roger always printed instrumental music from engraved plates and this method produces music pages that are much easier to read. This improved quality of the publication will have helped Roger to sell his editions, but raised the price at the same time: engraving is a more expensive method to print music than letterpress.

In general, one may suppose that Roger faithfully reproduced the original work in its typographically new look. But so far, only very few cases have been studied, and these tell us that one cannot rely on truly faithful reproductions. Roger's reprint of Antonio Vivaldi's *Sonate a violino e basso per il cembalo [...] Opera seconda* (Venice, Antonio Bartoli, 1709; reprint Roger, 1712) has added ornamentation in comparison with the Venetian original,[2] and Roger's reprints of Corelli's trio sonatas Opera 1-4 add articulation.[3] Figuring may also be more extensive in the Amsterdam reprints.

Roger also reprinted works of Italian composers active in the Western European diaspora, mostly in London and Paris. Italian composers resident in London whose works were reprinted by Roger without authorization include Martino Bitti, Giovanni Maria Bononcini, Nicola Cosimi, Francesco Geminiani and Nicola Matteis. Michele Mascitti and Giovanni Antonio Piani "des Planes" worked in Paris, Francesco Maria Veracini in Dresden. These composers normally had their works published in the city where they worked, i.e. London, Paris or Dresden. These editions were always engraved, which made it easier for Roger to produce his reprint. Also here detailed studies about Roger's way of reprinting are small in number. In the case of the reprint of Geminiani's *Sonate a violino e violone o cimbalo* (London, 1716; reprint Jeanne Roger, 1716) it can be said that Roger's reprint contains a few mistakes, left out dynamic markings, changed the figuring frequently, replaced 4/2 *alla breve* bars with 2/2 bars and misunderstood the notation of double sharps. In this case, Roger's reprint cannot be considered a faithful reproduction of the original edition: an editor must have been at work to "modernize" the edition.[4]

There are also editions published by Roger outside of the composer's reach that must have been prepared with the help of circulating manuscripts. These may be first editions, but are as unauthorized as the reprints of earlier editions. The many anthologies of sonatas and concertos published by Roger seem to belong to this category, but there are also editions of works by Johann Jacob Froberger, Tomaso Albinoni, Antonio

---

2   Personal communication by Fabrizio Ammetto.
3   See RASCH, 2007, pp. 381-417.
4   Research by the author of this article.

Vivaldi, George Frideric Handel and Giuseppe Tartini that are not known from earlier editions and, at the same time, do not look like an authenticated edition. The only choice then left is to consider them to be works printed according to circulating manuscripts. How Roger had got hold of these manuscripts is impossible to say.

The "Italian department" is certainly the largest of Roger's publishing house; the "French department" takes a good second place. The list of reprinted composers includes the following names: Jacques Boivin, Jean-Baptiste de Bousset, Louis de Caix d'Hervelois, André Campra, François Chauvon, Jean-François Dandrieu, Jean-Henri d'Anglebert, François Dieupart, Louis Francœur, Louis Heudeline, Michel de La Barre, Michel Lambert, Nicolas Lebègue, Gaspar Le Roux, Jean-Baptiste Lully, Marin Marais, Louis Marchand, Charles Mouton and Jean-Baptiste Senaillé. In addition, Roger reprinted many anthologies of French airs, notably the series *Airs sérieux et à boire*, with annual volumes from 1701 to 1723.

English and German composers whose work was reprinted by Roger are lesser in number. Among the English composers, may be mentioned William Corbett, Matthew Novell, John Ravenscroft and William Topham and among the German Gottfried Finger, George Frideric Handel, Gottfried Keller, Johann Christoph Pez, Johann Joachim Quantz and Georg Philipp Telemann. Finger, Handel and Keller worked in London and had their works published there. Pez's music was also published in London. This all means that Roger mostly took a British edition as his example for the reprinted German works.

And finally, there is a category of Roger's publishing output that consists of authorized first editions. This category is not very large and probably covers not more than somewhere between 10 and 20 % of the total number of editions. An authorized edition presupposes direct contact with the composer which makes it interesting to see where these composers lived and what their place of residence meant for the contact between composer and publisher.

Local composers

A first group of composers who turned to Roger to have their works printed and published are the local composers, living in Amsterdam or other places in Holland. Mentioned may be Servaas de Konink, Johan

Schenck, Johan Snep, Pieter Bustijn, Reynoldus Popma van Oevering and Jacob Nozeman. But there were also composers of foreign extraction who lived in Holland and must be considered local composers in their relation to Roger: of those, Henrico Albicastro, Johann Christian Schickhardt and Pietro Antonio Locatelli are the most important. Local composers had the advantage that they could visit the publishing house, hand over a reliable score, discuss the details of the publication, read proofs and receive or buy copies when the edition was printed. The resulting editions should be considered as reliable and authentic.

Traveling composers

A second group of composers whose works were published by Roger in an authorized edition is formed by the traveling composers who visited Amsterdam.[5] They had principally the same advantages as the local composers: they could visit the publishing house and negotiate their works. The disadvantage was that they could not always stay long enough to follow the entire process; and if they could, it would be only for one or perhaps very few sets of works. Nevertheless, these cases are interesting because they are also episodes in the biographies of the composer.

The first example of a foreign composer traveling to Holland whose works were published by Roger is the English singer John Abell. He was in Holland in 1696 and gave concerts in various towns, among them Amsterdam and Utrecht. Roger published a small volume with a few airs composed by him with the title *Airs pour le Concert de Merc[r]edy, le 12 Décembre, Au Doule, Composés par Jean Abell Anglois*. In 1696, 12 December fell on a Wednesday. It is unknown whether the composer or the publisher had the initiative of this publication.

Giuseppe Torelli visited Holland in 1698, probably together with the castrato singer Francesco Antonio Pistocchi. Both worked in Germany at this time. Roger reprinted Torelli's *Concerti musicali a quattro [...] Opera sesta* (Augsburg, 1698) without authorization just before the composer's arrival, but this was apparently no obstacle for Roger to publish Torelli's *Capricci musicali per camera a violino e viola overo arcileuto [...] Opera settima*, which is most probably an authorized edi-

---

5   This phenomenon is dealt with in a broader context in Rasch, 2003, pp. 95-111.

tion: no earlier edition is known and Roger's edition contained a dedication, which is usually a sign of an authorized edition.[6] Pistocchi had his *Scherzi musicali* (a collection of solo cantatas) published by Roger, also most likely an authorized edition: it has a dedication to the Brandenburg Elector Friedrich III who shall become King of Prussia in 1701, and a brief preface by Pistocchi.

Johann Mattheson was in Holland in 1706 and Roger's edition of his *Sonates à deux et trois flûtes sans basse* [...] *Premier ouvrage* may be associated with this visit.[7] If the edition was authorized, and it looks like it was, Mattheson had left Amsterdam long before the publication, which probably appeared in 1709.

Domenico Silvio "Conte" Passionei was in Holland as envoy of the Holy Sea from 1708 onwards, first in The Hague, then in Utrecht as one of the negotiators of the Piece of Utrecht, in the years 1712-1713.[8] One is tempted to see a relation between this stay and the later publication of his cello sonatas by Jeanne Roger in 1718 as *XII Sonate a violoncello e basso continuo*.

Francesco Geminiani was in Holland in 1728 or 1729 and it seems impossible not to suppose a relation with the publication of the second volume of his concerto arrangements after Corelli's famous violin sonatas Opus 5 by Le Cène in 1729.[9]

There may be more cases of traveling composers having works published by Roger. But not always the biography of a composer is known into enough detail to be certain about this.[10]

Italian composers resident in Italy

Composers were not dependent on personal visits to the publishing house to have their works published. There was always the mail, and it

---

6 No copy seems to be extant, but see the description in WALTHER, 1732, p. 611.
7 See RASCH, 2012a, pp. 315-335.
8 See TALBOT, 2011a, pp. 189-215.
9 See RASCH, 2012b, pp. 113-158, in particular pp. 115-123.
10 The composer and cellist Giorgio Antoniotto is said to have traveled through Holland at which occasion he published his cello sonatas with Le Cène, but his journey to Holland lacks documentary support so far. See, for example, the article on him in *The New Grove Dictionary of Music and Musicians*, ed. by Stanley Sadie, London 2001, vol. 1, pp. 764f.

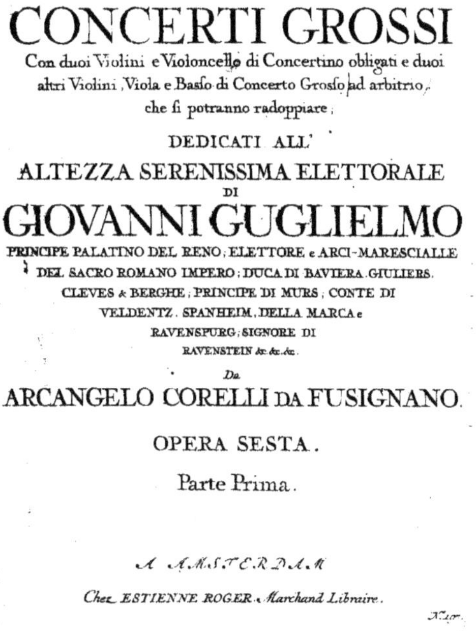

Figure 1

CONCERTI GROSSI
Con duoi Violini e Violoncello di Concertino obligati e duoi altri Violini, Viola e Basso di Concerto Grosso ad arbitrio, che si potranno radoppiare,

DEDICATI ALL'
ALTEZZA SERENISSIMA ELETTORALE
DI
GIOVANNI GUGLIELMO
PRINCIPE PALATINO DEL RENO; ELETTORE e ARCI-MARESCIALLE
DEL SACRO ROMANO IMPERO; DUCA DI BAVIERA GIULIERS.
CLEVES & BERGHE; PRINCIPE DI MURS; CONTE DI
VELDENTZ. SPANHEIM, DELLA MARCA e
RAVENSPURG; SIGNORE DI
RAVENSTEIN &c. &c. &c.
Da
ARCANGELO CORELLI DA FUSIGNANO.

OPERA SESTA.

Parte Prima.

A AMSTERDAM
Chez ESTIENNE ROGER, Marchand Libraire.

is remarkable to see how efficiently business was managed by mail over many hundreds of miles. Most remarkable are the contacts Roger must have maintained with Italian composers resident in Italy, particularly during the period from 1710 to 1720.

None less than Arcangelo Corelli himself opens the list of Italian composers resident in Italy who choose Roger as the publisher of his works. Reprints of Corelli's trio sonatas belong to the first publications of the publishing house; a second round of reprints, more luxuriously engraved and printed, was brought out in 1706.[11] Corelli's sonatas Opus 5 were reprinted by Roger in 1701 in an edition that carefully tried to copy also graphically Corelli's own 1700 edition (engraved by Gasparo Pietrasanta) and succeeded in that enterprise.[12] In spite of these unauthorized reprints, Corelli entrusted the publication of the ornamented version of

---

11 See RASCH, 2007.
12 Roger's reprint has a dedication to Jacob Klein "the Elder", dancing master of the Amsterdam Theater, father of the composer Jacob Klein "the Younger".

his violin sonatas Opus 5 to Roger, who published it in 1710 as *Sonate a violino e violone o cimbalo* [...] *Opera quinta, où l'on a joint les agréemens des Adagio de cet ouvrage, composez par Mr. A. Corelli comme il les joue*. In the twentieth century, doubts have been uttered about the authenticity of the edition,[13] but such doubts were totally absent during the eighteenth century. The strongest technical evidence in favor of its authenticity is perhaps the fact that the bass line at one point has a variant that occurs in later copies of the Roman edition, whereas the earlier Amsterdam and London reprints follow the older reading of this place.[14] Had the edition of the ornamented version of the sonatas been composed in Western Europe, it should have had this earlier reading.

After his ornamented Opus 5, Corelli published his concertos Opus 6 with Roger (see figure 1). Also here there have been doubts about the authenticity of the Amsterdam edition, but the surfacing of a contract between Roger and the merchant who maintained the contacts with Roger has removed all doubt that could possibly have existed.[15]

Two more major Italian composers followed Corelli's example in having their works published in Amsterdam: Antonio Vivaldi with his *L'estro armonico* [...] *Opera terza* (1711) and Tomaso Albinoni with his *Trattenimenti armonici* [...] *Opera sesta* (1712).[16] Both editions have dedications to Italian (Venetian) patrons and short texts explaining their publication in Amsterdam.

Neither Corelli nor Vivaldi or Albinoni have ever visited Holland or Amsterdam: all contacts between them – negotiating the conditions as well as the sending of scores to Amsterdam and the receiving of complimentary copies from Amsterdam – must have been established and maintained by mail. Unfortunately nothing of this has been preserved, and one can only guess about the role that mercantile or diplomatic contacts between Holland on one side and Venice and Rome on the other may have played.

The relation between Albinoni and Roger appeared to be a lasting one. Later authorized editions of Albinoni's works include *Concerti a cinque* [...] *Opera settima* (1715), *Balletti e sonate a tre* [...] *Opera ottava* (Jeanne Roger, 1722), *Concerti a cinque,* [...] *Opera nona* (Jeanne Roger,

---

13   See RINALDI, 1947, and RINALDI, 1953, pp. 221-223.
14   See the edition CORELLI, 2006, p. 163.
15   See RASCH, 1996a, pp. 83-136.
16   See RASCH, 1996b, pp. 89-137, reprinted in TALBOT, 2011b, pp. 241-289.

1722) and *Concerti a cinque* [...] *Opera decima* (Le Cène, 1736). Albinoni had sent his trios Opus 11 to Le Cène, but this was still unpublished when Le Cène died.[17]

The relation between Roger and Vivaldi was less stable. Roger's edition of *La Stravaganza* [...] *Opera quarta* (1715) is certainly authorized, but after *La Stravaganza* followed three volumes (Opus 5-7) probably based on circulating manuscripts. Then came two authorized editions, *Il cimento dell'armonia e dell'invenzione* [...] *Opera ottava* (Le Cène, 1725) and *La cetra* [...] *Opera nona* (Le Cène, 1727). The three volumes with six concerts each published in 1729 as Opus 10, 11 and 12 respectively, are probably unauthorized editions.[18]

Long before Roger had become the main publisher for Corelli, Albinoni and Vivaldi, he had established for himself a position as publisher of works composed by Italian composers in the diaspora. One can mention Pietro Antonio Fiocco (Brussels; *Sacri concerti* [...] *Opera prima*, 1701), Gasparo Visconti (London; *Sonate a violino e violone e cembalo* [...] *Opera prima*, 1703), Pietro Alberti (Kranenburg; *XII Suonate a tre* [...] *Opera prima*, 1703), Nicola Haym (London; *Dodeci sonate a tre* [...] *Opera prima*, 1703, and *Sonate a tre* [...] *Opera seconda*, 1704), Bartolomeo Bernardi (Copenhagen; *Sonate a violino solo col basso continuo* [...] *Opera terza*, 1706) and Pietro Evaristo Felice Dall'Abaco (Brussels; *Sonate da camera a violino e violone overo clavicembalo solo* [...] *Opera prima*, c. 1710, and later works until *Concerti a più istrumenti* [...] *Opera sesta*, Le Cène, 1735).

Further Italian composers, whose works were published in Amsterdam in editions of which nobody doubts their authenticity are Giovanni Mossi (*Sonate a violino e violone o cimbalo* [...] *Opera prima*, 1716 until *Sonate da camera per violino e violoncello o cembalo* [...] *Opera sesta/terza*, Le Cène, 1733), Giovanni Battista Somis (*Sonate da camera a violino solo e violoncello o cembalo* [...] *Opera prima*, Jeanne Roger, 1719), Giacomo Facco (*Pensieri adriarmonci o vero Concerti a cinque* [...] *Opera prima*, Jeanne Roger, 1720-1721) and Pietro Antonio Locatelli (*Concerti grossi a quattro e a cinque* [...] *Opera prima*, Jeanne Roger, 1721). From the diaspora Pietro Castruccci (*Sonate a violino e violone o cembalo* [...] *Opera prima*, Jeanne Roger, 1718) should not be forgotten.

---

17 See RASCH, 1995, pp. 1039-1070, in particular p. 1050.
18 See RASCH 1996b (see note 16).

German and English composers

Roger also published first and authentic editions of works by German and English composers, be it in lesser number than of Italian composers. Among the Germans may be mentioned Johann Adam Birckenstock, Johann Joseph Fux, Joseph Meck, Johann Melchior Molter, Johann Christoph Pez, Andreas Heinrich Schultze, Francesco Venturini and Johann Hugo von Wilderer; among the Englishmen, William Corbett, John Christopher (Johann Christoph) Pepusch, James Sherard and Robert Valentine.

Michel-Charles Le Cène

Le Cène followed Roger's example of publishing works by Italian composers. After first having published concertos by Giuseppe Tartini from circulating manuscripts in 1727-1729 (three volumes with six concertos each: *Sei concerti a cinque,* [...] *Opera prima, Libro primo-terzo*), he published Tartini's *Sonate a violino e violoncello o cimbalo* [...] *Opera prima* in 1734 as an authorized first edition.

Carlo Tessarini had the first two volumes ("Libro primo", "Libro secondo") of his *La Stravaganza, divisa in quattro parti [...] Opera quarta* published by Le Cène in 1735 and 1737 respectively. They contain a dedication to Cardinal Wolfgang Hannibal Count Schrattenbach. These editions followed three unauthorized publications of Tessarini's work, the *Concerti a cinque* [...] *Opera prima* (1724), the *XII Sonate per flauto traversie e basso continuo* (1729) and the *Concerti a più instrumenti* [...] *Opera terza* (c. 1730). The "Libro terzo" and "Libro quarto" of *La Stravaganza* were sent to Le Cène, but remained unpublished.[19]

And finally there is the case of Giovanni Battista ("Padre") Martini, whose *Sonate d'intavolatura per l'organo e'l cembalo* [...] *Opera prima* were published as one of the last editions of the publishing house, in 1742. This case shall be dealt with in more detail below.

Le Cène also published works by Italian composers in the diaspora such as Giovanni Antonio Brescianello (Stuttgart; *XII Concerti e sinfonie [...] Opera prima*, 1727), Giovanni Battista Sammartini (London; *Sonate*

---

19 The manuscripts of Libro terzo and quarto are listed in the inventory of the shop after Le Cène's death. See RASCH, 1995, pp. 1050f.

a solo, et a due flauti traversi col loro basso, Opera prima, 1736) and Giovanni Ferrandini (Munich; *Sonate a flauto traversiere solo e basso* [...] *Opera prima*, 1737-1742).

Giovanni Battista Martini's *Sonate d'intavolatura*

The case of Giovanni Battista Martini's *Sonate d'intavolatura per l'organo e 'l cembalo* [...] *Opera prima* has already been mentioned. This case is special because the correspondence between Martini and Le Cène about the production of this edition has been preserved, in the collection of the Museo internazionale e biblioteca della musica in Bologna. The way in which the edition of Martini's music was produced is not necessarily exemplary or typical, perhaps even rather atypical, but the production process contains a number of elements that must have belonged among the normal procedures when personal contact was impossible in case of an edition published a long distance from the composer (see figure 2).

Figure 2

Martini came into contact with Le Cène via Tartini.[20] Tartini had published his violin sonatas Opus 1 with Le Cène in Amsterdam in 1734. Martini knew that and asked Tartini how to proceed. He wrote his first letter to Le Cène on 15 November 1736, asking if the latter would be willing to publish his keyboard sonatas.[21] It took two and a half years, until 1 May 1739, before Le Cène could write to Martini that he indeed would publish them, but that Martini should have patience because he was busy with a second set of violin sonatas by Tartini and with the trio sonatas Opus 11 by Albinoni. Martini, in a letter of 17 June 1739, promises Le Cène that he would be patient.

Finally, in 1740, the moment for Martini to send his sonatas to Amsterdam had come. He sends them one by one, obviously a measure to prevent the loss of everything if the parcel would not reach its destination. Le Cène, or rather Le Cène's engraver, begins to engrave the pieces that have arrived. On 4 August 1741, Le Cène is able to write that 66 pages have been engraved and that the work as a whole will have more than 100 pages. The year 1741 passes by without major events. It is decided that Pietro Antonio Locatelli will do the proofreading in Amsterdam. This certainly means that no proofs were sent to Bologna. On 22 June 1742 Le Cène writes that Locatelli is correcting the second proofs. And then everything goes quickly. As early as on 30 July 1742, Le Cène can dispatch Martini's 30 complimentary copies plus two copies printed on large paper, one for Martini personally and one to give to the dedicatee, count Pepoli. *All is well that ends well.*

But there is a sequel to this story that does not end in a fairy tale. On 23 January 1743, Martini wrote a letter to Le Cène to propose the publication of a second set of keyboard pieces, much simpler than the *Opera prima*, which are indeed rather complicated (and somewhat old-fashioned) pieces. Le Cène has not sent an answer to this letter: the first months of 1743 were the last of his life and he died on 29 April 1743. After a couple of months, Martini gets slightly impatient and on 23 April 1744 he writes to Locatelli for a clarification of the situation.[22] In a letter of 21 May 1744, Locatelli tells Martini that Emanuel-Jean de la Coste

---

20 The letters of Tartini to Martini are preserved in I-Bc, Carteggio Martini, I.17.
21 The letters of Le Cène to Martini and the drafts of the letters of Martini to Le Cène are preserved in I-Bc, Carteggio Martini, I.19.
22 The letters of Locatelli to Martini and the drafts of the letters of Martini to Locatelli are preserved in I-Bc, Carteggio Martini, I.19.

now runs the music publishing business of Le Cène. In a letter of 8 July 1744, Martini addresses himself to La Coste with the same proposal as previously outlined to Le Cène more than a year before. After reciprocal communication, however, La Coste and Martini agree to publish twelve easy concerts for harpsichord with an accompaniment consisting of two violins and violoncello. These pieces (lost, unfortunately) are written in imitation of or as a response to Rameau's *Pièces de clavecin en concert*. By then, it was 1745.

Martini sends his concertos to La Coste from 7 April 1745 onwards, at a rate of one concerto every week. The last concerto was sent on 30 June 1745. These were sent as scores. In the meantime, the engraver had begun with his work. However, business was not going as La Coste had imagined and indeed, in 1746, La Coste sells the publishing business to Antoine Chareau, of which he informs Martini in a letter of 6 November 1746. According to this letter, it appears that the *Violino Primo* part of Martini's concertos had already been engraved. Martini writes to Chareau on 7 December 1746. Chareau promises Martini that he will do his best to complete the edition of Martini's music, in a letter dated 30 December 1746. That is, however, not what was going to happen. Chareau quits the business in 1748 by simply disappearing from Amsterdam, which marks the end of one of Amsterdam's most flourishing music publishing houses ever. Martini's *Pièces de clavecin en concert* was not published in Amsterdam or elsewhere.

Conclusion

This overview of Estienne Roger's editions of music by foreign composers shows us, first of all, the European dimension of his music publishing enterprise. Whereas music publishing in Italy, France, England and Holland before 1700 always focused upon the local production of music and the local dissemination of the editions published, Roger's publishing house had a truly European scope. His reprinting of music first published in Italy or France shows that he had found easy means to acquire publications from these countries. Later, he was able to maintain contacts by mail with composers resident in these countries, and these mail contacts sufficed to bring about a substantial number of important first editions of foreign, notably Italian composers. In general, very little or no information is available about what happened "behind the scenes"; often, we only know that the composer was living in Italy and that his music appeared in print in Holland. Only the preserved correspondence between Martini and Le Cène is available to obtain some insight into how the Italian composer and the Dutch publisher came into contact with one another, how they negotiated the details of the publication, the way the music was sent to the publisher and copies of the edition to the composer.

Literature

CORELLI, ARCANGELO, Sonate a Violino e Violone o Cimbalo Opus V, ed. by CRISTINA URCHUGUÍA in collaboration with MARTIN ZIMMERMANN, with a contribution by RUDOLF RASCH (Arcangelo Corelli, Historisch-kritische Gesamtausgabe der musikalischen Werke, vol. III), Laaber 2006.

LESURE, FRANÇOIS, Bibliographie des éditions musicales publiées par Estienne Roger et Michel-Charles Le Cène (Amsterdam, 1696-1743), Paris 1969.

RASCH, RUDOLF, The Music Publishing House of Estienne Roger and Michel-Charles Le Cène (My Work on the Internet, Volume Four), http://www.let.uu.nl/~Rudolf.Rasch/personal/Roger/Roger.htm.

ID., Johann Matthesons "Douze Sonates à deux et trois flûtes sans basse" (Amsterdam: Estienne Roger, 1709) und die Frühgeschichte des Duos und Trios ohne Generalbass, in: Johann Mattheson als Vermittler und Initiator. Wissenstransfer und die Etablierung neuer Diskurse in der ersten Hälfte des 18. Jahrhunderts, ed. by WOLFGANG HIRSCHMANN/ BERNHARD JAHN, Hildesheim 2012a, pp. 315-335.

ID., The Dutch Publications of Francesco Geminiani, in: Geminiani Studies (Ad Parnassum Studies 6), ed. by CHRISTOPHER HOGWOOD, Bologna 2012b, pp. 113-158.

ID., Migliorare il perfetto: Le edizioni delle sonate a tre di Corelli (ed altre edizioni corelliane) stampate ad Amsterdam nel Primo Settecento, in: Arcangelo Corelli fra mito e realtà storica. Nuove prospettive d'indagine musicologica e interdisciplinare nel 350° anniversario della nascita. Atti del Congresso Internazionale di Studi, Fusignano, 11-14 settembre 2003, ed. by GREGORY BARNETT et al., Florence 2007, pp. 381-417.

ID., The Dutch Republic in the Eighteenth-Century as a Place of Publication for Traveling Musicians, in: Le musicien et ses voyages. Pratiques, réseaux et représentations, ed. by CHRISTIAN MEYER, Berlin 2003, pp. 95-111.

ID., Corelli's Contract. Notes on the Publication History of the "Concerti grossi ... Opera sesta" [1714], in: Tijdschrift van de Koninklijke Vereniging voor Nederlandse Muziekgeschiedenis 46 (1996a), pp 83-136.

ID., "La famosa mano di Monsieur Roger". Antonio Vivaldi and His Dutch Publishers, in: Informazioni e Studi Vivaldiani 17 (1996b), pp. 89-137

ID., I manoscritti musicali nel lascito di Michel-Charles le Cène (1743), in: Intorno a Locatelli. Studi in occasione del tricentenario della nascita di Pietro Antonio Locatelli (1695-1764), ed. by ALBERT DUNNING, Luca 1995, pp. 1039-1070.

RINALDI, MARIO, Arcangelo Corelli, Milan 1953.

ID., Il problema degli abellimenti nell'Op. V di Corelli (Quaderni dell' Accademia Chigiana 10), Siena 1947.

TALBOT, MICHAEL, Domenico Passionei and His Cello Sonatas, in: Recercare 23 (2011a), pp. 189-215.

ID. (ed.), Vivaldi, Farnham 2011b.

WALTHER, JOHANN GOTTFRIED, Musicalisches Lexicon oder Musicalische Bibliothec, Leipzig 1732.

From "Sonate a quattro" to "Concertos in Seven Parts"
The Acclimatization of Two Compositions by Francesco Scarlatti

MICHAEL TALBOT

Among the musicians of the Scarlatti family Francesco (1666-1741 or later) has never enjoyed the highest reputation. Malcolm Boyd dismissed him as "third-rate",[1] and although recordings of some of his sacred vocal works have done a little to improve his standing, he remains a highly marginal figure. His biography marks him out as an abject failure in comparison with his elder brother Alessandro and his nephew Domenico. Like Alessandro born in Palermo, he studied in Naples in the early 1670s and in 1684 joined the viceregal court there as a violinist. In 1691 he returned to Sicily, where he remained until at least 1715, in which year he made an unsuccessful application to become *Vice-Capellmeister* at the imperial court. In 1719 he tried his luck in Britain, very possibly arriving there in the company of Domenico, whose long-doubted visit to London seems actually to have occurred in that year.[2] Turning down the offer of a position with the Duke of Chandos in 1720, Francesco remained in London, coming to public notice only rarely. It is very possible that in the period that followed he lived and worked for a while in the English provinces, to which the less successful among Italian immigrant musicians were apt sooner or later to gravitate. In 1733 he moved finally to

---

1   BOYD, 1986, p. 31.
2   IBID., pp. 28-31.

Dublin in Ireland, where he remained in obscure poverty until his death. He was indeed a rolling stone that gathered no moss.

Francesco's known compositions are relatively few. Most are vocal works, comprising four oratorios, one opera, one serenata, one Mass, three psalms, and perhaps a dozen chamber cantatas. His known instrumental output consists merely of a set of eleven sonatas for four-part strings discovered as recently as 2000.[3] These sonatas, the subject of this paper, were copied, probably during the late 1730s, into what has become known as "Workbook I" of the energetic Newcastle musician Charles Avison and are written entirely in his hand.[4]

It is clear that some if not most of the sonatas were composed after Francesco left Italy, since they collectively display *galant* characteristics that in 1719 were simply not yet current.[5] On the other hand, it appears probable that Francesco brought with him to England several of his own compositions with the hope of making use of them later. As many as 16 of his vocal works are preserved in British sources, 14 of which are unique and four (the Mass and psalms) autograph. In addition, Francesco

---

3   On the discovery of the sonatas and of Avison's two workbooks, see KROLL, 2005. Kroll is also the editor of *Francesco Scarlatti: Six Concerti Grossi*, Middleton 2010. The eleven sonatas by Francesco occupy folios 2r-28r of "Workbook I".

4   "Workbook I" and its continuation, "Workbook II", are both preserved without shelfmark in GB-NTp, In his article Kroll, following the earlier conclusion of Grace White, accepted the hand that copied out Francesco's sonatas as Charles Avison's, but he revised his opinion in the preface to the edition. However, since the same hand was responsible for notating what is indisputably a composition draft of Avison's Concerto in E minor, Op. 6 no. 8, there is no reason to doubt the original identification. How Francesco's sonatas reached Avison is unclear, but an anonymous early nineteenth-century annotation on the contents page of "Workbook I" stating that the works by Francesco and "Stephani" (to be mentioned shortly) Scarlatti were "no doubt from the MSS in Geminiani's possession" is at least plausible, given Avison's friendship with Geminiani and the latter's residence during much of the 1730s in the same city (Dublin) as Francesco Scarlatti.

5   These *galant* features embrace cadence forms, styles of melodic elaboration and ornamentation, dynamic contrasts and patterns of phrase structure. One also notes a high incidence of rounded binary form (featuring a tonic reprise of the opening theme mid-way through the second section) in preference to the simple binary form more common at the start of the eighteenth century.

seems to have brought to Britain various compositions by his brother and nephew with which he later parted, perhaps out of financial necessity. These may have included the well-known autograph set of twelve *Sinfonie di concerto grosso* composed by Alessandro in 1715-1716[6] and a group of twelve early keyboard sonatas by Domenico (K31-42) that later passed to Johann Christoph Pepusch and were sold by him to the publisher Benjamin Cooke, who in 1740 mixed them together with 30 sonatas pirated from the *Essercizi per gravicembalo* to create the strangely titled *XLII Suites de pièces pour le clavecin*.[7] Francesco could also have brought the autograph manuscript, or at least a copy, of the four *Sonate* (or *Sinfonie*) *a quattro senza cembalo* by Alessandro, with which his own sonatas display a degree of similarity, and on which they may even partly be modelled.[8] Avison's "Workbook I" likewise contains his copy of Alessandro's set,[9] their authorship disguised by the naming of the composer as the non-existent "Stephani Scarlatti" – partly, one suspects, as a ruse to keep the identity of the real composer hidden from other users of the volume, thus discouraging wider circulation of the sonatas, but also in playful allusion to the composer Steffani (his name often spelt "Stephani" in Britain), whose learnedly contrapuntal and consciously "antique" style Alessandro often parallels in these sonatas.[10]

---

6   GB-Lbl, R.M.21.b.14. The giga-like theme opening Francesco's eighth sonata is strikingly reminiscent of that opening Alessandro's first sinfonia, suggesting first-hand acquaintance.
7   On Cooke's acquisition of the Domenico Scarlatti sonatas and other works, see HALTON/TALBOT, 2015.
8   The sonatas are published as *Alessandro Scarlatti: Four "Sonate a quattro"*, ed. by ROSALIND HALTON, Launton, Edition HH, 2014. The earliest discussion of them in musicological literature is DENT, 1903. To Dent belongs the credit for discovering that the sonatas were in large part concordant with four of the *VI Concertos* published by Cooke. That an early source for the sonatas – possibly autograph, but at all events closely related to Scarlatti's original – had reached England is shown by a surviving copy of the set in GB-Lbl, R.M. 24.i.13.(1.), which was prepared around 1750-1760 by an unidentified Italian (his national origin emerges from various notational features) working in the orbit of the Academy of Ancient Music; this source largely corresponds textually to the early copy possibly by Cosimo Serio today in D-MÜs, Hs. 3957/1.
9   GB-NTp, "Workbook I", ff. 74r-81v.
10 Avison uses the Latinized name "Symphonia" in preference to "Sonata", a

This set of *Sonate a quattro* by Alessandro conforms to a basic formal template shared by other Neapolitan composers of the time (including notably his colleague Francesco Mancini) and embracing both quartet sonatas with a wind instrument added to the two violins and bass (such as found in Alessandro's twelve *Sinfonie di concerto grosso*) and ones including a viola instead. This design has three cardinal features:

1. The movements number at least four, generally five.
2. There is at least one regular fugue (often titled "Fuga") in moderate or quick tempo.
3. The last movement is brief, in binary form, and styled as a dance.

How well Francesco's sonatas conform to this template can be seen from Table 1, which gives basic data for his eleven sonatas. Their character is mixed: they show clearly both Francesco's indebtedness to his Neapolitan inheritance and his success at absorbing not only elements of the Roman and north-Italian traditions as represented by Corelli and Albinoni, among others, but also the new, *galant* incarnation of the Neapolitan style as cultivated by the generation around Leo, Porpora and Vinci, including a willingness to use the viola on occasion to reinforce the bass at the unison or upper octave (something that Alessandro's contrapuntally more rigorous quartet sonatas never do). The two five-movement sonatas, nos. 1 and 8, conform to the traditional Neapolitan plan; the eight four-movement sonatas resemble formally to a striking degree the six *Sonate* (or *Sinfonie*) *a cinque* of Albinoni's Op. 2 (1700), while the three-movement final sonata is an outlier. One also observes in the ninth sonata a composite opening movement wherein slow and fast tempos alternate on the pattern of the first sonata of Corelli's Op. 5. Since the eleven sonatas duplicate no key, one has good reason to suppose that they were conceived as a set. Perhaps a twelfth work (in G major or A major?) was omitted by Avison or never reached him.

The sonatas display great vigor and invention. If they have a weakness, it is that the writing of the inner parts, and particularly of the viola,

---

nomenclature probably taken over from his copy text. Although most other early sources of these compositions go under the title "Sonata", the parts for the last three in F-Pc (D-9171, D-9172, D-8967) have "Sinfonia". The Paris parts are interesting also for describing the works as "al tavolino senza cimbalo" (the first term denoting performance in the manner of Renaissance madrigals without keyboard continuo) and for mentioning lute or harp as alternatives to cello.

frequently runs into solecisms such as parallel fifths or octaves. Avison, who had an eye for such things, made many attempts to improve such passages, inking in new versions over the old, but not always with a successful outcome.

It appears that Avison tried out certain of the sonatas with local musicians, or at least brought them to the notice of others, since some of the scores have markings indicating where the breaks between systems should occur in a prospective fair copy. However, by the 1730s there was really no longer any market in Britain for sonatas employing an ensemble larger than a trio. Almost by definition, instrumental works in Italian style employing a viola had to be packaged as concertos or sinfonias. And in England – uniquely in Europe by this time – concertos for strings alone were customarily laid out neither in four parts (as *concerti a quattro*) nor in five parts (as *concerti a cinque*, with the addition of a principal violin), but in seven parts (with differentiated concertino and ripieno parts for both violins and a cello part distinct from the ripieno bass).

This situation had not always been so. Up to the time of the first publication of Corelli's *Concerti grossi* in 1714, England had become familiar first with Albinoni's *Concerti a cinque* (in Opp. 2 and 5), followed by those of Vivaldi and Giuseppe Matteo Alberti. Even after Corelli's concertos had won a huge following in England, no one thought initially to imitate their Roman-style orchestral layout in seven parts. Things started to change, however, in 1726, when the rising publisher Benjamin Cooke (d. 1743) advertised Francesco Geminiani's concerto arrangements of the first six violin sonatas in Corelli's Op. 5. In 1732 Geminiani published his own Opp. 2 and 3, which employed the same orchestral layout, whereupon the floodgates opened. Between 1734 (Michael Festing's Op. 3) and 1785 (a concerto by Charles Wesley) at least 25 concerto publications "in seven parts" for strings alone were issued in England, and all other species of string concerto, so far as one can tell, went into terminal decline.[11] As if to symbolize the change, William Corbett's collection of concertos entitled *Universal bizzaries*, which as originally published in 1728 had no concertino-

---

11 This is not to say that no such concertos were produced in manuscript in England before 1726 – Peter Holman has pointed out to me in correspondence the existence of specimens by Pepusch and Prelleur that may be earlier – but published works have special significance, since they were intended for general circulation.

ripieno differentiation, acquired extra partbooks for ripieno players when a second edition came out in 1742.

The rationale behind the insistence on a basic group of seven parts, to which extra obbligato parts for instruments other than violin could be added if desired, was a peculiarly British variation on the original Roman rationale. In the princely courts of Rome in Corelli's day the concertino-ripieno distinction generally coincided with that between a small group of salaried house musicians (a trio sonata ensemble, effectively) and the numerous professional musicians brought in from outside to swell the numbers and augment the splendor of an occasion. In British conditions, particularly within the music societies that were springing up everywhere, this very commonly transmuted into a distinction between paid professional musicians and the rank-and-file made up by amateur players, who would usually be glad to have less challenging and prominent parts to play. So the same layout was retained, but with a changed social meaning. It is a remarkable fact that no string concertos employing the traditional "Roman" layout seem to have been published on the continent after the appearance of the six concertos in Pietro Antonio Locatelli's Op. 4 of 1736 – at which point the baton passed, as it were, into the hands of the British.

Of course, not every movement or, indeed, every piece had to employ separate ripieno instruments. The options always existed to "double up" ripieno and concertino for the second or even both violin parts and to yoke together the cello and continuo bass. So we find a *de facto* ripieno concerto such as Handel's Op. 6 no. 7 (1740) masquerading as a "grand concerto", while the idea of doubling concertino and ripieno second violins while keeping the two first violin parts separate, thereby obtaining the texture of a solo concerto, has a pedigree stretching right back to Corelli's Op. 6.[12] Having seven parts to play with conferred maximum flexibility at the small cost of occasional wastefulness.

At some point, Avison conceived the plan of publishing the four Alessandro Scarlatti sonatas in his possession with the assistance of his old associate Cooke, who had already published his Op. 1 trio sonatas (c.1737), and would shortly become the London stockist of his Op. 2, the *Six Concertos in Seven Parts* (1740). The story has been told elsewhere,[13] and only the bare outlines will be given here. To convert

---

12   The second movement of Corelli's Op. 6 no. 12 is a perfect case in point.
13   In HALTON/TALBOT, 2015.

the original sonatas into the required concertos Avison needed to do little other than:

(i) remove the penultimate movement in 3/4 meter (perhaps thought redundant as there were already two quick movements) from each of the sonatas in C, G and D minor (nos. 2-4);

(ii) compose a new, slightly weightier finale (in a most un-Scarlattian mixture of binary and rondeau form) for the C minor work, using some of Scarlatti's original thematic elements;

(iii) provide a complete set of bass figures (thereby abandoning the original "senza cembalo" concept); and – very important –

(iv) momentarily reinforce the viola part with the cello or a violin whenever it became too exposed. As we know from his famous *Essay on Musical Expression*,[14] Avison was resigned to a common situation in eighteenth-century Britain where the viola part was assigned to the weakest player or players and therefore risked not being heard. Corelli had done something similar in his Op. 6 concertos as published, but there the motivation was very different: to make the pieces playable by concertino alone.

But four works were not enough to make up the six that were normally regarded as the minimum number of concertos in a properly constituted set. Moreover, Alessandro's cycle of four austere minor-key concertos progressing through the circle of fifths from F minor to D minor needed a measure of leavening, and also the provision of a few opportunities for solo display by the principal violinist and some solo-tutti contrast. Avison's solution, as inspired as it was also dishonest (for the concertos were marketed as works by "Alexander Scarlatti" *tout court*), was to coopt the first and eighth of Francesco's sonatas, the most "Neapolitan" in overall character, as the sixth and third concertos of the set, retaining Alessandro's works in their original sequence as Concertos I-II and IV-V. Francesco's two pieces required little reinforcement of the viola part, which was less prominent than in his brother's sonatas, but much more editorial work with regard to the finer details.

The resulting *VI Concertos in Seven Parts* enjoyed a measure of success when they appeared from Cooke in 1740, and the first two concertos were even published separately in France.[15] True, in modern times they

---

14 Avison, 1752, p. 19.
15 Concerto I, engraved and published by Louis Hue, was advertised as "Un Concerto Primo del Signor Scarlatti" in the *Mercure de France*, February 1742, p. 355; Concerto II followed at some point no later than 1745.

have sometimes been regarded, not without good reason, as spurious[16] – which in a sense they undeniably are (even disregarding Francesco's silent contribution) by virtue of appearing in a concerto rather than a sonata format. But only now have the specific roles played by Francesco Scarlatti and Charles Avison come to be recognized. Fortunately, the understanding of their complex origin is unlikely to dent their modern popularity, and may even do something for Francesco's reputation, not to mention Avison's (since his substituted movement is very attractive).[17]

In their own way, which is exceptional in its details but not in the wider circumstances to which they responded, these six sonatas by two different Scarlattis, skilfully transformed into concertos by a master *bricoleur*, Avison, and cunningly published by Cooke under the aegis of a royal privilege originally taken out on behalf of keyboard sonatas by Domenico Scarlatti, embody perfectly the idea that the migration of music and musicians from one local or national culture and milieu to another always entails the possibility of radical and unexpected change. Sometimes the outward form changes in order to preserve the meaning. Sometimes the meaning changes as the price of retaining the outward form. In the present case, what I have called in my title the "acclimatization" of the music has resulted in changes to both form and meaning via a complex and only partially reconstructable series of decisions and personal interactions. And the kind of synthesis that we have observed here is replicated countless times in the encounter of Italian music or musicians and the British marketplace during the eighteenth century.

---

16 For example, by Peter Holman in his review of a recording of the concertos in *Early Music Review* 81 (June, 2002), pp. 17f.

17 Avison went on to introduce surreptitiously many movements of his own composition in his published arrangements (as concertos) of keyboard sonatas by Domenico Scarlatti (1744).

Table 1: Plan of the eleven sonatas by Francesco Scarlatti in Avison's "Workbook I"

No.	Key	Tempo, Meter	Comments
1	E	Allegro, C	Imitative
		[Allegro], 4/2	Fugue
		Largo e puntato, 3/2	Through-composed, imitative, ends on V of c#
		[Allegro], C	Accompanied fugue
		Affettuoso, 3/8	Binary form, minuet rhythm, solo-tutti contrast
2	c	[Largo], C	Contrapuntal, ends on V of c
		Andante, C	Fugue on two subjects
		Grave, C	Starts in g. Homophonic, ends on V of c
		[Allegro], 3/8	Fugue
3	a	Allegro, C	Imitative, ends on V
		Andante, C	Fugue
		[Largo], 3/2	Homophonic, then contrapuntal, ends on V
		[Allegro], 2/2	Fugue
4	e	Largo→Andante, C	Contrapuntal, ends on V
		Allegro, C	Fugue
		Largo, 3/4	Starts in b. Homophonic, ends on V of e
		[Allegro], 2/2	Fugue
5	b	[Largo], C	Imitative
		Larghetto, C	Fugue
		Largo, 3/4	Starts in D. Imitative, ends on V of b
		Allegro, 2/2	Imitative
6	C	Allegro, 3/4	Homophonic, ends on V
		Allegro, 4/2	Fugue

		Largo, 3/2	Starts in a. Ends on V of a
		Allegro non presto, 3/8	Fugue
7	Bb	Grave, C	Imitative
		[Allegro], C	Accompanied fugue
		Largo, 3/2	Starts in g. Ends on V of g
		Allegro, 2/2	Binary form, gavotta rhythm, solo-tutti contrast
8	F	Allegro, C	Imitative
		Largo, 3/4	Starts in d. Ends on V of d
		[Allegro], [C]	Fugue with solos for Violin 1
		Largo, 3/2	Starts in a. Ends on V of d
		Allegro, 12/8	Binary form, giga rhythm
9	D	Grave, C→Presto, 3/4→Largo, 3/4→Presto, 3/4→Largo, 3/4	Composite form, with solos for Violin 1
		Larghetto, C	Fugue, with inversion of the subject in the second part
		Largo, 3/4	Starts in b. Ends on V of D
		Presto, 12/8	Fugue in giga rhythm
10	g	Grave, C	Imitative
		Allegro, 3/2	Accompanied fugue
		Siciliano, 6/8	Ends on V of g
		Allegro, 12/8	Accompanied fugue, with solos for Violin 1
11	d	[Adagio], C	Contrapuntal
		Largo e come sta, C	Starts in a. Ends on V of d, very brief
		Allegro, 3/4	Fugue

Note: Solo-tutti alternations marked in the score that are inessential to the structure and may have been inserted independently by Avison are ignored in the table above.

Literature

Avison, Charles, An Essay on Musical Expression, London 1752.
Boyd, Malcolm, Domenico Scarlatti: Master of Music, London 1986.
Dent, Edward J., The Earliest String Quartets, in: The Monthly Musical Record 33 (November 1903), pp. 202-204.
Halton, Rosalind/Talbot, Michael, "Choice Things of Value": The Mysterious Genesis and Character of the VI Concertos in Seven Parts attributed to Alessandro Scarlatti, in: Eighteenth-Century Music 12/1 (2015), pp. 9-32.
Kroll, Mark, Two Important New Sources for the Music of Charles Avison, in: Music & Letters 86, 3 (2005), pp. 414-431.

Spread of Italian Libretti
Maria Clementina Sobieska Stuart – a Patron of Roman Operas

ANETA MARKUSZEWSKA

The spreading or migration of different libretti is well-documented in the history of opera during the seventeenth and eighteenth century. A striking case in point is the popularity of Pietro Metastasio's libretti during the eighteenth century: numerous composers throughout Europe and beyond repeatedly set them to music. Sometimes, Metastasio's text was presented in its original form, but more often, it was modified and adapted to a given venue and performers. Many studies have been written on such adaptations of Metastasio's libretti.[1]

Another example of libretto migration is the incorporation of fragments of an older into an entirely new text. This was notably the case of the birthday cantata dedicated to the young Maria Clementina Sobieska Stuart in Rome in 1719. The title page of that composition, based on a text by Francesco Bianchini and music (now lost) by D. Giovanni Giorgi Veneziano, reads as follows: *CANTATA / PER IL GIORNO NATALIZIO / Della Sacra Reale Maestà Britannica / DI / CLEMENTINA / REGINA*

---

[1] The literature on the spread, multiple settings, and adaptation of Metastasio's libretti is sizeable. The majority of authors who focus on selected composers, operatic works, or themes indicate that Metastasio wrote the original text. Therefore, it is impossible to quote the entire literature: I shall list selected writings that analyze the adaptations of a given libretto, e.g. WEICHLEIN, 1956; DEMMEL, 1979; SPRAGUE, 1979; WILSON, 1982; ARSHAGOUNI, 1994; selected articles in HILSCHER/SOMMER-MATHIS, 2000.

D'INGHILTERRA &c. / In cui si allude alla unione delle due stelle, dette benefice, / che accade in quel dì 17. Luglio 1719. ed all' / Accademia tenuta, e stampata in Roma / l'anno 1687. dalla Maestà della fu / Regina CHRISTINA DI SVEZIA. / In occasione della solenne Ambasciata, spedita alla S. Sede / nell'assunzione al Trono d'Inghilterra della Maestà / DEL RE' GIACOMO SECONDO. / Di gloriosa memoria, / Con riferirsi i sentimenti della celebre Orazione, / e le parole de 'Versi allora composti / dalli Accademici Reali / DEDICATA A SUA MAESTA' BRITANNICA. / Da Monsignore Francesco Bianchini Cameriere d'Onore / di Nostro Signore.[2] The cantata composed for Sobieska is based on a fragment of a work performed during a musical celebration organized by Christina of Sweden in 1687 in honor of the English ambassador of King James II. Apart from illustrating a certain type of musical text migration, the example also shows that some circumstantial texts with a political character, held in large palatial libraries, continued to be known and reused for many years after their creation.

My MusMig project focuses on a group of selected Italian libretti from the *opera seria* genre that enjoyed great popularity in the Early Modern Era. My research investigates not the spreading of a single libretto set to music in different European centers, but rather the migration of a given operatic theme, usually under the same title. This approach was partly inspired by an article by Robert Freeman, *The Travels of Partenope*, which analyzed the mechanism of spreading of *Partenope*, one of Silvio Stampiglia's most popular texts, in thirteen adaptations.[3] Freeman notably analyzed the changes introduced into Stampiglia's original text and their character; the succession of scenes and *liaison des scènes*; the presence of Arcadian ideas in *Partenope*'s performances after 1699 (the premiere was at the Teatro di S. Bartolomeo in 1699); and the usefulness of substitute arias. He also addressed the question of who introduced changes to the original text and for what reasons. It is an important matter because the adapter's person is relevant to any analyzed libretto that adapts an existing text. Contrary to Freeman, however, the analysis of the above-cited issues constitutes only a part of my research; in fact, I am more interested in the phenomenon of popularity or fashion for some texts as well as their political potential. The key questions of my research are the following: Why did some stories in Early Modern opera

---

2   For more on this cantata see MARKUSZEWSKA, 2014.
3   FREEMAN, 1968, pp. 356-385.

become popular or fashionable? What was it that drew the attention of numerous authors and patrons to the multiple adaptations of some libretti over long periods? Of what exactly did the process of transformation of a theme consist? Could a well-known text be modified according to the current requirements of a patron, and how? What political aims or profits did patrons achieve? Were the libretti a vehicle for ideas, political or other, relevant in a given epoch?

Since the spread of Italian libretti is represented by a quantitatively enormous material, it is essential to find a reference point for my analysis. My choice is the character and patronage of Maria Clementina Sobieska Stuart, one of the most renowned, admired and intriguing women in Rome during the second and third decade of the eighteenth century.

Maria Clementina Sobieska Stuart

Maria Clementina Sobieska was born in 1701 in Macerata in Italy, the daughter of Hedwig Elisabeth von Pfalz-Neuburg and Jakub Sobieski, the eldest son of Marie Casimire and King Jan III Sobieski.[4] On her mother's side, she was related to many European courts, and her godfather was none other than pope Clement XI. In 1718, at the request of James III Stuart, pretender to the throne of England, Scotland and Ireland, Charles Wogan became interested in the young Maria Clementina. Wogan was James's devout courtier who traveled the European courts looking for an appropriate wife for his king. It was during the 1718 carnival that he arrived at Oława (Ohlau) in Silesia, where the Sobieskis resided. Of the many different princesses that Wogan came to know during his travels, Maria Clementina made the most lasting impression. After protracted and complex negotiations, with the participation of numerous spies, a wedding contract was signed and young Maria, with her mother and a small court, left for Italy in late 1718, where James resided. Unfortunately, James's wedding contradicted the political plans of the king of Great Britain, George I of the Hanoverian dynasty, who forced Emperor Karl VI to imprison Maria Clementina in the fortress of Innsbruck. Al-

---

4   About Clementina, see BORKOWSKA, 1874; MILLER, 1965; ROSZKOWSKA, 1984, pp. 106-119; and NOWAK-SOLIŃSKI's fictional biography (to be taken with a grain of salt), 1984; PLATANIA, 1993 as well as works by Edward Corp, a main scholar of the Stuarts in exile.

though the act met with surprise and outrage throughout Europe, the emperor remained impervious to requests to free the princess.[5] Wogan then decided to do so by ruse and succeeded thanks to an ingenious plan and the effectiveness of several allies. The bold escape of Maria Clementina was the talk throughout Europe,[6] with panegyric verses composed for the princess, printed accounts of the adventure[7] and numerous medals produced depicting Maria Clementina:

> "Some letters mention that in that city were issued many golden and silver medals, with on one side the portrait of Princess Sobieski, wife to the King of England, with the following words: *Clementina Maria Britannia, Francia, Hibernia, & Scotia Regina*, and on the other side, the same Princess fleeing toward Rome after having freed herself from Innsbruck, while her husband the King sailed from Spain to Rome, with the following motto: *Fortunam, causamque sequor* and underneath *Deceptis Custodibus Anno 1719*. It is said that those medals were and continue to be very sought-after, with everyone describing them according to their fantasy."[8]

---

5 Remember that on her mother's side, Clementina was related to the imperial court. The sister of Hedwig Elisabeth von Pfalz-Neuburg was the empress Eleonore Magdalene von Pfalz-Neuburg, mother of two future emperors: Joseph I and Karl VI, the latter to play an important role in Clementina's history.

6 Information on Maria Clementina appeared both in private correspondence and in the press; see notably *Diario di Chracas* and *Mercurio Storico e Politico*; Stuart Papers, vol. 7. Clementina continued to be remembered after her death: see LUBOMIRSKI; O'KELLY DE GALWAY, 1896.

7 GILBERT, 1894.

8 "Alcune lettere particolari dicono, che sono uscite in questa Città molte medaglie d'oro, e d'argento, sulle quali si vede da una parte il ritratto della Principessa Sobieski Moglie del Rè d'Inghilterra con queste parole. *Clementina Maria Britannia, Francia, Hibernia, & Scotia Regina*, e nel rovescio vi si vede pure questa Principessa, che fugge verso Roma, dopo essersi liberata da Inspruck, nel medesimo tempo, che il Rè suo Marito faceva vela dalla Spagna verso Roma con questa divisa. *Fortunam, causamque sequor*, e al di sotto *Deceptis Custodibus Anno 1719*. Dicesi, che queste Medaglie sieno state e sieno attualmente molto ricercate, e ciascuno ne parla secondo la sua fantasia." *Mercurio Storico e Politico* (October 1720). See also GUTHRIE, 2004, pp. 545f., especially note 9; ID., 2007, pp. 287-312.

Shortly after Sobieska's arrival in Bologna on 9 May 1719, the couple was married *per procura*,[9] and Maria Clementina shortly thereafter reached Rome[10] where she was greeted like a true queen and accompanied to the convent of the Ursulines, where she held an apartment prepared especially for her. There, she waited for James who was returning from an expedition to Spain:

> "On the 13th of the present month, this Princess arrived to Rome in the carriages of the Pretender who claims to be the King of England, and with which she is said to have been married in Bologna *per procura*. She was met outside the gates by the Cardinals Gualtieri and Acquaviva and several other persons of high rank, who retired after the first greetings, while the said Cardinals led her to the Convent of the Ursulines, where an apartment had been prepared for her and a number of refreshments were served to her in name of the Pontiff and that of Cardinal Gualtieri and Acquaviva, who also gave her in the name of the Catholic King a bond for twenty thousand *doppie*."[11]

During the following few days, Maria Clementina received visits from church officials and Roman ladies and walked the city with her numerous entourage, universally honored as a queen should be:

> "She went to the Capitoline Hill, where she was received at the sound of trumpets and drums, with all the honors due to crowned heads.

---

9 MILLER, 1965, p. 138. The marriage proper took place on 2 September in Montefiascone near Rome. The newly wed took residence in Rome at the Palazzo del Re on piazza SS. Apostoli. See CORP, 2010, pp. 180-205; Id., 2011.

10 *Diario di Chracas* 291.

11 "Adì 13 del passato arrivò questa Principessa in Roma nelle Carrozze del Pretendente, che si chiama Rè d'Inghilterra, col quale si dice sia stata maritata a Bologna per procura. Ella fu incontrata fuori della Porta da' Cardinali Gualtieri, ed Acquaviva, e da diverse altre persone di qualità, le quali si ritirarono dopo i primi complimenti, e i suddetti Cardinali la condussero poi nel Monastero del Orsoline, dove l'era stato preparato un Appartamento, e dove fù regalata d'una quantità di rinfreschi tanto in nome del Pontefice, quanto in quelli del Cardinal Gualtieri, e del Cardinal Acquaviva, il quale le diede per parte del Rè Cattolico una Cedola di venti milla doppie." *Mercurio Storico e Politico* (June 1719).

The same happened when, in the company of Cardinal Gualtieri, she visited the English College, where she was also hailed as Queen."[12]

Charles-François Poerson, director of the French Academy in Rome, wrote on the occasion of that celebration:

> "The Princess was admired on that occasion, as she is in any other. Her vivid and beautiful spirit is highly praised, supported, it is said, by a judgment that would be praiseworthy even with an elder person."[13]

Maria Clementina Sobieska Stuart and opera

Clementina's passion for operatic art is confirmed by one of the major events of her life. Her marriage to Stuart quickly proved to be a failure for a number of reasons.[14] Significantly, she decided to part with her husband in 1725 and seek refuge in the St. Cecilia convent in the Trastevere district. Baron Philipp von Stosch, a long-time spy of the King of England, wrote that only her passion for opera and the desire to see a new work staged at the Teatro d'Alibert could push her to leave the convent:

> "It appears at present that the desire to see the opera at Aliberti's would have more effect on the Princess's state of mind than all the

---

12 "Ella si portò a visitare il Campidoglio, dove fù ricevuta col suono delle Trombe, e de' tamburi, e con tutti gli onori, che si praticano alle Teste Coronate. Il medesimo è stato praticato, quando ella è stata a visitare accompagnata dal Cardinal Gualtieri, il Collegio degl'Inglesi, dov'è stata servita come Regina." *Mercurio Storico e Politico* (July 1719). Charles Poerson wrote about the noise of trumpets, drums, and oboes: "La Princesse Sobieski a été au Campidoglio, où les Sénateurs l'ont reçue au bruit des trompettes, tymbales, hautbois et tambours. Après y avoir vu ce qu'il y a de remarquable, elle fut régallée de magnifiques rafraîchissemens, ainsi que toute sa Suitte, qui estoit très nombreuse." See DE MONTAIGLON, 1889, vol. 5, p. 244.

13 "Cette Princesse se fit admirer dans cette occasion, comme elle a fait dans toutes celles où elle s'est trouvée. L'on loue extrêmement son esprit vif et beau, qui se trouve, dit-on, soutenu d'un jugement qui serait admiré dans une personne d'un âge plus avancé." DE MONTAIGLON, 1889, vol. 5, p. 244.

14 SKRZYPIETZ, 2008, pp. 238f.

reasoning of Cardinal Alberoni, which in vain seeks to inspire heroism in a lady entirely devoted to entertainment and spectacle."[15]

Another example of Clementina's fascination with opera, even her voracity in consuming every single operatic premiere, occurred in the year 1720. Late into pregnancy, she was unable to visit the theater, so a performance was arranged for her and her guests at the Palazzo del Re, the Stuarts' Roman residence. The evening opened with *Faramondo* with a text by Apostolo Zeno and music by Francesco Gasparini – a work actually dedicated to Clementina.[16] The performance coincided with her first labor pains. An extensive account of that event is given in *Diario di Chracas*; we shall quote but a fragment:

"Her Royal Highness, the Queen of England Clementina Subieski [sic], experienced the first slight labor pains on the evening of St. Stephen, at around a quarter to three Italian time, while she was being dressed to meet many Princesses and noble ladies, numbering over 100, at a rehearsal of the opera that is due to be staged at the Theater of Count d'Alibert. The following day, the Cardinals, Princesses, Prelates, the Magistrate of Rome and all other people selected to assist Her Royal Highness giving birth, who did not feel an increase of the labor pains before the evening of the 30th, when in the evening assistants were called to come to her Residence."[17]

---

15 "Il paroit présentement que le désir de voir l'Opera de Aliberti fait plus d'effet sur l'esprit de la Princesse, que touts les raisonnements fortes du Cardinal Alberoni, qui pretend en vain de semer un héroïsme dans l'esprit d'une femme infiniment adonné aux divertissements et spectacle." London, National Archives, SP 85/116 (21 January 1726).

16 *Il / Faramondo / drama per musica / da rappresentarsi / Nella Sala dell'Illm Sig. Conte D'Ali / bert nel Carnovale dell'Anno 1720. / DEDICATO / ALLA MAESTA' / DI / CLEMENTINA / Regina della Gran Bretagna &c / in Roma 1720.*

17 "Comminciate la sera di S. Stefano le prime doglie leggere alla Maestà della Regina d'Inghilterra Clementina Subieski, verso le ore due e tre quarti dell'orologia italiano, mentre si procurava vestirla in presenza di molte signore Principesse e Noblità numerosa di 100 e più persone, colla prova dell'opera che deve farsi al Teatro del Sig. Conte d'Alibert, furono avvertiti il dì seguente li Sign. Cardinali, le Sign. Principesse, li Signori Prelati, il Magistrato di Roma e tutti gli altri Personaggi scelti per l'assistenza del par-

Clementina was a frequent guest at the Roman opera theaters, but had a particular affinity for the Teatro d'Alibert. The Stuarts had three boxes reserved there, symbolizing the three kingdoms to which James pretended: England, Scotland, and Ireland.[18] It is also possible that her bond with the theater stemmed from the relationship with the d'Alibert family of her grandmother, Maria Casimira Sobieska, who resided in Rome between 1699 and 1714. It was in the printed libretto of the above-quoted *Faramondo* that Count Antonio d'Alibert referred to that long-time friendship:

> "And the ancient glory conquered by my ancestors who on many occasions served her Highness Maria Casimira, great Queen of Poland, and foremother of M.V., has assured me that She, in whom the virtue of her Husband and the magnanimity of her Foremother glow as the sun's rays, with no less clemency or goodness, she stood to appreciate the tribute of that second drama titled *Faramondo*, which will be performed at my theater."[19]

In total, nine operas were dedicated in Rome to Maria Clementina between 1720 and 1730:

1. *Faramondo*, libretto by Apostolo Zeno, music by Francesco Gasparini, 1720;
2. *Eumene*, lib. Apostolo Zeno, mus. Nicola Porpora, 1721;
3. *Flavio Anicio Olibrio*, lib. Apostolo Zeno, Pietro Pariati, mus. Nicola Porpora, 1722;
4. *Adelaide*, lib. Antonio Salvi, mus. Nicola Porpora, 1723;
5. *Scipione*, lib. Apostolo Zeno, mus. Luca Antonio Predieri, 1724;

---

to di Sua Maestà la Regina, la quale non sentì molto accresciute le doglie, se non la sera del 30, quando furono di nuovo avvertiti gli Assistenti sul tardi per rendersi alla di lei Abitazione." *Diario di Chracas* 544.

18 CORP, 2011, p. 82.
19 "e l'antica Gloria acquistata da miei Maggiori nel servire in molte occasioni la Maestà di Maria Casimira gran Regina di Polonia, ed Ava della M.V., mi hanno assicurato, che Ella, in cui, come in perfetto Parelio, tutta risplende la virtù dello Sposo, e la Magnanimità dell'Ava, con non minor Clemenza di questi, e con bontà non inferior dell'Altra, sia per gradire il tribute di questo secondo Drama intitolato il FARAMONDO, che pur debbe rappresentarsi nel mio Teatro *Faramondo*."

6. *Partenope*, lib. Silvio Stampiglia, mus. Domenico Sarro, 1724;
7. *Il Valdemaro*, lib. Apostolo Zeno, mus. Domenico Sarro, 1726;
8. *Siroe Re di Persia*, lib. Pietro Metastasio, mus. Nicola Porpora, 1727;
9. *Artaserse,* lib. Pietro Metastasio, mus. Leonardo Vinci, 1730.

Apart from *Partenope*, staged by the Teatro della Pace, the remaining works were performed at the Teatro d'Alibert, also known as Teatro delle Dame.

After 1727, Clementina gradually withdrew from secular life. She reconciled with her husband and resumed the tutorship of her sons, but she spent more and more time in church, mortifying her flesh and soul, immersed in prayer and talks with her confessor. Her rejection of all the pleasures she had previously embraced is illustrated in the documentation of her beatification, which actually never happened. In the section titled *Della Nascita, pia Educazione, / e Santa Vita / della Ven. Serva d'Iddio / Maria Clementina Sobieski / Regina della Gran Brettagna*, we find the following entry:

> "The truth is that after a few years, the God's servant parted with the convent, and moved to Bologna in the month of July 1727, but having not found His Royal Highness her husband there, who had left in the meantime, she continued to refuse any entertainment, leisure, and feast, be they public or private, which the City and His Eminence Buffo Legate had prepared, striving to receive her with the appropriate honors. She graciously answered the Noblemen that according to the teachings of St. Paul, when the Husband is far away, the wife should be withdrawn."[20]

---

20 "Gualm.te la Verità fù, ed é, che scorso qualche anno la Serva di Dio si partò dal Monastero, portarsi in Bologna nel Mese di Luglio 1727, e non avendo ivi ritrovato la Maestà di Rè Suo Consorte, il quale erasi(s) portato altrove, ricusò costante.te qualunque siasi divertimento, riecreazione, e festa, lo pubblica, come privata, che la Città, e l'Emo Buffo Legato preparate avevano, riceverla con quella proprietà, che convenivale, secusandosi? ella con la grazie, e dicendo a quella Nobiltà, che secondo l'insegam.to di S. Paolo, quando il Marito è lontano, la moglie deve star ritirata." *PROCESSUS ORDINARIA AUCTORITATE COSTRUCTUS SUPER ASSERTO MIRACULO A DEO PER INTERCESSIONEM DEL FAMULA MARIA CLEMENTINA SOBIESKI REGINA MAGNA BRITANNIA*. I-Ras, TRIBUNALE DEL CARDINAL VICARIO, BUSTA (VOL.) 338, fol. 640f.

Clementina died in 1735 in Rome, with the reputation of a saint. As one of only three women (the other two being Christina of Sweden and Countess Matilda of Tuscany), she was buried at St. Peter's Basilica in the Vatican. Her character, biography, her evolution from a young girl intoxicated with Roman entertainment to a mortified mystic are all interesting in themselves. In my present article, I shall nonetheless focus on the first period of her residence in Rome, when she was renowned as a patron of music and saw many new opera performances dedicated to her.

Libretti: *Adelaide*

The majority of the libretti dedicated to Clementina belong to a group of popular themes that were set to music with great frequency and presented on the opera stage of Italy and Europe. From these, I have selected the following:

1. *Adelaide*
2. *Eumene*
3. *Siroe, Re di Persia*

In the present article, I shall focus on the group of libretti titled *Adelaide*. In the history of Europe, there have been several outstanding women of that name. In opera, two have been portrayed frequently: Adelaide of Susa, also known as the Turin Adelaide, as well as Adelaide of Italy (or Burgundy; 931-99), also known as St. Adelaide, who was wife of the Holy Roman Emperor, Otto I. She appeared most of any Adelaide as an operatic character. Librettists were particularly intrigued by her early life, when Berengar, Duke of Spoleto, invaded the kingdom of her first husband, Lothair. The beauty, intelligence and intransigence of Adelaide who opposed the aggressors and the attempts at having her marry her own son, as well as her flight from prison and triumphant marriage to Otto I, provided some outstanding material for operatic plots.

Adelaide probably appears in opera for the first time in Venice in 1672 at the Teatro Vendramino (also known as Teatro San Salvatore or di San Luca).[21] The author of the first libretto dedicated to her was Giovanni

---

21 *L'Adelaide / Drama per musica / Da Rappresentarsi nel Teatro VEN-DRAMINO a San/Salvatore. / l'anno M.DC.LXXII / CONSACRATO / ALL'ALTEZZA SERENISS./ Del Prencipe / GIO: FEDERICO / Duca di*

Francesco Bussani, the music by Antonio Sartorio. Fortunately, both, the libretto and Sartorio's brilliant score, survived to our day at Venice's Biblioteca Marciana (I-Vnm). Subsequent productions included Siena, 1685; Munich, 1722; Rome, 1723; Palermo, 1724; Bologna, 1725; Florence, 1725; Genoa, 1725; Livorno, 1726; Venice, 1729; London, 1729; Mantua, 1730; Padua, 1732; Florence, 1735; Verona, 1735; Graz, 1739; Rome, 1743; Hamburg, 1744; and Prague, 1744.[22] In total, the group includes twenty libretti, set to music in the years 1672-1744 and for the most part available for musicological research.[23] We could add to the above-mentioned texts those that cite the story of Adelaide, but have other characters of the plots as title protagonists: Adalberto, Otto, Berengar, or Lothair (in the case of Handel). It is also worth noting that from the year 1722, the one libretto most often set to music is that by Antonio Salvi.

I have already discussed in detail the composition of *Adelaide* (text by Antonio Salvi and music by Nicola Porpora), performed in 1723 in Rome at the Teatro d'Alibert and dedicated to Maria Clementina Sobieska Stuart.[24] That analysis shows how a well-known text was used for the Stuart's case. In the present study, I would like to present a few observations that are more general. Antonio Salvi wrote the libretto of the short-lived *Adelaide* (not including the two productions in 1672 and 1685, the popularity of *Adelaide* spanned a period of slightly more than twenty years in 1722-1744).[25] What seems notable is that the original version of his libretto written for Munich (1722) was not used as a model for the later operatic productions. Instead, later productions were based on a text produced in Rome by Ignatio de Bonis whose name as an adapter of the libretto was

---

Bransvich / Luneburgo, &c / in Venetia M.DC.LXXII / Appresso Francesco Nicolini.

22 SARTORI, 1990-1994, vol. 1.
23 After this period, operas used the character of Adelaide increasingly rarely. She did not disappear completely, however, as testified by the composition of Gioacchino Rossini, *Adelaide di Borgonia* (1817) to a text by Giovanni Frederico Schmidt.
24 MARKUSZEWSKA, i.pr.
25 SARTORI, 1990-1994, vol. 1.

until now unknown,[26] set to music by Nicola Porpora in 1723.[27] This means that the later productions on the subject were based on a libretto dedicated to Marie Clementine Sobieska Stuart. It is possible to draw the following conclusions from that and two later, particularly interesting versions, namely Venice 1729 and Rome 1743. Firstly, the subject was deemed suitable for presentation to people connected with the unofficial English politics (the libretti were dedicated, in order, to Marie Clementine Sobieska, wife of James III Stuart; to the Jacobean prince George Hamilton; and to the Young Pretender or Bonnie Prince Charlie, son of Maria Clementina and James III).[28]

Secondly, the two later productions of *Adelaide* underwent various changes, reflecting the particular characteristics of their relevant locations. In the Venice production, most of the arias known from 1723 had been retained. For instance, eight out of the nine arias in Act One use the text of the Roman version. Act Two is different (only four arias out of nine share the same text), but Act Three again retains the same text in five of the seven arias. Although the Venice version retained many of the arias, it was also significantly abridged. In particular, the recitatives were trimmed, and some of the scenes were dropped, giving the Venetian *Adelaide* a more dynamic story arc. The Roman version (1743) retains most of the recitatives and the same sequence of scenes (with occasional word-level changes, though retaining the sense of the original), however most of the arias had been removed. Interestingly, the retained arias are mostly arias *di paragone*.

Thirdly, and perhaps most significantly for the resonance of *Adelaide* relative to the 1723 version in the other two productions and to those written for other places, the final scene underwent the most extensive modification. The closing scene of the 1723 Roman version is the only one to feature the appearance of "Italia in Macchina", praising the great hero Ottone, his marriage to Adelaide and their future offspring worthy of the parents' great deeds.[29] In the Venice production, the figure of Italy is removed, however a short fragment of her text is retained (the first five

---

26 "[…] ad Igniatio de Bonis […] per acomodare l'opera intitolata l'Adelaide", Rome, Biblioteca Magistrale e Archivi del Sovrano Ordine di Malta, entry CT 441, p. 38.
27 I present the explanation for such a situation in MARKUSZEWSKA, i.pr.
28 The story of Adelaide was also set by Handel in his *Lotario* (1729).
29 The scene is analyzed more deeply in MARKUSZEWSKA, i.pr.

lines, beginning with "Invitto Rè"). This passage is given to one of the characters, Clodimiro, a captain in the army of Berengario, Otto's opponent; this part in the Venice production is played by a castrato, Domenico Annibali, "virtuoso di S. M. il Rè Augusto di Pologna". The structural function of this recitative, however, was primarily to create an effective segue to a joyful *ballo,* choreographed by the eminent dancer and choreographer Gaetano Grossatesta. The final chorus comes after the *ballo,* containing quintessentially conventional praise for love ending in marriage. A quite different effect is produced by the ending in the second Roman version, addressed to Charles Edward Stuart, the Young Pretender and son of the deceased Marie Clementine. Another look at the libretto should prove helpful in interpreting the piece. The one person who repeatedly saves Adelaide from the envy and hatred of the usurpers, Matilde and Berengario, is their son Idelberto, who is in love with Adelaide. When the tables are turned and Adelaide is in a position to take revenge, she will be dissuaded from sentencing the usurpers to death by the insistence of Idelberto, who pleads with her to show mercy to his parents. Adelaide spares their lives and Idelberto hands over his father's kingdom to her. Ottone notes that "D'ogni paterno error la macchia orrenda / D'un Figlio illustre la virtude emenda." ("The horrendous stigma of every paternal error is corrected by the virtue of an illustrious son.") This ending portrays the son as the hero in this version of *Adelaide*, an impression that is not removed even by the closing chorus, which praises clemency, the virtue of good rulers. With his courageous heart of a warrior, Idelberto shall certainly be a clement ruler, no less so than Adelaide and Ottone.

It seems that this variant of the ending may have been related to the Stuart's changed circumstances in Rome compared to 1723. In 1723, the Young Pretender was only three years old, and his father James III was involved in a project calculated to regain the British throne by overthrowing a usurper monarch from the Hanover dynasty. Twenty years later, it was his son, then aged 23, who was preparing to fulfil his life's mission. Committed and self-confident, courageous and independent, he believed that he could regain the British throne with the help of a group of loyal Stuart supporters. Obviously, in 1743, nobody could foresee the details of his imminent involvement in the Jacobite rising, the battle of Culloden (1746), his expulsion from France and the failure of his life's project, a disappointment from which he never recovered. At this point, three years previously, the Roman sympathisers of Charles were still painting visions of his glorious future. Presumably, the 1743 production of the opera was part of that mood.[30]

Soon after 1743, the Adelaide theme disappears from Europe's opera stages. Why? It is difficult to offer a definitive answer. The changing tastes of the public are one possible answer: stories come and go, replaced by others. In the 1740s, operagoers became fascinated with stories by Metastasio, which pushed many earlier libretti into oblivion (with few exceptions, such as *Eumene* by Apostolo Zeno). However, the disappearance of *Adelaide* from opera theaters also appears to have had a political overtone. This political interpretation is suggested by the dedication in the libretto of the 1735 production of *Adelaide* in Verona with music by Antonio Vivaldi. It includes the following passage:

> "It was equally fitting that the work should be dedicated to a Venetian patrician, since the story upon which the action is based cannot be displeasing to a good Italian who, unlike many today, is not an enemy to his Nation. When, following the expulsion of the last Italian kings, poor Italy was brought back under the foreign yoke, never to be free again, the only thing that compensates for this deplorable misfortune is the existence of the most illustrious Venetian Republic, in which Italian liberty holds fast since its beginning to the present day and, God willing, until the end of time."[31]

This suggests that the story of Adelaide was associated with the history of Italy, whose various parts recognized a sense of shared past (though not shared statehood, despite the use of the word *nazione*). Vivaldi, a Venetian by birth who signed this dedication, regarded *La Serenissima* as a bastion of freedom not available to the other parts of Italy, which have

---

30 CLARK, 2003, pp. 91-100; CORP, 2011, pp. 240-257.
31 "Era parimente convenevole, che ad un Veneto Patricio fosse questo Dramma dedicato, imperciocchè non potendo la Storia, ond'è ricavata l'Azione, che sommamente dispiacere ad un buon'Italiano, che non sia, come tanti sono oggidì, di sua Nazione inimico, facendogli sovvenire, come discacciati gli ultimi Italiani Rè, ricadde la misera Italia, per non più liberarsene, sotto giogo straniero, a tale deplorabilissima sciagura solo dà qualche compenso l'inclita Veneta Republica, in cui dal suo nascimento fino a'nostri giorni l'Italiana libertà si conserva, e voglia Iddio sino al finire de'secoli conservarla." *L'Adelaide*, Verona 1735, p. A2.

been passed from hand to hand by a series of political powers including Spain, France and the Habsburg Empire. This may be one reason why the immense popularity of *Adelaide* on the stages of Italy and other countries, including Munich, London, Graz and Prague quickly waned with the realization of the story's import, so threatening to foreign powers. In the public theater, Metastasio's lamenting Didos were certainly a safer option.

Literature

ARSHAGOUNI, MICHAEL HRAIR, Aria Forms in the Opera Seria of the Classic Period: Settings of Metastasio's 'Artaserse' from 1760-1790, unpublished PhD diss., Univ. of Los Angeles 1994.

BORKOWSKA, ALEKSANDRA Z CH., Maria Klementyna Sobieska opowiadanie poświęcone młodemu wiekowi [Maria Clementina Sobieska. A narration dedicated to her young age], Warsaw 1874.

CLARK, JANE, The Stuart Presence at the Opera in Rome, in: The Stuart Court in Rome. The Legacy of Exile, ed. by EDWARD CORP, Aldershot 2003, pp. 85-93.

CORP, EDWARD, The Stuarts in Italy 1719-1766. A Royal Court in Permanent Exile, Cambridge 2011.

ID., The Location of the Stuart Court in Rome: The Palazzo Del Re, in: Loyalty and Identity. Jacobites at Home and Abroad, ed. by PAUL MONOD et al., Hampshire 2010, pp. 180-205.

FREEMAN, ROBERT, The Travels of 'Partenope', in: Studies in Music History: Essays for Oliver Strunk, ed. by HAROLD POWERS, Princeton 1968, pp. 356-385.

GILBERT, JOHN THOMAS (ed.), Narratives of the Detention, Liberation and Marriage of Maria Clementina Stuart Styled Queen of Great Britain and Ireland. With Contemporary Letters and Papers now for the First Time Published, Dublin 1894.

GUTHRIE, NEIL, The Art of the Jacobite Print, in: 1650-1750: Ideas, Aesthetics, and Inquiries in the Early Modern Era 14 (2007), pp. 287-312.

ID., The Memorial of the Chevalier de St. George (1726): Ambiguity and Intrigue in the Jacobite Propaganda War, in: The Review of English Studies, Vol. 55, No. 221 (2004), pp. 545-564.

HILSCHER, ELISABETH/SOMMER-MATHIS, ANDREA (eds.), Pietro Metastasio – uomo universale (1698-1782). Festgabe der Österreichischen Akademie der Wissenschaften zum 300. Geburtstag von Pietro Metastasio (Sitzungsberichte der philosophisch-historischen Klasse 676), Vienna 2000.

LUBOMIRSKI, HENRI, Lettres et Mémoire, concernant l'évasion de la Princesse Royale, Clementine Sobieska, promise au Prétendant d'Angleterre en 1719 [manuscript].

MARKUSZEWSKA, ANETA, Between the Sensuality of Music and Religious Ecstasy: Maria Clementina Sobieska Stuart (1702-1735), in: Revisiting Baroque (Report of the ENBaCH congress, Rome 2014), ed. by RENATA AGO, http://www.enbach.eu/content/between-sensuality-music-and-religious-ecstasy-maria-clementina-sobieska-stuart-1702-1735.

ID., "Queen of Italy, Mother of the Kings" or Adelaide on Opera Stages. A Case Study of Adelaide (Rome 1723) for Maria Clementina Sobieska Stuart, in: Music Migrations in the Early Modern Age. People, Markets, Patterns, Styles, ed. by VJERA KATALINIĆ, Zagreb i.pr.

MILLER, PEGGY, A Wife for the Pretender, New York 1965.

MONTAIGLON, ANATOLE DE (ed.), Correspondance des directeurs de l'Académie de France à Rome avec les surintendants des bâtiments, vol. 5, Paris 1889.

NOWAK-SOLIŃSKI, WITOLD, Klementyna Sobieska "Królowa Anglii" [Clementina Sobieska "Queen of England"], Warsaw 1984.

O'KELLY DE GALWAY, ALPHONSE (CTE.), Mémoire historique et généalogique de la famille de Wogan avec une relation inédite de l'évasion de la princesse Marie-Clémentine Sobieska femme de Jacques III roi de la Grande-Bretagne et d'Irlande (1719), Paris 1896.

PLATANIA, GAETANO, La politica europea e il matrimonio inglese di una principessa polacca: Maria Clementina Sobieska, Rome 1993.

ROSZKOWSKA, WANDA, Królowa Wielkiej Brytanii [The Queen of Great Britain], in: Oława królewiczów Sobieskich [The Ohlau of the Sobieski Royal Princes], Wrocław 1984, pp. 106-119.

SARTORI, CLAUDIO, I libretti italiani a stampa dalle origini al 1800. Catalogo analitico con 16 indici, 7 vols., Cuneo 1990-1994.

SKRZYPIETZ, ALEKSANDRA, Kłopoty małżeńskie Marii Klementyny Sobieskiej [Matrimonial problems of Maria Clementina Sobieska], in: Między Barokiem a Oświeceniem. Staropolski regionalizm

[Between Baroque and Enlightenment. Old Polish regionalism], ed. by STANISŁAW ACHREMCZYK, Olsztyn 2008, pp. 230-244.

SPRAGUE, CHERYL RUTH, A Comparison of Five Musical Settings of Metastasio's Artaserse, unpublished PhD diss., Univ. of Los Angeles 1979.

WEICHLEIN, WILLIAM JESSET, A Comparative Study of Five Musical Settings of 'La Clemenza di Tito', unpublished PhD diss., Univ. of Michigan 1956.

WILSON, J. KENNETH, L'Olimpiade: Selected Eighteenth-Century Settings of Metastasio's Libretto, unpublished PhD diss., Harvard Univ. 1982.

Migrations of Musical Repertoire
The Attems Music Collection from Around 1744

METODA KOKOLE

The owners: Countess Josepha and her husband, Count Ignaz von Attems

In 1744, an inventory of 98 Italian opera arias was compiled for their owner, Countess Josepha von Attems, née Countess von Khuen.[1] This inventory of arias, together with the music of the majority of the listed arias, was unearthed in the Provincial Archives of Maribor among a group of documents taken there after World War II from the castle of Slovenska Bistrica (Windisch Feistriz) which, until then, had been the seat of the noble family of Attems, the direct descendants of Countess Josepha.[2]

---

1 *Lista delle Arie dell'Illustrissima Signora Signora Giuseppa Contessa d'Atthembs Nata Contessa di Khuen. L'Anno 1744.* SI-Mpa, Gospoščina Bistriški grad, Musicalia, TE 67, AE 1. This document has no specially assigned number. It precedes music manuscripts that have recently been numbered and cataloged for the RISM A/II series: SI-Mpa, numbers SI_PAM/1857/010/00001-SI_PAM/1857/010/00102; the last three digits are new shelf marks running from 1 to 102, and these will serve as further marks of identification in this article; thus "Mpa 1" stands for the first listed surviving musical piece.

2 On the history of the castle of Slovenska Bistrica and its owners, see ŠERBELJ, 2005.

Countess Josepha von Attems was born as Maria Josepha Elisabeth Augusta Claudia Khuen zu Auer von Belasi-Lichtenberg on 4 July 1721 at Hall near Innsbruck[3] to Count Johann Franz Khuen zu Auer von Belasi-Lichtenberg (1690-1747), scion of an old Tyrolean noble family, and Maria Anna, by birth Countess von Thurn und Taxis (1696-1766), a member of a powerful German princely house. When the inventory of arias was compiled for her, she was 23 years old and already the mother of four small girls, all born in the Styrian capital of Graz, in the palace at Sackstraße which, at that time, was the seat of her husband's family.[4] She married in Vienna on 29 October 1739 at the age of 18, and her husband was Count Ignaz Maria von Attems-Heiligenkreuz.[5]

Countess Josepha – according to present knowledge – spent her early life in Hall near Innsbruck.[6] During the winter of 1738 to 1739 she met her future husband while visiting her uncle, the Archbishop of Sekau in Graz.[7] After her marriage she moved to Styria and was living between

---

3   A copy of Josepha's birth certificate is preserved in A-Gla, Familienarchiv Attems, K. 92, H. 949. The date of her christening is given there as 4 July 1721 in Brixen. However, in all modern family genealogies the referred date of her birth is 4 August in Hall; see for example the genealogy published online: http://gw.geneanet.org/cvpolier?lang=en&p=maria+josepha &n=khuen+von+auer, 20.11.2014.

4   For preliminary genealogical data on the Attems family, I am indebted to my colleague Dr Miha Preinfalk, the foremost Slovenian specialist on local aristocratic families, who also advised me on further research. Concerning the various members of the Attems family, see also the genealogy freely available on the following internet site: http://genealogy.euweb.cz/attems/attems4.html, 20.11.2014. On the family's Styrian branch in Graz, Ignaz's immediate family, see also WISSGRILL, 1794, pp. 189-192; ILWOF, 1897; FRANK/ŠERBELJ, 1990, pp. 146-148; and especially A-Gla, Familienarchiv Attems, Familiengeschichte, verfaßt von Maria Victoria Markgräfin Pallavicino-Attems, 1950ff., K. 3, H. 7 (3. Kapitel). I am extremely obliged to Dr Johannes Attems and to Dr Victor Attems-Gilleis for granting me a special permission to consult the last mentioned source in A-Gla.

5   See the marriage contract in A-Gla, Familienarchiv Attems, Ehekontrakte, K. 19, H. 86.

6   Josepha's taste for music and theater was probably acquired at her noble home with the aid of private tutors, and possibly also at one of the institutions in her town of birth. On music institutions in Hall see SENN, 1938.

7   A-Gla, Familienarchiv Attems, Familiengeschichte, verfaßt von Maria Victoria Markgräfin Pallavicino-Attems.

Graz and Slovenska Bistrica as well as in Vienna, where she was awarded the highest titles at the Imperial Court[8] and where she died in her sixty-third year, on 1 April 1784. However, all twelve of her children were born in Graz between 1740 and 1758.[9] Based on the evidence of her music collection we may assume that she was musically educated. She was most probably a soprano singer, or at least a fervent admirer of contemporary opera, as was also her husband Ignaz.

Figures 1a and 1b: Portraits of Ignaz and Josepha von Attems (Pokrajinski muzej Maribor, inv. nos. 29 and 30; by kind permission)

---

8   Josepha was made a member of the imperial order *Dames de l'ordre de la Croix de l'Étoile* on 3 May 1740 (see A-Gla, Familienarchiv Attems, K. 92, H. 950). Between 1765 and 1769 she was *Oberste Hofmeisterin* to the Austrian Archduchess Maria Elisabetha Christina.

9   Family portraits of both parents (depicted on horseback) as well as of most of their children, in paintings probably executed between 1784 and 1789 and originating from the castle in Slovenska Bistrica, are now housed at the Regional Museum of Maribor (Pokrajinski muzej Maribor). In the existing literature some of the family members are misidentified. See VRIŠER, 1974 (concerning the children), and VRIŠER, 1993, reproductions nos. 183 and 185 (Ignaz Maria II's uncle and father, respectively; these two are now exhibited at the Regional Museum at Ptuj) and nos. 147 and 148 (Ignaz Maria and his wife Josepha). The last two are inventoried under the numbers 29 and 30 (from the castle of Slovenska Bistrica). The portraits also receive discussion in CIGLENEČKI, 1997, pp. 47-51.

Ignaz, later known as Count Ignaz Maria II, was born on 27 February 1714 in the Styrian capital of Graz as Ignaz Maria Maximilian Dismas Josef Alexander Count von Attems-Heiligenkreuz. He was the first-born son of Count Franz Dismas Hermann von Attems, Freiherr von Heiligenkreuz (Graz, 6 August 1688-Graz, 10 May 1750), and Countess Maria Sophia Clara, née von Herberstein-Pusterwald (Graz, 12 August 1694-Graz, 28 July 1715). His mother died when he was just over one year old, and he was temporarily entrusted into the care of a local widow, Anna Maria Popp, who was his foster mother until his father remarried in 1717 and he was sent back to Sackstraße.[10] His mother's mother, Countess Christina Crescentia, by birth Countess von Herberstein, became the second wife of his grandfather, Ignaz Maria I in 1715. She brought into the family a lucrative new estate, Vurberk (Wurmberg), that she bequeathed directly to her grandson Ignaz Maria II, who was very attached to that property from the time of her death in 1737.[11] Ignaz, during his childhood called Ignaz Leander, received the best possible education in his youth. Initially, he was educated at home, for it is known that the family employed a resident tutor, *Praefectus* Johann Michael Kness,[12] and he was attending classes at the local Jesuit school in Graz from 1727 to 1729 where he finished the last two classes with distinction.[13] From another

---

10   A-Gla, Familienarchiv Attems, Familiengeschichte, verfaßt von Maria Victoria Markgräfin Pallavicino-Attems.

11   Ignaz was informed about his new property while in Leiden (he reacted to the death of his grandmother in a letter written on 14 May 1737) and enquired in a letter of 11 June 1737 on the state of the castle and its inventory: A-Gla, Familienarchiv Attems, K. 19, H. 87. On his special attachment to Vurberk, see also FEDERHOFER/SCHMEISER, 1971, p. 80.

12   Kness is described as a "Prafectus apud Excell. D. D. Comitatem ab Attembs" in the church records of Maribor, where in 1725 he got married. SLEKOVEC, 1895, p. 81.

13   His name is mentioned among pupils who were awarded prizes for their achievements in oration ("ex oratione soluta" and "ex oratione ligata") and Christian doctrine. The prizes were publicly awarded after the performance of a Latin play. The printed summary of the play with the names of all performers was for these occasions accompanied also by "Nomina eorum in arena literaria victorum". See the play *Urbis et orbis romani homagium Caesari Octaviano Augusto [...]*, Graz 1728, A-Gl, Tresor A 513549, and *Alphonsi Persii inaudita fidei constantia [...]*, Graz 1730, A-Gl, Tresor A 513546 I (xerox copy).

source we learn that he was additionally taught fencing and probably also dancing by the fencing and dancing master of the Styrian provincial estates in Graz, Johannes Baptista Robin (also known as Rubin), active as the principal dancing master at the same Jesuit school during the years of Ignaz's schooling there.[14]

From November 1734 to September 1738, Ignaz's father sent him, accompanied by a preceptor and/or tutor, *Hoffmaister* Westerhold, and an old servant,[15] on a Grand Tour typical of the time.[16] From his native Graz in Austrian Styria, he first traveled north to Würzburg and a few other German towns. During the first half of the year 1735, he studied in Prague and later enrolled at the University of Leiden as a *candidatus iuris*. In July 1737, he terminated his official university education and traveled on to Belgium, France and finally Italy. His itinerary is rather well documented by the 32 surviving letters sent to his father in Graz during his travels.[17] Besides providing other news, he kept his father informed of musical events that impressed him, such as a musical soirée at the court in Würzburg in July 1735, an exhibition of military music

---

14 Robin is recorded alternately as "saltuum instructore", "saltibus a provincia praefectus", "Tanzmaister", "Saltus et lanisticam instruente" and "provinciae Styriae saltuum et lanisticae magistro" in surviving printed librettos and programmes of the Jesuit dramatic productions in Graz between 1701 and 1734: see GRAFF, 1984, pp. 261-271. Ignaz von Attems mentions his old fencing master ("Kein fechtmeister ist auch nicht dorten, das muß ich anheur nothwendig lehrnen, weilen ich nur 3: Monat bey dem alten *Robin* zu gräz gelehrnet, und noch nichts contra gefochten habe, hier hätte ich eben die gelegenheit am besten.") in a letter sent from Prague on 29 October 1735 to his father in Graz: A-Gla, Familienarchiv Attems, K. 19, H. 87. Robin was most probably also a violinist, since this instrument was commonly played by dancing masters of the time.

15 A-Gla, Familienarchiv Attems, Familiengeschichte, verfaßt von Maria Victoria Markgräfin Pallavicino-Attems. In the letters the name of the *Hoffmaister* is, however, never mentioned.

16 On the Grand Tour in the eighteenth century in general, see BLACK, 2013, pp. 277-287, and BLACK, 2003, especially pp. 174-181 (dealing with the arts, notably music and theater, in Italy).

17 A-Gla, Familienarchiv Attems, K. 19, H. 87. The letters are mentioned in ILWOF, 1897, p. 21. A critical edition of the correspondence, edited by Metoda Kokole, Željko Oset, Miha Preinfalk and Luka Vidmar, is planned for publication by the Slovenian Eighteenth-Century Society within the next two years.

in Mainz in September 1735 and especially the musical performances – both instrumental and operatic – he witnessed in Rome and Venice during the year 1738.[18] From 1739 onwards, he was appointed to various high positions at the Inner-Austrian government and the Habsburg court in Vienna.[19]

Ignaz was heir to a large family fortune, including a sizable number of castles and palaces in addition to one of the richest local art collections of its time, accumulated by his homonymous grandfather, Ignaz Maria Maximilian Dismas Josef Leander Reichsgraf von Attems, Freiherr zu Heiligenkreuz, Lucinico, Podgora, Falkenstein und Tanzenberg (Ljubljana/Laibach 1652-Graz 1732), better known as Ignaz Maria I. During the first decades of the eighteenth century, the elder Ignaz Maria was the foremost Styrian patron and promoter of the arts. Between 1686 and 1717, he was busy buying numerous properties in Styria – in and around Graz, but mostly in Lower Styria, a geographical area belonging to Slovenia today. He had his newly acquired castles decorated by the best available artists in the new, fashionable style (Italian and French).[20] Symbols representing music are found in every place where he commissioned decorations, especially in the festive halls of his castles and palaces such as Brežice (Rann), Štetenberk (Stattenberg), Slovenska Bistrica. The castle of Slovenska Bistrica became the official seat of the branch of the family established by his grandson Ignaz Maria II (as the latter is called in family histories).[21] Ignaz Maria II died in Vienna on 15 July 1762.

18 On the subject of Ignaz's reports concerning music see KOKOLE, 2015, pp. 57-79.
19 On 7 April 1739 Ignaz was appointed by Karl VI *Regierungsrath* in Graz; in 1741 he became imperial *Kämmerer*, and in 1760 *Wirklicher Geheimer Rath*.
20 The patronage of contemporary artists by Ignaz Maria I and the commissioned works of art in his castles and palaces have been studied by a number of art historians in Slovenia and also Austria in recent decades. For Slovenia, see especially CIGLENEČKI, 1997, WEIGL, 2003 and 2006, and MUROVEC, 2000 and 2007; for recent Austrian literature, see especially LECHNER, 2010 (containing a complete bibliography up to that date that includes writings in Slovenian).
21 A comparison of the inventory compiled after Franz Dismas's death in 1750 with that compiled after his son's death in 1762 clearly testifies to the effort made by Ignaz Maria to transform the castle into a more permanent and commodious family residence; many pieces of furniture and everyday

Judging from the surviving music collection, both Josepha and her husband Ignaz von Attems were amateur musicians and enthusiastic admirers of contemporary opera. One or both of them possibly also played keyboard instruments, since one of these – "a new clavichord" – was listed after Ignaz's death in 1762 as standing in the sixth room in the family's castle at Slovenska Bistrica.[22] This may well be identical to a clavichord preserved in the Joanneum museum in Graz, which has the parchment label "Dismas Gf. Atthembs" and dates from the second half of the eighteenth century.[23] The person named Dismas was probably Ignaz's younger half-brother Dismas Maximilian Siegmund Engelbert Franz (1718-1765).

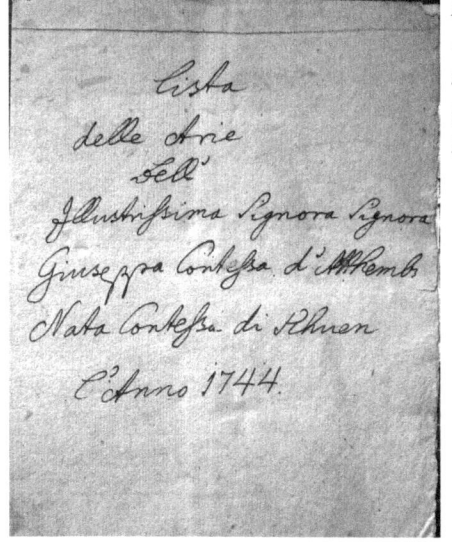

Figure 2: Title page of the 1744 list of arias belonging to the Countess von Attems (Mpa [without shelfmark]; by kind permission).

---

objects were added. See A-Gla, Familienarchiv Attems, Übergabsinventar nach den Ableben des Dismas Gr. Attems, 1750, K. 124, H. 1132, and Ignaz Maria Attems, Fideicommiss- und Allodial-Inventar 1762, K. 126, H. 1142. On the household of Ignaz Maria II at Slovenska Bistrica, see also ŠERBELJ, 2005, pp. 90-93.

22 A-Gla, Familienarchiv Attems, Ignaz Maria Attems, Fideicommiss- und Allodial-Inventar 1762, K. 126, H. 1142, fol. 26v. The instrument was valued at "4 gulden".

23 The clavichord was donated to the museum by the Attems family and, today, is located in the Section "Kunstgewerbe" under the inventory number 1340. See FLOTZINGER, 1980, p. 197 (no. 4.35).

Music, in general, seems to have been greatly appreciated in the Attems family. Ignaz's uncle Count Thaddäus Kajetan Bernhard Maria von Attems (1691-1750) apparently engaged some of the Graz civic musicians to provide and copy instrumental music for entertainment at his manor at Dornava (Dornau); his wife, Countess Crescenzia Maria Anna Francisca (1728-1801), was a keen harpsichordist; his son, Count Josef Bernhard Maria von Attems (1727-1772), was a lutenist.[24] To engage professional musicians for formal dinners, dances and other festivities, as well as to provide musical education, was common practice among the Styrian nobility during the first half of the eighteenth century. The relevant archival documentation lists many names of musicians who were members of formally constituted music companies with exclusive rights to perform in Graz.[25] Some aristocratic houses are known to have retained their own resident musicians during the early eighteenth century.[26]

The Attems music collection

The Attems music collection from the castle of Slovenska Bistrica consists of a total of one hundred pieces of music in manuscript, two compositions preserved only in incomplete form, two musical fragments, a further fragment containing cadenzas (an instructive or technical aid), an unidentified music print, and the already mentioned manuscript list of 98 soprano arias belonging to the Countess Josepha von Attems and compiled for her in 1744.

---

24   KOKOLE, 2012a, pp. 685f. On the subject of the connection with the collection of keyboard and chamber music from the mid-eighteenth century today housed at SI-Pk, see FEDERHOFER/SCHMEISER, 1971, and EYBL, 2012. On the instruments at Dornava manor, see KOTER, 2003, p. 357.

25   FEDERHOFER/SCHMEISER, 1971, pp. 74-78, and especially p. 90. On civic musicians in Graz in general and their names, see FEDERHOFER, 1951. On other musicians active in Graz during the first half of the eighteenth century and the repertory performed in Graz at that time, see likewise FEDERHOFER, 1971, pp. 634-641, and FEDERHOFER/FLOTZINGER, 1980, pp. 44-58. On the musicians connected with the operatic productions (in addition to Angelo and Pietro Mingotti, notably Pircker, Scalabrini and Locatelli), see KOKOLE, 2012b, pp. 73-77, and KOKOLE, 2013, pp. 152-155.

26   For instance, Count von Rosenberg in 1700; Count von Trauttmansdorff; probably also Count Joseph Leopold von Orsini Rosenberg and Johann Joseph von Webersberg. See FEDERHOFER/FLOTZINGER, 1980, pp. 53f.

The inventory of arias comprises four folios containing a title page followed by five pages that present a list with the following information: the serial number of the aria, the title of the aria (i.e., its textual incipit and the surname of the composer – unless it was not known, in which case the name is replaced by a horizontal line). The inventory has no assigned shelf mark, as is also the case with the two fragments, the cadenzas and the unidentified print. All remaining items, totalling 102, were cataloged for the RISM A/II database in 2012. Within the present article the titles and composers are presented in an annotated list forming the Appendix.[27]

Among the items without shelf mark is a small music print running to only six pages and lacking a title page. This contains three minuets, numbered in the French manner as "Menuet", "2ᵉ Menuet", and "3ᵉ Menuet". These initially appear in score format, the first two being for two violins and figured bass, and the third for "Flauto o Violini / Fagotto" and bass. They collectively make up a cycle of movements in the key sequence E major – E minor – E major, all three minuets having the time signature "3". The second half of the print (i.e., pages 4-6) is headed "PARODIE" and brings back all three minuets in arrangements for soprano voice with the following texts: "1ʳ Menuet / Quand je bois ce jus charmant"; "2ᵉ Menuet / Pour chasser la mélancolie"; and "3ᵉ Menuet / Brille a nos yeaux [sic]". Reaching the end, we are directed back to the beginning via the instruction "au 1ʳ Menuet". The print seems to be of French origin and was most likely intended for the practical purpose of accompanying dancing.[28]

All other musical items are properly cataloged. The first 77 pieces are for soprano solo with basso continuo and in some cases also additional instruments. With the exception of four compositions, they are all operatic arias. The exceptions comprise three pieces headed "Canzonetta"[29] and one piece taking the form of a short secular "Cantata" in four move-

---

27 See note 1.
28 In a letter sent from Mannheim on 24 September 1735 Ignaz actually mentions a "Menuet" danced at the Court (in mid-September), so this little print may well be a souvenir of that ball: A-Gla, Familienarchiv Attems, K. 19, H. 87.
29 All three are anonymous settings of the same text (*Grazie agl'inganni tuoi*) for voice and basso continuo. They are written by the same scribe on a paper of Venetian origin, but their music is different: Mpa 70, 72 and 74.

ments (recitative–aria–recitative–aria).[30] The arias on the Countess's inventory running from no. 22 to the end (no. 98) are today shelf-marked 1-77, reflecting the fact that the music of items 1-21 in the inventory is not present among the surviving music manuscripts. All of these 77 musical manuscripts probably received their numbering in 1744, when the name of either "Giuseppa Contessa d'Atthembs" or "Ignazio Conte d'Atthembs" was added on the title page or, alternatively, in the bottom right-hand corner of the first page of music. Ignaz's name in fact appears only on the first eight surviving compositions cataloged for his wife in 1744. The presence of his name indicates that these manuscripts were originally his personal property.

The remaining 25 recorded compositions in the present-day collection (Mpa 78-102) comprise further fourteen vocal pieces (eleven soprano arias, two duets and one *canzonetta*), two vocal pieces of which only instrumental parts are preserved,[31] four compositions for orchestra or smaller instrumental ensemble,[32] four compositions for transverse flute with basso or violoncello[33] and a lone soprano part for an *Amen*.[34] Only the four pieces for transverse flute plus three other manuscripts bear the name of the owner: Ignaz von Attems.[35]

The pieces for transverse flute – a "Sonatina" and three sonatas – merit special attention since they are written on completely different paper, feature distinctly different handwriting and thus constitute a separate section within the larger collection. Two of the sonatas have a composer indicated on the cover or title page, but both names were added only

---

30   Anon., *Cantata. Perdona o cara*: Mpa 75.
31   The parts for two violins with the title *Se libera non sono* (Mpa 90) have been identified as belonging to the lost no. 10 from the original list, an aria from Leonardo Leo's *Demetrio*, produced in the summer of 1738 at the Teatro San Carlo in Naples. The paper and the scribe are Roman, so one assumes that it originally formed part of the music brought back by Ignaz von Attems from his visit to Italy. Mpa 101 consists of parts for two violins and viola, probably the accompaniment of a so far unidentified aria.
32   Mpa 93-95 and 100.
33   Mpa 96-99.
34   Mpa 102.
35   Leaving aside the flute pieces, the remaining three manuscripts comprise two duets and an overture by Johann Adolf Hasse (Mpa 93), all copied by a Roman scribe on Roman paper.

Figures 3a and 3b:
Title page and page 1 of the flute part of Giuseppe Sammartini's Sonata à flutrav: solo e Basso *in the Attems collection*
(Mpa 98; by kind permission)

later: Domenico Sarri (or Sarro) and Giuseppe San Martino (Sammartini).[36] These two sonatas are in three and four movements, respectively. They belonged to the Count, and since his name is spelled in the French manner as "Ignace Compte d'Atthembs" they may well be a souvenir from one of the German and Flemish cities he visited, or perhaps even of Paris. The French spelling strongly hints at a Francophone court, while the upright format of the paper and the imperial double-headed eagle visible in the watermark seem to be leading us towards a German-speaking area of the Imperial territories. The prominence of the transverse flute in the collection – not only in these sonatas but also in the parts for transverse flute provided for a number of the arias – supports the hypothesis that Count Ignaz von Attems was a capable amateur flautist.

---

36   Mpa 97 and 98.

Among the orchestral pieces, we encounter parts for basso, two violins and viola of an "Ouverture Con VVi e Viola" by Johann Adolf Hasse, identifiable as the overture to Hasse's opera *Asteria*, written for Dresden in August 1737.[37] The title pages of the two orchestral concertos inform us that they are "Del Eccelentissimo Signor Duca di Santo Gemini"; the music, however, is identified by RISM as that of a Spanish composer, Alejsandro Fernandez de Cordoba y Lante, so the Duke of Santo Gemini was probably only a commissioner or patron.[38] The two concertos are copied on coeval Roman paper by Roman scribes – the same hands we recognize from the manuscripts of the arias belonging to Count Ignaz, brought home by him from his Grand Tour, that took him to Rome and Naples.

The arias of Countess Josepha's *Lista delle arie*

The bulk of the Attems collection, however, consists of soprano arias cataloged in 1744 for Countess Josepha von Attems. A rough dating for the manuscripts lies between the 1730s and 1744, the last possible year. The arias are mostly preserved in full or short score (for voice and basso continuo), but separate parts for instruments are added in many cases.[39] Sometimes, the parts were copied by a hand different from that responsible for the scores. There are also some instances of arranged parts that depart from the original scoring. These appear to reflect the wishes and special requests of the commissioner of the copied music – in this case, Josepha's husband Ignaz.

---

37 Mpa 93. The Count's name is spelled in the French manner.
38 Mpa 94 and 95. The Duke of S. Gemini indeed had musicians in his service. One of them, "Sig. Antonio Bragagna Virtuoso di s. Scc. il Signor Duca di S. Gemini", took the role of Bruscolo in the "drama giocoso per musica La comedia in comedia" composed by Rinaldo di Capua for a production in Rome during the Carnival season of 1738. The source of this information is a libretto in the Rolandi collection at I-Vgc (ROL.0574.19).
39 Short scores customarily written at the time as singers' parts (in self-accompanied performances with the singer seated at a harpsichord, the bass part would also be played by him/her), so the combination of a short score and violin/viola parts effectively equates to a set of parts.

Among the extant 92 arias (including in this total three duets and four *canzonette*), three major groups as determined by provenance have been identified through the investigation of repertories, paper types, watermarks and scribal hands. One group is southern Italian; another is apparently local, written by the same hand on papers of Styrian and Carniolan origin (34 pieces: nos. 22-55 listed in the Appendix); the third is possibly local or has a different, still undiscovered, provenance, probably connected to the German-speaking cultural area (nos. 56, 58, 60-67, 70, 72, 74, 75, 77, 87 and 89).

The names of fifteen composers had been identified by the end of the year 2014; some of these are indicated either in the inventory of the arias or on the musical manuscripts themselves. The dates of the compositions – in some cases written on the scores and in others inferred by relevant surviving documents such as librettos for the productions of the operas from which the pieces originated and/or the musical incipits in the RISM A/II database (in the list in the Appendix all secondary identifications are enclosed in square brackets)[40] – reveal the fact that the Attems household exclusively collected music popular at the time, never more than about ten years old. Among these composers are several well-known names, including those of Johann Adolf Hasse, Leonardo Vinci, Leonardo Leo, Gaetano Latilla, Niccolò Jommelli, Geminiano Giacomelli, Andrea Bernasconi, Niccolò Logroscino and Giuseppe Arena.

Over ten different hands and about ten principal paper types can be distinguished, which exhibit eight watermarks so far detected: the latter are mainly of Austrian and Venetian provenance, while the southern Italian manuscripts are, as one would expect, all copied on Roman paper. The single common element of the collection is that all the compositions are scored for soprano voice and basso continuo with or without additional instruments (two violins, transverse flute etc.).

---

40 I am especially grateful to Prof Reinhard Strohm, who kindly looked through the music and suggested many of the present identifications. Most of them were confirmed via concordances in the RISM A/II database and other digitalized original sources currently available online.

Known and identified composers of surviving arias in the Attems collection:

Composer	Count
Johann Adolf Hasse	14
Andrea Bernasconi	12
Leonardo Vinci	6
Giuseppe Arena	5 [+5 lost but indicated in the *Lista delle arie*]
Leonardo Leo	4 [+3]
Geminiano Giacomelli	4
Giovanni Battista Lampugnani	2
Rinaldo di Capua	2
Niccolò Logroscino	1 [+8]
Gaetano Latilla	1 [+3]
Niccolò Jommelli	1
Pietro Auletta	1
Pietro Vincenzo Chiocchetti	1
Rinaldo di Capua	1 [+1]
Giovanni Porta	1
Domingo Terradellas	1
Christoph Willibald Gluck	1
[Pietro Auletta]	[1]

The southern Italian group of manuscripts originally belonged to "Ignazio Conte d'Atthembs", whose name actually appears on the surviving manuscripts 1-8 and 91-92. They constitute the best documented portion of the present-day Attems collection. Considering first the music itself, the extant 14 pieces, as well as further 21 aria titles documented only in the list of 1744, can all be identified with operas Count Ignaz von Attems attended in Rome or Naples. The composer is named on most of the surviving pieces belonging to this group, as are generally also the year, the place and the title of the opera. The paper used is local: mostly Roman, featuring a water lily in a single or double oval frame as the watermark – the same as employed for the printed librettos of the operas by Giuseppe Arena, Niccolò Logroscino and Rinaldo di Capua produced in Carnival 1738 at the Teatro delle Dame and Teatro Valle in Rome.[41] Three of the

---

41 SARTORI, 1990-1994. The consulted examples of *Achille in Sciro* (no. 163), *Il Quinto Fabio* (no. 19390) and *La comedia in comedia* (no. 5952) are in the Rolandi collection at the Fondazione Giorgio Cini, Venice (I-Vgc).

Migrations of Musical Repertoire

Figure 4:
First page of Niccolò Logroscino's aria Questo che bagna *from the opera* Il Quinto Fabio, *I/4, copied in Rome during Carnival 1738 for Count Ignaz von Attems (Mpa 1; by kind permission).*

scribes were apparently professional musicians or copyists working in Rome.

The information offered by the music manuscripts themselves provides the names of two *drammi per musica* performed during the 1738 Carnival season in Rome at the then newly decorated Teatro delle Dame:[42] Giuseppe Arena's *Achille in Sciro* and Niccolò Logroscino's *Il Quinto Fabio*. There are additional traces of two comic operas produced at the Teatro Valle: Rinaldo di Capua's *La comedia in comedia* and Gaetano Latilla's *La serva padrona* at the same time. Other manuscripts point to two productions given during the summer season of 1738 in Naples: the pasticcio opera *Il Demetrio* at the Teatro San Carlo and Leonardo Leo's *Il conte* at the Teatro Fiorentino.

---

42 FRANCHI, 1997, p. 297 (citing reports in contemporary periodicals and chronicles). The new decorations are also mentioned in the two librettos for Carnival 1738.

These pieces must indeed date from 1738, since we are clearly informed by the already mentioned letters sent from Rome by Ignaz to his father that he spent January and February 1738 in the eternal city and would later travel to Naples. In his letter dated 4 January 1738 at Rome he explicitly mentions the comedies at the Teatro Argentina, without giving their titles, and also reports on the opening opera, *Achille in Sciro*, at the Teatro Alibert.[43]

The Count apparently brought back from Rome as many as nine soprano arias from this opera: among these were all six of Achille's solo arias, sung by the famous "Gioachino Conti detto Il Ghiziello", as well as his duet with Deidamia, whose role was sung in Rome by Giovanni Tedeschi, another well-known castrato singer.[44] However, only four of Achille's arias and a duet have survived in Maribor. The manuscripts comprise short scores for voice and basso continuo and parts for two violins and flute. It is indeed a testimony to the Count's personal preferences that he had parts for transverse flute specially arranged from the original parts for voice or first violin.[45]

Count Ignaz Attems was similarly enthusiastic about the other Carnival production at Teatro delle Dame: Niccolò Logroscino's first major opera, *Il Quinto Fabio*, given by the same company of singers with Gizziello in the title role.[46] He had nine arias from it copied for his per-

---

43 In the letter erratically styled "teatro liberta", probably through simple mishearing: A-Gla, Familienarchiv Attems, K. 19, H. 87; Rome, 4 January 1738. I discuss this operatic production and the arias surviving in the Attems collection in a separate article entitled *Giuseppe Arena's* Achille in Sciro *(1738): From Rome to a Styrian Private Household and Finally to the Public Theatre in Graz*, for publication in the forthcoming proceedings of the HERA MusMig conference in Zagreb, *Music Migrations in the Early Modern Age: People, Markets, Patterns, Styles*, Zagreb, 14 October 2014.

44 These arias are: (Achille, I/3) *Involarmi, il mio tesoro?*, (Achille, I/8) *Si Ben mio, farò qual vuoi*, (Licomede, I/13) *Intendo il tuo rossor*, (Deidamia, I/14) *Del sen gli ardori*, (Achille, I/14) *Risponderti vorrei*, (Achille, II/5) *Potria fra tante pene*, (Achille, II/6) *Dille che si consoli, (duetto*, II/4*) Non temer, sai quanto io t'ami*, (Achille, III/6) *Non paventar ben mio*.

45 All the items today preserved in Maribor (nos. 3, 4, 6, 7 and 91) include parts for transverse flute.

46 QUINTO FABIO Dramma per musica da rappresentarsi il carnevale dell'anno 1738 nel Teatro delle Dame nuovamente ristaurato e con pitture abbellito con architettura e disegno del Sig. cavaliere Ferdinando Fuga. Dedicato alla maestà di Giacomo III Re della Gran Bretagna. Rome 1738.

sonal use, but unfortunately only one has survived – Marco Fabio's aria from Act I, Scene 4: *Questo che bagna*. This aria is nevertheless interesting, since Ignaz Attems acquired two copies in the hands of different scribes. One was apparently taken directly from the original text, being scored for soprano and two violins and in the key of G major, whereas the other is transposed to D major and contains an additional part for flute.[47]

While in Rome, Ignaz also acquired copies of some delightful pieces from two other operatic productions, both given during the Carnival season at the Teatro Valle. The first was a "divertimento giocoso in musica" by Gaetano Latilla entitled *La serva padrona*,[48] the second being Rinaldo di Capua's satirical opera *La comedia in comedia*.[49] The latter was an outstanding success in its day, and its music became a much sought-after item even beyond the Alps.[50] Before departing from Rome, the Count made sure to add copies of four pieces by Latilla[51] and one by Rinaldo di Capua to his traveling case.[52]

After Rome, Ignaz von Attems made a detour from his originally planned itinerary and traveled on to Naples instead of proceeding north to Venice. We do not know exactly how long he stayed there, but it must have been long enough to visit at least two of the local theaters during the summer season of 1738. One of these was the splendid new Teatro San Carlo, and the other the smaller Teatro Fiorentino, reserved for the comic repertory. At the Teatro San Carlo, Ignaz heard the opera *Il Demetrio*, which was in part a pasticcio.[53] The

---

47 Mpa 1 – both versions. See also the facsimile reproduced as Figure 4.
48 FRANCHI, 1997, p. 295.
49 FRANCHI, 1997, p. 294. On the libretto, see note 41. Among the arias brought back from Rome by Count Attems was also one aria from this opera by Rinaldo: *Non così snella, la rondinella* (Act II, Scene 8). Today, the aria is lost, but was listed in the Countess's inventory as no. 7.
50 See note 70.
51 Only one, a duet, is preserved (Mpa 92); however, another three are listed in the Countess's inventory (nos. 3, 16 and 21).
52 See note 49.
53 *IL DEMETRIO Drama per musica dell'abate Pietro Metastasio da rappresentarsi in questo nuovo famoso real Teatro di S. Carlo nella està di quest'anno 1738*. SARTORI, 1990, no. 7362. "Musica del 1° atto e delle arie del 2° e 3° con + di Leonardo Leo, vice maestro della R. capp. Musica dell 2° atto di diversi autori. Musica del 3° atto di Riccardo Broschi". An example of the libretto in I-Mb, is freely available online (http://www.urfm.braidense.it/rd/02160.pdf). See Mpa 2 and Mpa 90.

libretto informs us that the first act plus the two arias in Acts II and III indicated by asterisks are by Leonardo Leo, the music of Act II by various (unnamed) composers, and the third act by Riccardo Broschi. The four arias of which our Count obtained copies were all by Leo.[54] Unfortunately only one has survived, as is also the case with the music from *Il conte*, likewise by Leo, of which the Attems collection preserves only the aria *Risolver non poss'io*.[55]

The other preserved arias listed in the Countess's inventory are not as easily classifiable as those of southern Italian origin. Only a handful of composers are named for them either in the inventory or on the music itself (see Appendix). At least seven different hands can be traced on various papers exhibiting six different watermarks. Their sole common feature is that they all display the name "Giuseppa Contessa d'Atthembs".

Figures 5a and 5b:
Title page and page 1 of Andrea Bernasconi's aria È vero, che oppresso la sorte *from the opera* Adriano in Siria *(Mpa 30; by kind permission).*

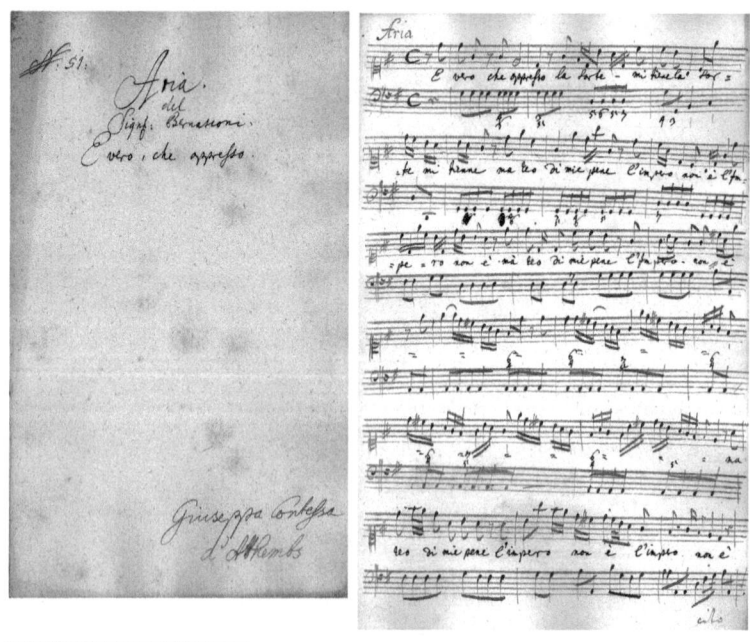

---

54 Mpa 2 and nos. 2, 10 and 19 in the Countess's inventory.
55 Mpa 5.

The most intriguing fact about the remaining arias is the presence of a surprisingly large group of as many as twelve attributed or attributable to Andrea Bernasconi,[56] a composer born in 1706 and generally identified in his earliest operatic works (from 1737 and 1743-1753) as Milanese. Between 1744 and 1753, Bernasconi was *maestro di coro* at the Ospedale della Pietà in Venice, and from 1753 a well-paid and fashionable *Kapellmeister* in Munich, where he remained until his death in 1784. Since the arias in the Attems collection date from before 1744, Bernasconi's early musical career becomes of special interest; unfortunately, little is known about this period of his life so far.[57] According to musicological literature, his earliest known operas were staged between 1737 and 1744 in Vienna, Venice, Padua, Lucca and Rome.

Arias by Andrea Bernasconi in the Attems collection:
Mpa
16. *Oh Dio! mancar mi sento* (Metastasio: *Adriano in Siria*)
22. *Se non ti moro allato* (Metastasio: *Adriano in Siria*)
25. *Ch'io mai vi possa*
27. *Parto, se vuoi così*
28. *Numi, se giusti siete* (Metastasio: *Adriano in Siria*)
30. *È vero, che oppresso la sorte* (Metastasio: *Adriano in Siria*)
39. *Il mio caro e dolce amore*
42. *Amor mio, la cruda sorte* (*Il giorno felice*, Vienna 1737)
47. *Ah! Che s'avessi il seno*
52. *La raggion, gli affetti* (Metastasio: *Adriano in Siria*)
55. *Digli, ch'è un infedele* (Metastasio: *Adriano in Siria*)*
68. *Dice che t'è fedele* (Metastasio: *Il Demetrio*)*

Among the arias attributable to Bernasconi, his name appears on five of the musical manuscripts (those with emboldened titles in the list above); his authorship of the remainder has been established mainly through matching with RISM incipits and identifications. The two asterisked attributions are not secure, being based solely on textual concordance. The aria *Dice che t'è fedele* is problematic, since the copyist of the music specified the act, scene and role as "Atto 2do; Scena 4ta; Mitrane", a descrip-

---

56 On Bernasconi, see the article by MÜNSTER/CORNEILSON, 2012.
57 The most recent and exhaustive account is the section "Andrea Bernasconi – Leben und Werk bis 1753" in SADGORSKI, 2010, pp. 47-51.

tion fitting the libretto for *Il Demetrio*[58] – but no such opera by Bernasconi is known to have been written before 1772. Other attributions are similarly puzzling. As many as six arias preserved in this collection – assembled up to the year 1744 – use Metastasio's aria texts for his *Adriano in Siria*, but Bernasconi's known setting of *Adriano in Siria* was only 1755 in Munich, over ten years later than the *terminus ad quem* of the Attems collection's compilation!

It would appear that the only entirely plausible identification is that for Bernasconi's aria *Amor mio, la cruda sorte*, which comes from the Viennese production of *Il giorno felice* at the Kärntnertortheater, which opened on 5 February 1737.[59] *Il giorno felice* was a pasticcio opera based on Vivaldi's *La fida ninfa*, or at least on its libretto. Since Bernasconi had his own opera *Flavio Anicio Olibrio* staged in Vienna during the Carnival season of 1737, his authorship of an individual aria for the Kärntnertortheater is conceivable. I would go even further and speculate on a possible Viennese provenance for the other Bernasconi arias in the Attems collection, since both Josepha and her husband were rather intimately connected to Viennese cultural life. Of course, the music could equally well have reached Graz via a third party, a musician or an impresario, only later being copied for the Countess.[60]

---

58   The aria is a textual match with the libretto for the Naples production of *Il Demetrio* in 1738, known to Count Ignaz (see earlier, note 53) and also fits the librettos for the productions of *Il Demetrio* in Graz and Ljubljana in 1742 under Pietro Mingotti (MÜLLER VON ASOW, 1917, pp. LXXIX-LXXXI, and KOKOLE, 2012b, pp. 75, 77 and 85; or KOKOLE, 2013, pp. 153, 155 and 163). So far, however, I have been unable to establish a connection between these productions and the manuscript Mpa 68; nor can Bernasconi's music be securely linked to the setting heard in Graz or Ljubljana, since in the Hamburg production of 1744 under Mingotti the same aria text was apparently set to music by Paolo Scalabrini. Similarly, I have not yet been able to compare the music for the 1744 score allegedly by Scalabrini with Mpa 68, attributed to Bernasconi. One must remain aware that attributions to composers in the scores of pasticcio operas are not always reliable.

59   See RISM-ID no. 450059470 and the attached comments.

60   The surviving documentation on the operatic repertoire produced in Vienna in the late 1730s and early 1740s does indeed show some striking similarities to the productions organized for the Estates Theater (*Ständisches Theater*) in Graz from 1736 to 1745 under the management of the impresarios Angelo and Pietro Mingotti. Although the connection of the Mingottis with

In view of the absence of detailed documentation for Bernasconi's years before 1744 and the large number of arias by him conforming to the libretto of *Adriano in Siria*, I venture the hypothesis of an earlier setting by him of this opera. This would, of course, imply that the well-documented production of 1755 in Munich was in fact only a revival or else another setting. There was indeed an anonymous *Adriano in Siria* staged at the Imperial Theater in Vienna in 1743,[61] as were others prior to that date. Of some relevance could be a further *Adriano in Siria* for which the composer – or, rather, composers – are not indicated: this was produced in Ferrara during the 1741 Carnival season.[62] Both Vienna and northern Italy were relevant to the operations of Graz impresarios during the years important for the present discussion.

In any case, it should be mentioned that ten out of the twelve arias by Bernasconi – seven of them linked to the *Adriano in Siria* texts – were

---

Vienna has not yet been securely established, it would seem that they at least had very good contacts there. I have been kindly provided with information on operatic productions in Vienna by Dr Andrea Sommer-Mathis, who shared with me information gathered during the "work-in-progress" stage of a database, for which I am deeply indebted to her. On the activity of the Mingottis in Graz, see MÜLLER VON ASOW, 1917; and for a wider perspective of the Mingottis' activities in the Inner-Austrian provinces, see also KOKOLE, 2005, KOKOLE, 2012b or KOKOLE, 2013.

61 SARTORI, 1990, no. 386, and especially the following information from Andrea Sommer-Mathis's database: "Hadrianus in Syrien: musicalische Opera, aufgeführet auf dem von Ihro zu Hungarn und Böheim Königl. Majestät Privilegirten Theatro in Wien. 1743, übers.von Joh. Leopold v. Ghelen. Wien, J. P. v. Ghelen, 1743." It would undoubtedly be worth cross-checking the aria texts with the Attems scores.

62 SARTORI, 1990, no. 385. It is interesting that two of the singers for that production were at some point also engaged by the Mingotti brothers: Filippo Finazzi by Pietro Mingotti from 1743 to 1744 (for Linz, Hamburg, Prague and Leipzig) and Carlina Valvasori by Angelo Mingotti for the 1740 Carnival production in Ljubljana. On Finazzi, see MÜLLER VON ASOW, 1917, p. CCIV (and references in the *Anhang* II); for Valvasori, see KOKOLE, 2012b, p. 67. It is interesting to note that one of the arias headed with Bernasconi's name and linked to his *Adriano in Siria* (Mpa 28, *Numi, se giusti siete*) in the Attems collection is attributed in Pietro Mingotti's production of *La finta cameriera* (Act II, Scene 7) for Hamburg in 1745 to the same Filippo Finazzi (the music is identical). See MÜLLER VON ASOW, 1917, pp. CCXII and XCVI.

most likely copied locally, possibly in Graz itself, by the same scribe.[63] For seven of them (Mpa 22, 25, 27, 28, 30, 39 and 42) the scribe used paper from the Seisenberg paper mill in Carniola (its watermark featuring the coat of arms of the Seisenberg mill, with the letters FAK as the countermark); he also wrapped the music – using the folders designed to indicate the number in the collection, the aria's title, in some cases also the composer and Countess Josepha's name (see Figure 5a) – in another kind of paper widely used locally (with a leaping stag as the watermark and the letters MIH as the countermark).[64] Another three Bernasconi arias were copied by the same scribe on a different locally used paper (with St Vitus in a cauldron of boiling oil enclosed by a pair of antlers as the watermark and the letters ZA as the countermark), this time without the use of separate folders (nos. 47, 52 and 55).

These arias all belong to a larger group of thirty-four manuscripts (Mpa 43-76) in the hand of the same copyist (I shall call him Scribe 1) employing two kinds of locally produced and/or used papers of Styrian and Carniolan origin, as described above. This group can be considered as forming the core repertoire of the Countess's aria collection. Leaving aside Andrea Bernasconi, the composers so far identified include Hasse (with eight arias), Lampugnani, Vinci and Porta (with one apiece). It is impossible to ascertain why these particular arias, including the ones by Bernasconi, were copied locally at the present stage of research.

However, one pointer, as hinted earlier, could well be the flourishing operatic life during the period 1736-1743 in Graz, where the two Venetian impresarios, the brothers Angelo and Pietro Mingotti, settled with their companies in 1736 and also erected a permanent theater. We have already learnt that both the Count and his wife were great devotees of opera, so they would surely not have neglected this kind of entertainment so close to home, especially since the Attems family had become one of the richest in the town by then, Ignaz's father being one of the leading members of the provincial estates, the patrons of Mingotti's theater. Although no documents have as yet surfaced to confirm Ignaz's personal involvement with this local theater, it is perhaps telling that his eldest son

---

63 Only two arias identified as being by Bernasconi do not belong to this larger group; both are copied on a variety of Venetian papers with three crescents in the watermark.

64 Paper with a stag in the watermark also appears in some of the printed librettos for operatic productions in Graz during the period around 1740.

Ferdinand, later elected provincial governor, took over the direction of the Graz opera theater in 1784, while the latter's son, Count Ignaz Maria III, was involved in the building of a theater to replace it in the early nineteenth century.[65]

How closely Ferdinand's parents were actively involved in the operatic life of Graz in their own time awaits investigation, as pointed out above. Precise documentation on the Mingotti *impresa* in Graz is scarce. In view of the complete absence of unequivocal related musical sources, the best available evidence at present comes from preserved librettos, which alone provide a solid basis for further deductions.

Nevertheless, even a cursory glance at the titles of the arias in the Attems collection and at those documented in opera librettos for the various productions overseen by the Mingotti brothers in Graz and Ljubljana, as well as for other productions following on immediately from their joint venture in Graz (in Linz, Hamburg, Leipzig and Dresden)[66] reveals a remarkable fact: no fewer than seventeen out of thirty-four arias occur in both repertories. An instructive example is the aria *No, non vedrete mai*. Its text was written by Pietro Metastasio for the opera *Ciro riconosciuto*. The composer of Mpa 33 (copied by Scribe 1) is not identified; the aria is scored for soprano, two violins and basso continuo. The same text occurs also in the libretto for the 1740 production in Graz of *Amor, odio e pentimento* as well as the Graz 1743 libretto for *Semiramide*. Strangely, in the libretto for *Amor, odio e pentimento* one encounters further arias with matches in the Attems collection: for example, the aria *Risponderti vorrei*, composed by Giuseppe Arena in 1738 for his *Achille in Sciro* (Mpa 3).

A close look at the librettos for the operatic productions in Graz in the two years following Count Attems's return from Italy (i.e., 1739 and 1740) uncovers an even more astonishing fact: as many as ten arias written variously by Latilla, Leo, Logroscino and Arena – the same as those brought back to Graz by Count Attems – may have been used in the pasticcio operas mounted by Pietro Mingotti. I hardly believe this to be a coincidence.

Any comparison based solely on textual factors is, however, potentially misleading, since the same text may well have been set by any

---

65 On Ferdinand Attems, see ILWOF, 1897, p. 27, and FEDERHOFER/SCHMEISER, 1971, p. 80; on his son, see SUPPAN, 2009, pp. 18f.
66 MÜLLER VON ASOW, 1917. For the productions in Ljubljana, see KOKOLE, 2012b or KOKOLE, 2013.

number of composers.[67] A case in point taken from the Attems collection itself (and belonging in both cases to the section copied by the local Scribe 1) is *Non vi piacque, ingiusti Dei*. There are two settings of this aria in our collection, both for soprano, two violins, viola and basso continuo. One has been identified as that of Hasse's *Siroe* of 1733 (Mpa 31); the other as that of Vinci's *Siroe* of 1736 (Mpa 43). The text itself appears in two librettos associated with Mingotti productions: that for the 1738 production of *La verità nell'inganno* in Graz and that for the 1746 production of *Lucio Vero* in Hamburg. These examples cause us to wonder whether the arias of the Attems collection sourced and copied locally originated mainly from the complex transmission tradition of pasticcio operas.

We may even speculate on some kind of special association between the opera producers in Graz and the opera-loving Attems couple. Perhaps they shared a common taste, or even exchanged music materials for further use, so that some of the pieces pleasing to the ears of Countess Josepha when she heard them in the Graz theater were subsequently copied for her own personal use. Further research into the Attems family archives will perhaps one day provide us with some answers, but at present this explanation must remain a mere hypothesis.

The third, larger group of arias that were possibly copied locally and which may likewise be connected with the Mingotti opera company is written on a variety of Venetian paper with three crescents in the watermark and a bow traversed by an arrow as the countermark. These copies were written by a scribe who could either be an 'Italianized' German musician or an Italian working in a German-speaking milieu. The handwriting is indeed the same as, or at least very close to, one encountered in some of the copies attributed to Graz musicians working during the mid-eighteenth century.[68]

---

67 Two cases of conflicting attribution have been discussed earlier in notes 58 and 62.

68 The handwriting seems very close to the one attributed to a local violinist and composer of Italian origin in Graz, Antonio Sgattberoni, who was the composer of some instrumental pieces possibly once belonging to a member of the same Attems family, such as Ignaz's uncle resident at Dornava castle; today, these manuscripts are held by the public library at Ptuj: SI-Pk, Domoznanski oddelek, inv. št. 9, 11, 29, 51, 56, 154 and 157. See also the literature cited earlier in note 24.

This group consists of 14 arias listed in the final part of the Countess's inventory (original numbers 77, 78, 80-88, 91, 93 and 95).[69] The repertoire – judging from the identified composers – Johann Adolf Hasse, Leonardo Leo and Leonardo Vinci – could indeed have been copied in Graz or else brought from Vienna or some other musical center visited by the young Count Ignaz Attems after returning from his Grand Tour and where he had maintained good connections. Such cities undoubtedly included at least Vienna and Prague. The Count is even known to have been involved in the import of Italian music to serve the needs of Czech aristocrats.[70]

Other papers and handwritings appear in smaller quantities. The paper used for these copies is mostly either Venetian (featuring different varieties of three crescents paper) or Austrian, from various Styrian paper mills. Some smaller groups of arias could well have been brought back

---

69   Mpa 56, 58, 60-67, 70, 72, 74, 75, 77, 87 and 89; the last two pieces do not appear in the original inventory.

70   He had, for example, been in touch with Count Johann Adam von Questenberg's *Hofmeister* Hoffmann in 1739, and was even acting as an intermediary for the acquisition of some music manuscripts. He was asked through Hoffmann to obtain music from the opera *La comedia in comedia* by Rinaldo di Capua (well known to Count Attems from the Roman premiere at Carnival 1738; see earlier, and also note 49) and Giovanni Battista Pergolesi's *La Salustia* (Naples 1732). See the letters by Hoffmann to Questenberg in the Moravian Provincial Archive, Fund G 436, carton 748, Inv. no. 6133. I am citing here the two letters concerning Count Attems by kind permission of Jana Perutková, to whom I am indebted for this information. Letter of 24 March 1739: "[…] Der junge Graf Athimis empfehlet sich Ewer Excellenz, zur nachricht dienend, er hatte schon in antworth bekommen, daß die opera La comoedia in comoedia genannt den 7. hujus seÿe angefangen worden zu copieren, und die Salustia, weilen ohne deme ein guter freund Mr. Henighen haushoffmeistern von Gr: Harrach nach Neapel gereist, will dieser allda auch copieren lassen, und nachdeme dem 2.te oster–feüertag ein gelegenheit von Rom anhero kommen solle, so hoffet H: Gr: Athimis beedes zu erhalten. […]" and the letter of 17 October 1739: "[…] der junge graf Atthymis aber, so wieder in Passauer Hoff logiert, empfehlet sich Ewer Excellenz, zugleich andienend, wie dass er glaube, die eine opera [= probably *La commedia in commedia*] seÿe schon auf den weeg, allein die Salustia könnte er nicht bekommen, ohngeachtet einer seiner guten freunden von Rom nach Neapolis gereÿst, solche allda selbst zu sollicitieren […]". See PERUTKOVÁ, 2015.

Figure 6:
The first page of the aria Se viver non poss'io *(Mpa 65; by kind permission).*

home by the Count from his numerous travels in Europe, or else were acquired from acquaintances, such as is probably the case with at least the aria *Dal sen del caro sposo* by Rinaldo di Capua (Mpa 8), composed in 1739 for the production in Rome of his *Vologeso, re de' Parti*. The manuscript copy of this aria was sent to Count Attems attached to a letter – probably in 1739, following its success on the Roman stage.

Whatever the case may be, the Attems collection of arias and its history provides a good illustration of some of the many possible ways in which musical repertoire could travel from one theater to another through personal initiative, as well as from public theaters to the sphere of private music-making, as exemplified by the Attems household in Graz (and also Slovenska Bistrica) during the mid-eighteenth century.

Appendix

The list of extant musical items belonging to the Attems collection from Slovenska Bistrica

Square brackets denote editorial identifications (as of November 2014).

Mpa no.	ARIAS – textual incipits	COMPOSER and OPERA
1	Questo che bagna	LOGROSCINO, Nicola Bonifacio *Il Quinto Fabio*, Rome, 1738
2	Scherza il nocchier talora	LEO, Leonardo [*Il Demetrio*], Naples, 1738
3	Risponderti vorrei	ARENA, Giuseppe *Achille in Sciro*, Rome, 1738
4	Potria frà tante pene	ARENA, Giuseppe *Achille in Sciro*, Rome, 1738
5	Risolver no[n] poss'io	LEO, Leonardo *Il conte*, Naples, 1738
6	Dille che si consoli	ARENA, Giuseppe *Achille in Sciro*, Rome, 1738
7	Non paventar, ben mio	ARENA, Giuseppe *Achille in Sciro*, Rome, 1738
8	Dal sen del caro sposo	[RINALDO DI CAPUA] [*Vologeso, re de' Parti*], Rome, 1739
9	Amo, sospiro, e peno	LAMPUGNANI, [Giovanni] Battista
10	Parto, se vuoi così	[HASSE, Johann Adolf] [*Issipile*, Rome, 1732] = RISM ID no.: 852022219 etc.
11	Cara, t'inganna	JOMMELLI, Niccolò
12	Amo te solo	HASSE, Johann Adolf (= Adolfo Sassone) [*La clemenza di Tito*, i.e., *Tito Vespasiano*, Pesaro, 1735] = RISM ID no.: 270000660 etc.

13	Tu m'offendi	[VINCI, Leonardo] [*Flavio Anicio Olibrio*, Naples, 1728] = transposition of RISM ID no.: 852028214 and 000140522
14	Spero per la germana	[GIACOMELLI, Geminiano] [music of the aria "Sposa non mi conosci" in *Merope*, Venice, 1734] = score; identified by R. Strohm
15	Amor, dover, affetto	[GIACOMELLI, Geminiano] [music of the aria "Amor dover rispetto" in *Merope*, Venice, 1734] = score; identified by R. Strohm
16	Oh Dio! mancar mi sento	BERNASCONI, Andrea [Metastasio: *Adriano in Siria*; not in Munich, 1755] = RISM ID no.: 703001893 and 200021411 (text only)
17	Speranza foriera	GIACOMELLI, Geminiano [*Scipione in Cartagine Nuova*, Parma, 1728] = score
18	Mio ben, ricordati	HASSE, Johann Adolf (= Adolfo Sassone) [? *Alessandro nelle Indie*, Venice, 1736]
19	La destra ti chiedo (duetto)	
20	Arse ormai	CIOCCHETTI, [Pietro Vincenzi]
21	Mi vuoi tradir, il sento	[VINCI, Leonardo] [*Ernelinda*, Naples, 1726] = score
22	Se non ti moro allato	[BERNASCONI, Andrea] [Metastasio: *Adriano in Siria*; different to Munich, 1755] = transposition of RISM ID no.: 451002381, 000110978 and 000101180
23	Madre diletta, abbracciami	[PORTA, Giovanni] = RISM ID no.: 150204742 [*Ifigenia in Aulide*, Munich, 1738]

24	Deh, deh, deh se piacer	HASSE, Johann Adolf (= Sassone) [*Tito Vespasiano*, Pesaro, 1735] = RISM ID no.: 451500558, 000122520, 703001519, and 452011892 (one of the versions of this aria written for F. Bordoni)
25	Ch'io mai vi possa	BERNASCONI, Andrea
26	Quanto mai felici siete	LAMPUGNANI, Giovanni Battista [*Ezio*, Venice, 1737 and 1743] – identified by R. Strohm
27	Parto, se vuoi così	BERNASCONI, Andrea
28	Numi, se giusti siete	BERNASCONI, Andrea [Metastasio: *Adriano in Siria*, Munich, 1755] = RISM ID no.: 702002522 et al.
29	Son sventurato	[Metastasio: *Adriano in Siria*]
30	È vero, che oppresso	BERNASCONI, Andrea [Metastasio: *Adriano in Siria*, different to Munich, 1755] = RISM ID no.: 851000191 and 840001029
31	Non vi piacque, ingiusti Dei	[HASSE, Johann Adolf] [*Siroe, re di Persia*, Bologna, 1733] = RISM many variants
32	Sù gl'occhi miei dolenti	
33	Nò, non vedrete	
34	Almen, se non poss'io	
35	Se tu mi vuoi felice	HASSE, Johann Adolf (= Sassone) [*Siroe, re di Persia*, Bologna, 1733] = RISM ID no.: 700001642 et al.
36	Che legge spietata	HASSE, Johann Adolf (= Sassone) [*Catone in Utica*, Turin, 1731] = RISM ID no.: 703001994 et al.
37	Pensa a serbarmi, ò cara	= RISM ID no.: 456011368 (*Ezio*)
38	Bell'alme fortunate	
39	Il mio caro e dolce amore	[BERNASCONI, Andrea] = RISM ID no.: 550018292 (sacred contrafactum)

40	Già presso al termine	HASSE, Johann Adolf (= Sassone)
41	Alla fida sua costanza	=RISM ID no.: 806930383; Carlo Arrigoni in RISM ID no.: 000101152 (transposed)
42	Amor mio, la cruda sorte	[BERNASCONI, Andrea] [*Il giorno felice*, Vienna, 1737] = RISM ID no.: 450059470
43	Non vi piacque, ingiusti Dèi	[VINCI, Leonardo] [*Siroe, re di Persia*, Venice, 1726] = score; transposed also in RISM ID no.: 850011608
44	Parto, mà tu, ben mio, ritorna	[HASSE, Johann Adolf (= Sassone)] [*La clemenza di Tito*, i.e., *Tito Vespasiano*, Pesaro, 1735] = RISM ID no.: 270000660 etc.
45	Non so frenare il pianto	= RISM ID no.: 452017151 (in a collection dated 1740)
46	Fissa ne' sguardi	[HASSE, Johann Adolf (= Sassone)] [*L'Ulderica*, Naples, 1729] = RISM ID no.: 451500501 etc.
47	Ah! Che s'avessi il seno	[BERNASCONI, Andrea] = RISM ID no.: 550018291
48	Se m'accosto bel ruscello	? [HASSE, Johann Adolf (= Sassone)] text "Se m'accosto al bel' ruscello" from *Il Sesostrate*, Naples, 1726 – identified by R. Strohm
49	Quel folle nocchierò	
50	Meco perche s'ingrata	
51	Di questo cor fedele	
52	La raggion, gl'affetti	[BERNASCONI, Andrea] [Metastasio: *Adriano in Siria*; not in Munich, 1755] = RISM ID no.: 851000189, 702002517 and 212008218; cf. also 806351387
53	Il Ciel mi vuole oppresso	
54	Basta talora un' sguardo	

55	Digli, ch'è un infedele	[BERNASCONI, Andrea] [Metastasio: *Adriano in Siria*, different to Munich, 1755] = RISM ID no.: 200021404 (text only)
56	Per così dolce amplesso	VINCI, [Leonardo]
57	Perder l'amato bene	[VINCI, Leonardo] = RISM ID no.: 212008254 (transposition)
58	Non vi dolga, ò piagge amene	HASSE, Johann Adolf (= Sassone) [*Asteria*, Dresden, 1737] = RISM ID no.: 190015001 et al.
59	Se la sorte mia tiranna	
60	Chi mai non vidde uniti	
51	Un lampo di speranza	
62	Dirti di più non posso	
63	Se a me sola fosse dato	
64	Non odo gli accenti	
65	Se viver non poss'io	
66	Dirti, ben mio, vorrei	[LEO, Leonardo] [*Alessandro in Persia*, London, 1741 – pasticcio] = RISM ID no.: 211005238 and 850032591
67	Se sciogliere non vuoi delle catene	[VINCI, Leonardo] [*Catone in Utica*, Naples, 1729] = score
68	Dice che t'è fedele	? [BERNASCONI, Andrea] [*Il Demetrio*], "Mitrane atto 2do, scena 4ta" = very close to RISM ID no.: 456008430
69	Voglio sperare, che'l nume arciero	
70	Grazie a l'inganni tuoi (canzonetta)	
71	Voglio sperare, che'l Nume arciero	
72	Grazie agl'inganni tuoi (canzonetta)	

73	Per pietà, voi, che vedete	
74	Grazie à gl'inganni tuoi (canzonetta)	
75	CANTATA – Perdona, ò cara amorosetta [Mira là quell'angue (Aria); Dunque se il Ciel dispose (Recit.); Vorrei potervi amare (Aria)]	
76	Quando sperava un dì	= Contrafactum *Veni o Jesu amor*, RISM ID no.: 551000832
77	Che bel diletto	[HASSE, Johann Adolf (= Sassone)] = RISM ID no.: 852024115 (transposition)
78	Io son qual pellegrino	[TERRADELLAS, Domingo] [*Artaserse*, Venice, 1744] = RISM ID no.: 450059318
79	Passaggier che su la sponda	
80	Sono innocente	
81	Se la tua fè mi rendì	
82	Vedi se grato io sono	[HASSE, Johann Adolf] [*Euristeo*, Venice, 1732] = RISM ID no.: 270000652 (transposition)
83	Vengo à darti, anima bella	[GIACOMELLI, Geminiano] [*Lucio Papirio dittatore*, Parma, 1729] = RISM ID no.: 703002271 and 190011430
84	Quanto mai felici siete	
85	Ch'io mai vi possa lasciar	[GLUCK, Christoph Willibald] [*La finta schiava*, Venice, 1744] = RISM ID no.: 400110572 and 400110700
86	Vorrei del caro bene	
87	Allegri sù bevemo (canzonetta)	
88	Pietà d'un core	

89	Aure lievi che spirate	
90	Se libera non sono	Only parts for vl1 and vl2 survive; probably belonging to an aria originally numbered 10 [LEO, Leonardo] [? *Il Demetrio*, Naples, 1738] = see libretto
91	Non temer sai quanto io t'amo (duetto)	ARENA, Giuseppe *Achille in Sciro*, III/4, Rome, 1738
92	Quando senti la campana (duetto)	LATILLA, Gaetano *La Serva Padrona*, II/13, Rome, 1738
93	*Ouverture con VV e Viola*	HASSE, Johann Adolf [*Asteria*, Dresden, 1737]
94	*Concerto* (vl1, vl2, vla, tr1, tr2, cor1, cor2, ob1, ob2, b)	[CORDOBA Y LANTE, Alejandro Fernandez de] "Del Ecc.mo Sig.r Duca di S.to Gemini"
95	*Concerto* (vl1, vl2, vla, cor1, cor2, ob1, ob2, b)	[CORDOBA Y LANTE, Alejandro Fernandez de] "Del Ecc.mo Sig.r Duca di S. Gemini"
96	*Sonatina* (fl, vlc)	
97	*Sonata* (fl, vlc)	SARRI, Domenico
98	*Sonata* (fl, b)	S. MARTINO, Giuseppe (SAMMARTINI)
99	*Sonata* (fl. vlc)	
100	*Partita à 5 voci* (vl1, vl2, cor1, cor2, cemb)	
101	[no title] (vl1, vl2, vla)	
102	*Amen* (S)	

Sources

I-Vgc, Fondo ROLANDI, ROL.0140.13 and ROL.0421.01.
http://genealogy.euweb.cz/attems/attems4.html, 20.11.2014
http://gw.geneanet.org/cvpolier?lang=en&p=maria+josepha&n=khuen+von+auer, 20.11.2014
Knjižnica Ivana Potrča Ptuj, Domoznanski oddelek, 'Ptujska zbirka'.
SI-Mpa, Gospoščina Bistriški grad, Musicalia, TE 67, AE 1.
RISM A/II SI-Mpa (RISM ID nos. 540002808-540002909)
A-Gla, Familienarchiv Attems, Ehekontrakte, K. 19, H. 86.
A-Gla, Familienarchiv Attems, Briefe des Grafen Ignaz Attems, K. 19, H. 87.
A-Gla, Familienarchiv Attems, Familiengeschichte, verfaßt von Maria Victoria Markgräfin Pallavicino-Attems, 1950ff., K. 3, H. 7 (3. Kapitel).
A-Gla, Familienarchiv Attems, Geburtsnachweiss der Maria Josepha v. Khuen – Persönliche Akten, K. 92, H. 949, 950.
A-Gla, Familienarchiv Attems, Ignaz Maria Attems, Fideicommiss- und Allodial-Inventar 1762, K. 126, H. 1142, 1143.
A-Gl, Tresor A 513549: *Urbis et orbis romani homagium Caesari Octaviano Augusto* […], Graz 1728.
A-Gl, Tresor A 513546 I: *Alphonsi Persii inaudita fidei xostantio* […], Graz 1730, (xerox copy).

Literature

BLACK, JEREMY, Italy and the Grand Tour, New Haven/London 2003.
ID., The British Abroad. The Grand Tour in the Eighteenth Century, Stroud 2013.
CIGLENEČKI, MARJETA, Oprema gradov na slovenskem Štajerskem od srede 17. do srede 20. stoletja [The interior equipment of the castle in Slovenian Styria from the middle of the 17th till the middle of the 20th century], PhD diss., Univ. of Ljubljana 1997.
EYBL, MARTIN, The Early Keyboard Concertos in Ptuj: Music Composed for the Dornava Court, in: De musica disserenda 4, 2 (2008), pp. 65-85.
FEDERHOFER, HELLMUT, Die Grazer Stadtmusikanten und die privilegierte Stadtmusikantenkompagnie, in: Zeitschrift des Historischen Vereines für Steiermark 42 (1951), pp. 91-118.

ID., Musikleben in der Steiermark, in: Die Steiermark. Land, Leute, Leistung, ed. by GERNOT D. HASIBA/BERTHOLD SUTTER, Graz 1971, pp. 614-660.

ID./FLOTZINGER, RUDOLF, Musik in der Steiermark – historischer Überblick, in: Musik in der Steiermark. Katalog der Landesausstellung 1980, ed. by RUDOLF FLOTZINGER, Graz 1980, pp. 15-85.

ID./SCHMEISER, M. GUDRUN, Grazer Stadtmusikanten als Komponisten vorklassischer Klavierkonzerte, in: Historisches Jahrbuch der Stadt Graz 4 (1971), pp. 73-90.

FLOTZINGER, RUDOLF (ed.), Musik in der Steiermark. Katalog der Landesausstellung 1980, Graz 1980.

FRANCHI, SAVERIO, Drammaturgia romana II (1701-1750), Roma 1997.

FRANK, ULRIKE/ŠERBELJ, FERDO, Kratka zgodovina grofov Attems [Short history of Counts Attems], in: Zbornik občine Slovenska Bistrica [Collectanea of the Slovenska Bistrica Municipality] 2, ed. by FERDO ŠERBELJ, Slovenska Bistrica 1990, pp. 144-161.

FRAS, IVAN, Inventar gospoščine Bistriški grad 1587-1944 [The inventory of the seigneury Windish Feistritz] (Inventarji 10), Maribor 2004.

GRAFF, THEODOR, Grazer Theaterdrucke. Periochen und Textbücher (16.-18. Jh.), in: Historisches Jahrbuch der Stadt Graz 15 (1984), pp. 245-286.

ILWOF, FRANZ, Die Grafen von Attems. Freiherren von Heiligenkreuz in ihrem Wirken in und für Steiermark (Forschungen zur Verfassungs- und Verwaltungsgeschichte der Steiermark 2, 1), Graz 1897.

KOKOLE, METODA, Glasba v plemiških bivališčih na Slovenskem od srednjega veka do konca 18. stoletja [Music at noble residences on the territory of today's Slovenia from the Middle-Ages to the end of the eighteenth century], in: Kronika 60, 3 (2012a), pp. 667-698.

ID., Glasbeni utrinki s potovanja štajerskega plmiča po Evropi 18. stoletja [Musical impressions from an eighteenth-century European Tour by a Styrian nobleman], in: Muzikološki zbornik [Musicological Annual] 51,2 (2015), pp. 57-79.

ID., Italijanska opera v notranjeavstrijskih središčih v 18. stoletju: repertoar in izvajalci [18th-century Italian opera in Inner-Austrian centers: repertory and performers], in: De musica disserenda 1,1-2 (2005), pp. 75-93.

ID., Two Operatic Seasons of Brothers Mingotti in Ljubljana, in: De musica disserenda 8, 2 (2012b), pp. 57-89.

ID., The Mingotti Opera Company in Ljubljana in the Early 1740s, in: The Eighteenth-century Italian Opera Seria. Metamorphoses of the Opera in the Imperial Age. Musicological Colloquium at the Brno International Music Festival, 42, Dietrichstein Palace, Congress Hall, Brno, 24-26 September 2007 (Colloquia musicologica Brunensia 42), ed. by PETR MACEK/JANA PERUTKOVÁ, Prague 2013, pp. 138-163.

KOTER, DARJA, Lutnja Andreasa Berra in likovne upodobitve glasbil v dvorcu Dornava [The lute by Andreas Berr and depictions of musical instruments in Dornava Manor], in: Dornava – Vrišerjev zbornik 2003 [Dornava – Vrišer's Festschrift], ed. by MARJETA CIGLENEČKI, Ljubljana 2003, pp. 341-357.

LECHNER, GEORG MATTHIAS, Der Barockmaler Franz Carl Remp (1675-1718), PhD diss., Univ. of Vienna 2010; available online: http://othes.univie.ac.at/9877/, 19.11.2014.

MÜLLER VON ASOW, ERICH H., Angelo und Pietro Mingotti: Ein Beitrag zur Geschichte der Oper im XVIII. Jahrhundert, Dresden 1917.

MÜNSTER, ROBERT/CORNEILSON, PAUL, Bernasconi, Andrea, in: Grove Music Online, article url: http://www.oxfordmusiconline.com.nukweb.nuk.uni-lj.si/subscriber/article/grove/music/02864, 18.11.2012.

MUROVEC, BARBARA, Antonio Maderni (1660-1702). Je bil pozabljeni Weissenkircherjev zet iz Capolaga prvi Attemsov freskant? [Antonio Maderni (1660-1702). Was the forgotten Weissenkircher's son-in-law of Capolago the first of Attems' fresco-painters?], in: Slovenska umetnost in njen evropski kontekst [Slovenian art and its European context], ed. by BARBARA MUROVEC, Ljubljana 2007, pp. 114-122.

ID., Wagingerjeva *Allegorija petih čutov* v gradu Brežice [J. C. Waginger's *Allegory of the Five Senses* in Brežice Castle], in: Vita artis perennis. Ob sedemdesetletnici akademika Emilijana Cevca [Vita artis perennis. Festschrift Emilian Cevc], ed. by ALENKA KLEMENC, Ljubljana 2000, pp. 403-408.

PERUTKOVÁ, JANA, Der glorreiche Nahmen Adami. Johann Adam Graf von Questenberg (1678-1752) als Förderer der italienischen Oper in Mähren (Specula Spectacula 4), Wien 2015.

SADGORSKI, DANIELA, Andrea Bernasconi und die Oper am Münchner Kurfürstenhof 1753-1772, München 2010.

SARTORI, CLAUDIO, I libretti italiani a stampa dalle origini al 1800. Catalogo analitico con 16 indici, 7 vols., Cuneo 1990-1994.

SENN, WALTER, Aus dem Kulturleben einer süddeutschen Kleinstadt.

Musik, Schule und Theater der Stadt Hall in Tirol in der Zeit vom 15. bis zum 19. Jahrhundert, Innsbruck etc. 1938.

SIETZENHEIM, ADAM SEBASTIAN VON, Newbegläntzter Zucht-Spiegel der Adelichen Jugend. Klärlich entweffend: wie die Edle Jugendt von ihren Wiegen-Jahren, biß zur anruckender reiffen Mannbarkeit mit schönen Tugenden Seelen-Ersprietzlich gezieret: Auch in goldseligen Sitten und höflichen Gebärden liebsbehäglich gepflanht werden sollte. Auß underschiednen Geist- vnd Weltlichen Lehrreichen Verfassern, unnd theils eygnen müglichisten Nachsinnen, in unser Teutschgebundne Helden-Sprach, trewlich zusamen gezogen und eyferigist gesambelt, Munich 1659.

SLEKOVEC, MATTHÄUS [MATEJ], Wurmberg. Topografisches-historische Skizze, Marburg [Maribor] 1895.

STAUDACHER, ILSE M., Musik in Graz, in: Kirche – Bildung – Kultur (Geschichte der Stadt Graz 3), ed. by WALTER BRUNNER, Graz 2003, pp. 664-668.

SUPPAN, WOLFGANG, Steierisches Musiklexikon, Graz 2009.

ŠERBELJ, FERDINAND, Bistriški grad [The castle of Slovenska Bistrica], Slovenska Bistrica 2005.

VRIŠER, ANDREJA, Noša v baroku na Slovenskem [Clothing and dress in the Baroque Era in Slovenia], Ljubljana 1993.

VRIŠER, SERGEJ, Iz zbirk Pokrajinskega arhiva v Mariboru. I. Skupina portretov rodbine Attems [From the collections of the Provincial Archives of Maribor. I. Group of portraits of the family Attems], in: Časopis za zgodovino in narodopisje [Review for history and ethnography] n.v. 10/1 (1974), pp. 136-144.

WEIGL, IGOR, Ignacij Maria grof Attems in slikar Johann Caspar Waginger - Clery [Count Ignaz Maria von Attems and the painter Johann Caspar Waginger - Clery], in: Zbornik za umetnostno zgodovino [Art history journal] 42 (2006), pp. 165-181.

ID., O francoskih grafikah, loparjih in grofičinem strelovodu. Oprema in funkcije dvorca Dornave v 18. stoletju [On French engravings, rackets and Countess' lightning conductors. Furnishings and function of the Dornava manor in the 18th century], in: Dornava. Vrišerjev zbornik [Dornava – Festschrift Sergej Vrišer], ed. by MARJETA CIGLENEČKI, Ljubljana 2003, pp. 180-244.

WISSGRILL, FRANZ KARL, Schauplatz des landsässigen Nieder-Oesterreichischen Adels vom Herren- und Ritterstande von dem XI. Jahrhundert an, bis auf jetztige Zeiten, vol. 1, Vienna 1794.

The Case of Juraj Križanić
(1619-1683?) – His Texts on Music.
From Artefacts to Cultural Study
(Croatian Writers on Music and The Transfer
of Ideas in Their New Environments)

STANISLAV TUKSAR

This essay describes the achievement, in the fields of music theory and history, of the outstanding Croatian seventeenth-century ecclesiastical writer, polymath and traveller Juraj Križanić (1618-1683?), whose name appeared during his lifetime variously in a Latinized form as Georgius Crisanius and in its Italian version as Giorgio Crisanio.

The discovery of Križanić's works, their bibliographical afterlife, the extent and character of what has already been done from a scholarly point of view and, finally, what should and could be done in the future in this regard together make for an exemplary case study fitting perfectly into the scheme suggested by the title of the workshop where the present contribution was presented as a paper. In placing Križanić within the very complex socio-historical context of his time and in mapping his most extraordinary migrations around Europe, it may be stated that his written legacy was created and survived exactly in the way that its author had lived: dynamically on the edge of extravagance, rich in fantasy and often with quite weak connections to reality, precariously balanced between full recognition and total oblivion.

Since Križanić's intellectual output both in the field of music and at large was closely linked to his general ideological vocation and to the behavior and actions resulting from it, one needs to obtain an insight into both the elementary facts of his life and the characteristics of his posthumous fate.

Križanić was born in 1617/1618 in Obrh, a small village in the vicinity of Zagreb, some 30 kilometers to the west, close to the present-day Croatian border with Slovenia. He was initially educated in the humanities by the Jesuits in Ljubljana (Laibach), later studying philosophy in Graz and theology in Bologna and Rome. Seized very early by the *idée fixe* of a would-be religious unity of the Slavic world, he studied Greek, eastern liturgies and theological controversies in Rome. In addition, he dreamed about a Christian alliance against the Ottomans in order to liberate the Slavic world from the Turkish yoke, deciding to travel to Russia in order to give a decisive impetus to both of his phantasmagorias, which are called "intentio moscovitica" in some documents. In 1646-1647 he traveled to Russia (Smolensk, Moscow) for the first time and returned full of enthusiasm for the young Tsar Aleksey Mikhailovich Romanov. Between 1647 and 1659 he stayed in Rome, mostly writing and publishing his works on the subjects of Orthodox controversies (*Biblioteca Schismaticorum Universa*) and music (*Asserta musicalia* and other texts). In the meantime, in 1651, he also visited Istanbul for three months as chaplain to a Viennese court deputation. In Rome Križanić's activities brought him into contact with such outstanding contemporaries as Athanasius Kircher, Juan Caramuel Lobkowitz, Virgilio Spada, Lucas Holstenius and Fabio Chigi, the future Pope Alexander VII.[1]

In 1659 Križanić went to Russia again, this time staying there for eighteen years – up to 1677. After a year or so of initial attempts to establish himself in the ecclesiastical and scholarly circles surrounding the court he succeeded in accomplishing only one project: work on an all-encompassing Slavic grammar, lexicon and spelling book. Working among many foreigners, especially German and Greek merchants and travelers, in the atmosphere of local controversies between church reformers and conservatives, he obviously acted incautiously in a political sense and was consequently sentenced in early 1661 to sixteen years of exile in Siberia. He served the full term in the town of Tobolsk, and his sojourn there could be characterized simultaneously as a curse and a blessing with regard to the course of his life. Tobolsk being at that time far from a Soviet-style Gulag, Križanić had considerable freedom of action and

---

1 GOLUB, 1976, pp. 91-144.

penned several texts there that turned out to be his life's work: *Razgowori ob wladatelystwu* (Conversation on governance), *Gramatično iskazânje* (Grammar), *O Promysle* (De Providentia Dei), *Ob svêtom kreščênju* (On holy baptism), *Tolkovanie istoričeskih proročestv* (The interpretation of historical prophecies), *O kitajskom torgu* (On Chinese commerce), *O preverstve beseda* (On superstition) and various others. In 1676 the new Tsar, Feodor III Alexeyevich Romanov, pardoned Križanić, who initially returned to Moscow. In March of the following year, 1677, he left for Vilnius in Lithuania, becoming Father Augustin of the Dominican Order there. It was in this city that he wrote the work *Historia de Siberia*, which was dedicated to the Polish King Jan Sobieski, whose army he soon joined (probably in Warsaw). He disappeared on campaign during the siege of Vienna in 1683.[2]

The crucial question about Križanić that occurs to every musicologist is: how and why did such a personality, dealing throughout his life both intellectually and existentially principally with history, linguistics, theology, economics and politics, come to occupy himself at all with music? In this essay we shall try to state briefly *how* he did it (the "artefacts" part); but the answer to *why* he did it (the "cultural studies" part) will have to remain in the sphere of optimistically plausible speculation pending the conclusion of all-encompassing research on Križanić.

Križanić produced several texts on musical matters. Here is a list of them according to the present state of knowledge:

Printed works

1. *Asserta musicalia nova prorsus omnia (Rome, 1656)*. This booklet has been found in six (seven) copies up to now: Rome (I-Rsc); Bologna (I-Bc); Vienna (A-Wn); Berlin (D-B); the Vatican (I-Rvat); Vigevano (Archivio Capitolare) – fragment; Paris (F-Pn).

2. *Novum instrumentum Ad cantus mira facilitate componendos* (Rome, 1658). This leaflet has been preserved in only one copy in Vienna (A-Wn), bound together with the Viennese copy of *Asserta musicalia*.

---

2 GOLUB, 1981, pp. 1-12.

Manuscripts

1. *Nova inventa musica or Tabulae novae, exhibentes musicam, Late augmentatam: Clare explicatam: Valde facilitatam* (Rome, 1657-58). This manuscript has been known to exist in two copies since December 2012, following my recent discovery: in Rome (I-Rn, Ms Mus. 167) – Križanić's incomplete autograph; in Paris (F-Pn, Rés. Vm. 11) – Križanić's complete autograph.
2. *De Musica* (Tobolsk, between 1663 and 1666). The manuscript *De Musica* exists in only one autograph copy, preserved in the Central State Archives of Old Writings (Centralni gosudarstveni arhiv drevnih aktov) in Moscow; it makes up part – as a separate chapter – of his more widely preserved work entitled *Razgowori ob wladatelystwu* (Conversation on governance; shelfmark: fund 381, ed. hr. 1799).
3. *O cerkovnom penju* (On church singing) (Tobolsk-Moscow, 1675). This shorter manuscript exists in only one autograph copy, also held by the Central State Archives of Old Writings in Moscow; it makes up part – as a separate chapter – of his more widely preserved work entitled *O preverstve beseda* (On superstition), written in Tobolsk in 1675 (no shelfmark known).

Opera dubia

1. *Sopra le proportioni musicali* (Rome, 1658?; MS; I-Rvat, Fondo Chigi, F.IV.73; uncertain authorship).
2. *Novi uzorak glazbe* (A new musical pattern) (Moscow, 1676; uncertain existence).

Information on, and appreciation of, Križanić as a music theorist dates back to the nineteenth century. Among outstanding lexicographers we may mention François-Joseph Fétis in 1866[3] and Robert Eitner in 1900;[4] and among Croatian scholars, Ivan Kukuljević Sakcinski in 1869,[5] Vatro-

---

3   Fétis, 1866, p. 391.
4   Eitner/Springer, 1900, p. 104.
5   Kukuljević Sakcinski, 1869.

slav Jagić in 1876,[6] the historians Franjo Rački[7] and Vjekoslav Klaić in 1892,[8] and Mirko Breyer in 1930.[9] Križanić was later included in the historical surveys of Croatian music by Božidar Širola[10] in 1922 and Josip Andreis in 1962, as well as in some more recent publications,[11] while his full recognition was confirmed in 1965 by Albe Vidaković in his dissertation *Asserta musicalia (1656) Jurja Križanića i njegovi ostali radovi s područja glazbe* (Yury Krizanich's Asserta musicalia [1656] and his other musical works).[12] Moreover, during the late 1960s and 1970s the ecclesiastical scholar and poet Ivan Golub published around 20 studies, mostly concerning Križanić's treatment of music, and in addition a book entitled *Juraj Križanić – Glazbeni teoretik 17. stoljeća* (Juraj Križanić – A music theorist of the seventeenth century).

Regarding the cultural studies dimension, questions should be put forward at this point on the internal and external aspects of Križanić's treatment of music. It is obvious that his musico-theoretical output was produced in two separate contexts: in the first place, the two printed ones (*Asserta musicalia* and *Novum instrumentum*) plus the manuscript *Tabulae novae* belong to his Roman period in the second half of the 1650s; in the second place, the two remaining manuscripts (*De Musica* and *O cerkovnom penju*) belong to his Russian-Siberian period, having been written some ten to twenty years later. The two existential contexts of Križanić differ substantially in character and are, consequently, reflected accordingly in the contents and profiles of his texts.

In the first, Roman, group of texts, Križanić obviously wished to prove to his intellectual and social environment his level of insight into musical matters. In *Asserta musicalia*, from 1656, he discussed in 20 "assertions" or propositions a series of musico-theoretical and musico-aesthetical problems such as scales, Pythagorean and Guidonian rules, notation, organ manuals, the breaking of rules in the composition of "enthusiastic songs", and intervals and chords. In the main part of *Nova*

---

6   JAGIĆ, 1876.
7   RAČKI, 1892.
8   KLAIĆ, 1892.
9   BREYER, 1930.
10 ŠIROLA, 1922, pp. 58f.
11 ANDREIS, 1962; ANDREIS, 1974, pp. 113-117.
12 Initial publication as an article: VIDAKOVIĆ, 1965. Later published separately in English: VIDAKOVIĆ, 1967.

inventa musica or *Tabulae novae, exhibentes musicam*, from 1657/1658, Križanić displayed 30 tables with complicated graphical drawings that deal with the problem of the classification of consonances on the one hand and propose a kind of "equal temperament" on the other; these can be understood as an expansion and more detailed elaboration of his short "assertions" published one year earlier. In *Novum instrumentum*, a published pamphlet from 1658, Križanić offered in five points instructions for a device intended for a "miraculously easy way of composing songs". The mechanical device, which was intended for use by both amateur and professional musicians, has itself not survived.

This Roman group of writings, though theoretical in character, took as their final goal the facilitation of specific aspects of practical music-making: composition and the notation of musical compositions. In a short period of only two years Križanić produced three separate, yet connected, musical writings. In the first, he used as sources older writers such as Boethius, Gioseffo Zarlino and Giovanni Battista Doni; in the second and third, elements from Marin Mersenne, Athanasius Kircher, René Descartes, Giovanni Valentini and Juan Caramuel Lobkowitz that have been identified by researchers from the 1970s onwards. The manuscript of *Tabulae novae* was written in two copies, one of which was presented as a gift to Pope Alexander VII. What does all this bespeak? For some reason, Križanić was eager to put himself forward both as an expert on questions of music theory and also as someone who desired to improve and facilitate the techniques and practices of composing, reading and performing music. Was he himself an unrealized composer? Was he thinking of a future need to teach somebody to compose up-to-date music? Was he thinking about his first Russian experience and the prospect of another Russian trip, a mission in which music-making could play a certain role? Or was the bull *Piae solicitudinis* concerning music, issued by Alexander VII in 1657,[13] somehow connected with Križanić's efforts to promote certain "puristic" ideas about music in general?

The Russian group of writings consists of two manuscripts (*De Musica* and *O cerkovnom penju*), both written in exile in the Siberian town of Tobolsk. The first text has additional information – it is captioned "Haeresis Politica 16. De Musica" – within a broader text dealing with eight false political beliefs or misconceptions (errors), and has been written in Latin. It consists of twenty "points" and four "questions". On the whole,

---

13 Cf. IBID., p. 44.

the "points" could be understood as a new series of propositions, following the twenty "points" of the 1656 *Asserta musicalia*. Much space is devoted to various aspects of music-making and to a characterization of music in ancient Greek and Roman practices, as well as among modern nations such as those of the Italians, Spaniards, Turks, Croats, Serbs, Czechs, Poles and Hungarians. Križanić's most intriguing thesis lies in the assertion that the sole purpose of the existence of music is to offer men pleasure, joy and relief from their troubles, all other concepts and beliefs, past or present, being merely false ones. The second part – four *Quaestiones de musica* – deals with the history of church music, the variety of European national musics, secular music and *tibiae*. In this part of the work the second and third sections seem to be the most interesting, since they put forward various suggestions or directions on what to retain and what to change in the Russian musical life of their day.

Thus – despite the fact that the Russian group of writings has not as yet been studied in detail – it may be asserted that a shift occurs between the Roman portion of Križanić's texts, which deals mostly with music theory and aesthetics, and the Russian portion, which deals mainly with the ethnographic and sociological aspects of music. Both orientations were very probably dictated by the particular and differing socio-cultural environments of Rome and Russia, respectively, and by the role Križanić imposed on himself in his position within these two very different cultural circles. However, some unifying aspects exist as well in these two poles of his musical thought: ones exemplified by his general attitude towards music as a useful pleasure-giving activity and by his personal ambition to participate actively in the religious and socio-cultural politics of his time.

At the most general level it should be pointed out that this phantasmagorian idealist, a man of exceptional culture and encyclopaedic knowledge, was commonly misunderstood by both his audiences: "in Rome he was considered an exaggerated Slav nationalist, while in Moscow he was considered a suspicious foreigner and, for the state, a dangerous man".[14] And yet, his œuvre was later studied by Peter the Great and the Russian nineteenth-century Slavophiles, as well as by South-Slavic nationalists of the nineteenth and twentieth centuries,[15] thus bridging past and present and making him "a man for all times" in terms of the relationship between the European West and East.

---

14 Cf. IBID., p. 9.
15 Cf. GOLUB, 2003, pp. 123-140; GOL'DBERG, 1976; PAVIĆ, 1974; SOLOVIEV, 1868.

Manuscript sources

KRIŽANIĆ, JURAJ, De Musica (Tobolsk, between 1663 and 1666), in: Razgowori ob wladatelystwu [Conversation on governance], Central State Archives of Old Writings (Centralni gosudarstveni arhiv drevnih aktov), Moscow, fund 381, ed. hr. 1799 (autograph).

ID., Nova inventa musica or Tabulae novae, exhibentes musicam, Late augmentatam: Clare explicatam: Valde facilitatam (Rome, 1657-58), I-Rn, Ms Mus. 167 (incomplete autograph), F-Pn, Rés. Vm. 11 (complete autograph).

ID., Novi uzorak glazbe [A new musical pattern] (Moscow, 1676; uncertain existence).

ID., O cerkovnom penju [On church singing] (Tobolsk-Moscow, 1675), in: O preverstve beseda [On superstition] (Tobolsk, 1675), Central State Archives of Old Writings (Centralni gosudarstveni arhiv drevnih aktov), Moscow, no shelfmark known (autograph).

ID., Sopra le Proportioni Musicali (Rome, 1658?), I-Rvat, Fondo Chigi, F.IV.73 (uncertain authorship).

Printed sources

KRIŽANIĆ, JURAJ, Asserta musicalia nova prorsus omnia, Rome 1656.
ID., Novum instrumentum ad cantus mira facilitate componendos, Rome 1658.

Literature

ANDREIS, JOSIP, Povijest hrvatske glazbe [History of Croatian music], Zagreb 1974.

ID., Razvoj muzičke umjetnosti u Hrvatskoj [The development of the art of music in Croatia], in: Historijski razvoj muzičke kulture u Jugoslaviji [Historical development of musical culture in Yugoslavia], Zagreb 1962, pp. 92-93.

BREYER, MIRKO, Neke muzičke epizode u Jurja Križanića [Some musical episodes by Juraj Križanić], in: Sv. Cecilija, XXIV/5 (1930), pp. 157-159.

EITNER, ROBERT/SPRINGER, HERMANN WILHELM, Crisanius, Georgius, in: Biographisch-bibliographisches Quellen-Lexikon der Musiker und Musikgelehrten der christlichen Zeitrechnung bis zur Mitte des neunzehnten Jahrhunderts, vol. 3, Leipzig 1900.

FÉTIS, FRANÇOIS-JOSEPH, Biographie universelle des musiciens, vol. 2, Paris 1866.

GOL'DBERG, ALEKSANDR L'VOVICH, Juraj Križanić in Russian Historiography, in: Juraj Križanić (1618-1683). Russophile and Ecumenic Visionary. A Symposium, ed. by THOMAS EEKMAN/ANTE KADIĆ, The Hague/Paris 1976, pp. 51-69.

GOLUB, IVAN, Contribution à l'histoire des relations de Križanić avec ses contemporains, in: Juraj Križanić (1618-1683). Russophile and Ecumenic Visionary. A Symposium, ed. by THOMAS EEKMAN/ANTE KADIĆ, The Hague/Paris 1976, pp. 91-144.

ID., Juraj Križanić – glazbeni teoretik 17. stoljeća [Juraj Križanić – A music theorist of the seventeenth century], Zagreb 1981.

ID., Počeci slavenske misli [The beginnings of Slavic thought], in: Hrvatska i Europa. Kultura, znanost i umjetnost, III: Barok i prosvjetiteljstvo (XVII-XVIII. stoljeće) [Croatia and Europe. Culture, science and arts, Vol. III: Baroque and Enlightenment], ed. by ID., Zagreb 2003, pp. 123-140.

JAGIĆ, VATROSLAV, Gradja za slovinsku narodnu poeziju [Materials for Slavic folk poetry], in: Rad JAZU 37 (1876), pp. 33-137.

KLAIĆ, VJEKOSLAV, Gjuro Križanić kao glazbenik [Gjuro Križanić as a musician], in: Gusle (1982), No. 4, pp. 25-27.

KUKULJEVIĆ SAKCINSKI, IVAN, Juraj Križanić Nebljuški, hrvatsko-ruski pisac [Juraj Križanić Nebljuški, Croatian-Russian writer], in: Arkiv za povjestnicu jugoslavensku [Archive for Yugoslavian history], book X, Zagreb 1869, pp. 11-75.

PAVIĆ, RADOVAN (ed.), Život i djelo Jurja Križanića [The life and work of Juraj Križanić], Zagreb 1974.

RAČKI, FRANJO, Odkrito glazbeno djelo Jurja Križanića [A musical work by Juraj Križanić discovered], in: Vienac, XXIV/12 (1892), p. 192.

ŠIROLA, BOŽIDAR, Pregled povijesti hrvatske muzike [A review of the history of Croatian music], Zagreb 1922, pp. 58-59.

SOLOVIEV, SERGEY MIKHAILOVICH, Istorija Rossii s drevneishih vremen [History of Russia since the earliest times], Vol. XIII, St Petersburg 1868.

VIDAKOVIĆ, ALBE, Asserta musicalia (1656) Jurja Križanića i njegovi ostali radovi s područja glazbe [Yury Krizanitch's Asserta musicalia (1656) and his other musical works], in: Rad JAZU, book 337, Zagreb 1965, pp. 41-159.

ID., Yury Krizanitch's Asserta musicalia (1656) and His Other Musical Works, Zagreb 1967.

People and Places in a (Music) Source. A Case Study of Giuseppe Michele Stratico and His Theoretical Treatises (Croatian Writers on Music and Transfer of Ideas in Their New Environments)

Lucija Konfic

Taking into consideration a particular (music) source means to have in mind the various interpretative aspects that it offers. It is a sort of (hi)story that can be told about a source itself, its author, context, connections, etc., based on research.

In this paper, I would like to propose a story/case study of Giuseppe Michele Stratico, a composer, violinist and writer on music from the 18th century.[1] Considering that the analytical work on Giuseppe Michele Stratico's theoretical treatises is still a work in progress, the conclusions in my article shall not be final.

There is not much literature on Stratico. Valuable sources are an article on his biography by Zdravko Blažeković (1990),[2] doctoral theses on his compositions by Michael Thomas Roeder[3] and Francia Fitch Mann,[4] an article on his theories by Mark Lindley,[5] and the catalog by Vincent

---

1 The subject is part of my doctoral project at the Kunstuniversität in Graz under the supervision of Prof Klaus Aringer.
2 Blažeković, 1990.
3 Roeder, 1971.
4 Mann, 1992.
5 Lindley, 1981.

Duckles and Minnie Elmer[6] of the collection in Berkeley, where most of his compositions are preserved today.[7]

Giuseppe Michele was a member of the noble Stratico family from Zadar (Zara, the family had Greek origins) that has produced a number of outstanding personalities. His brothers were Gian Domenico (1732-1799), bishop of Novigrad (Cittanova), later bishop of Hvar (Lesina) and professor in Siena; Simone (1733-1824), expert in the regulation of rivers and shipbuilding, and university professor at Padua and Pavia; Gregorio (1736-1806), lawyer, diplomat and poet. They all contributed significantly to the environment in which they worked. Giuseppe Michele was born in Zadar on July 31st, 1728. Already in 1737 (at the age of only nine), he moved to Padua where his uncle, Antonio Stratico, was rector at the Collegio Cottunio. Musical life in Padua during the mid-18th century was rich. Two dominant figures in the Paduan Basilica were Giuseppe Tartini (1692-1770), who also operated the famous music school (*Scuola delle nazioni*), and Francesco Antonio Vallotti (1697-1780), both not only composers but also music theorists. It is supposed that, besides his law studies, Stratico studied violin and composition with Tartini. Although he is not listed anywhere as one of Tartini's students, there are several indications supporting that assumption: the letter by Father Antonio Bonaventura Sberti mentions him as "Sig. Michele Stratico, insigne aluno del gran Tartini",[8] and Giordano Riccati in his (as yet disputable) *Memorie sul violinista G. Tartini* mentioned that "the young man was presented as Stratico Michele, Tartini's pupil in violin and composition".[9] The fact that Riccati did know Stratico is suggested by a letter from Giovennale Sacchi asking for an opinion on Stratico as a composer: "recently I have been told infinite praises about Mr Michele Stratico, vicar of Sanguinetto. Your Lordship, I presume, must know him."[10]

---

6   DUCKLES/ELMER, 1963.
7   Stratico produced more than 300 compositions that are preserved mostly in Berkeley (the *Manuscript Collection of 18th-Century Italian Instrumental Music*), and also in Padua (Cappella Antoniana), Venice (Biblioteca di San Marco, Fondazione Ugo e Olga Levi), Verona, Berlin (Deutsche Staatsbibliothek), Washington (The Library of Congress), Modena (Biblioteca Estense), Ancona (Biblioteca Comunale Luciano Benincasa).
8   SBERTI, 1814, p. 10., cited by BLAŽEKOVIĆ, 1990, p. 124.
9   "il giovane fu presentato come Stratico Michele allievo a Tartini in violino e composizione". RICCATI, 1969, p. 408.
10 "Ultimamente mi sono state narrate infinite lodi del signor Michele Stratico

Around 1760, Stratico moved from Padua to the small town of Sanguinetto (near Verona), where he worked as *vicario e giudice al maleficio* (vicar and criminal judge). Research during 2011 established 31st January 1783 in Sanguinetto as the date and place of his death.[11]

In the field of music theory, Stratico left behind three works. They are preserved only in the form of manuscripts in the Biblioteca Marciana in Venice (I-Vnm), under the signatures Ms. It. Cl. IV, 341 [= 5294], 342 [= 5347], 343 [= 5348].

These treatises are:

a. *Trattato di musica* – in nine versions and related sketches;[12]
b. *Trattato di musica – Nuovo sistema musicale* – in one version, clear copy, dialog;[13]
c. *Lo spirito Tartiniano* – in one version, clear copy.[14]

It is presumed that all of Stratico's treatises were written after 1770 (the year of Tartini's death). Leonardo Frasson supposed that *Lo spirito Tartiniano* had been written between 1771 and 1775, and the other two, far more complex, before his premature death from tuberculosis in 1783. All literature on Stratico mentions two of the treatises (a and c), probably considering the second (b) as a version of the first, but I venture that these are, in fact, three different works.

Taking into account persons connected to these sources, the first problem arises in connection with authorship, which is not precisely specified anywhere. No version with Stratico's name on it exists, but it was Giuseppe Valentinelli in 1868, *praefectus* of the Biblioteca Marciana in Venice, who attributed the work to the theorist/writer.[15] All the treatises were donated to the Marciana with the belongings of his more famous

---

vicario di Sanguinetto. Vostra Signoria illustrissima parmi che lo dovvia conoscere". The letter dated June 22nd 1776 is held in Udine, Biblioteca Comunale (I-UDc), Correspondence of Giordano Riccati, vol. 6, sign. Mss. 1025, f. 107, cited by BLAŽEKOVIĆ, 1990, pp. 128-129.

11 First published in: KONFIC, 2012.
12 Althought the first version (341a) is titled *Nuovo sistema musicale*, as well as the dialog (341b), the title in other versions is *Trattato di musica*. 342 contains another version of the *Trattato di musica*.
13 STRATICO, 341b.
14 STRATICO, 343e.
15 VALENTINELLI, 1868, p. 162.

brother Simone, whose wish it was to deposit his works in some public library. Thus, his nephews and heirs, Giovanni Battista Stratico and Giuseppe Bellori, gave them to the Marciana between 1831 and 1841. One of them could well be "amatissimo mio signor Cugino" ("my beloved Mr Cousin"), mentioned by Stratico in his *Fogli con dichiarazioni*:[16]

> "Principles and reasoning, with which presented Melody is deducted, are declared and explained on the leaves (folios) left in the hands of my dearest Mr Cousin, and the Writer reports to them."[17]

Another issue regarding authorship concerns the different handwritings in these treatises (even within the same version). More precise and detailed comparison with the existing Stratico's legal documents (and its copies)[18] could help to identify whether these handwritings belong to Stratico or to different persons/copyists. However, at the present state of research, we shall assume that all the treatises and their versions were written by Stratico, as suggested by Valentinelli.

Examining Stratico's theoretical work from the aspect of names of persons and places found within, our goal is to detect a set of sources that Stratico used in his work, as well as the tradition (resulting from school experience or knowledge acquired in a spiritual circle) in which he formed his thinking on music and music theory. Also, we aim to connect those names with already known facts about Stratico's life that may lead to our deeper understanding of yet unknown parts of his biography. Therefore, the references on people and places will be divided into several categories that shall help us to realize their greater or lesser im-

---

16   *Fogli con dichiarazioni* (Folios with clarifications) are explanations of the most important parts of Stratico's musical system, part of the 341c, fol. 157-168.

17   "I principj poi, ed i ragionamti, in forza dei quali deducesi la pr[ese]nte Cantilena, sono dichiarati, e spiegati ne' fogli lasciati nelle mani dell'amat[issi]mo mio Signor Cugino, e ad esseloro riportasi lo Scrittore." STRATICO, 341c, fol. 158r.

18   Some of the legal documents in affairs under the jurisdiction of vicar of Sanguinetto are preserved as originals written by Stratico, and some as copies transcribed with another hand. See for example Affari del feudo di Sanguinetto ove Michele Stratico era Vicario, I-Vnm, Ms. It. Cl. VI, 282 [= 5773], fols. 90-96.

portance. In this sense, it is important to determine which sources Stratico quoted and who he had seen as an authority figure, to which tradition he adhered, in which way ideas were transferred to him and in which way he used them.

In Stratico's treatises we can distinguish several types of references:

1. Quotations – 3 types:
   a. of sources in the text;
   b. of sources in the studies;
   c. of classical literature;

2. General references – referring to a group of people;

3. Other references – names (in the main text or at the margin).

1. Quotations

a. Quotation of sources in the text

These quotations are one of the main keys in understanding Stratico's starting points and they introduce changes in his theory. The most important source upon which Stratico bases his system is certainly Giuseppe Tartini (mentioned in all three treatises). Stratico quotes his *Trattato di musica seconda la vera scienza dell'armonia*, published in Padua in 1754 (in *Lo spirito Tartiniano, Nuovo sistema musicale, Tratatto di musica*), as well as *De' principj dell'Armonia contenuta nel Diatonico Genere* published in Padua in 1767 (only in *Lo spirito Tartiniano*). They are not only his sources, but the starting points for the development of his new musical system. As *Lo spirito Tartiniano* suggests, Stratico starts his reasoning within Tartini's system, but then proposes some changes and more consistent thoughts.[19]

---

19 It would also be very interesting to find out more about Stratico's connections with some others among Tartini's students. Beside the Berkeley collection, Stratico's compositions can be found in the Fondo della Biblioteca Comunale "Luciano Benincasa" in Ancona (I-AN) and the Fondo Malaspina dell'Archivio di Stato in Verona (I-VEas), among Tartini's own and (other) of Tartini's students' works. These are, for example, Pietro Nardini (1722-1793), Giuseppe Antonio Capuzzi (1755-1818), Domenico Ferrari (1722-1780), Lodovico Syrmen (1738-1812), Carlo Antonio Campioni (1720-1788), Carlo Ignazio Nappi (1723-1796) etc. However, fur-

Another name quoted in the treatises (in *Nuovo sistema musicale* and *Tratatto di musica*) is that of the Spanish theorist Antonio Eximeno (y Pujades, 1729-1808) and his work *Dell'origine e delle regole della musica colla storia del suo progresso, decadenza, e rinovazione* published in Rome in 1774. As David Damschroder and David Russell Williams state, Eximeno "attained notoriety not by creating new theories but by broadcasting his opposition to those of others. He criticized the use of rules and mathematical formulations as aids to the mastery of music"[20] (especially criticising Martini and Tartini). Thus, Stratico takes a stand against Eximeno and in favor of music as science.

b. Quotations of sources in the studies

The example of these quotations is a copy of parts of a treatise by another author, which is also an important source concerning the contents of Stratico's treatises. The name mentioned here is of another important composer, player and music writer of 18th century Padua – Francescantonio Vallotti (1697-1780). At the end of version 343a, we can find transcriptions of Vallotti's treatise *Della scienza teorica, e pratica della moderna musica* (Padua 1779). Vallotti's name is marked in the upper corner of the page. Together with the letter written to Vallotti,[21] this is the proof for Stratico's connections with the Paduan environment, even after his transfer to Sanguinetto (in the 1760s and 1770s).

c. Quotations of classical literature

These quotations show Stratico's (wide) knowledge, but are not important for understanding his theory. Stratico quotes or paraphrases only masters of classical literature in order to emphasize more vividly his position or statement, and always specifies the source of his quotations. They all appear in the treatise *Lo spirito Tartiniano*. On most occasions, he uses *Saturae* by Juvenal, then *De rerum natura* by Lucretius, and once also Virgil (*Aeneid*), Ovid (*Metamorphoses*), Persia (*Satura*) and Horace (*Sermones*).

---

ther research on this aspect would exceed the framework of this paper. Cf. CANALE, 2010.
20   DAMSCHRODER/WILLIAMS, 1990, p. 83.
21   Now in I-Pca, D.VI.1894/6-3.

For example:

"Est modus in rebus, sunt certi denique fines, quos ultra, citraque nequit consistere verum" ("Measure in everything: in short, there are certain boundaries, on neither side of which lies Right").[22]

2. General references

The syntagm "general references" in this paper refers to a group of people mentioned in Stratico's treatises. They do not offer specific data and require a contextual knowledge (partly) to identify them. They are interesting as a target audience (for whom the particular version is written, considering different styles in different versions of the treatises).

I am referring here particularly to Stratico's clear opposition of music theory and music practice: "What then the scholars say, and what is discussed among musicians?"[23] From this standpoint, throughout the entire treatise (*Lo spirito Tartiniano*), two ways of understanding general and specific issues in music theory arise, more or less applicable in practice. Because, as Stratico explains, scholars ("i Dotti") discuss the theoretical assumptions not knowing their application, and practical musicians ("i Musici") do not understand the theoretical studies and think that only that which can be put to practical use is important.[24] That is why only those

---

22 Stratico's quotation (variant) of Quintus Horatius Flaccus, *Sermones*, I, 106-107, STRATICO, 343e, fol. 190r. English translation by A. S. KLINE, http://www.poetryintranslation.com/PITBR/Latin/HoraceSatiresBkISatI.htm, 7.4.2014.

23 "Che dunque ne dicono i Dotti, e cosa si discorre frà Musici?" STRATICO, 341e, fol. 172v.

24 "I Dotti la negligono, e non vi badano perche manca loro quel grado tale pratico delle cose musiche, il quale rendesi necessario a ben intenderla, e perciò fare non possono la vera, e legitima applicazione della teoria, alla pratica [...]; I Musici per converso, mancando della cognizione de' principi teorici, non la curano, perche non la intendono. Al solo rimbombo di questa vostra espressione Diatonico Sestuplo Consonante Sistema, resta abbattuto il di loro spirito, e se poi s' incontrano nelle proporzioni della Dupla geometrica discreta, della Sesquialtera geometrica discreta etc. etc. chiudono in fretta il libro, per mai più affacciarvisi." ("The learned persons neglect it and don't care for it because they lack that practical level of musical things,

practical musicians who have theoretical knowledge, and only those theorists who are also practical musicians, can discuss music in a complete and proper way. Two such examples are, of course, both Tartini and Stratico.

In *Nuovo sistema musicale* and *Tratatto di musica* we can find similar statements – "Musicopratici" ("practical musicians") and "Musicoteorici" ("music theorists"), or "Persone illuminate e dotte" ("enlightened and learned persons"), as scientists. This is particularly present in the discussion on common terms of the different subjects of the music system. Another name for music theorists is also "parecchi autori più rinomati di questo secolo" ("several most reputable authors of this century").[25]

As a separate group, we can find the "Filarmonici", used in the introduction of the version 341a, with whom Stratico himself identifies:

> "The Philharmonics taught in it [music as science] will thus have greater incentive to discuss in this new study, which is exposed by me to them in the present short work, free from the difficulties which want to retain our minds [...]."[26]

That group also includes those "amanti e studiosi di tale scienza" ("lovers and scholars/researchers of this science"), mentioned in the version of the *Trattato* 343d.[27]

As ideas, these groups are very clear, but several questions arise: did Stratico have conversational partners also in Sanguinetto; did he only refer to past Paduan days or did he participate (at least through the cor-

---

which is necessary to understand it well, and therefore they cannot make the true and legitimate application of the theory into practice [...] Musicians conversely, lacking the knowledge of the theoretical principles, pay no attention to it, because they do not understand it. At a single rumble of your expression Diatonic Sextuple Consonant System, their spirit remains knocked down, and if they find themselves in the geometrical discrete proportion of dupla, geometrical discrete proportion of sesquialtera etc. etc. they close quickly the book, not to look at it ever again.") STRATICO, 343e, fols. 172v-173r.

25 STRATICO, 341a, fol. 2r.
26 "Avranno quindi più forte stimolo i Filarmonici addottrinati in essa di versare in questo nuovo studio, che da me lor si esibisce nella presente breve opera, sgombro dalle difficoltà, che arrestar soglion le menti nostre [...]." STRATICO, 341a, fols. 2r-v.
27 STRATICO, 343d, fol. 121r.

respondence, as the letter to Vallotti indicates) in music events or discussions in Padua or elsewhere ...

3. Other references

This group refers to the names/persons (in the main text or at the margin) that are mentioned by Stratico, but not in terms of the content. They are, however, important for understanding the context.

In *Lo spirito Tartiniano*, Stratico mentions (always in connection with Tartini's treatises) "Mr. le Serre, vostro [Tartini's] critico" ("Mr le Serre, your critique"),[28] i.e. Jean-Adam Serre (1704-1788), Swiss physicist, chemist, painter and music theorist who, in his work *Observations sur les principes de l'harmonie* published in 1763, questioned the theories of D'Alembert, Tartini and Geminiani.[29] One can also find the name of "Mr Rameau insigne Musico Francese" ("Mr Rameau, famous French musician").[30] Jean-Philippe Rameau (1683-1764) and his work in the field of music theory marked the entire century and he was widely known. His connections with the Italian (Paduan) circle, as well as similarities with and differences from Paduan theories were researched by Patrizio Barbieri.[31] One of the future tasks is to put Stratico in this context. Another name in this category is Andrea Zotti, who will be mentioned in more detail later in the text.

The mention of places/towns in Stratico's treatises is rare. We can distinguish either direct or indirect types of reference.

The crucial place for Stratico is Padua. From *Lo spirito Tartiniano*, we can understand the change of the environment and the influence on Stratico's life and work:

> "I, who live in an almost complete solitude, and what is worse, distant and distracted, because of my duties and occupations, from musical thoughts, that formed for a while my delights, I do not know surely and certainly what to answer you about your research."[32]

---

28   STRATICO, 343e, fol. 172r.
29   COHEN, http://www.oxfordmusiconline.com/subscriber/article/grove/music/ 25488, 7.4.2014.
30   STRATICO, 343e, fol. 174v.
31   See BARBIERI, 1987, 1991.
32   "Io, che vivo in una quasi solitudine, e quel ch'è peggio lontano, e distratto, a causa delle mie cure, ed occupazioni de' musici pensieri, che pur anno

Although he does not mention Padua or Sanguinetto here, connecting the information with the other data (of his employment as a "vicario" from 1760), we can assume that he talks about these two places. Another, even more important conclusion is that Stratico kept his (vital) connections with Padua even after his transfer to Sanguinetto, which is specifically important in Stratico's case for the acquisition of the literature (the books of Tartini and Vallotti).

> "I'll tell you the truth, and that is how I acquired your [Tartini's] Music treatise according to true harmonic science from a certain practical musician [on the margin: That was Mr. Andrea Zotti, violinist at the cappella of the Saint in Padua] who in desperation to come to his senses, begged me to take it as a gift, almost as if he wanted to unburden himself of a harassing and useless weight; and I've later found gladly this purchase, and I wanted resolutely to pay the right price."[33]

In this quotation, we can find the name of Andrea Zotti (or De Zotti), violinist of the Basilica in Padua from 1735 to 1788, member of the family of professional violinists with whom Stratico seems to have been in contact even after his transfer to Sanguinetto.[34]

The present study takes into consideration the names of people and places mentioned in the theoretical work of Giuseppe Michele Stratico. They are divided into several categories that indicate the importance of particular ways of referencing within Stratico's treatises and related writings. As it is shown, these references are important for understanding Stratico's position and his ideas behind his musical system. This especially applies to the quoted sources in the text and in the sketches. The

---

    formate un tempo le mie delizie, non sò che rispondervi di sicuro, e certo sopra le ricerche vostre." STRATICO, 343e, fol. 172r.

33 "Vi dirò cosa verissima, e si è, l' aver io, fatto acquisto del vr~o Trattato di musica secondo la vera scienza, dell'Armonia, da certo Musicopratico* [on the margins:] /*Questi fù il Sr Andrea Zotti, violinista nella capella del Santo di Padova / che disperando di giugnere[!] [giungere] alla sua intelligenza, pregòmi a riceverlo in dono, quasichè sgravarsi volesse di peso molesto, ed inutile; ed a me poi riuscì grato l'acquisto, ed hò voluto risolutamte pagarne il giusto suo prezzo." 343, fol. 173r.

34 BOSCOLO/PIETRIBIASI, 1997, p. 37.

two primary sources for Stratico's treatises are Giuseppe Tartini's and Francescantonio Vallotti's theoretical writings. But, Stratico also made a detachment from both authorities, seeking a different (even braver) approach to what was then common practice. The ideas of the musical system from which he started to develop his own musical thinking are, thus, changed and shaped into a new system, which was disseminated further (cf. the example of the *Fogli con dichiarazioni*). Given the relative scarcity of clearly stated sources, additional sources (and associated names) could be found in a more detailed analysis of the contents of the treatises (reading "between the lines"), which shall be dealt with in a further study. Particular general references, although they do not contain specific names, reveal the tradition in which Stratico formed his theoretical thinking and the audience with which he wanted to communicate. He considered himself a practical musician, not a scientist. However, in clear opposition to Eximeno's counter-scientific discourse and with his commitment to music as a science, Stratico wanted to balance the two (not necessarily opposite) sides. In some cases, although not often, some details of Stratico's biography or the context of his activities can be revealed. Thus, the idea in the MusMig project of creating an interactive map also offers a great possibility for the wider understanding of paths and overlaps in the (hi)stories with which we are dealing.

Manuscript sources

SBERTI, ANTONIO BONAVENTURA, Memorie intorno l'abate Ant.o Bonaventura Dr. Sberti, Padovano, scritte da lui medesimo in 9bre 1814, I-Pci, Ms. B. P. 1479/V.

STRATICO, GIUSEPPE MICHELE, Nuovo sistema musicale, I-Vnm, Ms. It. Cl. IV, 341a [=5294], fols. 1-22.

ID., Nuovo sistema musicale, I-Vnm, Ms. It. Cl. IV, 341b [= 5294], fols. 23-130.

ID., Fogli con dichiarazioni, I-Vnm, Ms. It. Cl. IV, 341c [= 5294], fols. 157-168.

ID., Trattato di musica, I-Vnm, Ms. It. Cl. IV, 343a [= 5348], fols. 1-49.

ID., Trattato di musica, I-Vnm, Ms. It. Cl. IV, 343d [= 5348], fols. 104-170.

ID., Lo spirito Tartiniano, I-Vnm, Ms. It. Cl. IV, 343e [= 5348], fols. 171-191.

Literature

BARBIERI, PATRIZIO, Martini e gli armonisti 'fisico-matematici' Tartini, Rameau, Riccati, Vallotti, in: Padre Martini. Musica e cultura nel settecento europeo, ed. by ANGELO POMPILIO, Florence 1987, pp. 173-209.

ID., Calegari, Vallotti, Riccati e le teorie armoniche di Rameau: priorità, concordanze, contrasti, in: Rivista Italiana di Musicologia 26, 2 (1991), pp. 241-302.

BLAŽEKOVIĆ, ZDRAVKO, Elementi za životopis Josipa Mihovila Stratica [Contributions to the biography of Giuseppe Michele Stratico], in: Radovi Zavoda za povijesne znanosti JAZU u Zadru [Papers of the Institute for Historical Sciences of the Yugoslav Academy of Sciences and Arts in Zadar] 32 (1990), pp. 109-138.

BOSCOLO, LUCIA/PIETRABASI, MADDALENA, La cappella musicale Antoniana di Padova nel secolo XVIII: delibere della Veneranda Arca, Padua 1997.

CANALE, MARGHERITA, I concerti solistici di Giuseppe Tartini. Testimoni, tradizione e catalogo tematico, PhD Università di Padova 2010, http://paduaresearch.cab.unipd.it/3658/, 20.8.2014.

COHEN, ALBERT, Serre, Jean-Adam, in: Grove Music Online, http://www.oxfordmusiconline.com/subscriber/article/grove/music/25488, 7.4.2014.

DAMSCHRODER, DAVID/WILLIAMS, DAVID RUSSELL, Music Theory from Zarlino to Schenker: a Bibliography and Guide, New York 1990.

DUCKLES, VINCENT/ELMER, MINNIE, Thematic Catalog of a Manuscript Collection of 18th-Century Italian Instrumental Music in the University of California, Berkeley 1963.

HORACE, The Satires. Book I: Satire I, translated by A.S. Kline, 2005, http://www.poetryintranslation.com/PITBR/Latin/HoraceSatires BkISatI.htm, 7.4.2014.

KONFIC, LUCIJA, Josip Mihovil Stratico u Sanguinettu – nova otkrića o skladateljevom životu i smrti [Giuseppe Michele Stratico in Sanguinetto – new discoveries on the composer's life and death], in: Arti musices, 43, 1 (2012), pp. 89-99.

LINDLEY, MARK, Der Tartini-Schüler Michele Stratico, in: Gesellschaft für Musikforschung: Kongress-Bericht, Bayreuth 1981, pp. 366-370.

MANN, FRANCIA FITCH, Michele Stratico: The Opus 1, "Sei Sonate", and an Edition of Sonatas No. 2 and No. 6 (Volumes I and II), DMA diss., Univ. of Nebraska 1992.

RICCATI, GIORDANO, Memorie sul violinista G. Tartini (1774), in: Il Santo 9 (1969), pp. 407-423.

ROEDER, MICHAEL THOMAS, Sonatas, Concertos and Symphonies of Michele Stratico, PhD diss., Univ. of California 1971.

VALENTINELLI, GIUSEPPE (ed.), Biblioteca manuscripta ad S. Marci Venetiarum, vol. 1, Venezia 1868, http://www.mdz-nbn-resolving.de/urn/resolver.pl?urn=urn:nbn:de:bvb:12-bsb10800292-1, 1.11.2014.

List of Contributors

Norbert Dubowy has held grants from the Centro tedesco di studi veneziani in Venice and the German Research Council (Deutsche Forschungsgemeinschaft). He has been a Research Fellow at the German Historical Institute in Rome (Istituto Storico Germanico di Roma) and has taught in various universities in Europe and the US. He currently holds the position of Managing Editor of the *Digital Mozart Edition* at the Mozarteum Foundation, Salzburg. His research interests include music of the 17th and 18th centuries, especially Italian opera, the orchestra and orchestral music, Alessandro Scarlatti, and textual criticism. Contact: dubowy@mozarteum.at.

Britta Kägler is a historian of early modern history with a special interest in regional and cultural history. She is a Research Fellow and Lecturer at the LMU (University of Munich) Department of Bavarian and Regional History, with a focus on medieval and early modern history. Her research interests include social and cultural history, transcultural and intercultural relations, and economic history. To satisfy these interests she has been working on early modern court culture and migratory musicians, and she is currently focussing on building history in the baroque period. Contact: b.kaegler@lmu.de.

Vjera Katalinić is the Scientific Adviser and Director of the Department for the History of Croatian Music, Croatian Academy of Sciences and Arts, in Zagreb, as well as a Full Professor at the Music Academy of the University of Zagreb. Since 2013 she has directed the HERA project "Music Migrations in the Early Modern Age: the Meeting of the European East, West and South" (2013-2016). Her fields of interest are 18th-

century instrumental music and 19th-century opera, as well as musical collections and archives in Croatia. Contact: fides@hazu.hr.

Metoda Kokole is a Research Adviser at the Institute of Musicology at the Scientific Research Centre of the Slovenian Academy of Sciences and Arts; from 2005 also Head of the Institute. Her research focuses on the history of music on the territory of present-day Slovenia from the 16th to the 18th century. She is the General Editor of the series *Monumenta artis musicae Sloveniae*, the leader of the national group for RILM in Slovenia and the author of seven music editions and numerous articles. She is the Principal Investigator of the Slovenian partner group in the HERA MusMig project (2013-2016). Contact: metoda.kokole@zrc-sazu.si.

Lucija Konfic is an assistant and a librarian at the Department for the History of Croatian Music, Croatian Academy of Sciences and Arts, Zagreb. In 2011 she started her PhD studies at the Universität für Musik und darstellende Kunst in Graz on the topic "Giuseppe Michele Stratico's theoretical treatises" (supervisor: Prof. Dr. sc. Klaus Aringer). She has a special interest in several subjects: G.M. Stratico's theoretical treatises, music theory in the 18th century, the digitization of musical materials, and the organization and preservation of music collections. Contact: lucijam@hazu.hr.

Joachim Kremer studied school music and music education at the Lübeck University of Music. Thereafter, he studied musicology, art history and philosophy at the Christian-Albrechts-Universität, Kiel. After his *Habilitation* at the University of Music, Drama and Media in Hannover he became, in 2001, Professor of Musicology at the State University of Music and Performing Arts, Stuttgart. His key research areas are: music und musical history from the 15th to the 20th century, French music 1870-1920, socio-historical, institutional historical, professional historical and local historical aspects and questions of historiography. Contact: joachim.kremer@mh-stuttgart.de.

Jan Kusber is a Professor of the History of Eastern Europe at the Johannes Gutenberg University, Mainz, since 2003. He is currently working on a book dealing with the political reforms of Catherine the Great. Contact: kusber@uni-mainz.de.

List of Contributors

Aneta Markuszewska studied musicology at Warsaw University, and harpsichord at the Frédéric Chopin Academy of Music in Warsaw and the Hochschule für Musik in Würzburg. In July 2011 she received a doctorate for her thesis *Festa and Music at the Court of Maria Casimira Sobieska in Rome (1699-1714)*. This study was published in December 2012 as *Festa i muzyka na dworze Marii Kazimiery Sobieskiej w Rzymie (1699-1714)*, Warsaw 2012. The book received an award from the association of Polish musicologists, ZKP (Society of Polish Composers) and by the Rector of Warsaw University and the Dean of the Department of History. She was a member, in the years 2012-2014, of the European project ENBaCH (European Network for Baroque Cultural Heritage), and from 2013 a member of the HERA (Humanities in the European Research Area) project. She is interested in music of the 17th and 18th centuries. Contact: amarkuszewska@hotmail.com.

Gesa zur Nieden is a Junior Professor of Musicology at the Johannes Gutenberg University, Mainz. After completing her German and French doctoral studies on the Théâtre du Châtelet in Paris, she worked for the German Historical Institute in Rome. She was the German director of the ANR/DFG project "MUSICI" from 2010 to 2013, and has been a leader of the HERA project "MusMig" since the middle of 2013. The main focus of her research is on the cultural history of music and on the sociology of music, especially in relation to music and mobility in early modern Europe, and on ethnographical research into the contemporary reception of Richard Wagner and his music. Contact: znieden@uni-mainz.de.

Berthold Over is a Research Associate at the University of Mainz. He wrote his PhD on music at the Venetian *ospedali* in the 18th century. Before joining the HERA project "MusMig" in 2013 he worked for the research project "The Cantata as an Aristocratic Medium of Expression in Rome during Handel's Time (c. 1695-1715)", funded by the Fritz Thyssen Foundation (2010-2013). His main research interests lie in the cultural history of music in a European context. In addition, he concerns himself with the economic background of music, especially with regard to the Munich court. He has discovered unknown autographs by Antonio Vivaldi and George Frideric Handel. Contact: over@uni-mainz.de.

Rashid-S. Pegah (born in 1978) is a cultural historian. He has worked as a research assistant on projects organized by the Bach-Archiv Leipzig (sponsored by the Alfried Krupp von Bohlen und Halbach Foundation), the Bavarian Academy of Sciences, Munich, and the Foundation "Prussian Palaces and Gardens Berlin-Brandenburg Potsdam". Between 1993 and 2003 he collaborated on several broadcasts by the editorial department for early music of the former radio station Sender Freies Berlin. Contact: eskender.dishar@gmail.com

Jana Perutková teaches at the Institute of Musicology, Faculty of Arts, Masaryk University, Brno (from 1996 as an Assistant Professor, since 2013 as an Associate Professor). Her research and teaching activities focus primarily on music of the 18th century. Her current theme is Italian opera and oratorio in Moravia and the Habsburg Empire in the early 18th century. Her *Habilitation* study is the book *František Antonín Míča in the Service of Count Questenberg and Italian Opera in Jaroměřice* (Prague, 2011). In the past she has been a coordinator of the internationally successful projects "The Italian Opera in Moravia in the First Half of the 18th Century" and "Research of the Opera Repertoire in Bohemian Lands during the Baroque Period". She is currently involved in the project "Research Probes into the History of Musical Culture in Moravia, Especially in Brno" at the Masaryk University. She also participates in the organization of various conferences. Contact: perutkov@phil.muni.cz.

Barbara Przybyszewska-Jarmińska is Professor and Head of the Department of Musicology in the Institute of Art of the Polish Academy of Sciences in Warsaw, and editor-in-chief of the series *Monumenta Musicae in Polonia*. Her main area of research is the history of music of the late Renaissance and Baroque periods in the Commonwealth of Poland and Lithuania in relation to neighbouring countries and to Italy. She is also interested in the theory and practice of the critical editing of early music. Contact: barbara.przybyszewska-jarminska@ispan.pl.

Rudolf Rasch is a musicologist who for many years taught the theory and history of music at the Department of Musicology of Utrecht University (Netherlands). Since his retirement he has remained affiliated to Utrecht University as a "guest" researcher. Among his interests are the musical history of the Netherlands, especially in the 17th and 18th centuries, the history of music printing and publishing, and the works of composers such as Corelli, Vivaldi, Geminiani and Boccherini. He has published books, articles and editions related to those topics. He is the General Editor of the Complete Edition of the Works of Francesco Geminiani published by Ut Orpheus Edizioni (Bologna). Contact: r.a.rasch@uu.nl.

Torsten Roeder has worked as a digital humanities specialist in the editorial project "Richard Wagner Schriften" at the Institut für Musikforschung of the Julius-Maximilians-University, Würzburg, since 2014, and participated earlier in the music migration research projects "MUSICI" and "MusMig". His major fields of research are music criticism in the 19th century, choral music and conducting, and Italian studies. Contact: torsten.roeder@uni-wuerzburg.de.

Matthias Schnettger is Professor of Early Modern History at the Johannes Gutenberg University, Mainz. His research interests embrace the Holy Roman Empire and small principalities and republics in Germany and Italy as well as diplomacy and the processes of transfer and exchange in early modern Europe. Contact: schnettger@uni-mainz.de.

Jana Spáčilová graduated in musicology at the Charles University, Prague (2001). She subsequently received her PhD degree from the Masaryk University, Brno (2007). At the Masaryk University she has participated in research projects concerning baroque opera in the Czech Lands. Between 2007 and 2014 she has worked as curator for early music in the Department of Music History, Moravian Museum, Brno. Since 2014 she has been an Assistant Professor in the Department of Musicology of the Palacký University, Olomouc. She specializes in baroque music in Central Europe, predominantly Italian opera and oratorio. Contact: jana.spacilova@upol.cz.

Michael Talbot is Emeritus Professor of Music at the University of Liverpool. He is best known for his studies and editions of Italian, particularly Venetian, music between 1650 and 1750, his most recent book being *The Vivaldi Compendium*. More recently, he has begun to explore the byways of music in 18th-century Britain and Ireland, in particular that written by Italian visitors and immigrants, as well as that of English musicians who settled in Italy. Contact: mtalbot@liverpool.ac.uk.

Colin Timms is a Professor Emeritus at the University of Birmingham, where he held the Peyton and Barber Chair of Music from 1992 to 2012. He is a trustee of the Handel Institute and of the Gerald Coke Handel Foundation, and Honorary President of the Forum Agostino Steffani. His publications include books and articles on Steffani, essays on Stradella and Handel, and editions of music by all three composers, including *Theodora* (Hallische Händel-Ausgabe) and the first edition of Handel's *Comus* (Novello, forthcoming). Contact: c.r.timms@bham.ac.uk.

Stanislav Tuksar is a retired Professor of Musicology at the Department of Musicology, Academy of Music, University of Zagreb, Croatia, and a participant in the HERA project "Music Migrations in the Early Modern Age: the Meeting of the European East, West and South (MusMig)". He has published 24 books and over 200 articles in Croatian and international journals and proceedings, dealing mostly with the history of Croatian music from the 16th to the 19th century and the aesthetics of music. Since 2000 he has been Editor-in-Chief of the *International Review of the Aesthetics and Sociology of Music* and a full member of the Croatian Academy of Sciences and Arts. Contact: stanislavtuxar@gmail.com.

Alina Żórawska-Witkowska is a Professor at Warsaw University's Musicological Institute, where she directs the Department of General Music History. Her research focuses on baroque and classical music history: in particular, the musical culture of Poland and the dissemination of Italian opera. She is the author of four books – *Muzyczne podróże królewiczów polskich* (Warsaw, 1992), *Muzyka na dworze i w teatrze Stanisława Augusta*, (Warsaw, 1995), *Muzyka na dworze Augusta II w Warszawie* (Warsaw, 1997), *Muzyka na polskim dworze Augusta III*, (Lublin, 2012) – and of over 150 articles published in Poland, Italy, Germany and other European countries. Contact: azorwit@plusnet.pl.

Index of Persons

A

Abell, John 299
Adelaide of Susa, Adelaide of Italy (or Burgundy), (Cath. Saint) 332
Alberti, Amalie Antonie 262
Alberti, Giuseppe Matteo 296, 315
Alberti, Giuseppe Nicola (Josephus Nicolaus) 259, 262, 268, 270
Alberti, Pietro 303
Albertini, Gioacchino 157
Albicastro, Henrico 299
Albinoni, Tomaso 258f., 296f., 302f., 306, 314f.
Albrecht V of Bavaria, Duke 77-79
Albuzzi, Ottavio 257, 270, 279, 286
Albuzzi-Todeschini, Teresa 154
Aldrovandini, Giuseppe 296
Aleksey I Mikhailovich Romanov, Tsar 380
Alembert, Jean-Baptiste Le Rond, d' 397
Alexander VII (Chigi, Fabio), Pope 380, 384
Alghisi, Paris Francesco 139
Alibert, Antonio d', Count 329f.
Ambrosini 222
Ammetto, Fabrizio 297
André, Louis 153
Andreides, Rosalia → Holzbauer, Rosalia
Andreis, Josip 383
Anerio, Giovanni Francesco 136
Anet, Jean-Baptiste 101, 117
Anfossi, Pasquale 181
Anglebert, Jean-Henri d' 298
Anna Ivanovna, Empress of Russia 153, 159-161
Anne of Austria, Queen of Poland 136
Annibali, Domenico 154, 335
Antoniotto, Giorgio 300
Apollini, Salvatore 161
Araja, Francesco 160
Arco, Johann Baptist von, Count 104, 121
Arena, Giuseppe 353-356, 363, 367, 373
Arrigoni, Francesco 281, 370
Attems, family 28, 341-342, 347, 351-354, 356, 358-366
Attems, Christina Crescentia von, Countess, née Herberstein, Christina Crescentia von 344
Attems, Crescenzia Maria Anna Francisca von 348
Attems, Dismas Maximilian Siegmund Engelbert Franz von, Count 347
Attems, Ferdinand von 363
Attems, Ignaz Maria I Maximilian Dismas Josef Leander von, Count 344, 346, 362
Attems, Ignaz Maria II (Ignaz Leander) von, Count 341-352, 354-357, 360, 362-365

Attems, Ignaz Maria III von, Count 363
Attems, Johannes 342
Attems, Josef Bernhard Maria von, Count 348
Attems, Maria Josepha von, Countess, née Khuen zu Auer von Belasi-Lichtenberg, Maria Josepha 341-343, 347f., 350, 352, 360, 362, 364
Attems, Maria Sophia Clara von, née Herberstein-Pusterwald, Maria Sophia Clara von 344
Attems, Thaddäus Kajetan Bernhard Maria von, Count 348
Attems-Gilleis, Victor 342
Attems-Heiligenkreuz, Ignaz Maria Maximilian Dismas Josef Alexander von → Attems, Ignaz Maria II von, Count
Attems-Heiligenkreuz, Franz Dismas Hermann von, Count 344f., 362
Aubin, Hermann 54
Augerneder, Veith 109, 122
Augustus II Wettin, King of Poland (Frederick Augustus I of Saxony) 151-153, 159, 161, 217, 335
Augustus III Wettin, King of Poland (Frederick Augustus II of Saxony) 151f., 154-157. 160-164
Auletta, Pietro 354
Autgartten, Franz 223
Autgartten, Maximilian 222
Avison, Charles 312f., 315-320
Ayala, Sebastiano d' 175

B

Baab, Jerrold 141
Bach, Carl Philipp Emanuel 208f.
Bach, Johann Christian 208, 219
Bach, Johann Sebastian 46, 53, 66, 209, 228
Bade, Klaus J. 74
Baglioni, Antonio 155

Bajamonti, Julije (Giulio) 178-180
Balatri, Ferrante 110f.
Balatri, Filippo 109-111, 113, 121, 232, 241-251
Balbi, Lorenzo 296
Baldassini, Antonio Luigi 296
Balthasar, Ignaz 105, 119
Baltzar, Thomas 37
Bambini, Eustachio 257, 260f.
Bambini, Laura 257-259, 270, 284
Banti, Brigida 155
Barberini, Maffeo → Urban VIII, Pope
Barbieri, family 220
Barbieri, Antonio 285
Barbieri, Faustino 219f.
Barbieri, Livia 285
Barbieri, Maria (Marietta) 219f.
Barbieri, Patrizio 397
Barez 222
Barthel, Rosemarie 227
Bartoli, Antonio 297
Bartoli, Bartolomeo 103, 118, 120
Bartscher, Matthias Valentin 101, 117
Bassani, Giovanni Battista 296
Bassegli, Tommaso (Toma) 171
Bassi, Luigi 155
Battaglini, Domenico 259, 270
Battistini, Giacomo 296
Bees-Majerin, Rosalia 264
bei der Wieden, Helge 62
Bellisani Buini, Cecilia 283
Bellori, Giuseppe 392
Benda, Franz (František) 153
Berengar of Spoleto, Duke 332f.
Berg, Adam (Adam Montanus) 79
Berglund, Lars 141
Bernabei, Ercole 42, 80, 94
Bernardi, "Senesino", Francesco 228
Bernardi, Bartolomeo 296, 303
Bernardini, "di Capua", Marcello 174
Bernasconi, Andrea 28, 81-84, 353f., 358-362, 368-371
Bernasconi, Antonia 83f.
Bernhard, Christoph 138, 143
Bernina, Veneranda 263
Bernucci, Anna Davia de 155

Bertolusi, Vincenzo 137
Besozzi, Carlo 156
Bianchi, Giovanni 263, 269
Bianchini, Francesco 323f.
Biarelle, Johann Adolph 212
Biarelle, Johann Franz (Giovanni Francesco) 211f., 223
Biarelle, Paul Amadé 212
Biffi, Gioseffo 64
Binetti, Anna 156
Birckenstock, Johann Adam 304
Bitti, Martino 297
Blažeković, Zdravko 389
Blichmann, Diana 218
Blovy, Gregoire 101, 117
Bluemb (Pluemb), Johann 158f.
Boenicke, Jonas Friedrich 227, 229-238
Boethius 384
Böhmer, Lorenz 104, 121
Boivin, Jacques 298
Bombarda, Giovanni Paolo 94, 99-101, 114
Bonafini, Caterina 155
Bonaventura Sberti, Antonio 390
Bonel 101, 116
Bonis, Igniatio de 333
Bononcini, Giovanni Maria 297
Bonporti, Francesco Antonio 296
Bordoni, Faustina 81f., 217f., 369
Borosini, Francesco 277-279
Bošković, Ruđer (Boscovich, Ruggiero), Abbot 176, 178
Bousset, Jean-Baptiste de 298
Boyd, Malcolm 311
Brade, William 37
Brambilla, Antonio 172, 280
Braubach, Max 212
Brescianello, Giovanni Antonio 304
Brescianello, Giuseppe 103, 112, 118, 120
Breunich, Johann Michael 154
Breyer, Mirko 383
Brivio, Giuseppe Ferdinando 288
Brocchi, Giovanni Battista 155
Brogniez 222

Broschi, "Farinelli", Carlo 162-165, 210
Broschi, Riccardo 357f.
Brühl, Heinrich von, Count 155, 161-163
Brunerio, Michelangelo 143
Bruscolini, Pasquale 154
Buini, Giuseppe Maria 283
Bull, John 37
Burger, Johann Caspar (Hans Kaspar) 100, 117, 119
Burney, Charles 173f.
Bussani, Giovanni Francesco 333
Bustijn, Pieter 299
Butir, Leonid Mironovich 158
Bütner, Crato 143f.
Buxtehude, Dietrich 141, 143f.

C

Caix d'Hervelois, Louis de 298
Cajo, Bartolomeo 258, 270
Caldara, Antonio 258, 261, 275, 296
Camati Brambilla, "La Farinella", Maria 280, 283, 285
Campioni, Carlo Antonio 393
Campra, André 298
Capua, Rinaldo di 173f., 352, 354f., 357, 365-367
Capuano, Angela 283
Capuzzi, Giuseppe Antonio 393
Caramuel y Lobkowitz, Juan, Bishop 380, 384
Cardini, Rosa 259, 270
Carissimi, Giacomo 141-143
Čart, Jiří → Zarth, Georg
Casanova, Giovanna 154f., 160f.
Casarini, Domenica 263, 271
Casarini, Giacobbo 263
Castrucci, Pietro 303
Catherine Jagiellon, Queen of Sweden 135
Cattani, Dario Luca 259, 271
Cavalli, Francesco 37
Cecilia (Cäcilia) Renata of Austria, Queen of Poland 138, 142

Chareau, Antoine 296, 307
Charles II, King of Spain 99
Charles III Philip, Elector Palatine 193, 195, 218
Charles III, King of Spain → Charles VI
Charles Theodore of Pfalz-Sulzbach, Elector Palatine, Elector of Bavaria 193, 195f.
Charles VI of Austria, Holy Roman Emperor 108, 325f., 346
Charles VII, Holy Roman Emperor (Karl Albrecht, Elector of Bavaria) 105, 109
Chastelin 222
Chauvon, François 298
Chigi, Fabio → Alexander VII, Pope
Chiocchetti, Pietro Vincenzo 354
Christian IV, King of Denmark and Norway 136f.
Christian IV of Pfalz-Zweibrücken, Duke 195
Christian of Saxe-Weißenfels, Duke 229f.
Christina I Vasa, Queen of Sweden 324, 332
Cignoni, Francesco 103, 118, 120
Cimarosa, Domenico 156f.
Clark, Brian 227
Clavareau, Victoire 155
Clement IX (Rospigliosi, Giulio), Pope 325
Clérambault, Nicolas 93
Clossé, Clementina 214
Colbeaut 222
Comans 223
Constance of Austria, Queen of Poland 136
Conti, "Il Ghiziello", Gioachino 356
Conti, Ignazio Maria 275, 288
Cooke, Benjamin 313, 315-318
Corbett, William 298, 304, 315
Corbisier 222
Cordoba y Lante, Alejandro Fernandet de 352, 373
Corelli, Arcangelo 296f., 300-303, 314-317

Cornillor (Cornillio) 222
Corradi, Vincenzo 103, 118, 120
Cosimi, Anna 258, 262, 271
Cosimi, Nicola 297
Cosimo III de' Medici, Grand Duke 109, 241
Costantini, Antonio 160, 258, 260
Costantini, Giacinta → Spinola Costantini, Giacinta
Coste, Emanuel-Jean de la 296, 306f.
Couvin, Franz 103, 118
Crisanio, Giorgio → Križanić
Crisanius, Georgius → Križanić
Cron (Krenn) 223
Cuzzoni, Francesca 286f.
Czanczik, Józef 154
Czirenberg, Constantia 142
Czirenberg, Hans 142

D

D'Alay, Mauro 296
Dall'Abaco, Pietro Evaristo Felice 98, 100, 116, 303
Damschroder, David 394
Dandrieu, Jean-François 298
Dandrieu, Jeanne-Françoise 93
Danzi, Franziska → Le Brun, Franziska
Dauflise, Bonne 105, 120
Dechars (de Chars, Deschars), Pierre (?) 101, 117f.
Dedekind, Constantin Christian 138
Degli Antoni (Antonii), Pietro 296
Degrimon 222
Deibner (Teybner), Felix Emanuel Cajetan 94f., 99, 111, 114
Deibner (Teybner), Hans Caspar 95
Deibner (Teybner), Johann Anton Franz 95
Deibner (Teybner), Sigmund Joseph Victor Amadee 95
Delfini (Dolfini), Cecilia → Ramis, Cecilia
Della Parte, Anna Caterina 271, 288f.

Index of Persons

Delvincour 222
Demović, Miho 181
Denzio, Antonio 258-261, 283
Deridder 222
Descartes, René 384
Deseschaliers, Louis 153
Desprez, Josquin 36
Devoti, Andrea 267
di Bologna, Teresa → Zanardi, Teresa
di Capua, Marcello → Bernadini, Marcello
Dieupart, François 298
Dithmar, Dorothea 12f.
Döbel, Heinrich 144
Domenico, Don 272
Doni, Giovanni Battista 384
Donnini, Girolamo 222
Dowland, John 37
Draghi, Giovanni Battista 37
Drese, Adam 138
Du Breil, Jean Pierre 105, 119
Du Breil (Dubreil), Pierre 105, 120
Du Clos, Catherine 120
du Croux 222
Du Fay, Guillaume 36
Düben, Gustav 143f.
Dubowy, Norbert 26
Dubuisson, Gabriel 106, 119
Duckles, Vincent 389f.
Dupré, Louis 153
Dussek (Dusík), Jan Ladislav (Johann Ladislaus) 156

E

Ebenpöck, Abraham 100, 116
Eckhardt (Eckardt), Maria Anna 281
Edzard II of East Frisia, Count 54
Eitner, Robert 382
Eleonora Maria of Austria, Queen of Poland 139
Eleonor Magdalene of Pfalz-Neuburg, Holy Roman Empress 326
Elisabeth I, Queen of England 63
Ellmer, Johann Conrad 234f.
Elmer, Minnie 390
Engelhardt, Christoph 227
Erben, Balthasar 144
Ernst August I of Saxe-Weimar, Duke 230
Ernst Friedrich II of Saxe-Hildburghausen, Duke 233, 234
Ernst III of Holstein-Schaumburg, Count 56f., 61-65
Eschwiller, Wilhelm 223
Evelyn, John 220
Eximeno, Antonio 394, 399

F

Fabio, Marco 271, 357
Fabri 223
Fabris, Abbate 289
Facco, Giacomo 303
Fadini, Andrea 296
Fagniani 222
Fantasia, Filippo Neri del 256, 258, 260, 269
Fantasia, Rosalia 258, 271
Fanti, Mauro 265
Farinel, Jean Baptiste 210
Farinella → Camati Brambilla, Maria
Farinelli → Broschi, Carlo
Fasch, Johann Friedrich 234
Favier, Jean 153
Federhofer-Königs, Renate 55
Feodor (Theodore) III Alexeyevich of Russia, Tsar 381
Ferdinand III, Holy Roman Emperor 18
Ferrandini, Giovanni 305
Ferraresi Del Bene, Adriana 155
Ferrari, Domenico 393
Fétis, François-Joseph 382
Filonardi, Mario 142
Finazzi, Filippo 361
Findeizen, Nikolai 159
Finger, Gottfried 37, 298
Fink, Johann Franz 100
Fink, Matthias Anton 100, 117, 119

Finscher, Ludwig 56
Finsterbusch, Ignaz 259, 271
Fiocco, Pietro Antonio 93, 303
Fiorè, Andrea 296
Fiorè, Angelo Maria 296
Fischenschildt, Paul → Führschildt, Paul
Fischer, Johann Christian 155
Fivé, Peter 94, 96, 114
Flaccus, Quintus Horatius 395
Flemment 223
Flora, Margarita 258, 271
Fonpré, Jean de 153
Fornarini, Antonio 265-267
Förster, Kaspar the Elder 142
Förster, Kaspar the Younger 135, 138, 140, 142-145
Fortis, Alberto, Abbot 171
Franchi, Giovanni Pietro 296
Francœur, Louis 298
Frederick August I, Elector of Saxony → Augustus II Wettin, King of Poland
Frederick August II, Elector of Saxony → Augustus III Wettin, King of Poland
Frederick I of Wurttemberg, Duke 55, 59f., 61-63, 65
Frederick I, King of Prussia (Frederick III, Elector of Brandenburg) 300
Frederick I, King of Prussia 44
Frederick II of Saxe-Gotha-Altenburg, Duke 229-231
Frederick II, King of Prussia 181
Frederick III Jacob of Hesse-Homburg, Landgrave 229-231
Frederick III of Saxe-Gotha-Altenburg, Duke 233, 237
Frederick III, King of Denmark and Norway 137, 143
Frederick IV, Elector Palatine 54f.
Frederick V, Elector Palatine, King of Bohemia 61
Freeman, Robert 324
Frezza, Angiolo Maria 182

Frilli, Stefano 100, 116
Friedrich → Frederick
Froberger, Johann Jacob 18, 27, 297
Fugger, Christoph 66
Fugger, Marcus 66
Fugger, Paul, Graf zu Kirchberg und Weißenhorn 125
Führschildt (Fischenschildt), Paul 100
Fürstenau, Moritz von 159
Fux, Johann Joseph 304

G

Gabbiati, Giuseppe 271
Gabrieli, Giovanni 37
Gabussi, Giulio Cesare 136
Gaggiotti, Pellegrino 271
Galetti, Filippo 271
Galliard, Johann Ernst (John Ernest) 37
Gallieni, Giuseppe 154
Galuppi, Baldassare 179, 259, 261
Ganspöck, Johann Kaspar 108, 122
Ganspöck, Matthias 108, 122
Gardiol, Cantor 21-24
Gaspardini, Gasparo 296
Gasparini, Francesco 172, 329f.
Gasparini, Maria Giovanna 285, 287
Gebel, Georg 155
Geminiani, Francesco 297, 300, 312, 315, 397
Gentili, Giorgio 296
George I, King of Great Britain (Georg Ludwig, Elector of Hanover) 37, 41, 43, 325
Gerber, Ernst Ludwig 54, 81, 282
Gerbl, Cornelius 101, 117, 119
Getzmann, Wolfgang 63
Ghelen, Johann Leopold van 280, 361
Ghigiotti, Gaetano 164
Ghiziello → Conti, Gioachino
Giacomelli, Geminiano 353f., 368, 372
Giorgio, Giuseppe 263
Giornovichi, Giovanni → Jarnović, Ivan

Index of Persons

Giusti, Maria 271
Glatz, Martin 60
Gluck, Christoph Willibald 162f., 176, 179f., 354, 372
Goldberg, Johann Gottlieb 155
Goldoni, Carlo 154
Golitsyn, family 245
Golitsyn, Alexander M., Prince 241f.
Golitsyn, Boris 247f.
Golitsyn, Petr Alekseyevich, Prince 241, 243, 245, 248-251
Golitsyna, Darya 250
Golub, Ivan 383
Gori, Antonio 161
Gouvillet, Carl 106, 120
Gozze, family 176, 179, 181
Grabbe, Johann 64
Grabu, Luis 37
Graeb 223
Grandi, Alessandro 296
Gravier, Pierre 105f., 120
Greber, Jakob 37
Greber, Johann 218
Grepaldi, Cecilia 263
Grossatesta, Gaetano 335
Grossi, Andrea 296
Grossi, "Siface", Giovanni Francesco 220
Gualandi, Margherita → Moretti, Margherita
Guazzini (Guaccini), Pietro 228
Günther I of Schwarzburg-Sondershausen, Prince 237

H

Hader, Clementin → Hadersberg, Clementin von
Hadersberg, Clementin von 97, 100, 112, 114, 116
Hager, Christoph 281, 283f., 286f.
Hagius, Konrad 51-67
Hainhofer, Philipp 59f.
Hakenberger, Andreas 137
Hamilton, George 334
Handel (Händel), George Frideric (Georg Friedrich) 37f., 46, 67, 74f.,189f., 195, 208, 217, 278, 280, 298, 316, 333f.
Harrach, Franz Anton von 276
Harrer, Gottlob 155
Hasse, Johann Adolf 74f., 81, 154, 161, 192, 198, 217f., 261, 350, 352-354, 362, 364f., 367-373
Hauer 281
Haussmann (Hussmann), Valentin 59
Haveck (Havek), Anton Alexius 107f., 113, 121, 222
Haydn, Joseph 176
Haymerle, Franz 287
Hedwig Elisabeth of Pfalz-Neuburg, Countess Palatine, Princess of Poland 325f.
Heinichen, Johann David 75
Heinrich Julius of Brunswick-Wolfenbüttel → Henry Julius of Brunswick-Lüneburg
Heissler-Heitersheim, Franz Joseph von 262, 279
Helwig, Barbara 144
Henricus, Nicolaus the Younger 79
Henriette Adelaide of Savoy, Electress of Bavaria 42
Henry Julius of Brunswick-Lüneburg, Duke 62
Henry VIII, King of England 36
Henry, Pierre 105, 120
Herberstein, Christina Crescentia von → Attems, Christina Crescentia von, Countess
Herberstein, Sigismund von 242
Herberstein-Pusterwald, Maria Sophia Clara von → Attems, Maria Sophia Clara von
Heudeline, Louis 298
Heuser, Johan Christoph 12f., 15
Hiller, Johann Adam 213, 218
Hindermair, Franz Anton 106, 113, 121
Hintze, Maria 142
Hintze, Martin 142

415

Hirschmann, Wolfgang 59
Hochpain, Hyacinth 100, 117, 119
Hoffkuntz, Tobias 64
Hoffmann, Leopold 277
Hoffmann, Georg Adam 261, 275, 277-289
Holland, Johann David 157
Holstenius (Holste), Lucas 380
Holzbauer, Ignaz 257, 280, 287
Holzbauer, Rosalia, née Andreides, Rosalia 257, 270, 281, 287
Horn, Christian Friedrich 155
Hoyoul, Balduin 59
Hue, Louis 317
Humfrey, Pelham 37
Hussmann, Valentin → Haussmann, Valentin
Huwet (Heuwett, Howett), Gregorius 65

I, J

Imer (Immer), Giuseppe 280
Imer (Immer), Marianne 280
Isola, Anna 271
Ivan III, Grand prince of Moscow 244
Ivan IV, Tsar 244
Ivan V Romanow, Tsar 243
Jäcklin, Johann 79
Jacobi, Daniel 144
Jagić, Vatroslav 383
James I Stuart, King of England 40
James II Stuart, King of England 324
James III Stuart, King of England 325-327, 330, 334f.
Jamet 211, 223
Jan II Casimir (Kazimierz) Vasa, King of Poland 135, 139, 143f.
Jan III Sobieski, King of Poland 102, 135, 139, 153, 325
Jacquet de La Guerre, Élisabeth 93
Jarnović (Giornovichi), Ivan (Giovanni) 156
Jaroszewicz, Stefan 154

Jarzębski, Adam 143
Jaziomski, Dominik 154
Jenisch, Paul 55, 63, 66
Johann Friedrich of Württemberg, Duke 56, 59
Johann Theodor of Freising and Regensburg, Prince-Bishop 241
Johann Wilhelm of Pfalz-Neuburg, Elector Palatine 40f., 43, 109, 193, 195, 218, 229
Johann Wilhelm of Saxe-Eisenach, Duke 229
Johann Wilhelm of Jülich-Kleve-Berg, Duke 54
John (Johan) III Vasa, King of Sweden 135
John, Anton 264
Jommelli, Niccolò 353f., 367
Joseph Clemens of Bavaria, Archbishop-Elector of Cologne 95, 107, 194
Joseph Ferdinand of Bavaria, prince 99
Joseph I of Austria, Holy Roman Emperor 326
Joseph II of Austria, Holy Roman Emperor 174
Josquin des Prez 36

K

Kägler, Britta 26, 99
Kamieński, Maciej 156
Kämpfer, Joseph 156
Kaplan, Benjamin 246
Karl → Charles
Karll III, King of Spain → Charles VI
Karl Albrecht, Elector of Bavaria → Charles VII
Karl of Württemberg-Bernstadt-Oels, Duke 233
Kaspar, Johann 108, 119
Katalinić, Vjera 26, 186
Katarzyna Jagiellonka, Queen of Sweden → Catherine Jagiellon, Queen of Sweden

Index of Persons

Keller, Gottfried 298
Kerckhoven, Johann Philipp 93
Kerll, Johann Caspar 95, 108, 121
Kerll, Johann Christoph 108, 121
Kern, Lorenz Bruno 107, 121
Kevorkian, Tanya 73
Khan, Ayuka 247f.
Khuen zu Auer von Belasi-Lichten-
    berg, Johann Franz, Count 342
Khuen zu Auer von Belasi-Lichten-
    berg, Maria Josepha Elisabeth Au-
    gusta Claudia → Attems, Maria
    Josepha von, Countess
Kircher, Athanasius 222, 380, 384
Klaić, Vjekoslav 383
Klain 223
Kness, Johann Michael 344
Koch, Heinrich Christoph 174
Kokole, Metoda 28, 268
Konfic, Lucija 28
Konink, Servaas de 298
Korb, Johann Georg 242
Kossołowski (Kozłowski), Antoni 154
Kremer, Joachim 26
Krenn → Cron
Krieger, Johann 143
Križanić (Crisanio), Juraj (Giorgio) 379-385
Kröner, family 76, 84
Kröner, Anton 85
Kröner, Franz Karl 85
Kröner, Johann 85
Kröner, Johann Nepomuk 85
Kröner, Joseph 85
Kröner, Maria Josepha 85
Kuhnau, Johann 53
Kukuljević Sakcinski, Ivan 382
Kusber, Jan 27

L

La Barre, Michel de 298
La Grange d'Arquien, Marie Casimire
    de, Queen of Poland → Marie
    Casimire
Lamberg, Ferdinand von 288
Lambert, Michel 298,
Lambert (Lampert), Vinzenz 95, 97, 99, 101, 111, 114, 116, 222
Lampe, John Frederick 37
Lampugnani, Giovanni Battista 354, 362, 367, 369
Landmann, Ortrun 159
Lasso, Orlando di 78f.
Latilla, Gaetano 353-355, 357, 363, 373
Lauffensteiner, Wolf Jacob 106, 113, 121
Laurent, Marie 105, 120
Laurent, Pierre 105, 120
Lavigne, Pastor 22f.
Le Brun (Le Brüne), Ludwig August 84
Le Brun (Le Brüne), Franziska, née Danzi, Franziska 84
Le Cène, Michel-Charles 300, 303-308
Le Cerf 222
Le Cocq, Franz Anton 94, 96, 99f., 112, 114, 116
Le Clerc, Laurent 101, 117
Le Comte, Johann Ferdinand 106, 113, 121
Le Doux, François-Gabriel 156
Le Fevre, Marie 105, 120
le Long 222
le Petit 222
Le Picq, Charles → Picque, Charles
Le Roux, Gaspar 298
Le Teneur 222
Le Vray, Peter 97, 99f., 112, 114
Lebègue, Nicolas 298
Lebon, Gideon 65
Lechner, Leonhard 59
Leers, Consul 21-25
Lefort, François 247
Legrand 101, 116
Lehner, Anton 281, 286
Leitenroth, Johann Georg 104, 121
Lemoles, Pietro 102, 118,
Leo, Leonardo 350, 353-355, 357f., 365, 367, 371, 373

417

Leopold of Anhalt-Köthen, Prince 209, 228
Leopold Wilhelm of Austria, Archduke 93, 95
Leser, Johann Michael 104, 121
Lindley, Mark 389
Locatelli, Pietro Antonio 299, 303, 306, 316, 348
Loeillet, Jacques 106, 119
Logroscino, Niccolò 353-356, 363, 367
Loli, Dorotea 280
Lolli, Antonio 156
Lomazzo, Filippo 142
Lombé, Maria Anna 86
Lorenz, Franz Xaver 101, 117, 119
Lorenz, Johann Anton 101
Lorenzini, Sante 266
Lorme, Jean-Louis de 295
Louis XIV, King of France 40, 42
Louis-Alexandre de Bourbon, Count of Toulouse 104
Lubomirski, Theodor Constantin, Prince 215
Lucchini, Giovanni Matteo 261, 271, 278f., 289
Ludwig of Württemberg, Duke 54
Lully (Lulli), Jean-Baptiste (Giovanni Battista) 37, 112, 298
Lüttgenhausen 223

M

Maccioni, Giovanni Battista 80, 82
Madonis, Girolama 271
Maillien, Johann Joseph 101
Majerin, Teresia 264
Markuszewska, Aneta 27
Mancini, Francesco 314
Manfredi, Alessandro 256, 269f.
Manfredini, Francesco 296
Mann, Francia Fitch 389
Manzini, Dario 102
Manzini (Mancini), Massimiliano Gaetano 102, 118

Marais, Marin 298
Marcello, Benedetto 296
Marchand, Johann Anton 101, 104, 117, 119
Marchand, Louis 298
Marchesi, Luigi 155
Marenzio, Luca 135
Mareschi, Marc' Antonio 263, 271
Maria Amalia of Austria, Archduchess 105
Maria Anna Josepha of Austria, Archduchess 82
Maria Anna Luisa de' Medici, Electress Palatine 109
Maria Feodorovna (Fyodorovna), Empress of Russia 165
Maria Josepha of Austria, Queen of Poland 106, 161f.
Maria Josepha of Bavaria 82
Maria Theresa of Austria, Holy Roman Empress 175
Marie Casimire, Queen of Poland 139, 325
Marie Jeanne Baptiste of Savoie-Nemours, Duchess 42
Marie Louise Gonzaga, Queen of Poland 138, 144
Marini, Carlo Antonio 296
Marini, Giuseppe (Josephus) 60
Marpurg, Friedrich Wilhelm 15, 213
Marquier 222
Martín y Soler, Vicente 157
Martínez, Marianne von 176
Martini, "Padre Martini", Giovanni Battista 163, 165, 218f., 304-308, 394
Mascitti, Michele 297
Matilda of Tuscany, Countess 332
Matteis, Nicola 37, 297
Mattheson, Johann 16, 18, 141, 143f., 300
Mauro, Bartolomeo Ortensio 38
Maximilian I of Austria, Holy Roman Emperor 244
Maximilian I Joseph, King of Bavaria 193
Maximilian II Emanuel, Elector of Bavaria 36, 124

Index of Persons

Maximilian III Joseph of Bavaria, Elector 196
Maximilian Karl von Löwenstein, Prince 107
Mayer, Georg 60
Mayerin, Catharina 259, 272, 280, 284
Mayr, Dominique (Dominicus) 95
Mazzioli, Giuseppe 272
Mazzoni, Anna 288
Meck, Joseph 304
Menghini, Carlo 172
Menshikov, Alexander 250
Merlis, Jacobus 137
Mersenne, Marin 59, 384
Metastasio, Pietro 163-165, 176, 323, 331, 336f., 357, 359f., 363, 368-371
Meuris 223
Míča, Franz Anton → Mitscha, Franz Anton
Micelli, Caterina 155
Michael I Korybut Wiśniowiecki, King of Poland 135, 139
Michaeli, Giovanni 258, 272
Michalak, Jerzy 141, 143
Mielczewski, Marcin 143
Miller, Maxmilian 281
Mingotti, company 28, 267
Mingotti, Angelo 256, 258-260, 267, 269, 348, 360-364
Mingotti, Pietro 267, 286, 348, 360-364
Mira, Pietro Adamo 151, 158-166
Mitscha (Míča), Franz Anton 275
Moch, Leslie Page 74
Moe, Bjarke 141, 143
Molter, Johann Melchior 304
Mons, Anna 245, 248
Montanus, Adam → Berg, Adam
Montée 222
Monteverdi, Claudio 36, 136, 141, 209
Monteviali Rubini, Angelica 272
Monti, Cecilia 258, 272
Mooser, Robert Aloys 158, 160

Morcelli, Pietro 172
Moretti, Lorenzo 261, 272
Moretti, Margherita, née Gualandi, Margherita 261, 272
Moritz of Hesse, Landgrave 62
Morley, Thomas 45
Moro, Elisabetta 285f.
Moser, Hans Joachim 55
Mossi, Giovanni 303
Motta, Artemio 296
Mouton, Charles 298
Mozart, Wolfgang Amadeus 84, 155f., 218
Mucciolanti, Domenico 93
Muffat, Georg 217
Müller, Carl 275

N

Nanteuil, Denis 153
Nappi, Carlo Ignazio 393
Nardini, Pietro 393
Negri, Domenico 259, 272
Neighbour, Oliver 37
Neuner, Georg Elias 95
Niedermayr, Adam 103, 119
Normand, Remy (Remi) 96, 155
Novell, Matthew 298
Nowak, Rainer 227, 238
Nozeman, Jacob 299

O

Obrecht, Jacob 36
Oevering, Reynoldus Popma van 299
Olearius, Adam 242
Ories, Franciscus (Franz) 100
Orlandi, Angela 84
Orlandi, Luigi 84
Orologio, Alessandro (Alexander) 64f.
Orschler, Georg 260
Orsini und Rosenberg, Joseph Leopold von, Count 348

Ortes, Giammaria 218
Oset, Željko 345
Ossoliński, Jerzy 142
Otto I, Holy Roman Emperor 332
Over, Berthold 14, 21, 26, 209, 232

P

Pacelli, Asprilio 136
Paisiello, Giovanni 156
Pallavicini, Stefano Benedetto 153
Pallavicino, Carlo 44
Pallavicino-Attems, Maria Victoria, Marquess 342, 344f.
Pampini, Teresa 272
Pancino, Livia 218
Panizza, Jacob Anton 109
Panizza, Lucrezia 109, 122
Pantani, Filippo 97, 99, 112, 115
Paolini, Aurelio 296
Pariati, Pietro 330
Pasquali, Rosa 281
Passionei, Domenico Silvio 300
Paul I Romanov (Pavel Petrovich), Tsar 165
Pegah, Rashid-Sascha 26, 212
Pękiel, Bartłomiej 139, 143
Pellegrini, Valeriano 100, 116, 194f., 200
Penzenauer (Pientzenauer) 223
Pepusch, Johann Christoph (John Christopher) 37, 304, 313, 315
Pepys, Samuel 220
Pera, Girolamo 265
Pergolesi, Giovanni Battista 179, 365
Personè, Catterina 272
Perti, Giacomo Antonio 218f.
Perutková, Jana 27, 255, 365
Peruzzi, Teresa 259, 272
Peruzzi, Vittoria 280
Peruzzino 216
Peter I Romanov, Tsar 241-245, 249
Petit, Louis 94, 99, 113,115
Pez, family 76, 84, 86
Pez, Anna Maria 86

Pez, Christina Theresa 86
Pez, Franz Anton 86
Pez, Johann Baptist 86
Pez, Johann Christoph 86, 98, 107, 115, 194, 298-200, 304
Pez, Theresia Christina 86
Philipp V Bourbon, King of Spain 108
Philips, Peter 37
Piani (des Planes), Giovanni Antonio 297
Piani, Giovanni Battista 104
Piani, Tommaso (Thomas) de 103f., 119
Picque (Le Picq), Charles 156
Pierre, Jean 105
Pietrasanta, Gasparo 301
Pilaja, Caterina 154
Pircker, Josepha Susanna 280, 282
Pirker, Franz Joseph Carl 209, 348
Pirker, Marianne 348
Pirro, André 141
Pischlin, Teresia Danese 271
Pisendel, Johann Georg 154, 217f.
Pistocchi, Francesco Antonio 299f.
Pitrot, Antoine 154
Piubelin, Johann Romedi 106, 120
Piva, Antonio 160
Piva, Gregorio 223
Pleyel, Ignace 181
Pocorni, Johann 100
Poerson, Charles-François 328
Poli, Camilla 263
Poll 223
Pollarolo, Carlo Francesco 139
Pollarolo, Orazio 139
Pollarolo, Paolo 139
Polsator, Ignaz (Ignatius) 264
Ponziani, Felice 155
Popp, Anna Maria 344
Porfireva, Anna Leonidovna 158f.
Porpora, Nicola 314, 330f., 333f.
Porta, Giovanni 354, 362, 368
Poulain, Toussain 94, 96f., 99, 115
Pourveu, Marin 104f., 119
Predieri, Luca Antonio 330

Index of Persons

Preinfalk, Miha 342, 345
Price, John 59f.
Przybyszewska-Jarmińska, Barbara 26
Pugnani, Gaetano 156
Pürfüscht (Purfürst) 211
Puttini, Bartolomeo 155

Q

Quantz, Johann Joachim 15, 17, 153, 212, 298
Questenberg, Johann Adam von, Count 255, 261, 275-279, 284, 286-288, 395

R

Rački, Franjo 383
Radziwiłł, Karol 157
Rameau, Jean-Philippe 307, 397
Ramis, Cecilia, née Delfini (Dolfini), Cecilia 258, 263f., 268, 271
Ramis, Giuseppe 264
Rampe, Siegbert 108
Raphael, Johannes Antonius 263
Rasch, Rudolf 27, 228
Rault 222
Rauschning, Hermann 141
Ravenscroft, John 298
Reali, Giovanni 296
Rees, Franz Philipp 223
Reggio, Pietro 37
Reininger, Paul 109, 122
Reling (Röhling) 223
Resti, Tommaso 182
Rey, Pierre 105, 120
Riccardini, Giovanni Giacomo 97, 99, 112, 115
Riccati, Giordano 390f.
Ricciardi, Domenico 156
Richter, Johann Christian 218
Rigoli, Paolo 217
Rinaldi, Francesco 280-282, 284

Rissack 222
Rist, Johann 61f.
Ristori, Giovanni Alberto 153f., 161
Ristori, Tommaso 153
Ristorini, Caterina 155
Ritzarev, Marina 159
Robin (Rubin), Johannes Baptista 345
Rochetti, Ventura 154
Rockstroh, Andreas 108
Rodenin de Hirzenau, Antonia, née Salawin de Lippa 263
Rodier, François (Franz) 98f., 115
Roeder, Michael Thomas 389
Roeder, Torsten 26
Roger, Estienne 16, 27, 46, 295-304, 307
Roger, Françoise 296
Roger, Jeanne 295, 297, 300, 302f.
Roger, Nicolas 105, 120
Rolland, Romain 53f.
Romani Bartoli, Angela 285
Rosenbusch, Johann Conrad 18, 25
Rospigliosi, Giulio → Clement IX
Rossi, Luigi 37
Rossini, Gioacchino 333
Rottal, Franz Anton von, Count 256
Rottal, Maria Caecilia von, Countess 256, 262
Różycki, Jacek 139, 153
Ruggieri, Giovanni Maria 296

S

Sacchi, Giovennale 390
Sacco, Gennaro 153
Saint-Huberty, Antoinette 155f.
Salawin de Lippa, Antonia → Rodenin de Hirzenau, Antonia
Salvai, Maria Maddalena 280, 283
Salvi, Antonio 330, 333
Salvo, Maria di 242
Sammartini, Giovanni Battista 304
Sammartini (San Martino), Giuseppe 351, 373
Santer, Gottfried Ludwig 101, 117, 119

Sarri (Sarro), Domenico Natale 258f., 351, 373
Sarti, Giuseppe 181
Sartori, Claudio 219, 265, 283f.
Sartorio, Antonio 333
Sassi, Barbara 214
Scacchi, Marco 137-139, 142f.
Scalabrini, Paolo 348, 360
Scapitta, Vincenzo 143
Scarlatti, Alessandro 313, 316f.
Scarlatti, Domenico 27, 313, 318
Scarlatti, Francesco 27, 311-313, 318f.
Scheibe, Johann Adolph 66
Schering, Arnold 141
Schickhardt, Johann Christian 299
Schilling, Gustav 54
Schlafly, Daniel 242
Schmidt, Giovanni Federico 333
Schmidt, Johann Christoph 153
Schmoll, Michael 20f.
Schneider, Johann Valentin 233
Schneider, Ludwig Michael 233
Schnettger, Matthias 27
Schnoebelen, Anne 219
Schobser, Johann Andreas 79
Schönborn, Lothar Franz von, Archbishop-Elector of Mainz 44
Schrattenbach, Wolfgang Hannibal, Cardinal 255-257, 264-267, 276, 304
Schuechpaur, Franz Simon 97, 99, 102, 112, 115, 118, 124
Schultze, Andreas Heinrich 304
Schütz, Heinrich 36, 138, 143
Schweickhart, Johann, Arch-Bishop and Elector of Mainz 63
Schwöller 222
Seerieder, Philipp Jacob 97, 99, 112, 115
Sękowski, Józef 154
Selliers, Joseph Carl 277
Senaillé, Jean-Baptiste 298
Senesino → Bernardi, Francesco
Senfl, Ludwig 77
Serio, Cosimo 303
Serre, Jean-Adam 397
Sgattberoni, Antonio 364
Sherard, James 304
Sidon, Samuel Peter von 143
Siefert, Paul 137, 139, 143
Siface → Grossi, Giovanni Francesco
Sigmund (Zygmunt) III Vasa, King of Sweden, later King of Poland 135-137, 139
Simon VI of Lippe, Count 55, 58, 64
Simon VII of Lippe, Count 61
Simpson, Thomas 64
Širola, Božidar 383
Snep, Johan 299
Sobieska Stuart, Maria Clementina (Marie Clementine), Wife of the Pretender of the British throne 28, 323-328, 330f., 333-335
Sobieski, Jakub 325
Somis, Giovanni Battista 303
Sommereis 223
Sommer-Mathis, Andrea 268, 276, 361
Sophia Alekseyevna, Regent of Russia 243
Sørensen, Søren 141
Sorgo, family 176
Sorgo, Antun (Antonio) 178f., 182
Sorgo, Kata 173
Sorgo, Marija 173
Sorgo, Miho 173, 178
Sorgo (Sorkočević), Luca (Luka) 171, 173-182
Sové (Sauvé), Gerhard 95f., 99, 111, 113, 115
Spáčilová, Jana 27, 288
Spada, Virgilio, Cardinal 380
Spinola Costantini, Giacinta 258, 260, 272
Stabile, Annibale 135
Stadler, Anton 156
Stählin, Jacob von 158
Stamitz, Johann 53, 181
Stampiglia, Silvio 228, 324, 331
Stanisław August Poniatowski, King of Poland 151f., 155-157, 164f.

Index of Persons

Stefani, Jan 156
Steffani (Stephani), Agostino 35, 38-47, 313
Stichweh, Rudolf 25
Stosch, Philipp von, Baron 328
Straparappa, Bartolomeo 263
Stratico, family 390
Stratico, Antonio 390
Stratico, Gian Domenico 390
Stratico, Giovanni Battista 392
Stratico, Giuseppe Michele 389-399
Stratico, Gregorio 390
Stratico, Simone 392
Strohm, Reinhard 267f., 278, 288, 353, 368-370
Strutius, Thomas 144
Stuart, Charles Edward, Pretender to the British throne 334f.
Stumpff 223
Subissati, Aldebrando 143,
Susanni, Antonia 272
Sweelinck, Jan Pieterszoon 137
Syrmen, Lodovico 393

T

Taglietti, Giulio 296
Taglietti, Luigi 296
Talbot, Michael 27
Tartini, Giuseppe 25, 28, 298, 304, 306, 390f., 393-399
Taselli (Tasseli), Domenico 259, 272
Taufkirchen, Ferdinand Johann von 104
Taunickh, Elias Anton 107, 121
Tedeschi, Giovanni 356
Telemann, Georg Michael 53
Telemann, Georg Philipp 46, 53, 67, 233, 298
Terradellas, Domingo 354, 372
Tessarini, Carlo 266, 304
Teuber (Teyber), Elizabeth (Elisabeth) 154
Teubner, Wolfgang 95
Teybner → Deibner

Theodore III Alexeyevich of Russia → Feodor III Alexeyevich of Russia
Theresa Kunegunda Sobieska, Electress of Bavaria 91, 102f., 118
Thirreur 223
Thomas, Ferdinand Matthias 108, 121
Thomas, Nikolaus Joseph 108, 113, 121
Thrane, Carl 141
Thurn und Taxis, Maria Anna von, Countess 342
Thurn-Valsassina, Johann Matthias von 263
Tibaldi, Giovanni Battista 296
Timms, Colin 26
Tonini, Bernardo 296
Topham, William 298
Torelli, Giuseppe 296, 299
Torri, Pietro 36, 94, 98, 100, 103, 109, 112, 115f.
Toselli, Giuseppe 281
Trauttmansdorff, Franz Ehrenreich von, Count 348
Trevisani, Giuseppe 95, 99f., 112, 115f.
Tuksar, Stanislav 28

U, V, W

Ugolini, Vincenzo 136
Urban VIII (Barberini, Maffeo), Pope 142
Valente (Valenti), Giuseppe Antonio 173
Valentine, Robert 304
Valentini, Giovanni 384
Valentinelli, Giuseppe 296, 391f.
Vallotti, Francesco Antonio (Francescantonio) 390, 394, 397-399
Valsisi, Aloisio 172
Valvasori, Carlina 361
Van der Linden, Jean-François 93
Van der Haque 222

Vanhal (Vaňhal), Johann Baptist (Jan Křtitel) 156
Vaurenville, Louise de 153
Veneziano, Giovanni Giorgio 323
Venturini, Francesco 304
Venturini, Francesco Maria 103, 118, 120
Veracini, Antonio 296
Veracini, Francesco Maria 297
Vestris, Apollino Baldassare 156
Vidaković, Albe 383
Gonzaga, Vincenzo, Duke 36, 209
Vinci, Leonardo 266-268, 314, 331, 353f., 362, 364f., 368, 370f.
Vinciguerra Collalto, Thomas 283
Violante Beatrix of Bavaria, Duchess 103, 109
Viotti, Giovanni Battista 156
Visconti, Antonio Eugenio 164
Visconti, Gasparo 303
Vivaldi, Antonio 103, 258f., 283, 296-298, 302f., 315, 336, 360
Volumier (Woulmyer, Woulmier), Jean-Baptiste 153
Von der Horst 223
Vulcani, Bernardo 160
Vulcani, Isabella 160
Wagele, Maria Josepha 82
Walther, Johann Gottfried 138
Wanning, Johannes 142
Warnecke, Berthold 141
Wastizky 223
Webersberg, Johann Joseph von 348
Weckmann, Matthias 143
Weckschmidt, Anton 264f.
Wendling, Johann Baptist 194-196
Werner, Christoph 139, 143
Westerhold 345
White, Grace 312
Wierzbicka-Michalska, Karyba 159
Wigboldt, Ursula 143
Wilderer, Johann Hugo von 304
Willaert, Adrian 36
Wille, Heinrich Conrad 15
Williams, David Russel 394

Wiśniowiecki, Michał Korybut → Michael I Korybut Wisniowiecki, King of Poland
Władysław IV Vasa, King of Poland 135, 137f., 142-144
Wogan, Charles 325f.
Wölffl, Joseph 156

Z

Zanardi, "di Bologna", Teresa 280
Zane, Catarina 259, 272, 280
Zangius (Zange), Nikolaus 55, 142
Zarlino, Gioseffo 384
Zedler, Johann Heinrich 67
Zarth (Čart), Georg (Jiří) 153
Zehetner (Zehentner), Dominikus (Dominicus) 100, 117
Zeno, Apostolo 329-331, 336
Ziani, Marc'Antonio 210
Żórawska-Witkowska, Alina 26, 135
Zotti (De Zotti), Andrea 397f.
Zotti, Giovanni de 296
zur Nieden, Gesa 186
Zygmunt III Vasa, King of Poland → Sigmund III Vasa, King of Poland

Index of Places

Adriatic region 24, 28
Altona 12f.
America 36, 52
Amsterdam 16, 24, 27, 46, 137, 295, 297-303, 306f.
Ancona 390, 393
Ansbach 84, 212
Antwerp 42, 96, 115, 123
Arbroath 227
Augsburg 43, 55, 234, 238, 299
Austria 37, 55, 92, 99, 107, 121, 139, 181, 187, 194, 279, 295, 345f., 351, 353, 361, 366
Baltic region 52
Bamberg 44f., 84
Bavaria 36, 38, 39f., 42, 75-80, 82-84, 86, 91-93, 99f., 103, 107-109, 113, 121, 124, 193f., 196, 234
Belgium 212, 345
Bensberg 44
Berg, duchy 40, 54
Bergedorf 198
Berkeley 390, 393
Berlin 16f., 22, 44, 144, 188, 190f., 196, 234, 238, 276, 285
Bohemia 27, 55
Bologna 36, 162-165, 171, 178, 195, 216, 219f., 280, 283f., 305f., 327, 331, 333, 369, 380
Bonn 42, 95, 100, 107, 114f., 194, 211f.
Bratislava (Pressburg) 259, 281, 286
Brescia 139, 220

Breslau → Wrocław
Brežice (Rann) 346
Britain 37, 173, 311, 313, 315, 317
Brno (Brünn) 27, 255-265, 267, 269f., 276f., 279, 284, 289
Brünn → Brno
Brussels 20, 36, 39f., 42, 91-100, 111-115, 194f., 303
Bückeburg 58-62, 64-66
Bützow 21-24
Caen 295
Carlsbad 209
Carniola 353, 362
Castelfranco Veneto 38
Celle 44
Cleves (Kleve) 54
Cologne 20, 42, 44, 86, 95, 98, 194, 211-213
Copenhagen 23, 59, 66, 136, 138, 141, 143
Cracow (Kraków) 135f., 140, 143f., 153, 263, 267
Cremona 228
Croatia 186, 379f., 382f.
Czech Republic/Czechia 257
Danzig → Gdansk
Den Haag → The Hague
Denmark 19, 37, 141, 143f.
Dessau 227, 234
Detmold 59, 61
Dillingen 66
Dornau → Dornava
Dornava (Dornau) 348, 364

Dresden 16f., 44, 100, 106, 138, 143f., 151-154, 157, 161, 163-165, 212, 217f., 249, 261, 297, 352, 363, 371, 373
Dublin 312
Dubrovnik (Ragusa) 26, 171-176, 178f., 181f.
Düsseldorf 35, 39-44, 47, 54, 98, 109, 195
Eichstätt 84
Eisenach 229, 238
Emden 54, 63
England 16, 27, 35, 61, 63, 73, 249, 278, 295, 307, 311-313, 315, 318, 325, 330, 383
Ferrara 36, 44, 361
Fiume → Rijeka
Florence 43, 142, 162, 241, 285, 333
Forlì 220
France 14, 16, 35, 37, 51, 73, 91f., 99-101, 103f., 106, 111, 113, 116, 119f., 143, 153, 175, 181, 187, 249, 295f., 307, 317, 335, 337, 345
Frankfurt am Main 43-45, 65, 217, 230, 237f.
Gdansk (Danzig) 55, 57, 137-144
Gedern 237f.
Geneva 22
Genova 216
Germany 11, 14, 19, 21f., 35, 37, 40-42, 53, 61, 79, 86, 92, 102, 105, 143, 153, 185f., 193, 217, 228, 232, 234-236, 238, 249, 267, 276, 295, 299, 345, 353
Ghent (Gent) 106, 119
Glückstadt 12f., 15, 18, 20-25
Gotha 66, 227, 229-233, 237f.
Graz 27, 106, 121, 195, 267, 279, 282, 284-286, 333, 337, 342-348, 356, 360-366, 380, 389
Grenoble 198
Gröningen 230-232, 238
Güstrow 22
Halberstadt 44, 229-232, 238
Hall in Tirol 342

Halle 37
Hamburg 20f., 23, 37, 46,138, 143, 228, 257, 284, 286, 333, 360f., 363f.
Hanover 35, 37-44, 46f., 210, 335
Heidelberg 44, 56, 61
Herten 44f.
Hesse 237
Holešov (Holleschau) 255-264, 267-270, 279, 284
Holland → Netherlands
Holleschau → Holešov
Holy Roman Empire 76, 92, 124, 187
Hungary 36, 55, 209
Hvar (Lesina) 390
Innsbruck 43, 212, 325f.
Ireland 312, 325, 330
Istanbul 380
Italy 16, 36f., 41, 43f., 59, 63, 75f., 80, 82, 84-86, 92, 102f., 112, 120, 136, 138, 143, 153, 159-164, 171-174, 176-178, 181f., 187, 198, 208f., 217, 234-236, 238, 249, 255, 267, 275, 278, 283-285, 289, 296, 300f., 307f., 312, 314, 325, 332-334, 336f., 345, 350, 361, 363
Jaroměřice nad Rokytnou (Jaromeritz) 255, 257, 267, 275f., 286, 288f.
Jaromeritz → Jaroměřice nad Rokytnou
Jena 12f.
Jülich, duchy 40, 54, 65
Kaliningrad (Königsberg) 137, 249
Kassel 59
Kempten 234
Klagenfurt 106, 121, 195, 267, 285
Kleve → Cleves
Koblenz 42f.
Kolberg → Kołobrzeg
Kołobrzeg (Kolberg) 138
Königsberg → Kaliningrad
Köslin → Koszalin
Koszalin (Köslin) 137
Köthen 66, 228
Kraków (Krakau) → Cracow

Index of Places

Kremsier → Kroměříž
Kroměříž (Kremsier) 255, 257, 264f., 267f.
Laibach → Ljubljana
Lauingen 55
Laxenburg 288
Lecce 182
Leiden 344f.
Leipzig 44, 65f., 187, 235, 238, 276, 361, 363
Lesina → Hvar
Liège 42, 213
Lille 20
Lindenberg 44
Linz 361, 363
Lisbon 275
Lithunia 55, 143, 152, 381
Livorno 333
Ljubljana (Laibach) 266-268, 346, 360f., 363, 380
London 37, 41, 195f., 208, 217, 220, 228, 276, 297f., 302-304, 311, 316, 333, 337, 371
Lucca 159, 165, 275, 359
Lusatia 142
Macerata 325
Madrid 108, 121
Magdeburg 44, 234
Mainz 9, 43, 45, 346
Mannheim 52, 84, 193, 195f., 257, 276, 349
Mantua 195, 333
Maribor 28, 341, 343f., 356
Mecklenburg 21f., 24, 44
Meiningen 276, 280
Memmingen 234, 236, 238
Merseburg 16, 232, 234, 236
Milan 36, 136, 142, 215, 282
Modena 390
Monselice 44
Moravia 255-257, 259f., 262f., 266-268, 275f., 281, 288f.
Moscow 27f., 153, 159f., 241, 243-251, 380-382, 385
Munich 35f., 38f., 41f., 44, 46, 59, 73, 75-87, 91-110, 112-115, 118, 123, 193-196, 200, 241, 257, 276, 305, 333, 337, 359-361, 368-371
Namur 212f.
Nancy 42
Naples 75, 104, 154, 157, 159, 164, 171, 173, 186f., 220, 255, 275, 311, 350, 352, 354-357, 360, 365, 367f., 370f., 373
Napoli → Naples
Netherlands (Holland) 16, 35, 37, 51, 63, 100, 113, 116, 124, 295, 298-300, 302, 307f.
Neuötting 86
Nesvizh (Nieśwież) 157
Nieśwież → Nesvizh
Novigrad 390
Nuremberg 64f.
Obrh 380
Ohlau → Oława
Oława (Ohlau) 325
Oliva 144
Olmütz → Olomouc
Olomouc (Olmütz) 255, 257, 264-266, 276
Orvieto 80
Padua 28, 38f., 41, 43f., 171, 178, 215f., 333, 359, 390f., 393f., 397f.
Palermo 311, 333
Paris 37, 39, 42, 46, 52, 59, 95, 117, 153, 156f., 176, 179, 196, 276, 297, 314, 351
Pavia 390
Pesaro 258, 270, 275, 367, 369f.
Piacenza 195
Poland 16, 19, 26, 55, 67, 135-143, 151-158, 161f., 186, 215, 217, 233, 238, 277
Portomaggiore 220
Prague 27, 57, 66, 258-261, 264, 267, 282f., 285f., 333, 337, 345, 361, 365
Pressburg → Bratislava
Prussia 44, 51, 55, 300
Ptuj 343, 364
Ragusa → Dubrovnik
Rann → Brežice

427

Regensburg 59, 107, 121, 227, 241
Riga 53
Rijeka (Fiume) 175
Rinteln 54, 58, 64
Rome 25, 28, 36, 39, 41-43, 46f., 75, 80, 82, 86, 102, 114f., 135-138, 142f., 171-173, 175, 179, 182, 186f., 192, 194f., 215f., 275, 302, 316, 323, 325-330, 332-335, 346, 352, 354-357, 359, 366f., 373, 380-382, 385, 394
Russia 37, 73, 153, 158-162, 164f.
Salzburg 211-213, 276
Sanguinetto 390-392, 394, 396, 398
Savoy 35
Schwerin 14, 20
Scotland 325, 330
Sebenico → Šibenik
Šibenik (Sebenico) 198
Siberia 380, 384
Sicily 175, 311
Siena 103, 333, 390
Silesia 67, 233, 325
Slovenia 75, 186, 342, 345-346, 379
Slovenska Bistrica (Windisch Freistritz) 28, 341, 343, 346-348, 366f.
Smolensk 247, 380
Sondershausen 66, 237
Sønderborg 67
Spain 36, 51, 73, 92, 108, 121, 187, 326f., 337
Spanish Netherlands 36, 40, 91-93, 96f., 99, 103f., 106, 111-113, 118f., 194
St Petersburg 159f., 165, 250f.
Stade 12f., 22
Stattenberg → Štetenberk
Štetenberk (Stattenberg) 346
Stockholm 23, 143f.
Stuttgart 54-65,103, 120, 195, 257, 284
Styria 342, 344-346, 348, 353, 362, 366
Switzerland 171, 295, 353
The Hague (Den Haag) 24, 42, 249, 300
Thorn 57, 63
Tobolsk 380, 382, 384

Turin 39, 42, 286, 288, 369
Udine 391
Ulm 40, 234
Urbino 266-268
USA 185
Utrecht 24, 299f.
Vatican City 332
Venice 36, 41, 43f., 60, 64, 74f., 82, 91,102f., 118, 143, 156f., 160f., 165, 178, 186f., 195, 197f., 210, 216-220, 241, 259, 264, 275, 277, 282f., 288, 297, 302, 332-335, 346, 354, 357, 359, 368-370, 372, 390f.
Verona 43, 217f., 333, 336, 390f., 393
Vicenza 44, 258
Vienna (Wien) 18, 27, 42f., 59, 77, 97, 104, 106, 109, 119, 12f., 138, 152f., 156f., 163-165, 175-177, 182, 195, 216, 241, 248-250, 257, 261f., 265, 267f., 275-278, 282-289, 342f., 346, 359-361, 365, 370, 381
Vilnius 140, 143, 157, 381
Vyškov (Wischau) 255, 257, 264, 266f.
Wallonia 106, 120, 212
Warsaw 136-140, 142f., 151-157, 161f., 164f., 381
Washington 390
Weissenfels 143
Westphalia 54
Wien → Vienna
Windisch Freistritz → Slovenska Bistrica
Winterburgen 12f.
Wischau → Vyškov
Wismar 22
Wolfenbüttel 44, 62, 66, 228
Wrocław (Breslau) 261f., 267, 285
Wurttemberg 54-59, 63-65, 195
Würzburg 43, 212, 345
Zadar (Zara) 390
Zagreb 356, 380
Zara → Zadar
Zieckau 142